LEGACIES AND AMBIGUITIES

LEGACIES AND AMBIGUITIES
Postwar Fiction and Culture in West Germany and Japan

Edited by Ernestine Schlant and J. Thomas Rimer

The Woodrow Wilson Center Press
Washington, D.C.
The Johns Hopkins University Press
Baltimore and London

Editorial Offices:
The Woodrow Wilson Center Press
370 L'Enfant Promenade, S.W.
Suite 704
Washington, D.C. 20024 U.S.A.

Order from:
The Johns Hopkins University Press
701 West 40th Street
Baltimore, Maryland 21211-2190
Telephone: 1-800-557-JHUP

© 1991 by the Woodrow Wilson International Center for Scholars

Printed in the United States of America
∞ Printed on acid-free paper

9 8 7 6 5 4 3 2 1

Library of Congress Cataloging-in-Publication Data

Legacies and ambiguities : postwar fiction and culture in West Germany
  and Japan/edited by Ernestine Schlant and J. Thomas Rimer.
    p. cm.
  Evolved from a conference held at the Woodrow Wilson International
Center for Scholars, Washington, D.C., Sept. 16–19, 1988.
  Includes bibliographical references and index.
  ISBN 0-943875-30-7 (case : alk. paper) : $35.—ISBN
0-943875-32-3 (pbk.) : $13.95
    1. German fiction—20th century—History and criticism—
Congresses. 2. Japanese fiction—20th century—History and
criticism—Congresses. 3. World War, 1939–1945—Literature and the
war—Congresses. 4. Holocaust, Jewish (1939–1945), in literature—
Congresses. 5. Atomic bomb in literature —Congresses.
I. Schlant, Ernestine. II. Rimer, J. Thomas.
PT772.L395 1991
833′.91409358—dc20   91-18654
                                                                                         CIP

WOODROW WILSON INTERNATIONAL CENTER FOR SCHOLARS
BOARD OF TRUSTEES
William J. Baroody, Jr., Chairman; Dwayne O. Andreas, Vice Chairman;
Robert McC. Adams; Lamar Alexander; J. Burchenal Ault;
James A. Baker III; James H. Billington; Henry E. Catto; Lynne V. Cheney;
Gertrude Himmelfarb; Eli Jacobs; John S. Reed; William L. Saltonstall;
Louis W. Sullivan; John H. Sununu; Robert H. Tuttle; Don W. Wilson

The Center is the "living memorial" of the United States of America to the nation's twenty-eighth president, Woodrow Wilson. The U.S. Congress established the Woodrow Wilson Center in 1968 as an international institute for advanced study, "symbolizing and strengthening the fruitful relationship between the world of learning and the world of public affairs." The Center opened in 1970 under its own presidentially appointed board of directors.

In all its activities the Woodrow Wilson Center is a nonprofit, nonpartisan organization, supported financially by annual appropriations from the U.S. Congress, and by the contributions of foundations, corporations, and individuals. Conclusions or opinions expressed in Center publications and programs are those of the authors and speakers and do not necessarily reflect the views of the Center staff, fellows, trustees, advisory groups, or any individuals or organizations that provide financial support to the Center.

Woodrow Wilson International Center for Scholars
Smithsonian Institution Building
1000 Jefferson Drive, S.W.
Washington, D.C. 20560
(202) 357-2429

CONTENTS

Preface ix

1 Introduction 1
Ernestine Schlant

I HISTORICAL OVERVIEWS

2 West Germany as We Know It—An Episode? 35
Arnulf Baring

3 The "Long Postwar": Japan and Germany in Common and in Contrast 63
Carol Gluck

II THE POSTWAR INTELLECTUAL CLIMATE

4 The Challenge of the Past: Turning Points in the Intellectual and Literary Reflections of West Germany, 1945–1985 81
Walter Hinderer

5 Post–World War II Literature: The Intellectual Climate in Japan, 1945–1985 99
Irmela Hijiya-Kirschnereit

III LITERATURE UNDER THE OCCUPATION

6 Literature under the Occupation in Germany: Memories of a Contemporary 123
Peter Demetz

7 Literary Reorientation in Occupied Japan: Incidents of Civil Censorship 135
Marlene J. Mayo

8 The Japan Communist Party and the Debate over Literary Strategy under the Allied Occupation of Japan 163
J. Victor Koschmann

IV POSTOCCUPATION LITERARY TRENDS

9 Postoccupation Literary Movements and Developments in West Germany   189
Judith Ryan

10 Postoccupation Literary Movements and Developments in Japan   207
Van C. Gessel

V THE CRITIC AND CRITICAL INSTITUTIONS IN THE POSTWAR ERA

11 Opening and Closing the Past in Postwar German Literature: Time, Guilt, Memory, and the Critics   227
Dagmar Barnouw

12 Mechanisms of Ideas: Society, Intellectuals, and Literature in the Postwar Period in Japan   249
Katō Shūichi

VI THE WRITER AS PUBLIC CONSCIENCE?

13 A Writer in the Present World: A Japanese Case History   263
Oda Makoto

14 German Postwar Strategies of Coming to Terms with the Past   279
Peter Schneider

Annotated Bibliography and Suggestions for Further Reading   289

About the Authors   311

Index   317

Preface

This book evolved from a conference on "World War II and Its Legacies: A Comparison of West German and Japanese Literature" at The Woodrow Wilson International Center for Scholars, Washington, D.C., September 16–19, 1988. Ernestine Schlant and J. Thomas Rimer organized the conference under the general direction of Michael Haltzel, Director of the West European Program at the Woodrow Wilson Center. The conference was made possible by generous grants from the Ford Foundation and the U.S. Congress Special Wilson Conference Fund.

The conference, which dealt with a variety of responses to political, intellectual, and spiritual problems, brought together a wide spectrum of participants from the United States, Japan, and West Germany. Some participants spoke in the scholarly terms of their discipline (literature, historiography, social or political science); some articulated their own experiences. This mixture of voices made the conference compelling for those who participated, and we have attempted to preserve that diversity in the juxtaposition of the essays that follow. In preparing the manuscript for publication, however, certain changes in the original presentations were made for reasons of continuity and length.

We also found a symbolic significance in the fact that the conference took place in the United States and was hosted by an American institution. While the focus of the presentations and discussions was on Japan and West Germany, it goes without saying that the United States as a military power, a political force, and a cultural impetus influenced both countries in profound ways. These influences are, in a way, the subtext to our comparisons, but not the explicit topic of this exploration. The role of the United States in this undertaking is that of an éminence grise. The complete manuscript was prepared for publication before the unification of Germany on 3 October 1990. Because Germany was divided during the time we discuss in this study, our references to West German literature remain pertinent.

Many thanks are owed to friends and colleagues whose generous advice and critical insights helped shaped the program, particularly David Goodman, Walter Hinderer, Irmela Hijiya-Kirschnereit, Ronald A. Morse, Daniel I. Okimoto, Fritz Stern, Frank Trommler, Janet Walker, and Alan Wolfe. Special thanks also go to Susan Nugent and

Charlotte Thompson of the West European Program of the Woodrow Wilson Center for their indefatigable and expert help in putting the conference together.

Japanese names are given in the standard Japanese format, that is, family name first, given name second.

1

Introduction

Ernestine Schlant

THE SETTING

The purpose of the Woodrow Wilson Center conference, "World War II and Its Legacies: A Comparison of West German and Japanese Literature," was to gain a better understanding of the present, younger literary generations in Japan and the Federal Republic of Germany.

Politicians and political scientists, economists, journalists, opinion makers, and poll takers all form their conclusions according to some "objective" criteria, but rarely, if ever, is literature consulted. Yet literature is the seismograph of a people's dreams and nightmares, hopes and apprehensions. Even when it pretends, it reveals. Literature reflects the interplay between conscious opinions and unconsciously held assumptions; it interprets and criticizes even while the tools of interpretation are themselves subject to analysis. The multilayered subtexts that constitute the density of literary discourse may be at odds with one another; yet these apparent contradictions powerfully highlight the tensions between dream and fantasy, desire and reality, between mirages of perception and self-perception. The literatures of Japan and West Germany reveal more intimately and, perhaps, more accurately, the contemporary Japanese and West Germany peoples' intellectual outlook and provide information that is not part of the official cant, of vulgar stereotypes, or of simplistic clichés. In short, literary truth often goes deeper than political or economic analysis, and it reflects the conditions and values of the society under which it was created.

The conference planners hoped to chart ways of inquiry that would suggest further comparative studies to explore more deeply what we have only begun to sketch.[1] In order to give focus to the vast subject matter, we concentrated on only one literary genre, the novel, and limited the inquiry to one specific topic. The legacy of the war still constitutes one of the most vibrantly sensitive areas of contemporary intellectual life and, at the same time, seems to facilitate comparisons since it emphasizes a similar nadir in each country's history.

"World War II and Its Legacies" may sound like a benign euphemism. Yet the objective was not to channel discussions immediately in previously established directions, where geographical names would function as shorthand for atrocities committed and suffered. This was all the more important since, on the German side, *Auschwitz* has become the code word for concentration camp atrocities and genocide and it loomed, inexorably, behind all discussions. On the Japanese side, it was equally mandatory that a discussion of the various legacies would include, but not be confined to, the horrors suffered and encoded in *Hiroshima* and *Nagasaki*, with the war crimes perpetrated in *Nanking* or *Manchuria*.

The structure of the conference was considered Western in the sense that a concern with historical epochs and periods informed the organization of the individual sessions. It was also Western in the sense that literature should be understood and interpreted in its social context. If a literary work pointed inward, if its concerns were apolitical and even ahistorical, if aesthetic considerations and psychological portraits stood in the foreground, then these characteristics could still be viewed in a variety of ways as signs of withdrawal from the complexities of historical reality, as rejections of an unacceptable present (or of a past-as-present), and as retreats into a self-made, autonomous world.

Yet for scholars of Japanese literature, such a reading of the literary text may not always seem appropriate.[2] Before the censorship of the military dictatorship, there existed a strong proletarian and Marxist-inspired literature. When this tradition re-emerged after 1945, there was little evasiveness and, as Victor Koschmann shows in Chapter 8, the question of war responsibility was clearly raised, at least until Allied censorship and the cold war imposed different directives. At the same time, however, other writers continued to follow intellectual traditions in which aesthetic imperatives occluded political and/or historical considerations. These apolitical novels with a preponderantly psychological focus might be considered documents of a literary tradition that cannot be evaluated by the same criteria as the German tradition. But traditional patterns are breaking open, and the strict rules of earlier aesthetic canons no longer apply. J. Thomas Rimer exemplified this point during the conference when he referred to the Japanese "I" novel (*shishōsetsu*). Works in this literary category had traditionally sought the closest possible approximation between actual author and the narrative voice without, however, having to be written in the first person singular. This type of novel focuses above all on the communication of a personal event or crisis, but by literary convention could not give an analytic account, much less an interpretation, of the war. Now, this canon is no longer immutable. In Chapter 5, Irmela Hijiya-Kirschnereit specifically addresses this point when she quotes Katō Shūichi saying that even "the narrowly personal genre of *shishōsetsu* relates to the times." Oda Makoto, a writer of distinction and a political activist, identifies himself in Chapter 14 as a socially committed writer, but similarly acknowledges the existence of this detached, apolitical tradition.[3] Thus, great care must be taken when interpreting literary silence relating to specific issues: in the Japanese context, the literary canon may have some bearing on excluding certain topics, whereas in the German context silence may indicate avoidance since, at the extreme, any literary text is a political statement.

For readers new to Japanese culture, another distinguishing characteristic in the intellectual approaches bears on the Japanese preference for "compartmentalization." Compartmentalization demands specific behavior in a specific context; outside that context, the same behavioral rules do not apply. Japanese compartmentalization stands in opposition to universalism, with its assumption that sets of principles remain universally applicable under the most diverse sets of circumstances. Indeed, compartmentalization in a Western context carries heavy ethical and psychological undertones by implying that universal principles can no longer be attained and that only item-by-item solutions are free of inner conflict. In scientific research, compartmentalization and segmentation may be considered necessary procedures, but intellectual attempts usually strive for synthesis and contextual interplay and pride themselves in demonstrating the unfolding of multiplicity out of a few universal principles.

In Japanese culture, by contrast, these self-contained units (Ruth Benedict calls them "circles"[4]) are the fundamental elements of social structures (including cultural, aesthetic, political, military, bureaucratic, interpersonal, and family organizations). Japan's immediate adjustment to democracy after military dictatorship has, for example, been explained as the effect of such compartmentalized behavior.

Although cultural differences still hold true in some important respects and are encouraged in a politically conservative atmosphere, there can be no doubt—and again the writers and the literature they create offer ample documentation—that many of these assumptions no longer rigorously hold. These differences in cultural and intellectual style[5] between Japan and West Germany contrast with striking similarities in the political and economic developments; yet, as Carol Gluck cautions in Chapter 3, it is the meaning rather than the structure of these similarities that should engage our attention. During the conference, it seemed therefore all the more interesting, even urgent, to inquire to what extent comparisons are feasible and the results useful.

Similarities, whether in politics, economics, or literature, that seem obvious at a first glance may upon closer analysis lose their compelling force; they offer a first, cursory survey and inevitably invite differentiation and correction. The introduction to this volume attempts to establish some rudimentary guideposts for comparisons, while the essays by the individual scholars elucidate specific topics. At this juncture in the project, it was clear that true comparative studies by any of the participating scholars could not yet be undertaken. Rather, we felt that the choice of topics, and juxtapositions made of the ideas and issues that emerged from our discussions of those topics were meant to serve as a first step toward producing a sketchmap of the problematics involved. The reader is challenged, in this first venture into unchartered territory, to participate in making the comparisons. We hope that as this territory is further explored, many detailed comparisons from a variety of points of view will take their departure from this present volume.

THE PAST IN THE PRESENT

Reaching Political Adulthood in the Age of Imperialism

Many reasons have been offered for the meteoric rise of the two countries. Both came of age politically and entered the world stage at about the same time after effecting momentous internal changes: the Meiji Restoration of 1868 abolished the political insularity of Japan; it adopted Western political institutions, particularly Prussian ones,[6] and started to industrialize. Germany, under Bismarck's leadership, united as a state three years later and continued the momentum of rapid industrialization based on existing tariff unions. Both countries emerged on the world stage as ambitious nations, and both expressed their aspirations in the terms of the late nineteenth century—as colonial expansionism and imperialism.[7] Both supported their aspirations with expert, highly respected bureaucracies, a thoroughgoing militarism, and a well-trained labor force.

After World War I, Germany's outrage and humiliation over the terms of the Versailles Peace Treaty, which included the loss of its colonies, was echoed in the "Japanese Versailles." Although Japan was among the victors, the Japanese believed themselves to have been treated at the nine-power conference in Washington in 1922 as if they had been conquered.

Japan watched the Chinese Revolution of 1911, the rise of the Kuomintang, and the founding of the Communist Party of China with great apprehension. The Bolshevik Revolution of 1917 and the temporary revolutionary Soviet republics established in central Europe at the conclusion of World War I shocked many governments and peoples into realizing, and sometimes exaggerating, the threat of communism. The territorial aspirations of leaders in Germany and Japan played on this fear of communism. Ultimately, in 1936, it resulted in the two countries' signing of the Anti-Comintern Pact.

The economic and social turbulence of the decade following World War I was not reserved for the vanquished alone. The stock market crash of 1929 and the Depression of the 1930s exacerbated the internal turmoil of many countries, but in both Germany and Japan, these internal difficulties were manipulated in the service of nationalism, chauvinism, and racism.

The Manchurian Incident of 1931 proved that Japan had no interest in abandoning its goal of establishing a "Greater East Asia Co-Prosperity Sphere." It continued to pursue a policy of territorial acquisitions started in 1895 with the war against China and in 1905 with the war against Russia. For Japan, the attack on Pearl Harbor and entry into World War II marked only the last four years of an expansionist war effort that was continuous from 1931. In all the wars prior to World War II, Japan had never been defeated, and the nation prided itself on its military strength and prowess.

After Germany's defeat in World War I, the Versailles Peace Treaty demanded a drastic reduction of Germany's military machine precisely to avoid a possible resurgence of its expansionist aspirations. Clever circumvention of the treaty's stipulations allowed the military structure to remain virtually intact, however, while the defeat in war was rationalized as a "stab in the back" by the socialists and other "subversives." Once Hitler came to power in 1933, he found an impressive reservoir of a trained military force to give substance to his grandiose design of the "Great German Empire" and world conquest.

The Allies imposed unconditional surrender on both countries to end World War II. While Japan regained its autonomy in 1952, even though it remained militarily dependent on the United States, West Germany has only in the last few years started to free itself from U.S. dominance. Economic success is forcing a reassessment of the two countries' political leadership roles, even though both have been reluctant, as a result of their histories, to confront these new political realities.

Unequal Continuities

In 1945, Japan was exclusively occupied by the United States, whereas Germany was divided into four occupation zones. Both countries were reeducated for democracy, and in today's world they constitute two of the most successful examples of democracies grafted onto authoritarian pasts. Both countries were, presumably, purged of their nefarious past leadership, in the Nuremburg trials and the Tokyo war crimes trials of 1946. These trials were meant not only to let justice prevail, but also to let the two democracies start out with a clean slate. In addition, Germany went through denazification. Yet the difficulty of administering justice in the denazification trials, given the huge number of people implicated and the fact that many of the judges had also served in the prior system, prevented the realization of a radically clean start. Within a few years there were men in high positions of the new governments in both countries who had also served before 1945. In Japan, the imperial system was retained, if modified, with Emperor Hirohito providing continuity rather than radical change.[8]

To this day, the debates continue over responsibility for the war and the atrocities committed; indeed, they flared up most vehemently in the "historians' debate" (*Historikerstreit*) in Germany in 1986, and they gained new impetus in Japan in 1989 with the death of Emperor Hirohito. These renewed debates testify that the attempts at a fresh start fell far short of their intended purposes, but they also demonstrate that the past can never be simply forgotten but eventually must be acknowledged and integrated into the present.

Literary and intellectual matters during the occupation were handled differently for the two countries, as Chapters 6, 7, and 8 in this volume, by Peter Demetz, Marlene Mayo, and Victor Koschmann, make abundantly clear. What impresses at a first glance is the great vitality of the Japanese literary and intellectual scene in comparison to the relative silence in the four occupied zones of Germany. The lively literary debates that Victor Koschmann outlines in Chapter 8 resulted from the excitement associated with a new beginning, and writers and intellectuals of many different ideological persuasions argued their hopes for democracy. During Japanese military rule, censorship had excised all Marxist literature. The writers either "converted" or remained silent, and some went to jail.[9] After the war, they were among the first to speak about war responsibility.

In Germany, however, the division into occupation zones had its early literary consequences: Marxist and Communist intellectuals who had managed to escape into exile returned after 1945, and they chose predominantly the Russian occupation zone and East Berlin as their new homes. Those who had fled because they were Jews did not return at all, nor were they invited back. (Restitution, when it came, was primarily a financial matter, addressed to Israel.[10]) The writers of the "inner emigration," those who had continued to live in Germany during the Hitler regime and who professed to write for posterity, had nothing to show in 1945. Much attention has been given to the founding of Group 47 in 1947 as a response to the Allies' revocation of the license to publish the periodical *Der Ruf* (*The Call*). The group was composed of writers of diverse political outlooks, united in the hope for a consistent and thorough establishing of democracy and, like their counterparts in Japan, they showed disappointment with Allied censorship practices. Japan could boast of many literary groups and factions, and members of the older generations fully participated in the debates, reaffirming earlier positions; in contrast, Group 47 became a unique focal point that contained many of the literary debates within the group and above all, it served primarily as training—and learning—grounds for young writers who found little they could identify with in the productions of the older generations living among them.

If one looks for possible explanations for the Japanese vitality versus the relative silence in Germany, several answers suggest themselves. Insular Japan contained all the voices of the most divergent opinions within its undivided boundaries, and living together facilitated confrontations of opinion and articulation. Meanwhile, Germany's political division entailed an ideological division and deprived writers of an essential ferment for debate. Another answer may be that although Japan had suffered severe shortages and deprivations during the war and the atomic bombings of Hiroshima and Nagasaki at the end of the war, it never had to tolerate war on its own soil. As a result, the civilian population had little first-hand knowledge of war crimes committed in faraway places. The end of the war meant an end to the hardship of war and a concentrated turn to the many, and often painful, changes accompanying democratization. The Japanese novels of these years document an intensive search into individuals' roles and options during and after the war. They can be read as explosions and as efforts to track the shattering of value systems. Perhaps motivated by the defeat, they saw the sufferings of war as meaningless; induced by the dissolution of traditional bonds of allegiance and power structure, and perhaps also the unequal justice of the Tokyo war crimes trials, they saw the survival of the individual as a matter of arbitrariness; fatalism and passivity, often couched in ironic terms, were the ingrained and powerfully reactivated response to circumstances beyond control.

Germany, on the other hand, had undergone a "total" war which had decimated many cities, torn families apart, and uprooted entire populations. The end of the war also, and finally, opened the gates of the concentration camps. When they opened, Germans were confronted with crimes committed on their own soil and of an enormity that defied comprehension. Denial, avoidance, silence became part of an arsenal of defense mechanisms that did not break open until the 1960s. In Chapter 14, Peter Schneider describes aptly how this silence worked. Peter Demetz speaks in Chapter 6 of the tendencies in the early postwar novel to avoid or annihilate history, and to take refuge in nature, precisely because the mass annihilation had not been arbitrary or meaningless. (A comparison of Demetz's observations on this literary withdrawal with those of Irmela Hijiya-Kirschnereit as she notes the same phenomenon in Japanese literature, could provide the impetus for one of many fruitful comparative analyses of the two cultures.) A preoccupation with formal problems in literature likewise signaled a retreat in German literature from the complexities of defeat and from the realization of the atrocities committed. (It may, of course, also have indicated the need for guidance in the midst of devastation, and may have reflected an emotional and intellectual exhaustion.) The denazification trials only reinforced cordoning off aspects of the immediate past. Presumably they addressed a wide range of questions from fellow traveling to overt leadership in the Nazi regime, and they tried to assign degrees of participation and resultant punishment. They did bring into the open the question of guilt, although they were inept mass procedures that only hardened recalcitrance and denial. Few were the voices like that of the philosopher Karl Jaspers who had among his first postwar publications a long inquiry into the "question of German guilt."[11]

In the Russian occupation zone, and in analogy to American efforts at "education for democracy," the so-called antifa-schools (antifascist schools) converted those who had been willing (and not-so-willing) instruments of Nazism to communism. Since communists and socialists had been persecuted by the Nazi regime even before the genocide of the Jews, they identified themselves as victims. East German writers questioned the role of Germans during the Hitler regime later than those in the West (e.g. Christa Wolf in *Kindheitsmuster* [*A Model Childhood*], 1976) and their quest was not as pervasive as it came to be in the Federal Republic of Germany.

Here perhaps should also be mentioned that in organizing the conference, we did not include East Germany in the comparisons, since, as a communist country, its legacies and its manner of coming to terms with the Nazi regime varied significantly from West Germany. Our comparisons were premised on the rapid economic recovery of the two newly constituted democracies in the orbit of American directives. Our goal was to feel the pulse of their literature as a way of finding the intellectual responses and assessments of these developments. In East Germany, this situation (exacerbated in later years by varying degrees of censorship and the exodus of artists to the West) simply did not apply.

The Cold War as Rallying Point

The fight against communism had been one of the major continuities from the troubled and turbulent 1920s through the totalitarian Hitler regime, and in Japan through the military dictatorship. Up to 1945, both Germany and Japan used the fight against communism to justify their territorial acquisitions. For a short period of time immediately after the war, with the Soviet Union one of the Allies, anticommunism was not an ideological issue, as both Peter Demetz and Victor Koschmann emphasize.

This political openness began to disappear in 1947. Challenged by Soviet pressure on Greece and Turkey, the United States conceptualized its mission abroad as a call to build a bulwark against Communist advances and formalized this foreign policy in the Truman Doctrine of spring 1947. During the same time, Italy, France, and other West European countries were threatened with social turmoil if they could not manage economic recovery. In order to fight postwar poverty and the destitution from which Communist revolutions could spring, the Marshall Plan was initiated in late spring and early summer of the same year. The Russian occupation zone was excluded from the plan since the Soviets would not meet its criteria. The currency reform in June of 1948 set up clear economic divisions between the Soviet and Western occuapation zones. The Berlin blockade was the immediate Soviet retaliation. The blockade and the Berlin airlift lasted into May of the following year and confirmed the breakup of the World War II alliance. A few months later, having already lost much territory to Poland and the Soviet Union, Germany broke into two parts. The Federal Republic of Germany was established in the West, and about one month later, developments in the East followed suit with the establishment of the German Democratic Republic. The cold war had led to the division of the country.

The Marshall Plan did not extend to Japan. In 1949, Japan had watched the end of the civil war in China with Mao's victory. But only in 1950, with the beginning of the Korean War, did Japan start to benefit from U.S. assistance in a substantial manner. The Korean War drove home the strategic importance of Japan to the United States and the need to strengthen it as an ally.

The tensions of an escalating cold war and the need to secure allies made it inexpedient for the United States to insist on thorough accountability for war crimes and crimes against humanity. In the highly diversified field of literary production in Japan, there were voices that demanded inquiries into the role of Japanese aggression during World War II; yet these voices were soon excised by Allied censorship. Similar questions were raised about the continuation of the emperor system and the role of Emperor Hirohito during the war. Many novels described the hardships of war and the sufferings at home and on the battlefield. A-bomb literature, focused on the horrors of the nuclear bombings of Hiroshima and Nagasaki, falls within this category and has, over the decades, become a major instrument for pacifist positions. Its early articulations, too, fell victim to American directives.

In Germany, the so-called *Trümmerliteratur* (literature of the rubble) similarly described the hardships of war and of living among ruins and rubble. Yet there were no literary voices that addressed the concentration camp atrocities and inquired, not only into the role of blatantly active Nazis, but more subtly into the conditions of passive tolerance, silent complicity, and ineffectual resistance. Instead, much was made of the *Stunde Null* (zero hour), which implied a complete break with the past and the Hitler regime, and a totally new start as a democracy. Yet there was no complete break, as perhaps there could not be without an entirely new population. Zero hour as a concept was perhaps invented out of the ardent desire to leave the past behind, out of reluctance to face the past. Popularized as a slogan, it briefly served a political purpose but was soon discredited. By contrast, as Carol Gluck mentions in Chapter 3, the Japanese have consistently and across generations adhered to the "founding myth" of a new beginning on 15 August 1945, even when that myth is at odds with demonstrable continuities.

The debates in the early 1950s in both countries over rearmament and remilitarization further exemplify the multiple standards that are acceptable when political expediency is the issue. The Korean War brought these inconsistencies most vividly to the open. Six years after the end of World War II and unconditional surrender, the Japanese were in a position to insist on their national autonomy in the Peace Treaty signed in San Francisco on 8 September 1951. While this date assured Japan's political recovery, it also carried and continues to carry signs of accommodation to the purposes of U.S. foreign policy. In the Security Treaty, signed on the same day, Japan agreed to permit U.S. bases on its soil.

In contrast, West Germany's consolidation was much slower and was accompanied by the watchful attention of the Western Allies. In 1955,

West Germany became a member of NATO, and East Germany joined the Warsaw Pact. In 1957, West Germany entered the European Economic Community, while East Germany moved into the socialist economic bloc. For West Germany, integration into a West European context and carefully balanced systems of dependence were the political prescriptives. To this day, there is no peace treaty.

The Economic Miracle as Cover-Up

Ironically, the cold war can be seen as responsible for the speedy economic recovery of both Japan and West Germany, yet the magnitude of the recovery—indeed the forging ahead into positions of world leadership—far exceeded the initial U.S. investments in the two countries. Various reasons have been proffered for these "economic miracles": On the German side, the influx into drastically reduced territories of a homogeneous population eager to resettle, and hence the availability of a highly skilled and disciplined work force; the technological advances made during the war; the dismantling of old plants as part of reparation payments and the resultant installation of far more sophisticated equipment; the desire of workers to lose themselves in work and thereby forget the traumas of the war years; or, inversely, the sublimated attempt to dominate the world economically instead of militarily.

In the case of Japan, agricultural land reform, as one of many reforms listed by Carol Gluck in Chapter 3, acted as a catalyst for economic change. As expected, it had an enormous effect on traditional social structures and the process of democratization. The demise of the rich landholders was paralleled by the demise of other traditional lines of authority. The dwindling of rural communities; the erosion of family hierarchies and allegiances and individuals' attempts to free themselves from family expectations; the situation of the elderly, the handicapped, and the sick in urban settings without traditional support systems—these were some of the evolving problems, and they found expression in Japanese literature.[12] They, too, are an integral part of the legacies of World War II.

The lively literary scene in Japan in the postwar years was not an expression of hope or confidence in a new beginning, but rather the expression of a vast taking stock and sorting out of the war, the defeat, and its consequences in the present. Release from prior intellectual constraints and the impact of military defeat cleared the path for powerful antiwar literature which gained ever more impetus with the outbreak of the Korean war. The search to give voice to these complexities burst the bounds of literary conventions. Analogous to the breaking up of social and familial hierarchies, established literary forms broke open as writers groped for new ways to accommodate new perceptions of reality. This was above all apparent in the "I" novel (*shishōsetsu*) where an experimenting with multiple perspectives, splits in the narrative consciousness, and Romantic irony with its *Doppelgängertum*, pioneered narrative techniques for complex experiential relations. Van C. Gessel explores the portent of these innovations in Chapter 10. Equally momentous developments occurred in other genres as well.

In West Germany, there was of course literary activity, but no excitement. For about a decade and a half, until the late 1950s, literature reflected the devastations wrought on language by the Hitler regime, and the mechanisms of blanking out specific aspects of the past. Instead of groping to find literary expression for a heinous past, the younger generation sought to rediscover the achievements of high modernism in the first three decades of the twentieth century, and to expurgate Nazism from a compromised language. They chose Hemingway as their model for a lean language, but also Faulkner and a newly discovered Kafka for laying open the descent into the labyrinthian caves of the human mind. Wolfgang Koeppen was one of the very few writers in the early 1950s not discredited by the Nazi regime and he poured forth works of great literary achievement. He alone might be comparable to those Japanese writers who had fallen silent during the military dictatorship, but who injected their pent-up energies into postwar literary life. Koeppen, however, lacked resonance among his peers or an audience ready for his critical portrayals, as Dagmar Barnouw discusses in Chapter 11. Yet when one looks at these novels with the specific purpose of identifying legacies, one notes that even a writer as sharp-eyed as Koeppen does not explore the blind spots or tear away the pious veils of silence to dignify the victims by giving a name to genocide. Like many other writers, he couches his criticism of the past in criticism of the present. But pointing out the continuity of unsavory characteristics, and suggesting that zero hour was a hoax (since the past is alive in the present) constitutes evasion, not an acceptable confrontation. Koeppen's despair is genuine and poignantly expressed in the suicide of one of his characters. Yet the despair is not over crimes committed in the past; it is not sorrow and mortification and mourning for the victims and even, perhaps, for oneself; the despair arises over the absence of change.

To the extent that generalizations are permissible and even suggestive, one may speak in the case of West Germany of divisions and polarizations, in the case of Japan of ambivalences, ambiguities, and, in the words of Ōe Kenzaburō, of "synchronic" dualisms.[13] Japanese ambivalences were shared by all age groups and can be seen as a common bond, not a polarizing one. The ambivalences focused on practically all postwar issues and their interpretation, such as on the end of the war as defeat or liberation; on a clearly perceived need for political reform that welcomed democracy, yet smarted under its "imposition" by the Allies; or, inversely, on democracy as a "betrayal of national identity" coupled with a "kind of nostalgic admiration for the defeated imperial army"[14]; or on new, mutually contradictory attitudes toward the emperor system when Emperor Hirohito had been formally responsible for all war activities, yet was never held accountable; similarly ambivalent, social reform took away the power of patriarchy, yet many benefited from the concomitant new opportunities. These ambivalences continue into the present where they help to define Japanese self-perceptions in clearly conceived dualities. Thus, Oda Makoto speaks in Chapter 13 of the simultaneous, dual role of a person, group, or nation as victim/aggressor and subsumes Japan's position as a "first" as opposed to a third-world country under the same overriding concept.

East and West Germany emerged in the cold war geographically divided as the result of ideological divisions. This radical severance was compounded in West Germany by the vast areas of silence sensed correctly by the younger generations as repression and denial. These divisions and excisions became socially activated in the 1960s as generational polarizations. With Marxism segregated into the East, and the Communist Party forbidden in West Germany in 1956, the younger generation seized upon leftist ideologies and a parent's presumed Nazi past as polarizing weapons to combat their elders.

Existentialism, the main intellectual current in the 1950s, lent an oblique voice to these inconsistencies; it cast an air of doom over materialistic accumulation and expressed the disillusionment over hopes gone sour; it articulated the absurdist position of "being thrown" into an existence of irreconcilable opposites, of hypocrisies and outright lies. Criticism of materialism and consumerism as the most visible achievements of democracy implied an early criticism of American values and for some intellectuals suggested Communist ideologies as more palatable alternatives.

Nevertheless, the citizens in both West Germany and Japan clearly liked the economic prosperity and voiced their preference in their continued votes for conservative governments that promised—and delivered—material progress. Many writers in their discontent saw themselves as outsiders. They discovered older writers such as Kafka, and in Japan in particular they found new resonances in long-popular Dostoyevsky. In these writers, novelists in both countries recognized exemplary voices for the alienation and the estrangement they felt.

Coming of Political Age

The demonstrations against the renewal of the Security Treaty in 1960 proved the strong, antimilitaristic positions of the Japanese and placed them in the vanguard of the international protest movements. These positions became more militant and better organized toward the end of the decade, as the war in Vietnam escalated. The Japanese felt particularly implicated in this war, and therefore particularly eager to protest it, as the U.S. military bases in Japan were used to launch attacks against North Vietnam. Using a Japanese base to perpetrate what was seen as imperialistic aggression appeared as a clear violation of the Japanese Peace Constitution. Oda Makoto, one of the most active Japanese anti–Vietnam War organizers, explained at the conference that for him, accepting responsibility for the past war necessitated the fight against all further militaristic aggressions.

The avowed and actively committed Japanese pacifism must, of course, be viewed as a response to the sufferings and the defeat in World War II. This pacifism is understood as an identification with the victims, legitimized by Hiroshima and Nagasaki, and sometimes projected on the international plane as solidarity with the third world. The antiwar demonstrations offered the opportunity to demonstrate that the lessons had been learned, and that the best way to make amends for an unpalatable past was to make sure that it would not be repeated.

The relative paucity of works that attempt to sort out the atrocities committed by the Japanese military in other Asian countries could also be explained in terms of the victim/victimizer model, where the role of the victimizer has been balanced by that of the victim.[15] This cultural bookkeeping may have worked in a closed society, where everybody was held to the same standards. Yet the atrocities were committed outside Japan, in territories Japan was now becoming eager to engage economically. These countries were not bound by Japanese idiosyncracies and have given impetus to Japan's self-confrontation.

In West Germany, the generations could not unite in their opposition to political dictates. The split was inner-directed. The 1960s mark the progressive stages of a generational conflict that erupted in full force in 1968.

In the late 1950s, novels had begun to appear that went beyond the confines of suffering related to the war, or the moods expressed in the *Trümmerliteratur*. Technically and stylistically, they had found a new voice that acknowledged the heritage of high modernism in the literature before the Third Reich, while the social and political panoramas now widen sufficiently to encompass the years of the Hitler regime. Yet even these "first peak" novels, as Judith Ryan calls them and analyzes them in Chapter 8, were full of distancing devices, such as relativizing narrative frames, and they preferred picaresque heroes that could not be held accountable.

The Eichmann trial of 1961 in Jerusalem, and the Auschwitz trial from 1963 to 1965 in Frankfurt brought some of the Nazi criminals to court. The documents of these trials provided a first and vigorous impetus to documentary literature, and this literature produced works of political and social impact into the 1980s. The early practitioners of documentary literature hoped to force a confrontation with the Nazi crimes against humanity, yet the older generation, implicated, if by nothing else than by cotemporaneity and tacit complicity, persevered in postures of silence and denial. They were frozen in an "inability to mourn"[16] and had developed a culture of avoidance, as Walter Hinderer highlights incisively in Chapter 4. Documentary literature contributed significantly to the next generation's less restricted awareness of the many devastating aspects of the Hitler regime and of the individual's role in it.

From the mid-1960s on, this next generation, which was no longer implicated in the war, came of age. Political activism, spiced liberally with interpretations of Marx and Freud, fueled the young generation's militancy and hoped to provoke their elders to respond. In this respect, West German youth were part of a protest movement that spread through all developed countries (including the United States), and though each country may have had a different political agenda, they were united in their attack on the "system," which in most instances meant the cultural and military hegemony of the United States. The civil rights movement in the United States and the demonstrations against the war in Vietnam provided techniques and substance to act out grievances against democracies that were considered falling far short of their inherent promises.

In this respect, one of the most salient differences between Japan and West Germany bears on the attitudes of the successor generations. For Arnulf Baring, the West German generational consensus of 1945 was broken by the generation of 1968 with as yet unchartable consequences, and Peter Schneider suggests some of the reasons for this break. In the case of Japan, however, Carol Gluck speaks of transgenerational continuities throughout the postwar era; and she points to Japan's more recent efforts to claim even larger historical continuities by extending the present further into the past—a view that would see the military dictatorship as a interlude in a development continuous since the end of the last century.

In the late 1960s and into the early 1970s, young West Germans saw leftist ideology as the tool with which to battle the older generation; anti-Americanism was viewed as a proper counterbalance to the older generation's pro-American materialism. Sensitized to the cover-ups and the denials of their elders, and by now better equipped with knowledge about the crimes committed during the war, they went for the jugular. In this confrontation it became clear that the Holocaust was of the greatest importance in any relation between the generations and it clearly had the farthest-reaching consequences for the self-perception of young West Germans in their search for identity. Blind with rage, they used "Nazi" and "fascist" as the most condemning expressions of vilification, but only succeeded in diluting the precise, historical impact of these words.

The vehemence of the official reaction to the demonstrations and the political activism of the generation of 1968 confirmed the impression that the generation "gap" was indeed an abyss. The West German government invoked "emergency laws" in 1968, and in the "decree against the radicals" of 1972 excluded "radicals" from the civil service.[17]

Persistent, if Subdued, Progress

The generation of 1968 with its intellectually leftist underpinnings could not sustain itself. The economic consequences in the United States of the war in Vietnam and the worldwide oil crisis of 1973 dampened optimism about infinitely sustained economic growth globally. These shocks also silenced the attacks of many leftist intellectuals who had assumed that prosperity would continue to increase polarization and would suggest leftist solutions to social problems. When the United States withdrew from Vietnam, another important rallying point was lost. In addition, the Left in both countries had no cohesive party program that would attract and keep a constituency. In West Germany, the Greens, although initially successful with ecological and antimilitary issues, could not solidify their gains into a lasting political force. In Japan, ecological and locally concerned action groups have disintegrated whenever the ruling Liberal Democratic Party has addressed their goals even partially.

As the protest movements dwindled in the 1970s, individual terrorist groups appointed themselves to carry on. Although terrorism[18] as an international phenomenon has many different causes and philosophies, it seems fairly clear that the German (and Italian) and Japanese terrorists held somewhat similar objectives. As Red Army factions, they seemed primarily motivated by the inordinate desire to destroy "symbols" of so-called American imperialism and anyone allied with it. This meant attacks on American personnel and installations abroad; in the case of the West German terrorists it also meant attacks on some of those persons who symbolized the continuity from the Hitler era into the postwar years and the failure to purge German society of its past.

Coming to terms with the legacy of World War II has continued into the present. In 1979, the American television series "Holocaust" engaged a wide audience in West Germany and facilitated public discussion. The medium of television and the serial presentation of the Holocaust, replete with sentimental appeal, created the large audience.[19] The favorable public reception of this memorial-turned-soap-opera may also have to do with the fact that by 1979 (as distinct from the trials in 1961 and 1963 to 1965) yet another, younger generation had come of age and was eager to be informed. About the same time, and for roughly a decade, many autobiographical novels were published in which the authors tried to reconstruct their parents' lives during the Hitler years in an attempt to define themselves in relation to this past and the present. These novels of psychological introspection are documents of turbulent and frequently agonizing polarizations between love and hate, attachment and revulsion; they are not novels in which author or character ever achieve peace of mind.

Throughout the 1980s, West Germany's intellectual and political life was punctuated by events and debates that made it clear that recognition of the crimes against humanity during the Hitler regime remained the overriding legacy of the war. This legacy still has not been settled and it remains an active political and psychological force.[20]

Repression, momentary glimpses, and variously renewed denials mark the postwar fever curve of West German confrontations with the Holocaust; yet, to paraphrase Dagmar Barnouw, anamnesis, the "undoing of forgetting," persistently challenged amnesia. Rationalizations and "relativizations" still abound, as the historians' debate made clear, yet even these sophistic subterfuges must accept the undeniable reality of the Holocaust and participate in the continuing intellectual attempts to come to terms with these crimes.

Although running the danger of oversimplification, one may suggest that in Japan the important breaks were less between generations than along political lines. Successive governments and the large segments of the population that vote for them have continued to show a decidedly conservative bent, whereas the opposition is consistently vociferous and clear in its promotion of alternative sets of ideas. Given the contextual nature of society in Japan, individuals work within a larger and mutually agreed upon group framework; it is not surprising that in a country like West Germany such divisions are significantly less pronounced. This split in the Japanese intellectual and political consciousness has repercussions in the manner in which the war has been viewed. It has been primarily the writers on the Left who have reminded the public of the atrocities committed by the Japanese military during World War II, and they have most pointedly demanded that the public should have a genuine knowledge of the extent of these crimes. Impelled by rapid economic developments since the early 1950s, the conservative factions, however, have been more concerned with the implications of economic success and have focused their attention on developing their relationships with Europe and the United States, often putting behind them any examination of the ambiguities of Japan's position in postwar Asia. The war and defeat came, more than anything else, to be symbolized in Hiroshima and Nagasaki. This powerful symbol of victimization has overshadowed other aspects of the war.

There can never be any comparison between the Holocaust, the systematic extermination of an entire people, and the Japanese atrocities, brutal though they were, committed during their overseas conquests. Yet it seems equally clear that the Japanese will surely, at one point or another, find themselves as a people forced to examine these burdening aspects of their past and to face in turn the implications of that past in their historical relationships with their neighbors in Asia.

The Future in the Present

Democratic pluralism and the ethnic and cultural diversity of the United States make for heterogeneous literary articulations even during politically conservative periods. In contrast, both Japan and West Germany have focused on cultural homogeneity and have frequently rejected the suggestion that ethnic diversity offers a better path to break out of a confining present. During the 1970s and into the 1980s, intellectuals in both countries turned inward as a response to the vicissitudes of global economic prominence and the demise of an activist Left. The labels of "New Subjectivism," in the case of West Germany, and of the "Introverted Generation," in the case of Japan, testify to the persuasiveness of this preoccupation. The focus of this introspection is most frequently the search for a definition of the self, and a quest for identity in a rapidly changing society and world.

Van C. Gessel sees the past forty years of Japanese literature as a fluid interplay between two literary camps that date to the early part of this century and that reconstitute themselves in ever new variations and gradations. The two camps consist of the ideologically committed writers on the one hand, and, on the other, of those of a primarily asocial bent. The "Introverted Generation," consonant with West Germany's proponents of "New Subjectivism," represent the latest swing of this pendulum.

Oscillations between predominantly conservative positions relating to a variety of issues and the voices of criticism with their demands for openness follow similar patterns. A case in point can be found in the field of education, specifically in the textbook controversies that have ignited opposite points of view from 1952, when Japan regained its sovereignty, to the present. In this regard, the Japanese arguments seem couched in altogether internal, contextual terms; issues relating to Japan's role in a larger world are seldom put at the core of the dispute, where common sense would suggest they surely belong. The arguments involve the need for a more positive assessment of Japan's twentieth-century past. The official position wished to institute a more positive assessment of this past, in which specific incidents of the war and the defeat are minimized, some would say trivialized, while the teaching of "traditional values" and "moral education"[21] moves to the foreground. This position holds that after forty years of consistent progress, the time has come to shed a past that is no longer in harmony with more recent accomplishments, and to emphasize those aspects that serve the present well. These endeavors to institutionalize cultural traditionalism (through control of the textbooks by the Ministry of Education) elicited new debates about war crimes and war responsibilities among many writers and intellectuals unwilling to accept the past uncritically or to paper over the war atrocities.

Yet even beyond these debates, as Irmela Hijiya-Kirschnereit points out, there has been a renewed emphasis on a Japanese cultural exclusivity, often termed Nipponism. Central to some of these attitudes is an understanding of the Japanese language as a common cultural bond. Reliance on language as a dominant, culturally unifying factor, and the insistence on cultural homogeneity may, as some critics have suggested, reflect a need for protective measures in the face of rapid and possibly frightening changes. Yet the Japanese language itself keeps changing, revealing ever greater degrees of democratic and internationalizing alterations in its structures and vocabulary; in this regard, the cultural critics remain impotent against the rush of time and change.

In the wake of this renewed emphasis on tradition and homogeneity of culture, it is all the more important that the new emperor made it clear in 1989, the very year of the beginning of his reign, that he would not revert to old models of nationalism and cultural conservatism when he stated his firm intent to abide by the postwar constitution. In another significant event, he apologized to the Koreans for the harshness of the

Japanese colonization of Korea during World War II,[22] and Japanese Prime Minister Kaifu Toshiki similarly expressed his regrets. These conciliatory gestures may have upset some conservative nationalists in Japan, but the acknowledgement bodes well for a more open assessment of past actions and raises hopes that the future will be approached with greater sensitivity to other nations in Asia and around the world.

Greater openness toward the past is an economic as well as a moral imperative, since insistence on insularity and Nipponism are at odds with a sustained position of world prominence. As an economic world leader, Japan cannot avoid profound encounters with other cultures or thorough appraisals of its own past. To withdraw into a comfortable acceptance of Nipponism might very well endanger the realization of Japan's future economic potential.

West Germany had increasingly been looking to its severed half, the German Democratic Republic, in efforts to reestablish cultural bonds and in October 1990 achieved national unity. The difficulties attending unification will be quite staggering since, as Peter Schneider has stated: "After the first thrill of unity, it will become clear that, on either side of the Wall, not only two states but two societies have developed."[23] In view of East Germany's prior position that assigned the Nazi crimes to capitalism and therefore to West Germany, and that maintained that, as Communists, many of its leaders and people had been equally persecuted by the Hitler regime, it is therefore significant that then-Prime Minister de Maizière, in his first speech before the newly elected People's Chamber, asked Jews and the Soviet Union to forgive East Germans for their role in the Nazi atrocities.[24]

Notwithstanding the German-German problems, the Federal Republic of Germany and other European countries are forging ahead with the concept of "Europe 1992." This far-reaching economic integration will imply cultural diversity and necessitates a tolerance of ethnic minorities that will clearly test the extent to which the nefarious past with its xenophobic excesses and crimes has been overcome.

Europeanization and globalization provide opportunities not only to advance economically, but to grow beyond cultural confines that, in the past, only brought disaster. For both countries, then, the manner in which they relate to minorities will be a gauge that can measure the sincerity of their attempts to face themselves in relation to the past, to make amends for it, and to give evidence of changed behavior. This may provide a clearer picture of the past-in-the-present, indeed of the future-in-the-present, than political speeches or current trade balances. The writers in both countries have begun to chart this territory.

The Writer as Public Conscience

In both countries, the memories of their nationalistic and militaristic aspirations need to be kept alive, precisely because the momentum of the present could so easily obliterate what is painful and inconvenient. It is essential to work the insights gained and the memories retrieved from the past into a contemporary sense of national identities. This is an arduous, ongoing task, with no end in sight. Indeed, Katō Shūichi perceives it as one of the main tasks for Japanese intellectuals.

Surrounded by the ubiquitous presence of television and a mass culture that prefers comic books to "high literature," Japanese writers may now feel peripheral to the society of which they are part, as Katō Shūichi maintains. In West Germany, the situation is not very different. Peter Schneider, for example, questions the role of the writer as public conscience in today's democracies. And yet both writers give evidence, in the very statements in which they sound the alarm, that they *are* the public conscience. (Nevertheless, it should be pointed out that, from the perspective of the United States, readers in both cultures still hold high allegiance to their great literary traditions; books of quality are widely available at inexpensive prices and continue to sell well. Cultural judgments made within one national framework may well look differently when measured by another culture's scales.)

Undoubtedly, and despite all reservations, writers remain the public conscience. Without them, their societies would become blind and obtuse. The writers may have limited visions, faulty memories, narrow obsessions, but they speak to the ills of the past and of the present that are otherwise so frequently ignored amid the glitter and the superficial urgency of the present. Uninterested in what is politically expedient, they address the issues as they perceive and understand them, and in doing so they reveal the motivating values of their times. They do battle with the present, and project their visions of despair and of hope in a future. Without them, we would be people without nightmares—and without dreams.

THE CHAPTERS

This volume is arranged topically and chronologically. Under each of the six headings, complementary and/or contrastive papers present the Japanese and West German points of view.

In the historical overview, which serves as a background for the literary discussions, fundamental questions were asked as to whether comparisons of countries as vastly different as Japan and the Federal Republic of Germany are valid and where the limits to generalizations must be drawn. The comparative approach was clearly affirmed with the caveat that comparisons highlight the differences as much as the similarities. Overall, the discussions emphasized the realization how fertile and extensive a field of studies these comparisons promise to be.

In this section, both Arnulf Baring and Carol Gluck make a case for the uniqueness of each country's experiences of defeat, occupation, reconstruction, and subsequent economic prominence. Nevertheless, they develop their arguments against the background of perceived similarities.

Baring stresses the fact that the two countries were "unequally defeated," since Germany lost its Eastern territories, had to absorb a large influx of refugees and expelled people, and experienced what amounted to a "social revolution," in that there was a complete change of power structure: not only was the dictatorship of the Hitler regime destroyed, but the old aristocratic elites vanished as well. Gluck, too, points to the many differences between the two countries, yet concedes that "the meanings attached to those histories were sometimes so alike as to seem uncanny."

These similarities were particularly evident immediately at the end of the war, when Germany hoped for a *Stunde Null* (the zero hour for a fresh beginning); indeed, Japan even pinpointed this beginning of the present to "noon, 15 August 1945."

Periodization, though frequently problematic, sets similar accents for both countries. For both, the end of the first postwar phase occurred in the mid-1950s, when the New Liberal Democratic Party came to power in Japan, West Germany regained its sovereignty, and both governments had to confront a long period of popular opposition to remilitarization. Both authors agree on the profound caesura to economic recovery caused by the oil crisis of 1973. In the case of Japan, the crisis separated the period of high economic growth from that of "post-high-growth," and in the Federal Republic of Germany it signaled the end of the *Wirtschaftswunder*.

Among the differences that may have implications for the future developments of both countries, Gluck sees a "transgenerational" continuum that extends through the entire postwar period and that rallies around the "founding myth" of the new Japan that began in 1945. This myth is not perceived to be a contradiction to the increasing preference to forget the prewar years and to focus on a continued, if interrupted period of modernization that dates back to the nineteenth century. In contrast, Baring holds that in West Germany the "generational consensus of 1945" ended with the coming of age of the 1968-generation. He expresses concern about the young generations' political priorities. These concerns, stated before the fall of the Berlin Wall, have lost none of the poignancy, although the future may now offer new options.

Section II presents in outline the intellectual climate in both countries during the last four and a half decades and offers some models of periodization. The limits of meaningful comparisons are here particularly pronounced, yet the options chosen in each country mutually illuminate culturally available alternatives.

The realization of the crimes committed during the Hitler regime may be said to represent a constant presence in German life, although the manner in which this realization has been repressed, denied, avoided, yet also acknowledged and confronted, has varied over the decades. Walter Hinderer connects his schematization with the sociopsychological interpretations of Alexander and Margarete Mitscherlich, who noted the "inability to mourn" of the postwar Germans, and with the early postwar analyses of Karl Jaspers and Theodor W. Adorno, in which they express doubt that the Germans are taking up the challenge of the past in order to confront its legacies.

Hinderer suggests five phases in the intellectual climate of the past forty-five years. He dates the first phase from the end of the war to the currency reform of 1948 and the creation of the Federal Republic in 1949. During this period, writers attempted to find a voice to express their war experiences; they took refuge in the aesthetically reassuring categories of parable, myth, and allegory looking for "tranquilizers" rather than critical enlightenment. His second phase lasts for about a decade, until 1959–60, when Adenauer's restoration and the years of the economic miracle began to show signs of crisis and a young generation of writers began "an increasingly critical dialogue with the West German past and present." The third phase, from 1959 to 1969, is marked by shifting political allegiances, Adenauer's departure from office, an upsurge in neo-Marxist thinking, the student revolts and demonstrations, and political activism on the part of the literary intelligentsia. Hinderer dates the fourth phase from the chancellorship of Willy Brandt in 1969 to the election of Helmut Kohl in 1982, during which time he notes a gradual retreat of the intellectuals into the private sphere. The last phase coincides with the new restoration era, that is, the chancellorship of Helmut Kohl. Here, trivialization and sentimentality characterize the approaches of the media and popular literature, while the "historians' debate" of 1986 acquainted a larger audience with the controversy as to whether the Holocaust was unique or should be considered in a context relative to genocide perpetrated by other countries. Although opinions may differ widely, there is no doubt that in public intellectual discourse, the legacy of the Hitler regime is not considered to be primarily the war and its scars, but rather the Holocaust and the crimes against humanity.

In Japan, as Irmela Hijiya-Kirschnereit makes clear, "the war" does not represent a euphemism for crimes committed against humanity nor does it raise questions as to what made it possible. Instead, it provides a context for sufferings experienced. In the years immediately after the war, Marxist writers addressed the "responsibility of war," but the debate soon lost force. Indeed, with the economic recovery in the 1960s, a reversal set in that found expression in "a surge of compassion for the victims" of the [Tokyo] war crimes trials. Protests against the war in Vietnam combined with self-perceptions as victims of the A-bombs and obscured the need to look more closely at Japan's own actions during the war.

Hijiya-Kirschnereit offers five different models that categorize literary reflection on the war and its legacies. In describing the literary strategies and the unconscious value systems they represent, she provides an informative portrait of Japanese sensitivities and cultural indoctrination.

Her first model offers a modified version of the Japanese classification by generation, in which an older generation of writers, established even before the war, is followed by a generation from which the recruits for "patriotic services" were drawn. They are followed by the war generation proper, those who grew up during the war but were too young to serve in the military forces: these represent the third generation of new writers. Her fourth category comprises those writers who were still children at the end of the war, and her last category refers to the most recently maturing writers, the "postwar babies." These categories give no indication as to the outlook, commitments, or development of any individual writers in the context of their time: obviously, each age group may encompass writers of the most divergent persuasions.

Hijiya-Kirschnereit then offers another, topical model, one that takes up the war as a central issue, either on the battlefield; in its effects on civilian life (here she includes the large subgroup of A-bomb literature); or, finally, in the hardships of the aftermath of the war. In a third paradigm she classifies according to the degree to which the novels focus on the war experience: war can represent the main topic, war can be a secondary or side aspect, or, as in her last and most interesting group, war can figure as omission (that omission being an unstated presence). Important for a comparison with the West German situation is her emphasis on the fact that such topical categories do not manifest trends that reflect social or political concerns. In yet another model she differentiates in the prose genre among "pure literature," mass literature, personal records, and documentary accounts.

In her discussion of fictional strategies adopted to present the war, she mentions sentimentalizing life, accepting disaster as fate, concentrating on aesthetics, and transforming history into nature. These strategies cut across the boundaries of other models and contribute, for a Western reader at least, to a sense of lack of historical dimension. Many such readers may consider these strategies as avoiding the issues or rationalizing them.

The American occupation policies vis-à-vis Japan and Germany, the subject of section III, differed in significant respects and were administered under quite diverse circumstances. Peter Demetz, speaking about the situation in Germany, reminisces "as a contemporary" and provides a personal account of these confusing, yet promising times. Germany was divided into four occupation zones with each zone administered according to different views on the future of Germany. Although the ideology of the cold war hardened during these years, it remains remarkable that the rules governing intellectual matters, such as literary censorship, remained fluid and open. (A case in point involves the repeal by the American censors of the license to publish the literary magazine *Der Ruf* [*The Call*] because the magazine had criticized communism.) After his discussion of literary policies and their implementation by the Allied occupation authorities, Demetz looks at the literature produced by the German authors of the period; here, he finds sparse evidence of a liberation or renewal of spirit. Rather, he notes a turning inward and a predominant concern with problems of form.

Because Japan was not divided into zones of influence or geography, the uniform administration of U.S. policies under General MacArthur, as well as the retention of the emperor system, provided a certain continuity. Still, in Germany as well as in Japan, "education for democracy" was a common goal.

The chapters by Marlene Mayo and Victor Koschmann complement each other in the sense that Mayo addresses the American, and Koschmann the Japanese perspective of the U.S. occupation policies. Mayo gives a detailed presentation of certain U.S. policy positions with respect to censorship and the ideological reeducation for democracy of the Japanese people. Her careful research has uncovered inconsistencies and shifts as much in the planning of these policies as in their implementation, and she is able to show sometimes amusing, sometimes baffling consequences that result from a lack of knowledge of the Japanese language on the part of the censors.

Koschmann focuses on the Japanese response to occupation policies and provides a close reading of the most important literary debates of those years. As authors and intellectuals alike struggled to find their own voices in the postwar era, they frequently attempted to do so by linking up or taking issue with certain prewar positions, indeed with clusters of attitudes predating the Japanese military dictatorship and its censors. In contrast to the muted tones prevalent in Germany, where the ideological split sorted out the Marxist writers and relegated them to the Russian occupation zone, the debates in Japan were lively. Koschmann draws attention to the continuation of some of these issues into the present, the most important being that of the "resistance to Westernization."

All three authors agree on the openness of the debates and the fluid intellectual boundaries that characterized this short span of years, before the cold war imposed the borders within Germany and initiated the Korean conflict. They agree as well on the importance of the hopes and expectations invested at that time in the promise of American democracy.

The two papers on "Postoccupation Literary Trends" in section IV cover a large territory and essentially sketch the literary currents of the past forty years under our specifically selected topic.

Judith Ryan finds the consistently political and social significance of postwar German literature to be its distinguishing characteristic. Hence, an awareness of the challenge of the past represents a continuous concern, in which peaks of intensity can be discerned. According to Ryan, the earliest of those peaks occurred in 1959, which saw the publication of the first major novels of authors who had by then absorbed the high modernism of the early decades of this century. With this achievement they finally overcame the deep abyss cut by the Hitler regime with its imposition of a language drenched in the jargons of National Socialism and of a literature cut off from international discourse. She finds that all these "first peak" novels share an interest in perspectivism, a concern to analyze the "suppression of memory" phenomenon, and a continuing interest in the nature of the relationship between the Nazi past and the postwar present.

She dates the second peak at about 1968, the time of the student revolts and the conjunction of political and intellectual activism that continued into the 1970s. She identifies a third, and admittedly minor, peak around 1985, flanked chronologically on both sides (that is, back into the late 1970s and forward into the present) by novels of generational conflict. These conflicts revolve, sometimes in imaginative projections, sometimes in autobiographical fiction, around the confrontations of the younger generation with their parents and the Nazi past.

Ryan concludes with the observation that this Nazi past is not an illness that can be cured but a historical fact that needs to be analyzed anew by each generation.

With reference to the postoccupation literature in Japan, Van C. Gessel notes two strands, both of which represent a direct continuation of the literary scene in the 1920s. In the immediate postwar years, Marxist writers vigorously reaffirmed their social commitment through the composition of proletarian novels; this group was superseded during the Korean War by the writers of the asocial "Third Generation," who produced a "literature of anxious tension." In Gessel's opinion, Japanese literature of the past forty-five years can be viewed as a constant interplay between these two camps. He notes in the 1960s a resurgence of the socially committed writers, and in the 1970s the development of a new "generation of introverts," whose literature is one of quiet desperation. At the same time, however, withdrawal and introversion are an affirmation of tradition, because the "I" novel is an established and, to its practitioners, a comfortable literary genre. Yet, as Gessel also notes, double perspectives and the use of irony have modernized this genre and shattered its self-contained world.

Another, equally ambiguous means of affirming tradition in a modern context can be seen in the revitalization of the classical heritage. Similarly, the many philosophical "changes of mind" on the part of the intellectuals can be seen in the context of a "legacy of ideological conversions."

In reference to the war and its legacies, Gessel specifies that although the war is viewed and presented with revulsion, the writers pose few questions concerning guilt and make no mention of the atrocities committed. In his well-balanced evaluation, Gessel is careful to mention also "the long-standing tradition in Japanese prose to focus tightly upon the narrow, introspective moment and the individual confession, removed from social context." This practice has far-reaching implications when the absence of such probing questions is considered.

Dagmar Barnouw and Katō Shūichi adopt two different approaches when they speak in section V about the role and function of the critic in society, and they suggest several equally fruitful perspectives.

Barnouw applies the framework suggested by theories of critical reception and reader response to the works of Wolfgang Koeppen and Ernst Jünger in order to show the shifts in intellectual perception over the past forty years. She selects these two writers to represent extreme positions in a literary spectrum that ranges from Koeppen's early postwar novels, where the author insists on reflecting the past-as-present in fictional form, to Ernst Jünger's aestheticism, cultural conservatism, and transhistorical elitism.

The history of the critical reception of these two writers and the possible causes for reader preference—which appear to be scarcely guided by the discussions of the literary critics—suggest the existence of various attitudes toward "undoing the forgetting" of the German past. The recent reevaluation and the development of a more broadly based esteem for Jünger among the critical establishment may give pause to those who believe that aestheticizing terror or war, and permitting aesthetic considerations to overrule ethical ones, is not the best way to look at a deeply troublesome past.

Katō Shūichi illuminates the position of the intellectual or writer in contemporary Japanese society. He identifies important factors that have profoundly influenced the general public and, to a lesser extent, the critical establishment, and intellectual production. The first of these is consumerism, with a corresponding decline in the reading of literature in favor of television and comic books. The second is the commercialization of the book-publishing world, with an ever-increasing trend toward larger publishing houses, a development that leaves increasingly less room for the middle range of authors and critics. The third is a depolitization of the public; as the public has become less interested in politics and more interested in material goods, it has moved toward political conservatism.

Katō gives interesting explanations of traditional Japanese behavior patterns that persist despite the fact that other long-established patterns were broken after 1945. The mix of change and tradition creates tensions that, in a sense, are characteristic of an economically international and pro-Western society such as Japan.

Katō sees Japan as facing a new turning point, because the country's economic goals have been reached and a new agenda must now be formulated for the future. For this purpose, he upholds the mission of the intellectual, who must not be co-opted by the pervasive culture industry that can involve the media, the various cultural bureaucracies, and the lecture circuit. The intellectual must keep an increasingly complacent public alert.

In the last section, two writers, Oda Makoto and Peter Schneider, speak with passion and eloquence of their personal memories of the war and the postwar period, and of the significance of the past for the present. Both writers insist that they cannot speak for their countries or for their generation, but only for themselves. Yet they give vivid testimony to the continued importance of the writer as public conscience in our societies.

Oda Makoto sees antimilitarism as one of the most important legacies of the war, and during the Vietnam conflict he translated these convictions into political action. For him, the dialectically operating concept of victim and victimizer serves to illustrate the dual role played by the Japanese during the Pacific War. Oda expresses great solidarity with third-world countries, thus extending his militant pacifism beyond the national boundaries of Japan. He delivers his credo in vividly evocative images, and he argues for a literature of "commitment."

For Peter Schneider, the writer as public conscience can thrive only in repressive societies; he believes that in a democracy, the media and public opinion groups have taken over the position of a "public conscience." Schneider sees four modes of behavior as representing expressions of the various attempts that have been made to deal with the legacy of the past: (1) maintaining silence; (2) evoking the past through artistic and intellectual means; (3) rebelling against the past, as epitomized in generational conflict; and, among the younger generation, (4) defining oneself as a victim. In opposition to recent attempts to "revitalize" this legacy, he suggests that the only means to deal with the issue is to abandon any pretense that it can be "resolved," and to admit that it must always be kept in the open.

These two writers offer contrasting perceptions of the legacies of the past. Oda speaks with abhorrence of Japan's aggressions during the war, but he embeds them in the concept of victim/victimizer and so vows to remain on the alert to battle against any recurrence of such ideas. For Schneider, as for many thoughtful and sensitive Germans, the one legacy of the Hitler years that cannot be accommodated is the Holocaust. He believes that each generation will have to face up to this legacy in new ways.

In the last decade of the twentieth century, the Federal Republic of Germany and Japan, as indeed many countries around the globe, are challenged by new and rapidly shifting developments. Only when they can accept themselves in the present because they have confronted their pasts, can Japan and Germany expect to enter a future of political adulthood that is commensurate with their current economic success. If they find that degree of self-knowledge, there is good reason to believe that fear of repeating the past will be replaced by hope for a better future.

NOTES

1. An example of a detailed and tightly focused comparison is Neil H. Donahue's "An East-West Comparison of Two War Novels: Alfred Andersch's *Die Kirschen der Freiheit* and Shohei Ooka's *Fires on the Plain*," *Comparative Literature Studies* 24, no. 1 (1987): 58–82.

2. See the illuminating article by Ito Sei, "Die geistigen Ausdrucksformen des modernen Japaners," in Karl Friedrich Zahl, editor and translator *Japan ohne Mythos* (Munich: Iudicum Verlag, 1988), 159–205. Among many excellent insights, Ito clearly connects the Japanese insistence on social harmony with an increasing loss of reality, and he correlates the ideal of purity and justice with resignation and flight from the world.
3. Although *detached* may carry negative connotations in a Western culture, this is not so in Japan. See the introduction by J. Thomas Rimer to his book *Modern Japanese Fiction and its Tradition* (Princeton, N.J.: Princeton University Press, 1978). See also in a wider cultural and social context Ruth Benedict's classic *The Chrysanthemum and the Sword* (Boston: Houghton Mifflin, 1946).
4. Benedict, *The Chrysanthemum and the Sword*. Takeo Doi, in his *The Anatomy of Dependence*, translated by John Bester (Tokyo/New York: Kodansha International, 1973), disagrees with Benedict on some of her interpretations, but he, too, stresses consistently the importance and function of "circles."
5. For an account of the complex and fascinating research on intellectual styles, see Johan Galtung, "Structure, Culture, and Intellectual Style: An Essay comparing Saxonic, Teutonic, Gallic, and Nipponic Approaches," *Social Science Information* 20 (1981): 817–56. Walter Hinderer pointed out this article to me.
6. Arnulf Baring mentions the "pseudo-constitutionalism" and the legal system of Bismarck's Prussia as models for a modernizing Japan. Compare the "Vorbemerkungen" to Arnulf Baring and Masamori Sase, eds., *Zwei zaghafte Reisen? Deutschland und Japan seit 1945* (Stuttgart/Zurich: Belser Verlang, 1977), 9–10. It is unfortunate that this seminal work, comparing the political and economic development of the two countries from 1945 to about 1975, has not been translated into English. The volume comprises twenty-two articles by German and Japanese scholars on a wide range of topics, from reeducation for democracy, the political party systems, and the question of remilitarization to the origins and consequences of the "economic miracle."
7. This parallel is essentially the thesis of Eberhard Jäckel's "Der gleichzeitige Eintritt in die Weltpolitik," in Baring and Sase, eds., *Zwei zaghafte Riesen?*, 38–57.
8. Chapters 7 and 8 in this volume give a clear intimation of the complexities of this process of democratization in the literary field alone. For a recent publication in the political context, see Robert E. Ward and Sakamoto Yoshikazu, eds., *Democratizing Japan: The Allied Occupation* (Honolulu: University of Hawaii Press, 1987).
9. Donald Keene, "Japanese Writers and the Greater East Asia War," in his *Appreciations of Japanese Culture* (New York: Kodansha International, 1971), especially p. 300.
10. See Lily Gardner Feldman, *The Special Relations between West Germany and Israel* (Boston: George Allen and Unwin, 1984).
11. Karl Jaspers, *Die Schuldfrage* (Zürich: Artemis, 1946).
12. Isoda Koichi discusses these changes in "The Historical Context of Postwar Japanese Literature," *Japan Foundation Newsletter* 12, nos. i and ii (June and August 1984): 1–9 and 1–8.
13. Ōe Kenzaburō, "Japan's Dual Identity: A Writer's Dilemma," *World Literature Today* 62,3 (Summer 1988): 359–69, esp. 365.
14. Isoda Kiochi, "The Historical Context of Postwar Japanese Literature," *Japan Foundation Newsletter* 12, no. 1 (June 1984): 1–2.
15. An example of such a balancing view is given by Donald Keene when he quotes Takami Jun: ". . . if one is going to bring up the matter of atrocities, it was an unspeakable atrocity to burn alive innumerable people in our cities with their incendiary bombs—not to mention the atomic bombs. But the atrocities of the victorious country are never subjected to examination; only the atrocities committed by the defeated country are pointed out in scorn." Donald Keene, *Dawn to the West: Japanese Literature of the Modern Era—Fiction* (New York: Holt, Rinehart, Winston, 1984), 968.
16. This phrase is the title of Alexander and Margarete Mitscherlich's study *The Inability to Mourn*, translated by Beverly R. Placzek (New York: Grove Press, 1975). The German original *Die Unfähigkeit zu trauern* (Munich: Piper) was published in 1967.

17. Peter Schneider addressed this situation in his novel . . . *schon bist du ein Verfassungsfeind* (Berlin: Rotbuch Verlag, 1975). For contextual presentations of these heavy-handed legislative measures, see Dieter Sterzel, ed., *Kritik der Notstandsgesetze* (Frankfurt/Main: Suhrkamp, 1968); and Peter Frisch, *Extremistenbeschluß* (Leverkusen: Heggen, 1976).
18. Among the many publications on contemporary terrorism, see in reference to terrorism in West Germany and Italy, Iring Fetscher's illuminating *Terrorismus und Reaktion* (Reinbek bei Hamburg: Rowohlt, 1981). Extremely pertinent to German terrorist activities in the context of this discussion is Leon Botstein, "German Terrorism from Afar," *Partisan Review* XLVI, no. 2 (1979): 188–204. On the international plane, terrorism and publications on its many different motives are reviewed by Shaul Bakhash in "The Riddle of Terrorism," *New York Review of Books* (24 September 1987): 12–16. The murder of Alfred Herrhausen, head of the Deutsche Bank, in November 1989 also follows this pattern.
19. Andreas Huyssen addresses this point in great detail in his "The Politics of Identification: *Holocaust* and West German Drama," *New German Critique* 19 (Winter 1980): 117–36.
20. Among the plethora of events, a few highlights should be mentioned: in 1985, on the fortieth anniversary of the end of the war and of the Hitler regime, the President of West Germany spoke of these dark years with sorrow and compassion and provided leadership that West Germans had been unable to accept in earlier statements by politicians such as Theodor Heuss or Willy Brandt, or in the writings of philosophers of the stature of Karl Jaspers, or in historians such as Karl Dietrich Bracher. The same year, President Reagan's visit to the cemetery of Bitburg reflected Chancellor Kohl's desire to force a symbolic forgiveness. (Geoffrey Hartman discusses the details in Geoffrey Hartman, ed. *Bitburg in Moral and Political Perspective* [Bloomington: Indiana University Press, 1986].) One year later, the historians' debate erupted, focusing on the question whether the Holocaust was a singular occurrence in history or could be "relativized" with respect to other genocides, such as those under Stalin's totalitarianism. (*Historikerstreit. Die Dokumentation der Kontroverse um die Einzigartigkeit der nationalsozialistischen Judenvernichtung* [Munich:Piper, 1987].) Charles S. Maier enlarges on this controversy in his penetrating book *The Unmasterable Past: History, Holocaust, and German National Identity* (Cambridge, Mass.: Harvard University Press, 1988). In 1988, Philipp Jenninger, president of the Bundestag, resigned after the controversy prompted by his speech on the occasion of the fiftieth anniversary of the *Kristallnacht*.
21. James Reston, Jr., "How Japan Teaches Its Own History," *New York Times Sunday Magazine* (17 October 1985).
22. On this aspect in the context of emperor Akihito's political position in general, see Steven R. Weismann, "Emperor Akihito: Japan's Imperial Present," *New York Times Magazine* (26 August 1990).
23. Peter Schneider, "Concrete and Irony," *Harper's Magazine* (April 1990): 56.
24. Marc Fisher, "New East German Legislature Asks Forgiveness for Holocaust," *Washington Post* (13 April 1990).

I
HISTORICAL OVERVIEWS

2
West Germany as We Know It—An Episode?

Arnulf Baring

The Allies' defeat of the Axis powers in 1945 destroyed the German Reich and led to a social revolution, a complete change in the traditional power structure of the country: the eastern territories were cut off or lost, the old capital lost its function, leadership and old aristocratic elites vanished, and social roots were shaken loose. The defeat of Japan, in contrast, meant no break with its history and tradition.

Germany's loss, however, gave the newly founded Federal Republic the chance for a fresh start. The catastrophe had persuaded the so-called '45 generation (comprising, in fact, several generations of Germans), who believed themselves to be at a "zero hour" of history (*Stunde Null*), to accept the rules of democracy and Western liberal principles. Economic and consequently psychological support by the United States led to the Americanization of the West German people.

In 1968, a new generation questioned the pact agreed to by the '45 generation and with it the conversion to Western ideals. The '68 generation's criticism has been adopted today by the Green movement—the most influential part of the new generations. The decline in the economy after 1973 supported this tendency to turn away from the existing foundations. Thus, in the long run, the political institutions and even the whole society, as it has emerged after the war on the basis of the generation pact of '45, might change fundamentally. The recent events in East Germany, which took place after this essay had been completed, might speed up this development. The merging of two societies, which had been separated over nearly half a century—and taken quite a different course—might well lead to a search for new and different fundaments that a future German state should be based on.

THE LEGACIES OF WORLD WAR II

The legacies of World War II have been profoundly different for Germany and for Japan, although at first glance the fates of both countries show some similarities: both fought a war with expansionist goals, they became allies and invaded large parts of Europe and Asia, and they suffered defeat almost simultaneously. Both were occupied and had the same postwar problems: the integration of people who had been expelled from their territories, the reeducation programs, and the imposed democracy. Both countries rose from the ruins to become economic world powers, although with relatively little political influence. Today both countries represent, after the United States, the two countries with the biggest economic potential in the capitalistic world. The picture appears simple: two countries with a similar fate, two timid (or cautious) giants.[1]

That picture, however, is misleading. Whereas Japan's defeat meant only a historical caesura, a severe blow but one with no radical consequences for the social structure of Japanese society and its national identity, Germany's defeat was total and led to a turning point in German history. With two lost wars, the German's quest to establish a united, centralized Germany as a dominating power in Europe had ended in a catastrophe. The basis of the Reich was broken, Germany occupied, and Berlin taken by the Russians. As Walter Hofer wrote in his book on National Socialism, a book that for decades was mandatory for every West German student, the historical outcome after the twelve-year period of Nazi rule and reign was horrible:

> Not only Germany and half of Europe were lying in shambles but the legacy of Bismarck, the unity of the country had been wasted, the achievements of the Prussian kings were destroyed: a many-centuries lasting development, the German colonization in the East, had been revoked. The soldiers of the Soviet Union are standing at the River Elbe and pose the gravest threat Europe has ever faced in its history. The German name was abused, burdened with the greatest crimes of mankind. And this all for the price of unimaginable suffering, sacrifices and ruins, not only of a material and physical but also of a spiritual and emotional nature.[2]

Facing the masses of rubble and ruins, as Hermann Glaser has written, the Germans believed that the rebuilding would take a half century.[3] However, amid the rubble, hope grew steadily. After that overwhelming experience the Germans wanted to start anew. They were convinced of being at a "zero hour." As one witness remembers:

> It was the beginning of a new era—I hope my words do not seem blasphemous—as at the outset of the world, when the earth lay waste and empty. But then God brought light and planted shrubs and animals and finally men. Back then we all suddenly felt newly created, newly reborn—finally free. Those who have never experienced this will hardly be able to comprehend it; and those who have will never be able to forget it. They will always feel the glow of gratitude for those things which succeeding generations regard as simply given—things which on the contrary are not at all matters of course. Never to be hungry! And always to have a roof over one's head. To be able to dress warmly in the winter and enjoy a heated home: A peaceful night of sleep, and security. No longer the officially promoted fanaticism—not to speak of the fairy tale prosperity which has descended upon us in the West.[4]

In 1945 a new generation emerged, although none in the usual sense of the word. What made them the '45 generation was the common experience; young and old, men and women, realized that the old German Reich was gone; turning back had become impossible. In 1945 Germany no longer existed. It was dissolved. Three states were to emerge from the broken pieces of the Reich: West Germany, East Germany, and Poland. Japan's situation was different. The defeat did not lead to a break in history. Defeat for Japan meant just a detour on the continuous course of Japanese national history.

TWO UNEQUALLY DEFEATED NATIONS

The defeat of Japan did not lead to division or even reduction of its national territory. Japan lost only colonies that it had occupied a few years, or at the most a few decades, earlier. Its losses did not compare with Germany's loss of territories that had been part of the German states for many centuries and, in some cases, since the Middle Ages.

By keeping its territories, Japan could preserve its national identity. As the German politician and writer Peter Glotz once said, an individual's identity is expressed in his capacity to integrate a great number of possible roles.[5] Accordingly, the identity and the strength of a nation can be measured by the opportunities this nation offers to its own people to find a valid way of life for themselves, a way of life they can affirm and shape according to their own inclinations within the framework of their country's stable boundaries, common history, language, and culture.

German national identity serves the German people in this sense to only a limited degree. For example, in the late 1970s the German author Martin Walser remarked in a discussion that

> one cannot suppress the concept of nation. I experience its division as a weakness, as something that is missing, a kind of persistent loss of blood. It is the feeling that I no longer belong to an organism that embraces Leipzig, Dresden and Weimar. It is a sense of pain; it can only hurt, if one is no longer part of it. When I look at other nations, I say to myself, in their case everything worked out well, even if they've been through God knows what kind of experiences—England, France, Italy, Spain, Poland. I can't help feeling that I come from Germany. The Germany of 1927—the year of my birth, i.e., an undivided Germany—is, in a sense, the map I go by. I cannot start redrawing it or correcting it.[6]

Japan's situation is different. Even though identity problems exist in Japan today, they derive from the nation's massive industrialization rather than from its defeat in World War II. The Japanese are conscious of the need to redefine themselves. They seek to establish an acceptable self-image as individuals, as a nation, and as a newly emerging power in the world community. "In many ways they (the Japanese) are new, different, westernized, modernized; in many ways they are old, traditional, oriental."[7] Other scholars support this view, even arguing that some of these changes had occurred before the war:

> The new education, the consumer society, new economic patterns, the rise in the status of women, the slow advance of the conjugal family ideal, unionization, the pursuit of happiness, the new religious freedom, all can be seen as quantitative change along lines begun in prewar Japan. Yet the changes are not simply linear. Rather, the total effect is a new social configuration.[8]

Although in Japan the transformation to a modern society caused an identity problem almost independent from defeat, in Germany the war led to a deeper identity crisis: besides the transformation that all industrialized countries experience, the collapse of the country, the division of the territory in three states, and the crimes committed by its former leadership struck at the very roots of the German national collective identity.

In many respects Japan after 1945 can be compared with post–World War I Germany. The Weimar Republic continued to exist almost (with the exception of its Polish border) in the borders of the former Reich. Berlin remained the capital. Weimar continued to be shaped largely by a preindustrial mentality. The eastern agrarian area and its Prussian-feudal elites and traditions still prevailed over the progressive western industrial social forces.

Because economic, and thus social, conditions and power relationships remained unchanged in Germany after World War I, continuity of leadership and bureaucracy was maintained. Military war leaders took over leadership positions in the republic. Erich Ludendorff played an important part in the rightist movement in Bavaria during the early 1920s, and Paul von Hindenburg became president of the Republic and, for many Germans, a substitute emperor.[9] At the same time judges, professors, and bureaucrats stayed in their offices and thus reproduced the values and goals of the Imperial Reich rather than shaping the new democratic values of the first Republic.

The still powerful conservative forces and large segments of the population of the Weimar Republic resented the changes in the form of government. Everybody understood that the kaiser had to step down, but did the monarchy have to disappear? One could perhaps argue that if the monarchy could have been preserved Hitler might not have come to power.

Strong support for monarchical government has continued to characterize Japan after 1945. The same conservative party has stayed in power with only one short interruption. The emperor did not even have to step down. As a poll showed in 1946, 86 percent of the Japanese people favored the monarchy; two years later the figure had even increased to 90 percent.

In Japan elements of the old political and economic system and its values survived and therefore could be sustained. Until the early 1960s, 40 percent of the Japanese were still working in agriculture and fishing industries.

After 1945 Germany was confronted with a totally new situation. Politically, socially, and economically, it started with a *tabula rasa*. First, there was the tremendous loss of its eastern territories, half of the country: one quarter of Germany within the borders of 1937 became Polish, another quarter a Soviet-dominated separate state. The seat of government had to move from Berlin to Bonn, where a new capital was founded, together with the new Federal Republic, four years later, in 1949. In American terms, imagine the area from the East Coast to Kansas City, from Miami to Dallas, from Boston to St. Paul, stripped from the United States; Washington, D.C., taken by a foreign power; and Denver named the new capital of the country.

Along with these geographic changes came the long stream of Germans expelled from their territories, refugees, bombed-out families, and evacuees. More than 16 million people—almost one-fifth of all

Germans—were expelled; they had to move to the West.[10] It has been argued that the compulsory exodus of 16 million Germans from the homes in which their ancestors had lived for centuries—in some regions, for nearly a thousand years—was a catastrophe with a historic dimension comparable only to the migration of nations at the end of the ancient world.

> While then the more daring and efficient groups of the population departed on their own will in order to find new land, now whole populations were expelled regardless of their abilities to survive, without supplies and almost without luggage, and were pressed into an economically and politically broken society, a society which did not seem to be able to place those millions of people, not to speak of, to feed them. Such a forced mass exodus could lead to nothing less, it seemed, but the end of the continent.[11]

The migration of millions toward the West profoundly changed the social structure of the new West German state. The traditionally strong "segregation" of "social-cultural milieus"—as Martin Broszat has called regions where, for example, one class or one religion dominated—disappeared. The distribution and absorption of millions of displaced persons, of refugees and those bombed-out threw the whole German society into disorder and destroyed centuries-old cultural boundaries. Even in Bavaria today, there is hardly a pure Catholic community anymore.

As often in life, however, a loss means also a gain. The "desegregation" proved to be an important advantage for the coming democratic state in West Germany. The traditional social-cultural milieus, as Broszat writes, "hampered inner unity and the capacity for consensus of the nation unified in 1871, as well as the acceptance of democracy in the Weimar period and produced an immense need for irrational-suggestive nationalistic integration that prepared the ground for the führer-messiah Adolf Hitler."[12]

The cutting off of the Reich's eastern territories also had an important effect on the future West German state. The agrarian-dominated territories with their traditional feudal-Prussian elites suddenly disappeared. Politically, these elites had represented a strong conservative force that has never accepted the democratic rules established by the Weimar republic. The East had long represented the opposite of the industrialized, progressive, democracy-oriented West.

Today the contrast between the two areas is even more obvious. East Germany has still cozy and quiet villages with ponds where storks still build their nests on top of the church; Germans driving west from southern East Prussia are still fascinated by the untouched nature, the unexpectedly preserved environment that seems not to have changed in a century.[13] In eastern Prussia and in East Germany the green fields, the long avenues with trees, often still without any pavement but sand, and the wooden houses prevail in the landscape. Desperate attempts at industrialization by East European socialist leaders have changed the character of the land and its people only in isolated areas. Not only the former eastern territories but also East Germany still presents a rather romantic picture, a picture that makes its visitors wish that Thuringia or Mecklenburg would be declared a national park.

In contrast, West Germany, with its fast economic progress, the growing net of autobahns through the countryside and woods, cities of constructed concrete, and transformed townlike villages, gives the impression of something completely new. Most houses there are no older than twenty or thirty years. History does not go beyond, tradition is missing. Industrialization has been thoroughly successful and has completely changed the shape of West German society. The West Germans after 1945 accepted democracy and Western liberal principles. But why?

FOUR GERMAN REVOLUTIONS?

There are at least four theories why Germans became converts to democracy, adopted Western liberal ideas, and, in contrast to their rejection of Weimar, wholeheartedly supported the new post–World War II republic:

1. The German sociologist Ralf Dahrendorf and the American historian David Schoenbaum have argued that the Nazis themselves unconsciously initiated a social revolution between 1933 and 1939.
2. The German political scientist Peter Graf Kielmannsegg has asserted that only the destructions in World War II themselves, not the changes of the six years preceding the war, caused revolutionary changes.
3. Another German political scientist, Theo Pirker, has suggested that the Allies halted revolutionary forces under way in 1945 thus thwarting an anticapitalistic revolution.
4. I believe that the real revolution was fulfilled by the Americanization of West Germany.

In 1965, Dahrendorf wrote that because the obstacles for the totalitarian state were also obstacles for the democratic form of government, Hitler unwittingly caused the transformation of German society, which made freedom and democracy possible.[14] In 1966, David Schoenbaum made much the same argument, declaring that the Nazis had accomplished a revolution that unintentionally prepared German society for the adoption of democratic rules. In *Hitler's Social Revolution*, he pointed out that by 1939 the Nazis had achieved exactly the opposite of what they originally had planned: cities had enlarged instead of being reduced; capital was more concentrated; land population had decreased not increased; women were working in factories and bureaus instead of staying at home and in the kitchen; industry's share of the gross national product (GNP) had increased while agriculture's role was reduced; industrial workers enjoyed good living conditions, while the small-business people ran into problems.[15]

The "brown revolution" changed society in different ways. For example, the army provided opportunities for young, lower-class people. Some of the most important leading politicians of West Germany, including Helmut Schmidt, chancellor from 1974–82, and Walter Scheel, the president of the Federal Republic in the 1970s, had been young officers in Hitler's army; their promotion to positions of responsibility while they were still in their early twenties was the first step on their way to the top of the Bonn republic.

The results of the changes during the Hitler regime were evident to everybody. Schoenbaum quotes a clerk:

> Formerly when I went to the theatre with my wife, there was always trouble. We got a seat in the twentieth row. But Huber, our chief accountant, and his wife were in the tenth row. And afterward all hell broke loose at home. Why can the Hubers afford the tenth row and we cannot, my wife asked. Nowadays, six nights a week, all the seats in the theatre cost the same. First come, first served. Sometimes the Hubers sit in the tenth row and we sit in the twentieth. But my wife knows that's because the Hubers live nearer to the theatre.[16]

Others, however, have contested Schoenbaum's thesis. In 1980, Peter Graf Kielmannsegg wrote that changes between 1933 and 1939 amounted not to a revolutionary, but to an evolutionary process. Real revolutionary change, Kielmannsegg said, meant the destruction of larger parts of the country and with it the old power elites, the "OffiziersKorps" and the east-Elbian aristocrats, as well as a change in the political consciousness. "The catastrophe of National Socialism, not the revolution of 1918," Kielmannsegg wrote, "has broken the domination of the elites of the Ancien Regime in Germany, has broken the domination of a political consciousness that was shaped by nationalism and hostility towards democracy." And, he says, it was the war, the bombs, and the catastrophe that led to that revolutionary development.

> What in the history of other nations successful revolutions have produced, had to be done in German history by two world-wide wars: the breakthrough toward political and social modernity. Two lost wars—that means: Germany was forced by two acts of giant self-destruction to break with its own history, and it thereby has broken the continuity of its history much more completely than is usually done by a revolution.[17]

The German sociologist Theo Pirker questioned this thesis. He suggested in 1977 that historical and social continuity had not been interrupted after 1945. On the contrary, the Western Allies supported restoration of capitalism and the "bourgeois class society." According to Pirker's view, 1945 could have meant a chance for a "democratic and anticapitalistic policy" if the working class, represented by the Social Democrats and the unions, had constituted the government, but Western Allies blocked this development.[18]

I believe that Pirker underestimates the profound transformation of German society during the Third Reich and in the postwar period. In addition to the restoration of capitalism West Germans have universally accepted democratic principles, in marked distinction to the situation in the Weimar Republic. This change of mind, together with a broad German adoption of American principles and values, has been the reason for the real revolution in Germany after the war.

AMERICANIZATION: THE REAL REVOLUTION

West Germany owes its real revolution to the American influence after the war. Although the leaders of the United States at first doubted whether Germans had the ability to absorb the Western way of life they tried to denazify and to reeducate the Germans, to acquaint them with rules of democracy, of political compromise, and of fair play. For them the authoritarian character of the Germans was responsible for fascism; therefore, it was important to change their ideas and their behavior in order to make them good democrats. This naive idea was totally different from the concept of the Soviets, who believed that capitalism was the fertile ground on which inevitably fascism grew. Thus, capitalism had to be destroyed and socialism established. Nearly all Americans questioned this conclusion because the United States, the heartland of capitalism, had not produced fascism. Therefore Americans prescribed basic political lessons: the Germans had to learn the rules of a free democracy and economic liberalism.

But neither reeducation nor denazification programs were enough to persuade the Germans to accept the liberal Western ideas. Instead, two other factors led to the Americanization of the Germans: first, as the West German writer Wolf Jobst Siedler has pointed out, "History itself has by force turned the face of Germany toward the west".[19] As a consequence of the defeat in 1945, the Germans had to abandon their traditional position between the East and the West. Prussia for centuries has been an eastern power, which had taken pride in colonizing the east; Prussian kings had been crowned in the easternmost city of Königsberg, now the Russian Kaliningrad.

Second, and equally important was the psychological assurance by the Americans, which came with the economic help of the Marshall Plan. In the beginning the West Germans doubted that the Americans would leave before long. In June 1945, for example, the journalist Margret Boveri was warned by a German Communist in Berlin not to collaborate with the Western Allies. "This would do one no good once the Soviets were alone in Berlin."[20]

Hope among Germans that the United States would not abandon them grew when Secretary of State James F. Byrnes spoke in Stuttgart in 1946. And hope finally became reality when his successor, George C. Marshall, announced the economic aid program for Europe in his speech of 5 June 1945 at Harvard University.[21] Finally, the Germans got what they had been seeking in vain for decades: a powerful ally.

Americanization was the consequence. West Germany identified itself with liberal democracy, with civil rights as the foundation of a constitution for free men, with the rule of law, with checks and balances, and with pluralism as the organizing principles of society, which through the distribution of powers and competitive forces guarantee liberty and progress. The West German political system, a completely new system, was based on something similar to the American model.

For the first time in its history, Germany—West Germany—became a society in which liberal economic goals, methods, and values played the dominant role. Patriarchal family businesses gave way to managerial companies; most businesses became corporations with limited liability. The extent to which German business followed its American model can already be inferred from terms such as *deficit spending*, *holding*, *trust*, *leasing*, *job-sharing*, or *know-how*, all of which the West Germans have borrowed from American English.

Today, the West Germans have Americanized to a much greater extent than the French, British, or Italians. East Germans or Germans who return from South West Africa after a long absence often go so far as to claim that the West Germans are not really German anymore—that they have discarded their "Germanness" (*Deutschtum*). "Genuine Germans," it is said, are to be found more commonly in East Germany, surprisingly the more conservative and traditional of the German states.[22]

TWO COUNTRIES UNEQUALLY OCCUPIED

Japan, although Americanized, insisted on retaining its national identity. Support for the monarchy remained strong in Japan. As in the Weimar Republic, officials and bureaucrats stayed in their offices, Tokyo remained the capital. The political purge was limited to high-ranking government officials and the military. Japan had no counterpart to the Nazi Party, with millions of members and huge mass organization.

Continuity was demonstrated in many ways. In 1957, Nobusuke Kishi, who had been sued after the war for crimes against peace while he was minister for munitions during World War II, became prime minister. It would have been unthinkable for his German counterpart, Albert Speer, who was sentenced to twenty years' imprisonment at the Nuremberg trials, to have become chancellor of West Germany. The main leaders of the Third Reich had either committed suicide or been hanged—the rest were discredited. The real reason for the astonishing Japanese tolerance toward Japan's war leaders seems to lie in the fact that after 1945 the Japanese people considered Japan's crimes of the 1930s and 1940s as merely regrettable side effects of the war. For the Japanese people they were, although unfortunate, understandable and therefore excusable.[23]

The continuities in Japanese society allowed the Japanese to handle the democratization process differently. The institutional compartmentalization of Japanese society implies a system of "special relations," which is too old and too strong to have been changed by Western individualistic rules of democracy. This system of special relations outranks the democratic system that was introduced by the American occupying power in 1945. The political systems of Japan and West Germany are different because the two countries had different reactions to defeat in 1945. Whereas the Japanese adopted the form of democratic rule imposed by the Americans and found a synthesis with traditional elements, West Germans adopted democracy totally. The complete integration of West Germany into the North Atlantic Treaty Organization (NATO) as well as the belief in the creation of a Western type of democracy, however, were possible only because the political attitude of the '45 generation in Germany had been completely changed by the total loss of the war.

THE '45 GENERATION: A FUNDAMENTAL CONSENSUS

In 1945 and for some time afterwards, there was no rebellion of the younger German generations against the old, even though such a squaring of accounts could have been expected. The shock obviously was too deep. Germans who in 1945 were old enough to understand the meaning of the end of the war, the collapse of everything, were shaken and converted, regardless of whether they were eight or eighty years old. They had experienced the results of a policy of high risks and fanaticism, and they had heard about the crimes. As a consequence, all generations tacitly agreed on a generational pact. No discussion was needed for the lesson from that experience: "Never again!" Everything that happened after 1945 and in the first decades of the Federal Republic can be understood by these two words. Never again dictatorship, never again isolationism, never again power politics.

The '45 generation turned to the West because it did not want Red dictatorship after it had just experienced the brown one. In addition, the frightening news about early Bolshevist terror during the 1920s had left a deep impression on the German people. The horrors of the Soviet invasion in 1944–45, the brutal transformation of the Soviet Zone into a "people's democracy" in the first years after the war, and finally the trauma of having Soviet soldiers standing at the Wartburg,[24] in the heart of Germany, made the Germans anti-Communist, anti-Soviet.

This feeling of fear helped prepare the generation of 1945 for the thorough Westernization of West Germany. Almost all the 1945 generation endorsed Konrad Adenauer's belief that only on the side of the United States could Europe stand up against the East. In the beginning of 1946 Adenauer, then chairman of the newly founded Christian Democratic Party in the British Zone, wrote to a friend in the United States: "The danger is grave. Asia stands at the River Elbe. Only an economically and politically healthy Europe under the guidance of England and France, a Western Europe, to which as an essential part the free part of Germany belongs, can stop further advancement of Asian ideology and power." He continued by asking his friend: "Please help to spread the opinion in the U.S.A. that Europe can be saved only with the help of the United States."[25]

As I have described elsewhere,[26] Adenauer wanted the Germans (or at least those who had come under Western occupation) to become a part of a West European federal state, included in the community of the older West European democracies, anchored in free Europe, for its own sake permanently bound into the West. The new West European federal state should be protected and guaranteed by the United States and by the presence of the Americans in Europe. He used the '45 generational pact to integrate the Federal Republic into the West. Thus Adenauer and Kurt Schumacher, the great leader of the Social Democratic Party who persuaded his party also to adopt an anti-Communist attitude, stand out in the history of the Bonn republic as the two most important West German founding fathers.

THE GROUP 47: A DIFFERENT VERSION

Some of the '45 generation, however, wanted a different policy. They felt that the opportunities of the "zero hour" in 1945 had been missed, that a harmful reconstruction—a regrettable Weimar restoration—was under way. They believed that Germany should again become a bridge between East and West, should develop a synthesis of Western democratic values and a socialist economy. They had in mind a Germany without the Soviet Union *and* without the United States; their political concept could be called liberal socialism and national independence.

The theory comes very close to that of Theo Pirker, who worked with Hans Werner Richter for the periodical *Der Ruf (The Call)*. The periodical served as an influential voice of the desired policies. Group 47 grew out of it. For a long time, the writers of this group shaped the literary scene in West Germany forming a kind of intellectual opposition to the newly established institutions, parties, and political trends. Group 47 also expressed a negative skeptical view of the Federal Republic in its literature. However, this assessment may also reflect the fact that literature tends to lament and criticize the deficits of society rather than to praise the existing situation.

Hans Werner Richter, who with Alfred Andersch had edited *The Call*, formed the group when the newspaper was forbidden in 1947, or at least, it has been argued, when Richter and Andersch were fired.[27] Young writers like Andersch, Richter, Heinrich Böll, Günter Grass and Wolfgang Koeppen, then twenty to forty years old, met regularly every year until 1967, seeking a completely remodeled Germany. In 1974, a more skeptical Richter wrote in retrospect:

> It was the so-called third way which we wanted to follow. We were not the first who tried that, and we should not be the last. But what was it, the third way? Socialism and democracy, that is easily

said, and we as well have said and written it easily. But did we have a clear conception of the building of a socialist economic order? No, we did not have it. There existed then as many ideas as today—and they were just as contradictory.[28]

The group gained no direct, immediate political influence. Its members soon had to realize that it was not the younger generation who steered the new republic but the older generations, men like Adenauer in West Germany and Walter Ulbricht in East Germany[29]—men who had received their political training during the Weimar period, some, like Adenauer, even earlier during the Imperial Reich before 1918. Above all, Group 47 feared the restoration of the prefascist period: "We spoke of the rule of the old men, Adenauer on the one side, Ulbricht on the other, men who tried to start after a collapse with no precedent at the point where during the Weimar Republic the social-political and party-political development had been interrupted."[30]

The Group 47 members resented the fact that they were excluded from political influence and, at first, even lacked recognition as authors. Probably because of this experience they never invited to their meetings any writers from other generations, such as Alfred Döblin, although his writings indicate that he would have fit into the group. Richter and the others feared that these already famous authors would dominate the meetings and the group. This is only one example of the truism that, in Germany, generational differences are often more important than ideologies or party loyalties. It was only much later, long after Döblin's death, that Günter Grass called him his "teacher."[31]

Disappointment and frustration soon set the members against the Federal Republic and the restoration thesis was born. Richter had already written in *The Call* in August–September 1946: "What is happening here seems to be a restoration, a repeat of what had existed before, a restoration of the constitutional conditions before 1933."[32] And Wolfgang Koeppen summed up the feelings of the group members in the beginning of the 1960s:

> If I think about 1945, I am of the opinion, that from there and then could have started a movement of the losers, a belief of those who broke with the world, those who felt remorse, those without flags, those who live above the nations, and finally of those brotherly human beings who have good will. Our imitation "Biedermeier" . . . is as absurd as repulsive. Sometimes I want to cry about the tender plant of our Democracy.[33]

But the Group 47 was wrong: Bonn was no restoration of Weimar. And as the writers came to realize the difference, most of them were slowly integrated into the establishment of the Bonn republic during the 1960s. While in the 1940s and 1950s they had voiced a kind of mild protest, during the sixties they were integrated into the political spectrum, together with the Social Democrats.

The differences between the Weimar and the Bonn republics are profound. The second republic, strangely enough, started under much better conditions than the first. As the next section details, Bonn has proved a lucky chance for Germany.

THE FEDERAL REPUBLIC: A WINDFALL

Bonn has become a success story, not only because of its economic prosperity but also because of its political stability. The republic has developed from a society marked by class distinctions during the Weimar times into a society of middle-class homogeneity. West German society has thus become more equal and harmonious. Regional differences have faded, and overall conditions equalized. Those who exercise the power of the state, such as bureaucrats and soldiers, have been democratized. Different classes, social strata, and the sexes are becoming emancipated.

The political system has been modeled on the American system at least to a certain extent. The trend toward a two-party system, as opposed to the multi-party system of the Weimar Republic, has gained strength and has forced the two major parties to be more flexible. They have become *Allerweltsparteien* ("catch-all" parties).[34] The Christian Democrats were the first party to dispense with ideology in the 1950s; in the 1960s, the Social Democrats followed suit. Even if this trend has, temporarily, slowed somewhat, the once long-term programs of the current West German parties have shrunk to mere campaign platforms. Public opinion polls, an American import, have become more important than firmly established links of class or religion between parties and certain groups of society.

Why has Bonn not become Weimar, as the Swiss expert on Germany, Fritz Rene Allemann,[35] noted as early as the 1950s? What are the reasons for the different development of the two German republics of Weimar and Bonn?

A number of factors helped to shape the emerging democratic West Germany; several cannot be ascribed to American efforts and others can be so ascribed only in part.[36]

1. The great land-owning class, which, even as late as the Weimar Republic, played a fateful role in German affairs, was permanently destroyed by the loss of the eastern regions of the German Reich.

2. German militarism under Hitler had obviously led to a catastrophe. The role of the army as a state within the state was accordingly discredited and destroyed. An autonomous Prussian-German military history also ended.

3. New elites—industrialists, managers, and bankers—gained power; West Germany became a middle-class society. Since 1945 the economy and liberal values decisively shaped Germany as never before. It is false to speak of a capitalistic "restoration," as the Left has been known to do; capitalism never was dethroned, and so could have never been restored. On the contrary, the increased significance of capitalism since 1945 far exceeds that of a restoration.

4. The lower middle class, small-business people, and shop owners have changed from their inferior position and their dependence on preindustrial models. Similarly, they have been cured of their inclination toward authoritarianism.

5. Since 1945, the workers have been increasingly integrated into society and have entered the middle class. Old rivalries among the workers were eradicated by the creation of a new federation of unions shortly after the war. The far-reaching share in decision making that West German factory workers enjoy today is widely regarded as a model in many countries of the world.

6. The importance of religious membership—indeed, religion itself—has disappeared. The secularization of the West Germans has contributed to their homogenization.

7. The creation of a functioning, parliamentary constitutional system, which enjoys support across the political spectrum, from the Right to the Left, has been especially important. Dolf Sternberger, a professor of political science and writer on public affairs, has suggested that the phrase "patriotism directed at the constitution" (*Verfassungspatriotismus*)[37] should serve as the rallying point for West Germans' national aspirations. And in fact this is the most important, the only appropriate form of German nationalism today.

8. Finally, one of the main reasons Weimar's democracy failed was the lack of support by members of the authoritarian-conservative Right. The Bonn republic was able to obtain their support.

> For the traditional, authoritarian-conservative right, the new direction was determined by the increasing terror of the Hitler regime, by the collapse to which it had led Germany, finally also by the threat of a communist dictatorship. . . . Even apart from all efforts of the allies to "reeducate," democracy seemed for these social groups more and more the only real alternative to a new,

this time communist dictatorship: the traditional followers of an authoritarian-constitutional state now preferred a democratic-constitutional state to an authoritarian-arbitrary state.[38]

The Federal Republic stood from the beginning on a different, more reassuring ground than its predecessor, but it took decades for the second German republic to become firmly established: Bonn was—economically, socially, politically, and culturally—built in stages.

THE FOUNDING OF THE BONN REPUBLIC: A LONG PROCESS

The foundation of the Bonn republic was laid during the war—in 1944—when the Allies decided to subdivide Hitler's greater German Reich into three, later four (including the French) zones. When Stalin, Truman, and Churchill met in Potsdam at the end of July and the beginning of August 1945, it became obvious that Germany would be divided if the war time coalition broke up. It was only a matter of time before this breakup occurred. Thus General Lucius D. Clay decided in May 1946 to stop the sending of dismantled machines from the U.S. Zone to the Soviet Zone. Simultaneously the decision was made to constitute a U.S.-British bi-Zone. With the Truman Doctrine and the debacle of the Moscow conference in spring 1947,[39] combining the three Western zones became unavoidable. Currency reform and the introduction of a free-enterprise economy (market economy) by summer 1948 laid a stable economic and social foundation for the forthcoming West German state. Subsequently, the Parliamentary Council prepared the Basic Law (*Grundgesetz*), a new constitution that was adopted on 8 May 1949, four years to the day after the Nazi capitulation. In August 1949, the Federal Republic held its first elections; in September, the first president and the first chancellor were elected. Until 8 May 1955, however, sovereignty remained with the high commissioners of the three Western powers. Once sovereignty was regained, the first phase of the founding of the Federal Republic was over.

The second phase began with the setting-up of an army, which had been discussed since 1950. In contrast, Japan remained unarmed. It had been forced by the United States to write this into its constitution. West Germany though became part of the defense system of NATO. Bonn used its offer to participate in a Western defense as a means to regain sovereignty. However, it would not be appropriate to talk of a *re*militarization. In fact an army was added to a state that originally had been planned and built unarmed. Accepting the new function of the republic meant a conversion.

In the third phase, after 1969, West Germany finally accepted its eastern border in the course of what became known as the *Neue Ostpolitik* (New Eastern Policy). The *Neue Ostpolitik* was pursued by a coalition of Social Democrats and Liberals which came into power after twenty years of Christian Democratic rule.

The new German state for more than twenty years had lacked this border, because for two decades it had not acknowledged the territorial changes—the amputations that had cut the former Reich into three parts. Now the chancellor of the Social Democratic-Liberal coalition of 1969, Willy Brandt, believed that the foundation of the Federal Republic, which had spanned above two decades, was completed with the acceptance of the status quo in the East. "Brandt continues what Adenauer began" was the slogan then; the New Eastern Policy meant the completion of Adenauer's Western state. It seemed that the foundation process had ended, the Bonn state was at last complete.[40]

Today, however, Brandt's New Eastern Policy can also be interpreted differently. Brandt's goals at that time, it seems, were more than just to complete the Federal Republic. When he spoke of achieving "good neighborhood with West and East," he was aiming at a new beginning. Brandt advised the West Germans to become partners of the East as well as of the West. Therefore, the chancellor's political position could indicate the beginning of a possible refutation of our pro-Western state. In this case, the New Eastern Policy represented the opposite, the revision of Adenauer's Western concept.

"WE SHALL OVERCOME": THE FEDERAL REPUBLIC AND THE '68 GENERATION

In 1966, when recession first shook the basis of the *Wirtschaftswunder* (economic miracle), twenty years after the currency reform, a new generation started to speak up, carried by a new consciousness.[41] Unlike the '45 generation, the '68 generation did not believe in the "zero hour" of 1945. Where their parents had seen a new beginning, the young saw continuity and subsequently asserted, "we don't have anything to do with the Nazi period."

For the first time since 1945 the generational pact was dismissed. Young people had two complaints: First, they regarded the economic achievements of the Federal Republic as shallow, because they themselves had been raised in an affluent society. They were *Wirtschaftswunder-Kinder*[42] and thus lacked not only the war experience but also a deeper understanding of the fundamentals of the Federal Republic. Second, they opposed their parents because of the Nazi past. Questions about the Nazi crimes were raised and discussions held. The young people demanded answers from their parents about their role in the Third Reich, about the Jews and Auschwitz.

The Auschwitz trial in Frankfurt from 1963 to 1965[43] was the beginning of a widespread public awareness in West Germany about what had happened in the death camps on Polish soil. Now it became a public topic. The Germans realized that something was fundamentally wrong with their history. The journalist Horst Krüger was one of the first to engage in that topic. In 1964 he reported from the Auschwitz trial in the monthly magazine *Der Monat*:

> Who is that? Who of the Germans comes here voluntarily? There are good, hopeful faces, lots of youth, students and pupils who watch with perplexity a show which their parents should have staged. Their parents? Well, no, certainly not theirs, but certainly others parents. My parents? Well, no, certainly not mine, but certainly other parents. Some old faces are also here, sixty or seventy years old, from which one can see that they did come out of sensationalism. What is missing here is my generation, the middle generation, which is concerned here, which took part. But they don't want to know anything about it, they know everything already. They have to work, to earn money at this time now shortly before noon, they have to keep the *Wirtschaftswunder* going. Who looks back is lost.[44]

For decades, the Nazi crimes had seldom been raised in the public at large. The '45 generation was a "quiet generation," a skeptical generation, which, during the Nuremberg trials, had watched the eradication of its former leaders. They did not speak about what had happened. They had gone through too much. Their first concern had been to survive, to look for a roof over their heads. Then they had to put their energies into the *Wirtschaftswunder*. Bitter discussions, condemnations, and executions at that time would have led to a new fragmentation of society. It would have been impossible to overcome successfully those twelve Hitler years. As Willy Brandt has pointed out several times, the integration of the Nazi generations into the Federal Republic represents one of the most important achievements of Konrad Adenauer.[45]

Only a new generation could start raising questions about the past. The '68 generation represented a new consciousness, different from the '45 generation and even from the socialists of Group 47. Members of the '68 generation felt that their parents had failed. They had missed the chances of a new beginning. Therefore the '68 generation tried anew to achieve a real, profound "zero hour."

On 7 October 1967, Group 47 met for the last time near Erlangen at *Pulvermühle* (Powder Mill)—an appropriate name for what happened there—in Bavaria. A radical student organization demanded a group resolution against the newspapers of Axel Springer—influential editor and owner of a chain of newspapers, among them the notoriously sensationalistic *Bildzeitung*—who represented one of the main targets of the young people's rebellion. Long and fierce discussions ensued in which Günter Grass became the speaker for the majority of the writers present who wanted to differentiate between their Group 47 and the politically naive, adventurous student group from nearby Erlangen University. Political differences of opinion within Group 47 could no longer be overcome.

As Rudolf Walter Leonhardt noted, "In *Pulvermühle*, Group 47 dissolved into two or three or even more political camps, which—and that was new—were feuding with one another."[46]

When it began, Group 47 had rejected the older generations; now Group 47 was rejected by a new, more radically minded generation. The '68 generation viewed the '45 generation and their contemporary adversaries, like Group 47, as belonging to the same camp. The younger students' final judgment on Group 47 was printed in *Kursbuch* of November 1968:

> As far as West Germany is concerned, one knows at the latest since Easter this year, that Group 47, notorious as a bulwark for discontent and a fountain of subversion, is not even a paper tiger but a lap dog. The group has given the students neither catchphrases nor applause. The students rather numbered them among the established people, in which before the group had seen the enemies of their own.[47]

The big difference between the Group 47 and the '68 generation was the experience of the war. The '68 generation, born after 1945, was no longer part of the postwar consensus. The '68 generation believed that the restoration of fascism was under way in the Federal Republic. They considered the emergency laws (*Notstandsgesetze*)[48] which were introduced by the Great Coalition in 1968 as Nazi laws. Thus they demanded a complete change, a radically new beginning, a revolution to stop the growing fascism they thought they discovered everywhere. Their aim was not a second phase of the existing Bonn republic but a completely new republic. They hoped for a new, true "zero hour" and tried hard to accomplish it.

Have they been successful? The '68 generation started early to complain about their failure, as we Germans obviously often do. In the long run, however, the movement had a profound impact on our society, our institutions, most of the country. A widespread new consciousness, which today is expressed in the Green movement, goes back to the '68 generation. Today the Greens have become important opinion leaders in the Federal Republic. And they, as well as the '68 generation, with their anti-Americanism and their condemnation of Western superpower politics, tend to seek a new position for Germany between East and West, as a neutral reconstructed national state.[49]

The integration of the Federal Republic in the Western Alliance is at risk. Even more, as a united Germany might feel the tendency to turn inward and away from former Allies. For some it might seem obvious that the two Germanies had to adapt to their respective allies, but that these times are over. So tomorrow, the united Germany might take a new course, adopt new ideas and values—which might well be very old ones—and regard the Adenauer Western state as just an interim stage in the long history of Germany.

THE END OF THE *WIRTSCHAFTSWUNDER*: THE BEGINNING OF A CRISIS FOR THE BONN REPUBLIC

The oil price shock in 1973 left a deep impression on the West German economy and even more on the West German mind. From 1974 the economy changed profoundly. Unemployment and inflation both increased in a development that was unforeseen by the experts. As the German economic historian Knut Borchardt asserts, however, the oil price shock was only one among many factors responsible for the deteriorating economic situation, but served as a handy scapegoat for the politicians. Borchardt considers the *Wirtschaftswunder* as a phase in which exceptional circumstances combined to support one another. In 1973 this phase ended, rather accidentally, with the oil price embargo.

What factors had made the *Wirtschaftswunder* possible?

1. After the war, West Germany had great potential for quick economic development. The backlog of demand for consumer goods was huge. Even before World War II the difference between the U.S. and German standard of living had been profound. In 1939 for example, 227 out of 1,000 Americans owned a car, compared with 25 out of 1,000 Germans. After the war, the Federal Republic seized the opportunity to adjust quickly to the American standard, but by the late 1960s the difference between Europe and the United States had declined, and economic development slowed.

2. The relative backwardness of West Germany in 1945 can also be seen in the agrarian sector. Whereas in the United States only 8 percent of all workers were farmers after World War II, in Germany 25 percent were still working in the rural economy. Then millions of Germans went into industry. By 1950 a worker in West German industry produced goods worth three times the value of production by a worker in agriculture. The gross national product climbed with incredible speed. But this movement too, came to an end. By 1973 only 7 percent of West Germans were still farmers—a figure that is normal for industrialized societies—and so this temporary fountain of growth was exhausted.

3. The highly motivated and flexible working reserve—those expelled and the refugees from the East—also helped account for the *Wirtschaftswunder*. The millions of qualified workers who arrived first from the former eastern territories, and later from the Soviet Zone, supported the continually expanding industry. Because these forces were willing to accept the governing conditions and wages, they guaranteed that during the 1950s the production costs remained relatively stable. As a result, investments in West Germany increased.

When the building of the Berlin wall in 1961 stopped the stream of refugees, the German economy sent out teams to the Mediterranean countries to recruit "guest workers." This strategy again proved to be successful for the economy, but—in contrast to the situation of those expelled—it was accompanied by many social, cultural, and political problems. Therefore in November 1973 the Federal Republic stopped accepting workers from non-European Community countries. The push came to an end.

4. The *Wirtschaftswunder* could never have happened without the low energy costs, without oil. Fast economic growth could not have been achieved on the basis of coal. From 1960 on, the use of cheap crude oil increased about 24 percent a year. In 1973, coal, originally *the* main source of energy in Germany, met only 22 percent of the need for energy in the Federal Republic, whereas oil accounted for 55 percent.

Beginning in 1973, when cheap production came to an end with the price embargo of the Organization of Petroleum-Exporting Countries (OPEC), other changes occurred which ever since have slowed down the growth of the West German economy. The main change was a growing public consciousness of the limits of economic growth as it had been formulated first in 1972 by the "Club of Rome."[50] The attitude of the public toward progress changed. The importance of environmental protection was slowly acknowledged and the first signs of a new, "Green" sentiment became evident, as demonstrated in the rapid growth of the Green movement.

As a result, environmental protection became a factor in production decisions. Cheap energy from other sources such as nuclear power could not play the role that oil had played in the 1960s; nuclear power has faced strong public resistance in the Federal Republic since the mid-1970s.

Together, these factors will tend to curb quantitative growth for a long time to come. The world may never again live under the same unique combination of factors favorable to economic growth. Therefore 1973 marks the turning point in economic development in two ways. As Knut Borchardt puts it, "It belongs to the greatest paradoxes of recent economic history that the call to stop economic growth came and received wide attention and consent at a moment when history itself started to fulfill the wish."[51]

CONCLUSION

The West German state was built on a broad consensus of the postwar generations. The experience of the Nazi collapse and the economic help of the United States led the West Germans to accept Western liberal principles. West Germany was integrated into the Western Alliance.

In the late 1960s a new generation began to question the political postwar consensus on which the only successful democratic republic on German soil had been created. Their criticism has subsequently been adopted by the Green movement, which still is the most influential voice of the new generations and which pursues a political concept contrary to Adenauer's Western integration policy. Germany should play again a role between West and East, the Greens believe. Although the Green Party lacks parliamentary influence, the movement has grown so strong that even the established parties have to keep a delicate balance between the '45 generation and the '68 generation in order to arrive at some political consensus and practical programs. It is, however, questionable whether the parties in the future will be able to integrate the new tendencies any further with the traditional Western concept.

Today there is a great danger that the raison d'être of the Federal Republic, as it was understood in its first decades, will dissolve. In the early 1980s the post–World War II generations became the majority of the population in West Germany. It will still take some years, even a decade or two, before these people will take over the political leadership, but they may well break the generational pact of 1945 and launch into something different by destroying the pillars on which the first successful democratic German state was built.

A new and rather unexpected force might precipitate the drift away from the fundamental principles of the West German state in the future. In the moment of a grand historic success a heavy burden is laid on the pillars of the Federal Republic. Will they endure it? The victory of free democracy in East Germany—as a consequence of the collapse of state socialism—also questions the existing West German state in many regards. In East and West Germany two different societies have emerged. Now that they will be united, the mixing will trigger off changes in both of them. It goes without saying that the appeal and the influence of the Federal Republic is much stronger. Nevertheless there will be tensions; institutions, values, concepts—tried and tested—will be questioned. If historically discredited ideas of Germanness fall onto the marshy ground, which has been prepared since 1968, it could lead away from the Western oriented culture and society as well as our Western style parliamentary democracy. Without any doubt it will require an enormous intellectual and political effort of all Germans to safeguard the fundamental principles and the underlying convictions of the most successful state on German soil to the present day.

NOTES

1. Arnulf Baring and Masamori Sase, eds., *Zwei zaghafte Riesen. Deutschland und Japan seit 1945* (Stuttgart, Zürich: Belser, 1977). See also Wilhelm G. Grewe, "Von der Besatzungsherrschaft zur Souveränität der Bundesrepublik Deutschland," in Manfred Funke, ed., *Entscheidung für den Westen. Vom Besatzungsstatut zur Souveränität der Bundesrepublik 1949–1955* (Bonn: Bouvier, 1988), 93–113. Grewe also compares the German and the Japanese experiences after 1945.
2. Walter Hofer, ed., *Der Nationalsozialismus. Dokumente 1933–1945* (Frankfurt am Main: Fischer Taschenbuch Verlag, 25th printing, 1975), 367.
3. Hermann Glaser, *Kulturgeschichte der Bundesrepublik Deutschland. Zwischen Kapitulation und Währungsreform 1945–48* (Munich, Vienna: Carl Hanser, 1985), 45.
4. Arnulf Baring, "8. Mai 1945," in Hermann Glaser, ed., *Bundesrepublikanisches Lesebuch. Drei Jahrzehnte geistiger Auseinandersetzung* (Frankfurt am Main: Fischer Taschenbuch Verlag, 1980), 40. In addition, see Wolfgang Malanowski, ed., *1945: Deutschland in der Stunde Null* (Hamburg: Rowohlt, Spiegelbuch, 1975).
5. Peter Glotz, "Über politische Identität," Merkur 391 (December 1980): 1177.
6. Martin Walser, "Glück der Gegenwelt," *Evangelische Kommentare* 14 (March 1981): 150.
7. Arthur G. Kimball, *Crisis in Identity and Contemporary Japanese Novels* (Rutland, Vermont; Tokyo: Charles E. Tuttle Co., 1973), 13.
8. John K. Fairbank, Edwin O. Reischauer, and Albert M. Craig, *East Asia: the Modern Transformation* (Boston: Houghton Mifflin, 1965), 828–29.
9. The Prussian generals Erich Ludendorff (1865–1937) and Paul von Hindenburg (1847–1934) were the most important military leaders in World War I. They dominated not only the military leadership but also played the decisive role in German politics. After the war, Ludendorff became a member of parliament for the Nazi Party from 1924–28, but later left it. Hindenburg was President of the German Reich from 1925 until his death in 1934.

10. Dietrich Hilger, "Die mobilisierte Gesellschaft," in Richard Löwenthal and Hans-Peter Schwarz, eds., *Die zweite Republik. 25 Jahre Bundesrepublik Deutschland—eine Bilanz* (Stuttgart: Seewald, 3d printing, 1979), 99.
11. Eugen Lemberg and Friedrich Edding, eds., *Die Vertriebenen in Westdeutschland. Ihre Eingliederung und ihr Einfluß auf Gesellschaft, Wirtschaft, Politik und Geistesleben,* 1 (Kiel: Ferdinand Hirt, 1959), 1.
12. "Am Ende des Sonderweges. Von Stalingrad zur Währungsreform: eine Epoche des gesellschaftlichen Umbruches in Deutschland," *Süddeutsche Zeitung, SZ am Wochenende* (18/19 June 1988), I–II. The article is a summary of the recently published, excellent book, Martin Broszat, Klaus-Dietmar Henke, and Hans Woller, eds., *Von Stalingrad zur Währungsreform. Zur Sozialgeschichte des Umbruchs in Deutschland* (Munich: R. Oldenbourg, 1988).
13. See Christian Graf von Krockow, *Die Reise nach Pommern. Bericht aus einem verschwiegenen Land* (Stuttgart: Deutsche Verlags-Anstalt, 1985).
14. Ralf Dahrendorf, *Gesellschaft und Demokratie in Deutschland* (Munich: Piper, 1965), 431–48.
15. David Schoenbaum, *Hitler's Social Revolution: Class and Status in Nazi Germany 1933– 1939* (Garden City, N.Y.: Anchor Books, Doubleday and Company, 1966), 283ff. Recently, Rainer Zitelmann has argued that far from being unaware of his revolution, Hitler supported that revolution: "The social revolution which was caused by national socialism was not inconsistent with Hitler's intentions. Hitler not only welcomed the process of industrialization and the increasing social mobilization, but consciously supported this development . . ." Rainer Zitelmann, *Hitler. Selbstverständnis eines Revolutionars* (Stuttgart: Klett-Cotta, 2d printing, 1989), 495.
16. Schoenbaum, *Hitler's Social Revolution*, 286.
17. Peter Graf Kielmannsegg, *Nachdenken über Demokratie. Aufsätze aus einem unruhigen Jahrzehnt* (Stuttgart: Klett-Cotta, 1980), 214 and 216.
18. Theo Pirker, *Die verordnete Demokratie. Grundlagen und Erscheinungen der Restauration* (Berlin: Olle und Wolter, 1977).
19. Wolf Jobst Siedler, "Was im Mai 1945 wirklich geschah. Längst bevor Europa seine Welt verspielte, verlor es seine Vernunft," *Frankfurter Allgemeine Zeitung,* 4 May 1985, supplement "Bilder und Zeiten," 1.
20. Margret Boveri, *Tage des Überlebens: Berlin 1945* (Munich: Piper, 1968), 188.
21. The American historian John Gimbel first asserted that the Marshall Plan was mainly created for the reconstruction of Germany. *The Origins of the Marshall Plan* (Stanford, California: Stanford University Press, 1976).
22. Why has society changed much less in East Germany? The Soviet Union could neither politically nor socially develop any attraction in East Germany. The economic order, forced onto this state, stagnated. The Soviet Union organized a strict control of the cultural life and never showed in the GDR any willingness to accept an international cultural exchange, except in limited and controlled state activities. So under the Communist surface German cultural life has remained much more original, and German traditions have been preserved more in the GDR than in the Federal Republic.
23. Akio Nakai, "Die 'Entmilitarisierung' Japans und die 'Entnazifizierung' Deutschlands nach 1945 im Vergleich," *Beiträge zur Konfliktforschung* 18 (1988): 6.
24. The Wartburg is one of the most symbolic places in German history. This castle in Thuringia was the scene of the legendary War of the Bards in the thirteenth century. In the nineteenth century the competition became widely known when Richard Wagner used it in his opera *Tannhäuser,* and the romantics Novalis and E. T. A. Hoffman in their poetry. This popularity was then used up by the national movement. Equally symbolic but also historically important was the time Martin Luther spent on the Wartburg in 1521–22, because during his stay he finished his translation of the New Testament into German. What came to be called Luther-German was the most language-creating and poetic achievement of his time and is today regarded as the basis for the New High German standard language. About two hundred years later, the

Wartburg celebrations of 1817 were a milestone of the German national movement. Students belonging to fraternities wanted to remember the Reformation and the wars of liberation against Napoleon. Today's national Colors also have their origins there.
25. Rudolf Morsey and Hans-Peter Schwarz, eds., bearbeitet von Hans-Peter Mensing, *Adenauer: Briefe 1945–47*. Rhöndorfer Ausgabe. Stiftung Bundeskanzler-Adenauer-Haus (Berlin: Siedler, 1983), 191.
26. Arnulf Baring in cooperation with Volker Zastrow, *Unser neuer Größenwahn. Deutschland zwischen Ost und West* (Stuttgart: Deutsche Verlags-Anstalt, 1988), 54.
27. That is the opinion of Jérôme Vaillant, *Der Ruf. Unabhängige Blätter der jungen Generation (1945–49). Eine Zeitschrift zwischen Illusion und Anpassung*, prefaced by Harold Hurwith (Munich, New York, London, Paris: K.G. Saur, 1978).
28. Hans Werner Richter, *Briefe an einen jungen Sozialisten*, prefaced by Leonhard Reinisch (Hamburg: Hoffmann und Campe, 1974), 107.
29. Walter Ulbricht (1893–1973) was a member of the Communist Party since 1919, emigrated in 1933, and lived in the Soviet Union after 1937. He returned to Soviet occupied Berlin on 1 May 1945 as the head of the "Ulbricht Group," to establish the Communist Party. Little by little he could get into all positions of power in the GDR, until he was gradually deprived of power by Erich Honecker with the help of the Soviets after 1971.
30. Richter, *Briefe an einen jungen Sozialisten*, 115.
31. In 1957 Döblin died. Eleven years later Grass published an article that began, "I never met him." Günter Grass, "Über meinen Lehrer Döblin," in *Über meinen Lehrer Döblin und andere Vorträge* (Berlin: LCB-Editionen 1, Literarisches Colloquium, 1968), 7–26.
32. Hans Schwab-Felisch, ed., *Der Ruf. Eine Deutsche Nachkriegszeitschrift* (Munich: Deutscher Taschenbuch Verlag, 1962), 251–52.
33. Wolfgang Koeppen, "Wahn," in Wolfgang Weyrauch, ed., *Ich lebe in der Bundesrepublik. Fünfzehn Deutsche über Deutschland* (Munich: Paul List, 1961), 36.
34. Otto Kirchheimer, "Der Weg zur Allerweltspartei," in Kurt Lenk and Franz Neumann, eds., *Theorie und Soziologie der Politischen Parteien* (Neuwied and Berlin: Luchterhand, 1968), 345–67.
35. The article first appeared in the periodical *Der Monat* 76 (January 1955): 337–41. Later the text was enlarged and became a book, *Bonn ist nicht Weimar* (Cologne, Berlin: Kiepenheuer und Witsch, 1956).
36. Jürgen Kocka, "1945: Neubeginn oder Restauration," in Carola Stern and Heinrich August Winkler, eds., *Wendepunkte deutscher Geschichte 1848–1949* (Frankfurt am Main: Fischer Taschenbuch Verlag, 1979), 141–68.
37. Dolf Sternberger, "Verfassungspatriotismus. Die Freunde des Grundgesetzes sollten sich zeigen und vernehmlich machen," *Frankfurter Allgemeine Zeitung* 31 August 1982, 9.
38. Richard Löwenthal, "Bonn und Weimar: Zwei deutsche Demokratien," in Walter Scheel, ed., *Nach dreissig Jahren. Die Bundesrepublik Deutschland—Vergangenheit, Gegenwart, Zukunft* (Stuttgart: Klett-Cotta, 1979), 78.
39. At the Moscow Conference in March/April 1947 the Four Allies talked seriously about Germany for the last time, looked for chances of a compromise. The conference did not yield any results, and was broken off. Immediately after that the American government decided to make West Germany the central point of an economic and political consolidation of the European continent. Wolfgang Krieger, *General Lucius D. Clay und die amerikanische Deutschlandpolitik 1945–1949* (Stuttgart: Klett-Cotta, 1987), 225ff.
40. It has been said, however, that the foundation phase of the new state ended perhaps even later. Ernst Nolte, for example, has argued that the refusal of the Bonn government to compromise with the terrorists who had kidnapped Hanns-Martin Schleyer, the president of the BDI, the Federation of German Industries, which resulted in the killing of Schleyer by the terrorists in 1977, marks such another date of the Federal Republic's foundation: It was not the only kidnapping at the time but part of a massive

attack against the state. Some time before, Jürgen Ponto, chairman of the board of the Dresdner Bank, and Siegfried Buback, the Chief Federal Prosecutor, had been killed in terrorist attacks. Schleyer's kidnapping was carried out with an unprecedented brutality. Nolte argued: "If the government had given in, a second sovereign would have constituted itself in the Federal Republic. The political leadership defended the basic foundation of statehood by rejecting the idea that preserving individual life should represent the first principle of its actions. In so far it made the Federal Republic a state." Ernst Nolte, *Was ist bürgerlich? und andere Artikel, Abhandlungen, Auseinandersetzungen* (Stuttgart: Klett-Cotta, 1979), 23–24.
41. Baring, *Unser neuer Größenwahn*, 77–80.
42. Ulf Preuß-Lauritz et al., eds., *Kriegskinder, Konsumkinder, Krisenkinder: Zur Sozialisierungsgeschichte seit dem Zweiten Weltkrieg* (Weinheim and Basel: Beltz, 1983).
43. In the so-called Auschwitz trial in Frankfurt 22 members of the guard had to face the court. For over 20 months new informations were constantly revealed about the horrible crimes of the Nazi regime. At the same time public anger was provoked by the possibility that these crimes might become statute-barred crimes if the penal law was not changed.
44. Hermann Glaser, ed., "Gerichtstag," in *Bundesrepublikanisches Lesebuch*, 251.
45. Willy Brandt, "Gespräch über Konrad Adenauer," in Helmut Kohl, ed., *Konrad Adenauer 1876–1976* (Stuttgart and Zürich: Belser Verlag, 1976), 58–59. Willy Brandt, *Begegnungen und Einsichten: Die Jahre 1960–1975* (Hamburg: Hoffmann und Campe, 1976), 58–60.
46. Rudolf Walter Leonhardt, "Aufstieg und Niedergang der Gruppe 47," in Manfred Druzak, ed., *Deutsche Gegenwartsliteratur: Ausgangspositionen und aktuelle Entwicklungen* (Stuttgart: Philipp Reclam Jr., 1981), 73.
47. Karl Markus Michel, "Ein Kranz für die Literatur. Fünf Variationen über eine These," *Kursbuch* 15 (November 1968): 177.
48. The emergency laws were the last constituent of the Basic Law. Originally there had been no emergency regulations, because the three Western Allies had kept these powers. The completion of the Basic Law needed, as all changes of the constitution in Germany, a two-thirds majority in both houses of parliament; that meant a great coalition of the leading parties (CDU/CSU and SPD). The constitutional articles created in 1968 only include state of emergency regulations in the case of international tension or in the case of defense, but not for interior emergency situations.
49. For details see Baring, *Unser neuer Größenwahn*, 197ff.
50. The "Club of Rome" was founded in 1968 and is a group of outstanding personalities of more than 30 countries. It is the aim of the club to discover reasons and correlations of urgent problems of mankind. Reports of the club are published regularly and they can often attract worldwide attention. The first report (Dennis Meadows et al., *The Limits to Growth*, 1972) has triggered off a revolution of the mind.
51. Knut Borchardt, "Die wirtschaftliche Entwicklung der Bundesrepublik nach dem Wirtschaftswunder," in Franz Schneider, ed., *Der Weg der Bundesrepublik. Von 1945 bis zur Gegenwart* (Munich: C. H. Beck, 1985), 210.

3

The "Long Postwar": Japan and Germany in Common and in Contrast

Carol Gluck

DIFFERENT HISTORY, COMMON MEANINGS

Comparison is far from the common coin of postwar history. Rather it is singularity, or even uniqueness, that characterizes most national renderings of war and postwar experience. In Japan and Germany there is reason enough for this in the particular nature of their fascisms, their culpability in the war, and the role that their respective pasts played in their subsequent history. A total war fought in terms of absolutes, World War II is also judged in absolute terms. Any German or Japanese attempt to relativize the past is met with strenuous objection at home and abroad, and comparability itself becomes suspect if asserted in connection with the Holocaust or the Rape of Nanking.

Both countries also conceive of their "postwar" as distinctive, situating defeat, occupation, and reform against both the immediate catastrophe of the war and the longer course of their modern history. Apart from the tendency, strong in both places, toward exceptionalist explanations of how and why modern Germany or Japan was different from what each calls "the West," they share an insistence on the special extent to which the postwar system was to break with the past and start anew. The subsequent scale of economic growth, foreseen by neither and termed miraculous by both, only made the postwar story seem that much more unusual, if not again incomparable.

Yet it is almost impossible *not* to compare Japan and West Germany in such regard. If the Japanese and the Germans have generally avoided comparison, they may perhaps be forgiven for shouldering the national burdens of a difficult recent past in predictably national fashion. But it is also true that frontal comparison of the two countries can easily seem outlandish, irrelevant, or worse, trivial. The Holocaust was singular; there were other divided countries, but Japan was not one of them;

63

nazism was politically structured and supported differently from Japanese fascism; Europe and Asia differed in both their regional and international relations; Japanese imperialism and racism originated in and operated on different historical grounds; the Allied occupations of the two defeated nations were neither institutionally nor functionally similar; and the cold war, postwar, and post-postwar international contexts were not the same for Germany and Japan. The list of contrasts is endless, seeming to confirm what each country was inclined to think in the first place: that its postwar history could properly be recounted only in its own terms.[1]

But granted the differences, great and small, in the twentieth-century histories of Japan and West Germany, the *meanings* attached to those histories were sometimes so alike as to seem uncanny. To the historical experience of fascism, aggression, war, defeat, occupation, reconstruction, economic success, political stability, rising power, and the uncertainties of the late-twentieth-century future, each country responded in its own way, but the responses themselves were homologous. However different in form and function, they occupied a similar structural position in the national discourse that related the past to the present. The strongly articulated break in 1945, for example, created a framework in which questions of continuity remained central in both countries, although the answers developed differently. The prominence of the United States in the two postwar histories generated a generically similar problem in domestic affairs and international relations, even if the details were not specifically congruent. And the besetting difficulty of dealing with an unmastered, perhaps unmasterable, past in the context of a present so much changed by the intervening decades has not yet disappeared in either country, both of which now confront their future in a post-postwar world.

A comparison of the ways these common meanings have been differently interpreted during the postwar decades can help to illuminate the particularities of literary expression in the two countries. Although my task here is to place postwar Japan in its own historical context, this volume as a whole suggests the potency of such a comparison. It may further serve somewhat to "denationalize" the two histories, a useful and appropriate approach to the cultural legacy of what was, in fact, not a national but a world war.

STARTING OVER

Much of the world in 1945 saw itself in departure, whether from fascism, war, or imperialism. The first legacy of World War II was the hope for liberation from the past, however uncertain the future. In West

Germany and Japan the hope was willed in particularly extreme form: history, severed, would begin again. As counterpart to the German "zero hour," the Japanese had "August 15." For them the present began precisely "at noon, August 15, 1945," when the emperor broadcast the news of surrender. Through the static and the strangeness of the previously unheard imperial voice crackling in an archaic language, few grasped the words accepting the terms of the Potsdam Declaration, the cosmic understatement of the war's having "developed not necessarily to Japan's advantage," the allusion to "a new and most cruel bomb," which could "lead to the total extinction of human civilization," or the resolve to move toward a grand peace by "enduring the unendurable and suffering what is insufferable." But they knew the war was over. And calm or weeping, relieved or betrayed, they were released.

An entire genre of "August 15" records and reminiscences now documents the moment when history intersected with autobiography and, in most renditions, liberated the personal from the public, the private from the state. The end of the war thus became the beginning of postwar remembrance and of its continued emphasis on "personal experience of the war" (*sensō taiken*) as the most reliably authentic voice of public memory. Without food, shelter, or any sure sense of what new oppression the occupation might bring, Japanese in the autumn and winter of 1945 thought nonetheless in terms of beginnings.

The surge of intellectual and cultural activity, which would have been striking at any time, was truly phenomenal against the background of extreme privation. Paper shortages and censorship notwithstanding, 434 magazines were founded or revived during the eight difficult months following 15 August. Of the many with born-again titles like *The New Age* and *New Life*, the most famous was the literary magazine *Shinsei*, with the parallel title *Vita nova* repeating its message in others' words.

> Setting out at these historic days that divide the century, we think of the many aspirations there are to express. . . . Let us put our sorrows behind us. Our course is clearly set. We must not err again. Deception and evasion no longer serve any purpose. The old Japan is completely defeated. Completely — . With these thoughts etched deep within us, let us strike out on the path toward a reborn Japan (*shinsei Nihon*).

The first issue of *Shinsei* sold 360,000 copies in three days in the fall of 1945, while its old liberal writers gathered down the hall from the editorial office to form the "private constitutional research association," which produced a revised draft of the imperial constitution by December. Toward more revolutionary ends, the Japan Communist Party revived its publication *Red Flag* (*Akahata*) in October, to offer guidance to the people in the "rapidly developing situation in Japan today which you yourselves must find surprising."[2]

The occupation meanwhile was speaking of little else but the "new Japan," using terms like the *democratic revolution* to mean something quite different from what the resurgent Left meant but sounding, for one brief moment, as if all stood on the same revolutionary brink. Even establishment politicians had to hone their public rhetoric on the whetstone of change and insist that every "reactionary force" would be eradicated now that the character of the nation had been entirely transformed. What a season of newness it was.

And what an illusion. It was scarcely likely that one day in August would inaugurate an utterly new Japan any more than it was possible for history to end, then start again. Indeed in the face of such strongly willed and radical discontinuity, the specter of continuity was never far from the thoughts of the political opposition or of the progressive intellectuals critical of the emerging conservative establishment. But neither they nor most other Japanese were willing to abandon the idea of a new beginning, for this was the founding myth of postwar Japan. The newness of the new Japan seemed to depend on its springing reborn from the "historic days that divided the century" and severed the past from the present.

It is correct, and absolutely necessary, for historians to point out the ways in which the two parts of Japan's twentieth century were, in fact, linked and continuous. It is also accurate for Arnulf Baring to suggest that the disjunction between postwar and prewar Japan was not so great as the discontinuity in Germany. He alludes to the loss of home territory, the division of the country, the fundamental change in social structure, and the discontinuity of political leadership that were the German results of nazism, war, and defeat. Japan, by comparison, emerged from its ordeal more intact territorially, socially, bureaucratically, and still in possession of its imperial institution. But the fact is that hardly any Japanese saw it this way right after the war, and few would accept this characterization even today.

It is not a matter of which caesura was historically stronger but of how that end/beginning was felt, interpreted, and woven into the mentality of the two "postwars." "Unequally defeated" or not, Japan understood its unconditional surrender as unconditional, its defeat as total, its political system and social relations as altered into a different, democratic form. On the individual level, the quick and sudden "conversions" (*tenkō*) from militarist to pacifist, imperial chauvinist to democrat, represented a personal equivalent of believing that the past could be buried by a loud and clear assertion of a change in direction. In the initial postwar years, although many Japanese lived their days in continuity, what they felt was change. The Left picked up where it had been cut off by the suppression of the prewar emperor system; old Anglo-American liberals became new American-style conservatives without having to convert much at all; established older writers resumed their introspective, aestheticized, or proletarian ways without a literary catharsis. Nonetheless, they did so in a context they saw as utterly changed. Utter change, that is what *sengo*, "the postwar," meant then and what it still largely means even now.

The "consensus of '45" in Japan may be summed up by this mythic sense of "starting over." Like most myths it was not true, and like most myths, it was "etched deep" enough that it long survived the circumstances that originally engendered it.

UNDER THE OCCUPATION

Starting over under foreign occupation meant that the United States was present at the creation of the allegedly new Japan. Quite apart from MacArthur's willingness to act the role of Creator, however, the postwar reforms (*sengo kaikaku*), as the Japanese call the wide-ranging institutional changes planned or implemented between 1945 and 1947, occurred in an atmosphere charged with an enthusiasm for "democratization" that did not emerge from the general's kit alone.

The Americans landed as occupiers but were welcomed as liberators, first because of the sudden freedom from the harsh wartime regime and then because of the enunciation of "peace and democracy" in sweeping but soon palpably concrete terms. Historians of the occupation stress the importance of Washington's presurrender plans in directing the occupation's program for aggressive change. But the Japanese saw mostly MacArthur, towering over their emperor in a September photograph designed to show who was now boss, or instructing the prime minister in October on the urgency of effecting the "Five Great Reforms," which seem to have emerged from the general's khaki pockets even before he landed in August. Give women the vote, encourage labor unions, liberalize education, abolish the secret police, and democratize the economy, pronounced the supreme commander, exuding a liberal air that surprised a few Americans and delighted many Japanese—Communists, progressives, and women among them.[3]

MacArthur's talent as a publicist notwithstanding, the Japanese enthusiasm for reform centered on democratization, not Americanization.

Japan had thought of itself as "Americanizing" twice before, once in terms of institutional "Euro-Americanization," which was the word used for modernization in the 1870s, and again in the 1920s, when "*Amerikanizumu*" swept over popular urban culture in Japan as it did in Europe. The post-World War II wave of American culture thus continued social trends that had been forcibly interrupted by wartime interdictions of American movies, jazz, and baseball language. Its significance was perhaps greatest for a younger generation of Japanese, who had grown up knowing only the propaganda of Japanist imperialism. To them the occupation brought not only an intoxicating freedom of intellectual access but also a sudden supply of American cultural products, which, if less inspiring, were not without ideological effect.

> I was about fourteen when the war ended. A year later, when I saw the American movies "His Butler's Sister" and "Madame Curie," I was able to accept our defeat for the first time because I learned that Americans were not devils, and I realized that Japan had suffered a moral defeat as well.[4]

From Bette Davis to moral defeat, the leap was easily made, and like other youth around the world in the 1940s, young Japanese gained part of their innocence about America at the movies. The rest they acquired from the ideals of freedom, democracy, and peace put forth by the occupation, which seemed to be about to make the movies come true in an entirely reformed Japan. When this did not happen and America the liberator turned the cold warrior and abandoned much of its own reform agenda after 1947, the progressives in this and other generations lost their innocence about the United States.

But their belief in democracy held. And that was because in Japan the "postwar reforms" were not initially conceived in terms of Americanization or of a "turning toward the West" in international relations. The issue was, rather, extirpating the domestic roots of fascism and imperialism, and the goal was expressed in so many variants of the word *democratic* that later commentators tallied their occurrences in the press as evidence of the ubiquity of the idea.[5] Just as they declined to become a Christian nation, despite MacArthur's gifts of free Bibles and other steadfast efforts toward this spiritual end, the Japanese could—and did—decline the aspects of the American reform program that did not suit them. The question is why so much did suit them, and the answer lay in the Japanese perception of the need for change. The reforms of 1945 to 1947 were real: land reform; a new constitution; social, legal, ideological reforms; and so on. Their provenance varied, from a land reform program similar to one that had been conceived within the Japanese bureaucracy years before the war to a constitution drafted entirely by Americans in days and forced through the parliamentary process in weeks.

Not everything changed, but not much promised to stay the same either. In 1946 intellectuals spoke of an "August revolution," when the defeat brought about the downfall of the imperial state and the Japanese people became "free and autonomous for the first time."[6] Although the commanding power of the occupation was never in doubt, these Japanese felt as if the Americans had liberated them so they could have the revolution (whether liberal, bourgeois, or socialist) they had hitherto been denied. And this was despite the fact that the Allies governed through indirect occupation, rather than direct rule as they did in Germany, which should have made the ancien regime seem quite potent, considering that its bureaucrats and ministries remained largely in place. Yet Maruyama Masao wrote of a "bloodless revolution" that had struck down the imperial order, and Japanese in 1946 felt paradoxically freer having gained popular sovereignty even under conditions in which their national sovereignty was, to say the least, severely compromised.

The word *democracy* belonged to the people in a different, although equally ubiquitous, sense. "From today is the age of democracy," announced circulars distributed to children who arrived at school in September 1945 to find, suddenly, *MINSHUSHUGI* (democracy) inscribed in large letters on the blackboard. In popular usage, democracy was not defined politically, but socially, and again it meant freedom. Sometimes it was freedom to buy in the "democracy market," as the black market everyone needed but could not afford was ruefully called. Sometimes it was freedom to do as one pleased, to crash a cinema line, for example. And most frequently, it was freedom to have as great a claim on food and goods as the once all-powerful officials. This definition of democracy as equalizing social access to livelihood was established early and remained more widely influential than the political definitions of social democracy or democratic revolution. And unlike the unfulfilled political hopes of the progressives, subsequent socioeconomic developments did little to undermine the popular notion that postwar democracy, once the early hardship was weathered, brought better living to more people.

In less than one year after the war, the constitution was promulgated and the first postwar elections held. Women, as MacArthur had promised, had the vote. Opposition parties were strong, the unions stronger, and the Left seemed to have a chance. Democracy, which had come packaged with peace, was popular. The watchword of the day was not the preservation of tradition but the achievement of modernity. Intellectuals viewed the postwar reforms as offering Japan another chance at the modern that it had bungled so badly before the war. Even the emperor, that most traditional of institutions, was trundling, democratized, around the countryside, greeting his people not as a god but as a symbol in a plain hat and suit. Most Japanese reacted with greater interest to this sudden civic mingling than they did to the so-called declaration of humanity, a rhetorical event much heralded by the occupation, which had staged it on New Year's Day 1946. That the imperial institution had survived, its tradition and person, if no longer sovereign or divine, nonetheless intact, occasioned less notice than the changes in the public management of the emperor. Compared with the founding of the two postwar German states, the institutional transformation of Japan had been rapid indeed. To Japanese of the time, it did rather seem as if a new age had dawned after the war and under the occupation. The myth of a new beginning now had the ideological and institutional garb of democracy, which was precisely what "the postwar" meant in its earliest manifestation.

That it soon developed differently than many had thought, hoped, or planned did not lessen the power of the idea of "postwar democracy," which remained the goal, however variously articulated or unfulfilled. This fact has doubled the conundrum for the Japanese, who had both to situate the postwar system against the prewar past, with which it was alleged to be discontinuous, and to legitimate a democracy, which, if not entirely imposed, was created under and by a foreign occupation. Note that the postwar puzzle here was posed almost entirely in domestic terms. Germany, East and West, was forced to define its postwar system in relation to other powers and as part of Europe. With help from the United States, Japan turned in on itself, hoping to withdraw from its Asian past and from the international stage in general. And although, unlike Germany, the occupiers of Japan governed indirectly, the historical effect was immediate and as if unmediated. If Japan and Germany were "unequally occupied," it was thus more likely in the direction of America's having invaded Japanese history in 1945 and having remained there, not only as the main all-powerful ally but as a simultaneously comfortable and discomfiting presence in Japan's domestic development and sense of its postwar self.

THE GENERATION OF LONG DOMINANCE

Seismic history tends to deepen the faults between generations, so that it is not surprising that the years of fascism and war produced strong generational identities in both Japan and West Germany and indeed in most other countries significantly affected by World War II. The patterns differ from place to place, but everywhere they seem particularly important in relation to culture, ideology, and political consciousness. When Arnulf Baring and Peter Schneider invoke the '45 generation and the '68 generation, they do not mean an entire chronological cohort, but an identifiable political and cultural voice that spoke with significant effect. The Japanese generational counterpart, those who were shaped by the war and by whom "the postwar" was shaped, entered the public stage immediately in 1945 and, either through itself or heritors of its consciousness, dominated the intellectual scene for nearly four decades.

Those progressive intellectuals, as they are called, ranged the political spectrum from communist through socialist to left-liberal, but all converged at the point after 15 August when their respective political goals seemed suddenly realizable and their collective task clearly set before them: to confront the past critically and march away from it resolutely toward an authentically modern future. From the beginning these influential intellectuals were a generational hybrid born of the war. The older figures came from two political generations, those old enough to have experienced the liberalism and socialism of the 1920s and those who came of intellectual age as the dark times grew ever darker. Whether they had recanted, like many of the communists, or retreated in a Japanese kind of inner emigration, like the scholars and writers who did not openly support the war, theirs were the generations that had submitted to, or at least failed to prevent, the fascism and militarism of the 1930s. Their awareness of this was reflected, and sometimes deflected, in the earnestness of their calls for fundamental postwar reform.

The younger members of these "prewar" generations were among the most effective spokesmen for the new Japan. Born in the 1910s and early 1920s, they were immediately vocal, some of them catapulted to intellectual and literary fame in their twenties, much younger than would have been the case in normal times. Partly because of their early prominence, this generation wielded influence across an extraordinarily long period, the bylines of figures such as Katō Shūichi having been as familiar in the media of the 1980s as they had been in the 1940s. And like Katō, most of them have changed neither their tune nor their tone.[7]

This steadfastness accounts in good part for their staying power. They initiated "the postwar" by invoking a democratic, modern, socially and politically reformist or revolutionary new beginning, and they remained faithful to this early "postwar" while others began to violate, abandon, or undo it. When the occupation and the Japanese government together veered away from reform and pacifism toward rehabilitation and rearmament from 1947 to 1951, the progressives denounced this "reverse course" as a subversion of the postwar goal. Thus they became their own Group 47, challenging the lost opportunity for change on behalf of their original vision. When the Security Treaty with the United States came up for renewal in 1960, the progressives joined forces across generational, sectarian, and social lines to protest the treaty and create a genuine democracy on a popular base. The 1960 protest, known as *Anpo*, was the Japanese counterpart of 1968 in Europe, a time when it seemed that the unfulfilled promise of postwar politics might finally be redeemed. But it was virtually the same promise, the same new beginning, that remained at stake. Thus the progressives became their own '68 generation as well. Or at least, they were present at the barricades as the torch passed to the younger generations whose political consciousness was defined by *Anpo*.

Of particular importance were those known as the "Shōwa single digit" generation because they were born between Shōwa 1 (1926) and Shōwa 9 (1934). Japanese of this generation had grown up knowing little else but war. Old enough to be indoctrinated but young enough not to be sent to the front, they had felt simultaneously repelled, betrayed, and liberated by the defeat. Many of the intellectuals among them lent their anguished voices to the condemnation of the imperial past and committed themselves viscerally to postwar democracy. They may have disagreed with the older progressives, for in Japan as elsewhere there were both a new and old Left, populist, radical, and liberal versions of democracy. But they shared the "postwar" world view, the belief in the zero hour of peace and democracy. And as the literary and political careers of men like Oda Makoto and Ōe Kenzaburō have shown, they were impelled to write and fight for it. Despair over the "death of literature" was not uncommon in postwar culture in Germany and other places, but in Ōe's case the cause was not the war but the failure of the "postwar." As he found it increasingly difficult in later years to believe in the possibility of democracy, he could no longer believe in literature either.[8] His is the progressive vision in its most acute and poignant postwar form.

It is both commonplace and true to point out that the progressives failed to realize their vision, standing divided among themselves and increasingly isolated from the majority of Japanese, as conservatism triumphed in politics, economics, and society. But they did stand fast, acting as an intellectual opposition and critical conscience against historical amnesia about fascism, the war, and postwar peace and democracy. And even younger generations, notably the student radicals of the late 1960s and early 1970s, shared a related stance. In comparison with Germany, there was in Japan a continuum of progressive opposition and influence across the postwar decades, which smoothed out generational differences on the issue of the legacy of the war.

Perhaps because the early postwar progressives had produced so strong and immediate an indictment of fascism, younger intellectuals did not blame the "generation of their fathers" on this particular count but instead became the carriers of the indictment to subsequent generations. Marxist in the academy, radical or populist in social action, and anti-American in foreign policy, the antiestablishment progressives had set themselves against the current of government policy and social trends. Thus the critical challenge that emerged in Germany in the 1960s had long been the intellectual status quo in Japan. The challenge to that status quo came not from the Left but from the Right, epitomized by Mishima exhorting his countrymen to a patriotic return to the lost samurai spirit before he committed ritual suicide in 1970, the event that for Ōe marked the death of postwar literature. In fact, however, it was Mishima who was eclipsed by the grand irrelevance of his gesture, while the progressives continued in fairly full voice.

Their fullness of voice was surely aided by the institutional continuity of the Japanese intellectual establishment—the so-called *bundan*—which helped to confer a longevity of influence on the early postwar progressives and their heirs. And even more important, the steady move of events in the direction of conservatism, the seemingly perpetual dominance of the Liberal Democratic Party, and the continually fading hopes for both social revolution and social democracy may well have strengthened the need to hold the progressive line in the face of Japan's historical retreat from its early postwar hopes and plans. Whatever the reasons, the progressive Japanese "consensus of '45" lasted across the decades in a strangely long and strangely strong transgenerational dominance.

THE "LONG POSTWAR"

This generational survival has a nomenclatural counterpart in the standard contemporary usage that refers even now in the 1990s to "postwar Japan." Japan has remained nominally and self-consciously "postwar" far longer than most other countries, which, however marked they still are by the configurings of the postwar world, have long since consigned their après-guerre to history. Since a government paper on the economy first declared in 1956 that "the postwar is over," the end of Japan's *sengo* has been reported many times, all to great exaggeration and little avail. Many said that the "postwar" would not end until the death of Emperor Hirohito, but that, too, occurred in 1989 without dislodging the epithet from general parlance. In this "long postwar" lies another legacy of the war for Japan.

Historians and commentators in Japan have by now agreed on a periodization of the "postwar" into three phases, which coincide quite closely with those of West Germany and other countries as well. There was first the period of recovery and reconstruction, from 1945 to 1955. Japan owed its economic recovery to the United States, although in a way different from what the original occupation planners had imagined, because it was the special military procurements that came to Japan during the Korean War that finally reestablished the economy on a positive footing. There was, it will be recalled, no Marshall Plan for Asia, just as there was no Pacific version of NATO, so that Japan's dependence on the United States in hot war and in cold was again less mediated than that of Europe. The San Francisco peace treaty ended the occupation and gave Japan its independence in 1952, at the same time that the Security Treaty tied that independence militarily to the United States, establishing what the Japanese know as the "San Francisco system."

A peace movement swept Japanese intellectuals in the early 1950s, directed against both the United States and against Japanese rearmament. Nationalism emerged on both the Left and Right, and for a time progressives hoped Japan might join the nonaligned nations of Asia, the first of several failed alternatives to the United States that were dreamt of in the postwar years. In domestic politics, 1955 saw amalgamation of both the leftist and conservative political parties, with the latter coming to power as the new Liberal Democratic Party. That it remained in power for the subsequent three-and-a-half decades suggests just how stable the so-called 1955 system proved to be.

The second phase, from 1955 to 1973, is known not as a system but as the "period of high growth," the Japanese equivalent of the German *Wirtschaftswunder*. In the wake of the *Anpō* protests of 1960 the government announced the "income doubling plan," which set the promotional emphasis on rising standards of living and new consumer prosperity. The rate of economic growth proceeded in double digits, and by 1968 Japan had the third highest GNP in the world, after the United States and the Soviet Union. The Tokyo Olympics of 1964 symbolized for the Japanese their newly regained sense of national confidence, and people reminisced about two decades of postwar peace and prosperity. Between 1971 and 1973 a series of events ended the period of high growth. Some, like the oil shock of 1973 and the pollution incidents that revealed the social costs of rapid economic development, affected West Germany in similar ways. Others, like the Nixon shocks of 1971, which normalized relations with China and freed the dollar from gold without informing Tokyo, America's closest Asian ally and trading partner, were peculiar to Japan. The rate of economic growth slowed, people again announced the end of "the postwar," and the years of "conservatization," Japan's *Tendenzwende*, began in earnest.

The third phase is called, simply, "post-high-growth." From the mid-70s until the present, this period has witnessed the completion of the alleged metamorphosis of Japan into a "new middle mass society," in which nearly everyone claimed to be part of a middle class that valued the status quo. In the strengthening conservative mood the long hegemony of the progressive intellectuals finally weakened, as conservative intellectuals celebrated Japan's postwar success and politicians dared to prettify the war in public. In a time of increasing economic friction with the United States and Europe, the Japanese, ever sensitive to foreign opinion and crushed by statements like that of the European Economic Community about their being "a nation of workaholics living in rabbit hutches," proclaimed the era of "internationalization," which was in fact the obverse of a rising nationalism. Now an economic superpower, Japan faced the future with great pride and greater uncertainty. Post-high-growth and *posuto-modan* (postmodern), the post-postwar period seemed to have arrived.

But when, after sixty-two years, the Shōwa era ended in January 1989, the founding myth of "the postwar" was rearticulated. In the endless public retrospectives, the new Japan always began in 1945, as unconnected from the old as it had ever been. Some of the sides had changed, as the progressives who had once criticized the American-written constitution for being imposed from outside now defended it against the conservatives who urged revision along nationalistic lines, while the new emperor on whose behalf the right wing denounced the constitution promised to uphold it in the first such imperial pronouncement in history. But the narrative of discontinuity remained the same, the status quo was reaffirmed, and Japan was still "postwar."

RESPONSIBILITIES, PAST AND FUTURE

Prewar/war/postwar: the key to the narrative is the war. Where Germans remember nazism, Japanese remember the war. The burdens of the past are similar, but they have been differently mastered. First, the chronology of mastery was different. A quiet generation in immediate postwar Germany was followed in the 1960s by a challenge to public memory to confront the Nazi past. In Japan not only was the prewar past openly confronted in 1945 but the postwar reforms were devised as its negative image, to remedy the structural flaws that had resulted in militarism and war. This early mastery of the past had genuine institutional consequences, but it may also have had its disadvantages, especially as time passed and the condemnation of the war settled into orthodoxy.

An event as cataclysmic as the war was bound to be viewed in stark terms by those who had only just experienced it, particularly when they had help from an occupying power intent on apportioning blame and bringing the guilty to trial. The original view of a wrong and unjust war emphasized the victimization of the Japanese people at the hands of a villainous leadership, which meant that "war responsibility," the Japanese term comparable to war guilt, or collective guilt, was clearly assigned from the first. There were debates over the emperor's war responsibility, but the people figured in a role that has often been called "victims' history," a view not much disturbed over the years. The focus on the Pacific War, which the Americans promoted during the occupation, meant the elision of the China War, which relegated the victims of Japanese aggression to the prologue of a story that ran dramatically from Pearl Harbor to the atomic bombs. For years the progressive intellectuals reminded people of the "Fifteen Year War," which began with the Manchurian Incident in 1931 and ended with the surrender in 1945, but there was little impulse for public memory to shift in that direction.

On the contrary, when officials and conservative politicians began publicly to revise the history of the war in the early 1980s, they left the tidy moral equation of Pearl-Harbor-to-atomic-bombs untouched, just as the U.S.-Japanese alliance it reflected remained undisturbed. Instead they chose to revise the China War, practicing comparative atrocities on the Rape of Nanking and finding it no worse than others, or sanitizing the "invasion" of China into an "advance" in national textbooks. In 1985, in a Japanese version of Kohl and Reagan's meeting at the cemetery at Bitburg, Prime Minister Nakasone paid the first official visit to the shrine of the war dead since the end of the war. Like the *Historikerstreit*, the Japanese revisions occasioned wide controversy, not only among the opposition at home, but more important, in foreign opinion, and particularly in Asia. Asia, for so long ignored by Japan as it nestled under the wing of America, was becoming increasingly important to Japan, and, if official Japan was able to forget Japanese aggression, Asia remembered. Just as the Germans had been watched by others as they watched, or neglected, their past, the Japanese were now coming under critical foreign scrutiny, not from the West but from Asia, where Japan had—with good reason—long felt uncomfortable. In terms of interpretive meaning, relations with Asia constituted a kind of Japanese Question, a legacy of the war that Japan had long avoided by virtue of the postwar world order, which in the 1980s was itself wearing down before Japan or Asia had found a mutually acceptable answer. In such times remembering the war became more than an academic issue.

The combination of early mastery, the long-dominant war generation, and the reliance on personal war experience (*sensō taiken*) as the medium of public memory has brought postwar Japan to a generational chasm somewhat different from that in Germany. The more than two-thirds of the Japanese born since 1945 are the "children who don't know the war," as the popular song has it, and it is likely that they never will. Personal experience is not transmissible, and the current mood of national pride does not incline the Japanese toward unpleasant self-reflection, at least not without prodding from outside. At the same time that the discontinuity of 1945 is maintained in public memory, a longer continuity is becoming more pronounced, one that elides the prewar years in much the way that the Nazi years are sometimes elided, and finds instead a single, slightly interrupted, period of modernization that turned out quite right after all.

In neither Japan nor Germany is this desirable, not only because of the anguish it causes to writers and others of conscience, but because the war, the postwar, and the post-postwar do not belong to these two countries alone but to a broader region and a wider world. If by looking in the postwar mirror of the other, Japan and Germany each sees the flaws in the distinctive legacy of the war viewed nationally, perhaps the common legacy of the war, which is an international one, will come more clearly into sight.

NOTES

1. For a narrative history from the establishment viewpoint, see Kosaka Masataka, *A History of Postwar Japan* (originally *100 Million Japanese*) (Tokyo: Kodansha International, 1972). For essays representative of the long-dominant progressive views, see Hidaka Rokurō, *The Price of Affluence: Dilemmas of Contemporary Japan* (Tokyo: Kodansha International, 1984).
2. *Shinsei*, *The New Age* (*Shin jidai*), and *New Life* (*Shin seikatsu*, with the English words also on the cover) all appeared in November 1945. See Fukushima Juro, ed., *Sengo zasshi hakkutsu* (Tokyo: Yōgensha, 1985), 45–52, 242–44, for *Shinsei*; 233–35 for *Akahata*.
3. Theodore Cohen, *Remaking Japan: The American Occupation as New Deal* (New York: Free Press, 1987), 53–78. The title of this book, written by a participant in the occupation, echoes the general tone set by MacArthur about the importance of the American role, which he made certain was echoed in the Japanese press. Hence the publicity given to the Five Great Reforms, rather than to the much more significant presurrender planning directive. See *Yomiuri shinbun* (12 October 1945) and *Asahi shinbun* (13 October 1945).
4. Sato Tadao, *Currents in Japanese Cinema* (Tokyo: Kodansha International, 1982), 36.

5. Katō Hidetoshi, "Shinbun to imiron: sengo Nihon no kii-shimuboru no rekishiteki henka," *Shisō*, no. 383 (May 1956): 77–97.
6. Hirata Tetsuo, "Kokkashi ni okeru 'hachigatsu kakumei,'" *Rekishi hyōron*, no. 446 (June 1987): 20–23. Miyazawa Tomoyoshi wrote of the August Revolution in "Hachigatsu kakumei to kokumin shukenshugi," *Sekai bunka*, May 1945; Maruyama Masao of the autonomy of the people in his famous article in *Sekai* in April 1946, translated as "Theory and Psychology of Ultra-nationalism," in Ivan Morris, ed., *Thought and Behaviour in Modern Japanese Politics* (London: Oxford University Press, 1963), 21.
7. Kazuki Kasuya, *Sengo shichō; chishikijintachi no shōzō* (Tokyo: Nihon keizai shinbunsha, 1981).
8. See Ōe Kenzaburō, "Japan's Dual Identity: A Writer's Dilemma," in Masao Miyoshi and H. D. Harootunian, eds., *Postmodernism and Japan* (Durham, N.C.: Duke University Press, 1989), 189–213.

II
THE POSTWAR INTELLECTUAL CLIMATE

4

The Challenge of the Past: Turning Points in the Intellectual and Literary Reflections of West Germany, 1945–1985

Walter Hinderer

Superficially, the two defeated countries, Japan and Germany, reveal a number of similarities. Both nations have enjoyed a remarkable recovery that has made them leading economic powers in the postwar world. This economic success has compensated for military defeat and healed the damaged national self-perception. In both countries, the emphasis on material success seems to have led to similar problems for the younger generation, whose misdirected attempts to fill the ethical void have resulted in extreme reactions and in terrorism. But the two states also manifest dissimilarities that are reflected in the different development of their political systems and of their literature. In Germany, the experience of World War II is overshadowed and burdened by the memory of systematic and unprecedented mass murder, whereas in Japan, memory is dominated by the deaths caused by the nuclear attacks at Hiroshima and Nagasaki.

In Germany, the legacy of World War II includes the question of guilt for the mass murders; the transition from fascist dictatorship to democracy; the reduction of the country's territory and its subsequent division into two Germanies; the relationship between culture and politics, and spiritual values and power; the dichotomy between the cultural and economic elites; the isolation of the intelligentsia and academics from society; and the generational conflict that emerged during the 1960s. Such internal German problems, which have their roots in both the Weimar Republic and the Third Reich, have belonged to the legacy with which the postwar German political, social, ideological, and cultural renaissance was burdened.

THE INABILITY TO MOURN

In the progressive magazine *Der Ruf* (*The Call*), the following curious "Acknowledgement of a Young German" appeared on 15 March 1947:

> I acknowledge the atonement that I together with my nation want to make for all our guilt. I do not acknowledge that the German people are the sole instigators of all crimes of these times. The extent of the catastrophe was too great for it to have been within the power of a single people to effect it and its repercussions. I believe that this second great war was a birth pang of a newly emerging era. Germany had the misfortune to represent the forces of the past against those of the future in this conflict.

Although the author concedes guilt and strives for atonement, and goes on in the article to plead for socialism, humanitarian beliefs, and democracy, this and other articles appearing in the magazine, edited by Alfred Andersch and Hans Werner Richter, show a suspicious "mixture of a democratic pathos of renewal and a militant-heroizing statement."[1] They also share a dangerous tendency to fix German responsibility in a more general context of the political world and thus to make it relative.

As can be deduced from the accounts of the Nuremberg trials after 1945, in addition to opting for unburdening strategies, the Germans suffered from a "severe lack of a *historical ability to imagine*."[2] They also seemed unable to attain an adequate perspective or to define their particular situation within the appropriate categories of human experience. These shortcomings impeded, and sometimes even prevented, a critical understanding of recent history. As early as 1946, in a noteworthy publication entitled *Geschichtsschreibung und Psychoanalyse* (*Historiography and Psychoanalysis*), Alexander Mitscherlich wrote of the impossibility of comprehending the German acts of inhumanity and translating them into human terms. In this study, he anticipated the socio-psychological thesis that he, with Margarete Mitscherlich, formulated in the mid-1960s as the "inability to mourn."[3] When both were alarmed by the absence of any sustained emotional feelings in postwar German society concerning the Nazi past and the crimes committed, they noted that neither mourning nor the "pathological intensification of mourning, that is, melancholy" was evident among the Germans.[4] Instead, the majority of the population experienced the period of national socialist ascendancy retrospectively "like the interruption [of life] by an infectious disease during the childhood years, although the collectively experienced regression under the protection of the Führer was at first pleasurable—it was wonderful to be a chosen people."[5]

In 1959, Theodor W. Adorno pointed out the social as well as the psychological motives of the repression mechanism in his important lecture entitled "Was bedeutet: Aufarbeitung der Vergangenheit" ("Coming to terms with the past: What does it mean?").[6] Since after 1945 the panic did not set in that Freud states will take place "when collective identifications crumble," Adorno argued in a 1970 work "that secretly . . . [collective] identification and collective narcissism were not destroyed at all, but continue to exist." In Adorno's view, only "coming to terms with the past as enlightenment" leads to maturity of the autonomous self and to a personal, independent self-identity.[7]

But, as Alexander and Margarete Mitscherlich observed, the path to maturity could become obstructed. Rather than taking the necessary steps to maturity, defined by Freud as "to remember, repeat, and work through,"[8] many Germans adopted defense mechanisms such as the denial and suppression of the past, resulting in an inhibited perception of reality and the spread of stereotypical prejudices, leading to an "orientation towards the unreal."[9] The Mitscherlichs also discussed the surprising fact that, after 1945, millions of Germans who had identified with the führer, the embodiment of the ego-ideal, did not even react to the sudden reversal of his qualities. The führer himself was now exposed "by the victors as a criminal of truly monstrous proportions," and one would have expected that the "ego of every German individual" would have consequently suffered a significant "devaluation and an impoverishment." As the Mitscherlichs commented: "The inability to mourn the loss of the Führer is the result of an intensive defense mechanism composed of guilt, shame, and fear; it is successful because of the retreat of a previously strongly libidinous occupation. The Nazi past is derealized, it is stripped of its reality."[10]

This indifference continued into the 1950s and manifested itself not only in the political and social life of West Germany,[11] but also in the fetishization of technology.[12]

As early as 1946, the emigrant Wolfgang Langhoff reported, not optimistically, after a visit to Germany: "I looked around for new people and colleagues with whom to undertake the cultural renovation—among actors, I found none, with very few exceptions. The old, narrow way of thinking: [there is] no consciousness of the catastrophe into which the German people fell [or] of the personal responsibility of each of them."[13]

OPTIONS AND DICHOTOMIES

It sometimes has been said that postwar German literature performed the mnemonic and mourning function that German society neglected,[14] yet many novels and stories written after 1945 show similar tendencies to "de-realize." The critic Hans Mayer, in his most recent book, *Die umerzogene Literatur* (*Reeducated Literature*, 1988), has called attention to two phases in the writers' reaction to the past:

> The short and vehement mourning by the writers around 1947 at the time of the first German writers' conference in Berlin had no repercussions, and amnesia replaced anamnesis. Only twenty years later did the discussion by writers of the younger generation concerning the guilt of the guiltless begin. Today, we must speak of the *Second Guilt*. It is no longer repression, but denial.[15]

This thesis of two phases—first, the failure to overcome the past, which operated as repression, and second, the "rehabilitation" of the past[16]—is associated with the two "restoration" eras as Mayer calls them: the "happy" restoration in the 1950s and the "sad" restoration beginning in the late 1970s.[17]

Although this thesis may oversimplify events somewhat, political apathy after 1945 was prevalent among the literary establishment. The cultural elite insisted, with Adorno, that poetry and politics were incompatible,[18] thus reaffirming the old dialectical model in which spiritual values and culture are separate from power and politics.[19] In 1962, Hans Magnus Enzensberger commented, "Poetry and politics, that was and is, in Germany, an always unpleasant and sometimes bloody theme, muddied by resentment and slave mentality, by suspicion and bad conscience."[20]

This dichotomy between the higher values of poetry and the dangerous devaluation of politics may reveal more of a "romantic attitude"[21] than Enzensberger perhaps realizes, and it shows little of the "critical attitude" of the intellectual who should understand his role as dynamic agent encompassing "distance and belonging, alienation and participation, criticism and agreement."[22] Participants in the meetings of Group 47, a loosely organized literary society founded by Hans Werner Richter after *Der Ruf* (*The Call*) ceased publication, demonstrated an unequivocally antifascist attitude but otherwise limited their political initiatives during the Adenauer era to the expression of a vague "discomfort."[23] If the discussions of the critics active in Group 47 can be taken as an indication of their intellectual concerns, aesthetic interests seem to have been far more important than goal-oriented political involvement. As Jürgen Manthey cynically wrote, "Defeat in a world war is absolutely necessary for the pursuit of culture, according to the motto: the Führer is dead, now the theatrical directors have their turn. It's as if the survivors had sworn with their last strength that *cultural* life would continue."[24]

The currency reform of 1948 introduced economic stability and facilitated the "economic miracle" of the years ahead. Concentration on economic matters and a concomitant disregard for politics had an analog in the cultural sphere. As discussed by Adorno in his 1950 essay "Auferstehung der Kultur in Deutschland" ("The Resurrection of Culture in Germany"), the pursuit of literature and cultural life that began in the late 1940s can be understood as a retreat by the intellectuals from the political arena into the aesthetic sphere. Many politically active publicists with literary ambitions retreated into the newly founded "Central Café of a literature without a capital city"[25] and concentrated on the display of various stylistic devices. Even Richter, founder of Group 47, commented the same year: "Thus the question is justified whether in our country a value-free intelligentsia has been discovered, a group that writes well, but that doesn't have much to say."[26] And Heinz Friedrich, a member of Group 47, suggested in 1970 that the decision on the part of the cultural elite not to participate in political activity may have been the "beginning of an inner emigration . . . an emigration into the domain of literature after political action had failed."[27]

In contrast, Hermann Glaser, the author of a detailed "cultural history of West Germany,"[28] has defended the "romanticism of the years of rubble," the new "turning inward," and the primacy of spiritual and cultural interests as the necessary regimen of a transition period that "strengthen[ed] the ego."[29] He opposed a "hasty rejection of escapism" and agreed with the two options pronounced by Peter Weiss in his play *Hölderlin*, two paths preparing "for basic change": the path of "analysis of the concrete historical situation" and the path of "visionary formulation of deepest personal experience."[30] Early postwar "analyses of the concrete historical situation" include Eugen Kogon's *Der SS-Staat* (*The Theory and Practice of Hell*, 1946) and Karl Jaspers's lectures on *Die Schuldfrage* (*The Question of Guilt*, 1946); they were, in my opinion, more important than the "visionary formulation of deepest personal experience," which only succeeded in a few exceptional cases.

As early as 15 November 1946, the editors of *The Call* suggested in an article entitled "Deutsche Kalligraphie" ("German Calligraphy") that the historically justified introversion "soon will become narcissism." And in an article published in *The Call* on 1 January 1947, Horst Lange made the following complaint about "books written after the war":

> What stagnation when it comes to ideas, what an educated desert, and what conventional boredom characterizes the new books that have most recently appeared here! This is not the first time that we have been witnesses of a regrettably regressive process in our

literature—of many evasions and aesthetic dodges, and of an overbred spirituality that was nothing but verbosity.

Later, Group 47 substantially helped to reduce what Adorno termed the "dangerous and ambiguous comfort of hiding in the provincial"[31] and the dominant tendency to write escapist literature. The group also tried to awaken sensitivity for the need to expurgate the language from the pollutions inflicted on Germany during the Third Reich. There is no question, however, that the general lack of analysis of the "concrete historical situation" was partially responsible for the failure to come to terms with the past.

Of course, one should not burden literature with demands that society and the political establishment were clearly unwilling to face. The public reception of Wolfgang Koeppen's trilogy, *Tauben im Gras*, (*Pigeons on the Grass*, 1951), *Das Treibhaus* (*Hothouse*, 1953), and *Tod in Rom* (*Death in Rome*, 1954), is a case in point. Koeppen described very astutely the "general political situation" in the postwar years and the failure to come to terms with the past. It is not surprising that he found no response.[32] Not coincidentally, Hannah Arendt wrote in 1950 after a trip to Germany: "Nowhere is the nightmare of destruction and terror less evident and nowhere is less said about it than in Germany. Everywhere one notices that there is no reaction to what happened, but it is difficult to say whether this is because of a somehow intentional refusal to mourn or the expression of true insensitivity."[33]

The Mitscherlichs have categorized the reactions "that prevent comprehension of the overwhelming burden of guilt" as being of three types: (1) an "obvious numbness of feeling" in the face of horrific events; (2) the "suddenly activated mechanism of de-realization" of the past to meet the requirements of the present"; and (3) the "manic attempt to take back" the past by concentrating on the reconstruction.[34] These psychosocial reactions find their political equivalents in the ideology of the cold war, expressed as early as 1947 in a speech in Stuttgart by the U.S. secretary of state, James F. Byrnes.[35] This ideology combines anticommunism, the introduction of the capitalist economic system, denazification, and the rather smooth incorporation of former Nazi officials in government positions in the new state as well as into the justice department, the police, national security, and the military.[36] In a poll taken in June 1961, 88 percent of the respondents said that they did not feel that they shared the guilt for the "genocide of the Jews."[37] No wonder Franz Josef Strauss, minister president of Bavaria, could still say in 1969: "A people that has accomplished these economic achievements has the right to want to hear no more about Auschwitz."[38] Against this background, Adorno's comment in 1959 continues to be pertinent: "We would come to terms with the past only when its causes had been removed."[39]

The tendency toward the "de-realization of the war and of the Nazi regime and its repercussions" can be traced as a phenotype to the current day, as Margarete Mitscherlich confirms in her 1987 book *Erinnerungsarbeit (The Work of Remembering)*.[40] But different phases in this process may be identified in the course of the development of West Germany, from the repression of the memory of the Third Reich in the 1950s to a critical confrontation with the reality of the Nazi regime and of West German society in the 1960s, to a historical relativity and the political challenge of the repressed problems of the past in the 1970s and 1980s. The formula expressed in *The Inability to Mourn*—"We developed from a nation that retreated aggressively from national socialism . . . into an apolitical conservative nation"[41]—no longer held true for the 1960s, when social upheaval caused the cultural elite suddenly to realize its political failures. In these years, the domestic political shortcomings of the "restoration era" under Adenauer, and the insufficiency of handed-down ideals became apparent. The search for new ideals, on the one hand, and the formation of the Great Coalition (November 1966), on the other, stimulated the organization of the APO or extraparliamentary opposition and the student revolts. Soon, German terrorists also appeared on the scene; they have been interpreted, somewhat superficially, as the product of the German process of repression—"Hitler's children."[42]

In summary, the social and political development of West Germany since 1945 demonstrates that the exclusively "consumption-oriented industrial nation . . . more or less lost its bond with the traditions, values, and cultural wealth of the old Germany when it emotionally denied its national socialist past."[43] The reduction or eradication of historical consciousness and the often noted general apathy were symptoms of this negative development. However, the analysis of neglected "mourning" and the inventory of the results of this omission, appear to relate to only one part—although an important part—of the German syndrome. The other part is the result of the German failure to work through their own history, to come to terms critically and relevantly with the past, to "grow to maturity," as Adorno sketched the problem in the 1960s.[44] Instead of openly discussing and analyzing World War II and the Third Reich, the industrial elite dedicated itself to reconstruction, the government established a new patriarchal order, and the cultural elite retreated into its own aesthetic realm. Government and society took over without complaint the ideological prescriptions of the occupation powers, who had become allies almost overnight in the cold war.

FIVE PHASES OF POSTWAR LITERARY REFLECTIONS

Postwar reflections on the Third Reich by the German literary and intellectual establishment can be divided into five phases, according to their contemporary political and economic contexts. Phase 1 dates from the end of World War II to the currency reform of 1948 and the creation of the Federal Republic in May 1949. Phase 2 extended from 1948–49 to 1959, the year in which the restoration era under Adenauer began to show signs of political and economic crisis and when a younger generation of novelists (Günter Grass, born 1927; Martin Walser, born 1927; and Uwe Johnson, born 1934) began an increasingly critical dialogue with the West German past and present. Phase 3 lasted from 1959 to 1969, during which time the CDU/CSU lost its absolute majority in the parliament for the first time (in the elections of 1961) and the literati's interest in politics grew considerably. In addition, the "*Spiegel* affair" not only created a governmental crisis but further stirred the literary elite to political activity.* In 1963, Adenauer stepped down and the father of the economic miracle, Ludwig Erhard, took over the government. After a new government crisis in 1966, the Great Coalition was formed under Chancellor Kurt Georg Kiesinger and the APO established itself at the same time. The political situation became polarized with the student revolt.** But the revolt showed increasing signs of exhaustion after the takeover of the government in 1969 by a social-liberal cabinet led by Willy Brandt. Phase 4 dates from 1969 to 1982, during which Brandt resigned, Helmut Schmidt headed the social-liberal government (from May 1974), and the so-called turning point in ideological attitude occurred.

After building slowly, the crisis in the coalition resulted in the creation of a new government under Helmut Kohl in September 1982, when phase 5 began. During phases 4 and 5, the literary intelligentsia re-

---

*Because of an article in the newsmagazine *Der Spiegel* on October 26/27 1962, the secretary of defense, Franz Josef Strauss, initiated the occupation and investigation by the police of the office of *Der Spiegel*. The editor in chief, Rudolf Augstein, and his director, Rolf Becker, were arrested. The events ultimately led to a political crisis in November 1962.

**In 1967 the so-called APO, or extraparliamentary opposition, developed outside of the parliamentary system. It included several leftist groups. An active student organization of the political Left (the SDS) was directed by Rudi Dutschke, who was shot and critically wounded in April 1968.

treated again from the public into the private sphere. In the public discussions of the 1970s and early 1980s, attempts to justify the past have increased. The new restoration era that began to take shape in the 1970s supported tendencies that emerged in Gerhard Zwerenz's novel, *Die Erde ist unbewohnbar wie der Mond* (*The Earth Is as Uninhabitable as the Moon*, 1973), and Rainer Werner Fassbinder's play, *Der Müll, die Stadt und der Tod* (*The Garbage, the City, and Death*, 1975), and that reached their climax in the "Historians' Controversy" of 1986.

In 1985 at Bitburg, Chancellor Kohl sought not only to make, in the words of Fritz Stern, "a gesture of symbolic forgiveness," but also to grant "an amnesty to the dead."[45] That same year, in a speech that received considerable attention abroad as well, however, President Richard von Weizsäcker challenged his fellow Germans "to face the truth, live with the memory of crimes committed and retribution suffered, and draw lessons from it."[46] Thus the themes of "memory" and "mourning" that Margarete and Alexander Mitscherlich introduced in 1967 into the discussion of the "coming to terms with the past" were finally put into the correct official perspective, after all the attempts over the previous three decades, and especially in the 1980s, to make a problematic past relative. "Anyone who closes his eyes to the past," said Weizsäcker of the problem, "is blind to the present. Whoever refuses to remember the inhumanity is prone to new risks of infection."[47]

EARLY RESPONSES

Although the literary establishment began to retreat from public into private life after the failure of the magazine *The Call* in 1947, postwar essays, short stories, and novels reflected critically on the experiences of the war and of the Third Reich. Even so conservative an author as Hans Egon Holthusen still asked in 1955 whether "the human and historical experience of the ominous 12 years [were] something quite unique and without precedent, something that had to be overcome and worked through in order not to miss living one's own reality."[48]

Nevertheless, Holthusen criticized the "sarcastic bitterness and despairing cynicism" of Wolfgang Koeppen's trilogy that pitilessly confronted the reader with these experiences.[49] Like many of the older generation of literati, Holthusen wanted to be edified or have aroused in him sentiments of apocalyptic doom, when quite to the contrary, fundamental criticism was called for and horror was the only appropriate response.

Holthusen was only one of many intellectuals for whom the actual subject of guilt often was transcended in postwar German literature by moral and physical arguments, so that the political responsibility of both the individual and the collective were relativized or even eliminated. Alfred Weber, for example, in "Abschied von der bisherigen Geschichte" ("Leave Taking from Past History," 1946), sought a "new human being." In *Doctor Faustus* (1947), Thomas Mann diagnosed the evil in German culture. In *Des Teufels General* (*The Devil's General*, 1945), Carl Zuckmayer dramatized a positive hero in bad times. Hermann Kasack, in the novel *Die Stadt hinter dem Strom* (*The City behind the Stream*, 1947), buried the experience of death in a timeless parable. Holthusen hoped for aesthetic victory over the "zero point of being" and Alfred Andersch for "existential self-realization" through literature. Other writers blamed supernatural powers or a Nazi criminal clique that finally had been unmasked after long fooling an innocent people. At the same time, such enlightening analyses appeared as Kogon's *Theory and Practice of Hell*, which discussed the "horror of evil" and the occurrences in the German mass extermination camps, and Jaspers's 1946 lectures, also mentioned earlier, defined the question of guilt and transposed it from the collective onto the individual. "Every German, without exception," Jaspers stated, "is politically liable."[50] As Jaspers later wrote in *Wohin treibt die Bundesrepublik?* (*Where is the Federal Republic Headed?* 1966), there was no dearth of intellectual witnesses who proposed to work on the past, but they remained without consequence for the "political thinking in the life of the population as well as of the government."[51]

Between 1945 and 1960 approximately 150 war novels were published.[52] For that reason, it might be interesting to look at them more closely, although the discussion here does not examine the so-called fact-oriented novels,[53] eyewitness accounts,[54] or the "trivial" war novels,[55] most of which are unconcerned with working through the past and instead prefer an unburdening of history and memory.[56] In the trivial novels, war is falsified and prettified as "the adventure of a highly stylized hero,"[57] while political reality serves as the context for war and as the condition that gave rise to it. Rather, the focus here will be primarily on literary texts that reveal a differentiated point of view.

Whereas novels with a critical perspective had only modest printings, the trivial novels with their more or less positive attitude toward the war and the Third Reich reached a broad public. For example, Koeppen's *Pigeons on the Grass* and *Death in Rome* had only about 6,000 readers, whereas the three volumes of Kirst's *08/15* (1954) reached some 1.8 million, and Konsalik's *Der Arzt von Stalingrad* (*The Doctor of Stalingrad*, 1963) was read by more than 2 million.[58] The complicated aesthetic techniques of the literary novels may account for some of the lack of their popular appeal, but the majority of readers were simply less interested in radical critical memories than in pleasant, conciliatory denial strategies. Günter Grass's Danzig trilogy (*Die Blechtrommel* [*The Tin Drum*, 1959], *Katz und Maus* [*Cat and Mouse*, 1961]), and *Hundejahre* [*Dog Years*, 1963]), Lenz's *Deutschstunde* (*German Lesson*, 1968), and last but not least, a series of prose works by Heinrich Böll, demonstrate that even successful novels did not need to neglect critical perspective. As Peter Demetz commented with resignation on the success of the American television series "Holocaust" in 1979: "Since 1945, the best and most thoughtful German writers have confronted the recent past, and yet it was a telecast with old-fashioned characterizations in black and white, realism and totally un-Brechtian empathy that shocked millions of viewers into thinking about German history more than any books or plays had been able to."[59] Demetz's statement reveals forcefully the longstanding division between literature and society, between intellectual discourse and the political consciousness of the masses.

THE "WORK OF REMEMBERING"

In phase 1 of the literary response to the war, as Peter Rühmkorf has remarked sarcastically, "stimulation [was not] desired, only tranquilizers . . . not flight into space and descent into hell, but comfort, reassurance, and the familiar."[60] This observation applies to a series of traditional prose texts that appeared before the currency reform. It is also true to a certain extent of some of the prose works of Wolfgang Borchert, who sought to articulate the postwar experience in a literary style between expressionism and reminiscences of New Objectivity.[61] The "literature of the war, of the returned soldier, and of rubble"[62] that Heinrich Böll addresses in his essay, "Bekenntnis zur Trümmer Literatur" ("Acknowledgment of a Literature of Rubble," 1962), is equally tradition-oriented despite contrary aesthetic demands.[63] In addition to realistic accounts such as Theodor Plievier's novel *Stalingrad* (1945), parables, allegories, and classical and Christian mythology were popular aesthetic prototypes until the 1950s, when foreign models such as Joyce, Hemingway, Faulkner, and Dos Passos were introduced. Although Wolfdietrich Schnurre declared, "We need no narcotic, we need the truth,"[64] writers at first avoided directly depicting the depressing reality in favor of a neoromantic, existential, surrealistic, or supernatural approach along the lines of the "visionary view" of Franz Kafka, Thornton Wilder, and Jean Anouilh, as Heinz Friedrich pointed out in May 1947.[65] Friedrich also argued that the surrealists "possess the metaphysical background against which our life is played out. [The surrealist] acknowledges in his 'Eternal Conversation' the irrational powers of the endlessness of life and thus affirms the present as well."[66] This statement could almost serve as a characterization of Ilse Aichinger's *Die grössere Hoffnung* (*Herod's Children*, 1948) and Elisabeth Langgässer's *Märkische Argonautenfahrt* (*The Quest*, 1950).

The novels of the 1950s adopted the narrative techniques used in Borchert's and Böll's short stories, which reduced political relations to a series of details that placed the terrible experiences of war, destruction, and hopelessness next to each other, like so many snapshots spread across a table for viewing. For example, in the novel *Wo warst du, Adam?* (*Adam, Where Were You?*, 1951), the most banal details are used to demonstrate the absurdity of the war. In contrast, Gerd Gaiser constructs in *Die sterbende Jagd* (*The Last Squadron*, 1955) the myth of the fighter pilots who possess "an intelligence without vocabulary."[67] At one point, one of the heros discusses the differences between the adventure of war, the "great time," with peace.[68] Peace, declares Vehlgast contemptuously, consists of "rank lists and promotions, frustrated ambition, lies, warehouses, wholesalers, and organized digestion. One man destroys another in order to live better himself. If he can't destroy him, he buys him, and that's called community."[69]

Wolfgang Koeppen's trilogy presents a rich dialogue on the Third Reich and the postwar situation. His collages reflect the influence of Joyce, Dos Passos, and Doeblin[70] and often parallel the phantasmagoria of Schnitzler. Like the works of Elisabeth Langgässer, Koeppen's books also refer to the mythological models of antiquity. *Pigeon on the Grass*, Koeppen's best novel, describes the atmosphere and problems of the postwar period. *Hothouse* represents a settling of accounts with the political conditions of the restoration era of the 1950s. In many details, this novel, which, like *Death in Rome*, at times degenerates into pulp fiction, anticipates parts of a fundamental criticism that Jaspers later presented in his *Where is the Federal Republic Headed?*

The achievements of Koeppen's novels in coming to terms with the past are particularly clear when compared with Alfred Andersch's 1957 novel, *Sansibar oder der letzte Grund* (*Flight to Afar*), in which several characters plan a rescue action to save a Jew—Judith—and a piece of sculpture from the Nazis. In this allegory, the only fascist character is the innkeeper, and Andersch does not analyze the threat in a political context as Koeppen does.

Except for Andersch's artificially constructed novel, there can be no question that, at the end of the 1950s, the literary depictions of German past and present became both sharper in style and perspective and more factual. The Eichmann trial (1960–61), the erection of the Berlin Wall (1961), the *Spiegel* affair (1962), the Auschwitz trial (1963–65), and the discussion of Hannah Arendt's thesis of the banality of evil, which based the question of guilt on a rational, historical foundation rather than a demonic or metaphysical one, helped change attitudes, particularly among intellectuals, and stimulated growing political involvement. Interest in the past is documented not only in innumerable publications on national socialism and in the attitude of such authoritative institutions as the church and the university, but also in plays like Rolf Hochhuth's *Der Stellvertreter* (*The Deputy*, 1963) and Peter Weiss's oratory *Die Ermittlung* (*The Investigation*, 1965); Grass's much discussed trilogy; and Alexander Kluge's *Lebensläufe* (*Attendance List for a Funeral*, 1962) and *Schlachtbeschreibung* (*The Battle*, 1964). Kluge's story, "Liebesversuch" ("An Attempt to Make Love," 1962) shows effectively the possibilities of the documentary method in the depiction of "inhumanity." In the case of *The Battle*, however, the antithesis of Plievier's *Stalingrad*, a historian's summary would have been welcome, since the documentary method alone could not organize the wealth of information. Whereas Grass uses irony and a distancing perspective, Kluge anticipates the awakening interest in information and factual depictions that is found particularly after 1966 and that at the beginning of the 1970s was to influence the aesthetic of a novel such as Böll's *Gruppenbild mit Dame* (*Group Portrait with Lady*, 1971).

Around the middle of the 1960s, after the parliamentary debates on the statute of limitations for Nazi crimes in March 1965, Karl Jaspers, as before him Wolfgang Koeppen, described the "political thinking in the life of the people and of the government" as "paralyzed." As in Kaiser Wilhelm's times, Jaspers wrote, an authoritarian state governs a population that believes itself inferior. The state structure is based on a "distrust of the people," and not on the responsibility of the individual. The German people are not yet "democratically minded." Writers and artists are denounced as "uncultured and resourceless" the instant they declare themselves politically, and only a "revolution in mental attitude" can lead the way out of the German misery. Jaspers demanded more insight not only into the present reality, but also into the past from which we have come. He rejected the economic ideology that shaped the restoration under Adenauer and warned that "if we consider national socialism to be an exception that already has been taken care of, we fill an interim stage with futilities that will be much more decisive for the coming catastrophe."[71]

The flagging of public interest in war novels that Jochen Pfeifer[72] notes at the beginning of the 1960s can be explained by the simultaneous ascendancy of nonfiction.[73] As West Germans' interest in socioeconomic, sociopsychological, and other nonfictional critical analyses increased, the demand for fiction fell. Soon the works of Walter Benjamin, Theodor W. Adorno, Alexander Mitscherlich, and Jürgen Habermas attracted more readers than the new publications of even well-known fiction authors. Kiesinger's election as chancellor in January 1966 also seems to have stirred to political activism the majority of the literary establishment who had hitherto been silent. The editors of *Kursbuch* 15 (1968) denounced all previous fiction as superfluous and challenged authors to devote themselves to the more worthwhile, practical task of increasing political literacy.

But just as the student mass demonstrators (1967–69) began to take their aesthetic fantasies as political actions, the action-oriented, positive beginnings revealed themselves as romantic substitutes; they had as little to do with reality as the literary "dreams of absolute" prevalent in the 1950s. Protests against the Nazi past, such as Beate Klarsfeld's political action against Chancellor Kiesinger, were increasingly buried beneath the echoes of the revolutionary dream that had gone unrealized in Germany and the growing dispute with the United States over the Vietnam War. The student revolution revealed problems that dated back to the Adenauer era, which Koeppen had depicted in his trilogy and Jaspers had described critically in his accounts. As Margarete Mitscherlich diagnosed in her book *The Work of Remembering*, a conformist younger generation had been in the majority in the 1950s, whereas in the 1960s opposition to the parents' generation began to increase "until in 1968 a particularly vehement generational conflict occurred."[74]

The formation of a social-liberal government by Willy Brandt in October 1969 marked a turning point and initiated what I have termed phase 4. Although the "emergency laws" (*Notstandsgesetze*) of May 1968 belonged to the period of government by the Great Coalition, the infamous "extremist decrees" (*Radikalenerlasse*) of 1972 were the work of a conformist Social Democratic Party (SPD) with reactionary tendencies. Many writers retreated from the political into the private sphere and the quotidian life of the individual. Soon the importance of the province, homeland, inner world, and depoliticized sphere was similar to that during the German Biedermeier and the Adenauer eras. Margarete Mitscherlich blamed the Germans' failure to work through "that which led to national socialism"[75] for many of the symptoms of crisis in West German society that intensified even further with the change in government in 1982. She also cautioned against attempts by historiographers to discuss the Third Reich in an aura devoid of emotional judgment and moral responsibility.[76] Such beginnings led in the 1980s to the "Historians' Controversy" in which these questions were discussed polemically.[77]

At the end of the 1970s, an even younger generation emerged and posed hard questions about the past to the older generation. In the majority of cases, the quest occurred in the form of autobiographical fiction and was guided by "paternal traces" and "childhood patterns."[78] In other instances, this trend in literature included "new insights into those ideological and micro-processes that permitted the bourgeois fathers to become opportunists or Nazis."[79] The younger generation of writers contributed to an understanding of the day-to-day aspects of fascism as well as an understanding of their own psychological situation as "Hitler's children."[80] Relevant titles include Bernward Vesper's *Die Reise* (*The Trip*, 1977), Siegfried Gauch's *Vaterspuren* (*Father's Traces*, 1977), Ruth Rehmann's *Der Mann auf der Kanzel* (*The Man in the Pulpit*, 1979), Christoph Meckel's *Suchbild* (*Picture-Puzzle*, 1980), and Peter Schneider's story, "Vati" ("Daddy," 1987).

Also since the 1970s the national socialist past has been reflected increasingly in film,[81] just as it had been in the novel and in drama during the 1960s. An exception is Hermann Lenz's trilogy, which appeared between 1961 and 1980: *Nachmittag einer Dame* (*Afternoon of a Lady*, 1961), *Im inneren Bezirk* (*In the Inner Sphere*, 1970), and *Constantinsallee* (*Constantine's Alley*, 1980). Whereas Grass in his Danzig trilogy clarifies the Third Reich from the perspective of a petit bourgeois, Lenz, who was born in 1913, places a Württemberg military attaché and his daughter in the foreground.

Several events—the success of the television series "Holocaust" in 1979, the renewed discussion surrounding Fassbinder's play *The Garbage, the City, and Death*, the Bitburg case, and the attempts on the part of conservative historians to redefine the function of the "work of remembering" in order to arrive at a positive historical assessment and evaluation—indicate that the Germans' reflection on the past is emerging from the narrow sphere of literature into the wider sphere of public life. In public discussion, fiction, and film, two reactions to the legacy of the Third Reich are distinguishable in what I have earlier termed phases 4 and 5. The first type of reaction in public discussion and literature is a tendency to minimize the crimes of the national socialist past and is found only among a minority of writers. The second type of reaction is based on critical self-examination and remembrance and applies to the majority of serious novelists, playwrights, film directors, artists, and scholars. The historian Christian Meier spoke for most German intellectuals when he reprimanded Chancellor Kohl and his facile attempt to distance himself from the past of the Third Reich since he had, mercifully, been born too late to feel responsible for any of the crimes then committed. Meier stated forcefully: "We will . . . never again have an unencumbered relationship to our own history. It is useless—rather, it is harmful—when a chancellor takes our history lightly, referring to the 'mercy of late birth,' since it is conservatives themselves who should be most conscious of [history]."[82] As Saul Friedländer has written with regard to the national socialist past, neither an "objective synthesis" nor a value-free view exists. On the contrary, "explicitly and implicitly, each depiction of the past must be based on a value system and finally such a depiction is not only a picture of this past but also a mirror of the society from which it comes."[83]

Surveying how Germans have come to terms with—or have avoided—the past since the end of World War II has been the aim of this report, which is its own mirror of the past and of ourselves.

NOTES

1. Hans Mayer, *Die umerzogene Literatur: Deutsche Schriftsteller und Bücher 1945–1967* (Berlin: Seidler, 1988), 19.
2. Klaus R. Scherpe, "Erzwungener Alltag: Wahrgenommene und gedachte Wirklichkeit in der Reportageliteratur der Nachkriegszeit," in *Nachkriegsliteratur in Westdeutschland 1945–49*, J. Hermand, H. Peitsch, K. R. Scherpe, eds. (Berlin: Argument, 1982), 68–74.
3. The first unpublished version dates from 1965–66.
4. Alexander and Margarete Mitschlerlich, *Die Unfähigkeit zu trauern* (Munich: R. Piper, 1967), 37.
5. Ibid., 25f.
6. Theodor W. Adorno, "Was bedeutet: Aufarbeitung der Vergangenheit," in his *Erziehung zur Mündigkeit: Vorträge und Gespräche mit Hellmut Becher* (Frankfurt am Main: Suhrkamp, 1970), 20.
7. Ibid., 28, 97, 145. See also Freud's essay, "Trauer und Melancholie," *Studienausgabe, III: Psychologie des Unbewussten* (Frankfurt am Main: Insel, 1975), 197–212.
8. Sigmund Freud, *Studienausgabe: Ergänzungsband* (Frankfurt am Main: S. Fischer, 1975), 207ff.
9. Mitscherlich and Mitscherlich, *Die Unfähigkeit zu trauern*, 16, 24.
10. Ibid., 34.
11. Ibid., 25f.
12. Ibid., 34; Adorno, *Erziehung zur Mündigkeit*, 104–6.
13. Quoted in Hermann Glaser, ed., *Bundesrepublikanisches Lesebuch. Drei Jahrzehnte geistiger Auseinandersetzung* (Munich: Carl Hanser, 1978), 90.
14. Jochen Vogt, ed., with cooperation of the Old Synagogue, *Die Vergangenheit ist nicht tot, sie ist nicht einmal vergangen: Nationalsozialismus im Spiegel der Nachkriegsliteratur* (Essen: Rigodon, 1984), 11–13.
15. Mayer, *Die umerzogene Literatur*, 12.
16. See also Jean Améry's thesis, cited by Norbert Mecklenburg, "Faschismus und Alltag in deutscher Gegenwartsprosa," in *Gegenwartsliteratur und Drittes Reich*, Hans Wagener, ed. (Stuttgart: Reclam, 1977), 11.
17. Mayer, *Die umerzogene Literatur*, 98.
18. H. M. Enzensberger, "Poesie und Politik," in his *Einzelheiten II* (Frankfurt am Main: Suhrkamp, 1970), 113–37.
19. Thomas Mann, "Kultur und Sozialismus" (1928), in his *Politische Schriften und Reden*, Hans Bürgin, ed. (Frankfurt am Main: S. Fischer, 1968), 165–73.
20. Enzensberger, "Poesie und Politik," 114.

21. Ralf Dahrendorf, *Gesellschaft und Demokratie in Deutschland* (Munich: R. Piper, 1965), 308–24.
22. Ibid., 318.
23. Walther Schmieding, "Der lange Marsch," in *Nach 25 Jahren: Eine Deutschland-Bilanz*, K. D. Bracher, ed. (Munich: Kindler, 1970), 197–99.
24. Jürgen Manthey, "Zurück zur Kultur/Die Wiedergeburt des nationalen Selbstgefühls aus dem Geist der Tragödie," in *Literaturmagazin 7*, N. Born and J. Manthey, eds. (Reinbek bei Hamburg: Rowohlt, 1977), 12.
25. Hans Magnus Enzensberger, "Die Clique," in *Almanach der Gruppe 47, 1947–1962*, H. W. Richter, ed. (Reinbek bei Hamburg: Rowohlt, 1962), 27.
26. Hans Werner Richter, ed., "Bilanz. Ein Nachwort," in *Bestandsaufnahme* (Munich, Vienna, Basel: Carl Hanser, 1962), 565.
27. Heinz Friedrich, "Das Jahr 47" (1962), in *Aufräumarbeiten*, Lutz-W. Wolff, ed. (Munich: Deutsche Taschenbuch, 1987), 201.
28. Hermann Glaser, *Kulturgeschichte der Bundesrepublik Deutschland*, 2 vols. (Munich: Carl Hanser, 1985–86).
29. Glaser, *Bundesrepublikanisches Lesebuch*, 755–57.
30. Ibid., 756.
31. Quoted in Manthey, "Zurück zur Kultur," 19–20.
32. See Margarete Mitscherlich, *Erinnerungsarbeit: Zur Psychoanalyse der Unfähigkeit zu trauern* (Frankfurt am Main: S. Fischer, 1987), 127–29.
33. Quoted ibid., 148.
34. Mitscherlich and Mitscherlich, *Die Unfähigkeit zu trauern*, 39–41.
35. Mayer, *Die umerzogene Literatur*, 38.
36. See Felicia Letsch, *Auseinandersetzung mit der Vergangenheit als Moment der Gegenwartskritik* (Cologne: Pahl-Rugenstein, 1982), 9–20.
37. Jürgen Weber, ed., *Geschichte der Bundesrepublik Deutschland*, IV (Paderborn: Ferdinand Schöningh, 1987), 339.
38. Quoted in Letsch, *Auseinandersetzung*, 12.
39. Adorno, *Erzeihung zur Mündigkeit*, 29.
40. Mitscherlich, *Erinnerungsarbeit*, 149.
41. Mitscherlich and Mitscherlich, *Die Unfähigkeit zu trauern*, 18–19.
42. Mitscherlich, *Erinnerungsarbeit*, 117.
43. Ibid., 115.
44. Adorno, *Erziehung zur Mündigkeit*, 20.
45. Fritz Stern, *Dreams and Delusions: The Drama of German History* (New York: Knopf, 1987), 18–19.
46. Quoted ibid., 19.
47. Richard von Weizsäcker, *Remembrance, Sorrow and Reconciliation* (Bonn: Press Information Office of the FRG, n.d.), 62.
48. Hans Egon Holthusen, *Der unbehauste Mensch* (Munich: R. Piper, 1955), 250.
49. Ibid., 285.
50. Karl Jaspers, *Hoffnung und Sorge: Schriften zur deutschen Politik 1945–1965* (Munich: R. Piper, 1965), 109.
51. Karl Jaspers, *Wohin treibt die Bundesrepublik?* (Munich: R. Piper, 1966), 150.
52. Jochen Pfeifer, *Der deutsche Kriegsroman 1945–1960* (Königstein/Ts.: Scriptor, 1981), 7.
53. Examples of this genre include Theodor Plievier, *Stalingrad* (1945); Walter Kolbenhoff, *Von unserem Fleisch und Blut* (1946); Hans Werner Richter, *Die Geschlagenen* (1945); Hans Helmut Kirst, *08/15* (1954); Willi Heinrich, *Das geduldige Fleisch* (1955); Josef Martin Bauer, *So weit die Füsse tragen* (1955); and Heinz G. Konsalik, *Der Arzt von Stalingrad* (1963).
54. On this topic, see also Hans Wagener, "Soldaten zwischen Gehorsam und Gewissen: Kriegsromane und -tagebücher," in Wagener, ed., *Gegenwartsliteratur und Drittes Reich*, 240–64.
55. See also Scherpe, "Erzwungener Alltag," 35–102.

56. Klaus F. Geiger, *Kriegsromanhefte in der Bundesrepublik* (Tübingen: Tübinger Vereinigung für Volkskunde e.V. Schloss, 1974); Walter Nutz, "Der Krieg als Abenteuer und Idylle: Landserhefte und triviale Kriegsromane," in Wagener, ed., *Gegenwartsliteratur und Drittes Reich*, 265–83.
57. Nutz, "Der Krieg als Abenteuer und Idylle," 277; Geiger, *Kriegsromanhefte in der Bundesrepublik*, 69–71.
58. Pfeifer, *Der deutsche Kriegsroman*, 49.
59. Peter Demetz, *After the Fires* (San Diego: Harcourt, Brace, Jovanovich, 1986), 29.
60. Peter Rümkorf, "Das lyrische Weltbild der Nachkriegsdeutschen," in Richter, ed., *Bestandsaufnahme*, 448.
61. Wolfgang Borchert, *Das Gesamtwerk* (orig. publ. 1949; Hamburg: Rowohlt, 1986), 313.
62. Heinrich Böll, *Werke: Essayistische Schriften und Reden 1952–1963*, Bernd Balzer, ed. (Cologne: Kiepenheuer und Witsch, 1978), 31–34.
63. Compare Urs Widmer, *1945 oder die "Neue Sprache"* (Düsseldorf: Pädagogischer Verlag Schwann, 1966).
64. Cited by Ludwig Fischer, *Literatur in der Bundesrepublik Deutschland bis 1967* (Munich: Deutsche Taschenbuch, 1986), 31.
65. Friedrich, "Das Jahr 47," 37.
66. Ibid., 38-39.
67. Gerd Gaiser, *Die sterbende Jagd* (Munich: Carl Hanser, 1955), 64.
68. Ibid., 170.
69. Ibid., 169.
70. Reinhard Baumgart, *Glückgeist und Jammerseele* (Munich: Carl Hanser, 1955), 64.
71. Jaspers, *Wohin treibt die Bundesrepublik?* 150, 154–55, 178, 180, 190, 192.
72. Pfiefer, *Der deutsche Kriegsroman*, 49.
73. The success of Lothar-Günther Buchheim's novel and film *Das Boot* (*The Boat*, 1973) illustrates that, despite everything, there is still a need for war literature.
74. Mitscherlich, *Erinnerungsarbeit*, 45f.
75. Ibid., 114.
76. Ibid., 113.
77. *Historiker-Streit: Eine Dokumentation der Kontroverse um die Einzigartigkeit der nationalsozialistischen Judenvernichtung* (Munich: R. Piper, 1987).
78. Reinhold Grimm, "Elternspuren, Kindheitsmuster," in *Vom Andern und von Selbst*, Reinhold Grimm and Jost Hermann, eds. (Königstein/Ts.: Athenäum, 1982), 176.
79. Michael Schneider, *Den Kopf verkehrt aufgesetzt oder melancholische Linke: Aspekte des Kulturzerfalls in den siebziger Jahren* (Darmstadt/Neuwied: Luchterhand, 1981), 22.
80. See Mitscherlich, *Erinnerungsarbeit*, 37–46.
81. Anton Kaes, *Deutschlandbilder: Die Wiederkehr der Geschicte als Film* (Munich: Edition Text und Kritik, 1987).
82. Christian Meier, "Verurteilen und Verstehen," in *Historiker-Streit*, 54.
83. Saul Friedländer, *Kitsch und Tod: Der Widerschein des Nazimus* (Munich: Deutscher Taschenbuch Verlag, 1986), 129.

5

Post–World War II Literature: the Intellectual Climate in Japan, 1945–1985

Irmela Hijiya-Kirschnereit

A common and not necessarily critical understanding of literature presupposes a relationship to general history as well as to the so-called intellectual climate. According to this view, both are "mirrored" in the literary creations of the time, and on the other hand they are, in some way or another, also influenced by history and virulent ideas. So far, so true—but how to establish these relationships in more concrete terms? This chapter first sketches aspects of the intellectual climate which appear to be of special relevance to our focus of concern, namely the corpus of literature dealing with the war experience. It then proceeds to propose a set of paradigms for screening and classifying the works and closes with observations on some widespread patterns of perception and attitudes in the Japanese literature dealing with the war experience.

THE GENERAL INTELLECTUAL CLIMATE IN JAPAN AFTER THE WAR

First, what does "intellectual climate" mean? Let us assume that this climate can be grasped through the observation of a succession of topics in public discussions on matters concerning society, the focus of media interest in certain issues, or the controversies of intellectuals and other public figures.

Despite the war damage and the shortage of food, housing, and all the materials necessary for printing, the publication industry revived almost immediately after the termination of the war in Japan. Since the early 1930s, rigid censorship and an extensive system of "advisorship" and control had marked Japanese literary creations, allowing nothing but the most conformist texts to appear. Even works as apolitical as Tanizaki Jun'ichirō's *Sasameyuki* (*The Makioka Sisters*) were held back after the first episodes had appeared in *Chūō kōron* in January and March 1943, on the ground that they ran counter to the national interest in time of emergency; Tanizaki's translation of the classic *Genji monogatari* into modern Japanese also was censored "because of the irregular ties it described in the succession to the throne."[1] Left-wing writers of the so-called Proletarian School had been forced to "convert" (*tenkō*) as early as 1933, and with the authorities' grip tightening on all spheres of public life, including literature, writers readily succumbed to the pressure in one way or another. The majority seemed to have regarded it as their duty to cooperate with the war effort in their field. They voiced no opposition to the system, emigration was out of the question for Japanese writers, and only rarely did they consider taking up jobs other than writing in order to avoid compromising. Only a few of the leftists, such as Kurahara Korehito, preferred going to prison rather than "converting."[2]

Writers eagerly volunteered to be sent abroad as war correspondents, and except for perhaps the established figures of Nagai Kafū, who lapsed into silence, and Tanizaki Jun'ichirō, who kept his cooperation to a minimum,[3] Japanese writers and poets seemed to have felt obliged to support what they, too, regarded as the national cause. The streamlining of the press and the "voluntary dissolution" of important general magazines such as *Chūō kōron* and *Kaizō* serve as further landmarks to indicate what Donald Keene has termed the "barren years," or, in the terminology of Marxist writers, the "dark valley" (*kurai tanima*) in the literary and intellectual history of modern Japan.

The emperor's broadcast on 15 August 1945, declaring Japan's acceptance of the terms of the Potsdam Declaration, caused different reactions in the population, but, while mourning and harboring deep feelings of shame at their nation's first defeat in history—even in the writings of intellectuals such as the author Dazai Osamu, "shame" (*haji*) is the central expression when describing his reaction at the end of the war[4]—the overwhelming majority of Japanese felt relief that the war had come to an end.

Within a few weeks, the Japanese people underwent a transformation of attitude, the rapidity and extent of which surprised members of the occupation so much that they found it hard to trust and feared a possible resurgence of militarism later. But these fears proved groundless. Busy with the task of sheer survival, people had turned away from matters of public concern, and the breakdown of the oppressive system of control inspired the press to write in an increasingly bold tone. The first new literary magazine, *Shinsei (Vita Nova)*, appeared, along with others temporarily suspended during the war such as *Shinchō* and *Bungei shunjū*. The following year saw a boom of already established or new magazines, beginning with *Chūō kōron* and *Kaizō* and the newly founded *Sekai, Ningen, Tenbō, Kindai bungaku*, all starting in January 1946, as well as *Shin Nihon bungaku* and *Sekai bungaku* following in March and April, respectively.

It may come as a surprise that in view of the radical changes in the political system and in the daily life of the people—and the abolition of the system of pressure and political-ideological claims on literature—literary historians insist on the power of continuity[5] rather than postulating a new beginning. Much evidence supports this view. Those authors who had been established before the war resumed their writing and publishing activities seemingly undisturbed by any sense of obligation to "explain" to themselves and others what had happened in the meantime. Continuity is also obvious in the ease with which the *bundan*, the literary establishment, revived, and in the "surprising tolerance" granted to writers who had closely cooperated with the militarists.[6] A beginning can be claimed only for that generation of younger writers who started their careers in the years after the war, the so-called *sengo ha* (Postwar School), but this fact sets the "beginning" off from any mere reorientation.

The writers generally appreciated the new air of freedom. Kawakami Hajime is reported to have observed that "the Americans and British had bestowed in the course of a few months freedoms that the Japanese could not have won unaided in ten or even twenty years."[7] Others such as Takami Jun expressed shame that this new liberty should have been given to his country by an occupying power,[8] and even the critical Nakamura Mitsuo, who in his history of contemporary Japanese literature chooses to speak of freedom after the war only in quotation marks and who insists in other places in calling postwar literature the "literature under the occupation" (*senryōka no bungaku*), admits that a new freedom in political and daily life formed the basis of a new and enlarged role of literature in society.[9]

THE DEBATE OVER WRITERS' WAR RESPONSIBILITY

The question of war responsibility and guilt of writers was first put on the agenda in the inaugural edition of another literary magazine, *Bungaku jihyō*, in January 1946, by Odagiri Hideo, who attacked the poet Takamura Kōtarō as one of the foremost figures in the world of poetry to carry "responsibility for the war" (*sensō sekininsha no iwaba dai ikkyū*).

The June 1946 issue of *Shin Nihon bungaku*, organ of the writers of the former proletarian literature movement, featured, again on Odagiri's proposal, a blacklist of twenty-five names of colleagues accused of intensive propaganda for militarist goals.[10] *Kindai bungaku*, founded by Marxist members but less orthodox than *Shin Nihon bungaku*, also brought up the question, this time voiced by Hirano Ken, Ara Masato, and others, but on the whole it seems to have been inseparably connected with Marxist writers who praised their liberation by the Allies, condemned their nonleftist colleagues who had willingly cooperated with the militarists from a moral standpoint, and sought to justify their second "conversion" immediately after the war.

The discussion seems never to have reached a substantial level, touching political or moral issues, but mainly ran to global accusations and reproaches, these being overshadowed by constant hostilities between the two Marxist groups, culminating in Nakano Shigeharu's verdict on the *Kindai bungaku* critics Ara Masato and Hirano Ken as "inhuman and anti-human."[11] Other writers tackled the question by attacking what they saw as the self-deception of the so-called democratic literary movement (leftist literature). Such criticism was voiced by Yoshimoto Takaaki and by Fukuda Tsuneari, who, in an article on "Literature and War Responsibility" ("Bungaku to sensō sekinin") in the February 1947 issue of *Asahi hyōron*, declared that he did not believe in anything like war responsibility for writers, adding that "the attitude of those who pursue the issue of war responsibility has nothing to do with literature."[12]

Needless to say, this dissociation of politics and history from literature, which as an implicit idea was widespread among intellectuals of the time even if it was not voiced in such a clear-cut manner, was also prevalent during the war, when a writer such as Nakajima Atsushi, while being sent to Micronesia by the government in 1941, could maintain that war and literature were completely separate and unrelated.[13] Other intellectuals and writers, such as Kobayashi Hideo or Dazai Osamu, self-indulgently declared themselves simple citizens without political interests or education, who could not have been expected to see through the machinations of the militarists.[14]

The debate over war responsibility soon ebbed away in literary circles, but the question was approached from a more fundamental angle in the works of the political scientist Maruyama Masao. He related the problem to Japanese political mentality in general as it was formed by centuries of social and intellectual history, and his contributions had exerted wide influence on critically minded Japanese intellectuals since the late 1940s.[15] Maruyama made important statements about the nature of Japanese political mentality.

On the whole, the early postwar years were tinged by a strong progressive current, which also reflected the fact that Japanese intellectuals had regained contacts with the international scene. The "almost completely uncritical acceptance of Marxist ideology" during these years, however, drove Donald Keene to suspect that the writers might have been motivated by the vague anticipation that sooner or later a socialist or Communist government might take over in Japan.[16]

Political developments, however, did not move in the expected directions. Although leftist groups obtained prestige and influence in the immediate postwar period, and the GHQ actively supported a coalition government of Socialists and leftist Liberals, the coalition suffered a severe defeat in the January 1949 elections. Under the strong influence of American policies, priorities shifted from democratization to reconstruction, paving the way for what the political scientist Ōtake Hideo recently described as an "anti-communist coalition between militant liberalism and traditional authoritarianism."[17]

From all that we know about it today, censorship under the occupation cannot have represented an important factor in the development of intellectual life. To describe its effects in Jay Rubin's phrasing,

> [It] may have come close to destroying the Kabuki theater and briefly inconvenienced a few determined believers in the imperial myth; it certainly did delay some of the more intense expressions of outrage at the use of the atomic bomb, and it reduced the number of mixed couples holding hands in the literary landscape. None of this qualifies as a general or systematic distortion of postwar literature.[18]

That this view differs markedly from the opinion of many Japanese literary historians is a point to which I must return later.

Under the liberal reactionism (*Ōtake*) of 1948–49, more often termed reverse course, and a government that increasingly represented traditional authoritarianism under the Yoshida cabinet, the economy made substantial progress toward recovery, further stimulated by the Korean War (1950–53). The prevailing mood in the early 1950s was one of optimism and privatism. People enjoyed consumption, and while one faction of intellectuals, the progressive liberals, were discussing the merits and demerits of Stalinism and while others were still attempting to understand what was by this time termed Japanese fascism (Maruyama Masao contrasted it with German fascism to explain its specific character[19]), the wider public had long accepted the return to office of wartime leaders. The selection of Kishi Nobusuke, former member of the Tōjō cabinet, as prime minister in February 1957 was only the most conspicuous case.

The question of writers' wartime responsibility was raised once more in 1956 in a study by Takei Teruo and Yoshimoto Takaaki, *Bungakusha no sensō sekinin* (*The War Guilt of Literary Writers*), but, again, their research dealt not with writers in general but only with those left-wing representatives who had been the focus of the discussion in 1946 and 1947. Yoshimoto took them to task for not facing the problem of collaboration among themselves. Leading figures of the democratic literature movement whose task would have been to explain themselves evaded the issue, while the rest of the members of the group merely closed their eyes during the decade after the war. Thus, according to Takei and Yoshimoto, they failed to face up to their wartime responsibility as well as their postwar responsibility; moreover, their avant-garde stance caused the failure of the "democratic revolution" (*minshu kakumei*). This seems to be the last contribution of some consequence to the issue under the heading of war guilt and the responsibility of writers.

THE INTELLECTUAL CLIMATE OF THE 1960S AND 1970S

The general public meanwhile enjoyed a period of high economic growth and increasing international attention with popular highlights such as the Tokyo Olympics in 1964, which the Japanese public viewed as the most conspicuous sign of international recognition. The nation also appears to have regained national confidence. At the same time, the 1960s and early 1970s represented a phase of sociopolitical activism in the form of mass demonstrations and citizen movements. The mass protest against the signing of the U.S.-Japanese Security Treaty in May and June 1960 was supported by a majority of intellectuals, as were the protests against the U.S. involvement in the Vietnam War and the support of that involvement by the Japanese government between 1965 and 1973. Student riots in the late 1960s, the fierce resistance of Sanrizuka farmers to the construction of Tokyo International Airport at Narita since 1966, the antimodern movement, and antipollution movements of which the Minamata case in the late 1960s and early 1970s is the most widely known, dominate the picture of Japan during these years.

Most of these citizens' movements appear to have parallels in other countries and thus to have international aspects as well as having concrete economic and ecological motives. Japanese cultural historians such as Tsurumi Shunsuke, however, tend to emphasize the indigenous, premodern roots of these citizen movements.[20] According to Tsurumi, these movements were issue oriented and thus disappeared with the issue. This characteristic seems to set them off, despite surface parallels, from phenomena like the " '68 generation" in Western Europe, which tackled more fundamental issues from an idealistic and socialist perspective. Issue orientation in the Japanese case also implies a spontaneous reaction to concrete problems. It does not grow out of a heightened political awareness as Tsurumi writes:

> Only when he [the ordinary citizen] feels his life affected by the political situation, or his life style hampered by it, does he rouse himself from political apathy and voice his political view in public. The citizen's political interest is in contrast to the political interest of the professional activists whose livelihood depends on being politically well informed.[21]

Writers took an active part in all these movements, and their activities were reflected in their literary works or essays, which often became bestsellers and gained the status of authentic condensations of the *Zeitgeist*, as did Oda Makoto's *Nandemo mite yarō* (*We will look at everything*, 1961) or Shibata Shō's *Saredo warera ga hibi* (*Those were the days, my friend . . .* , 1963). As the historical distance from the war years lengthens and the interest of the public turns to more immediate contemporary issues, this phase of Japanese history is hardly addressed. Those who do speak about the issue treat it in a clearly affirmative, noncritical manner.

One focus is the reevaluation of the Tokyo war crimes trials, which, according to the leftist liberal Tsurumi, were never accepted by the Japanese people but did serious harm to their notion of justice, although at the time of the occupation, they had to suppress their protests. Now, according to Tsurumi's slightly curious phrasing, "in the wake of the prosperity since 1960 there has been a surge of compassion for the victims of the War Crimes Trials."[22] As a matter of fact, documentary novels on wartime officials such as *Yamamoto Isoroku* (*The Reluctant Admiral: Yamamoto and the Imperial Navy*, 1965) by Agawa Hiroyuki, or Shiroyama Saburō's *Rakujitsu moyu* (*War Criminal: The Life and Death of Hirota Koki*, 1974) were widely acclaimed and won coveted prizes. Kinoshita Junji's play *Kami to hito to no aida* (*Between God and Man*, 1972), first staged in 1970, links Japanese doubts about the legitimacy of the Tokyo war crimes trials with the issues of the dropping of the A-bomb over Hiroshima and Nagasaki and the U.S. involvement in the Vietnam War. Thus, the roles of the accuser and the accused were reversed.[23] Writers who argued for a relationship between the contemporary Vietnam experience and the Japanese role in World War II usually reasoned in this way, using Vietnam as a means of Japan's exculpation.

Another, more extreme example for such a positive reevaluation of the war experience is Hayashi Fusao's *Dai Tōa sensō kōtei-ron* (*In Support of the Greater East Asian War*, 1964, with a sequel published in 1965),[24] which revived the wartime argument that Japan simply functioned as a liberating force against Western imperialism in Asia. According to Tsurumi, these views were widely acclaimed in the Japan of the 1960s.[25] Hayashi, by the way, is also notable as an example of a writer of originally Marxist inclinations who, after the war, never revoked his *tenkō*.

THE SWING TOWARD CONSERVATISM AND NIHONJINRON

Whether because the issues of the citizens' protests were settled, as Tsurumi maintains, or because people generally swung toward conservatism after a phase of political idealism and failed aspirations for direct democracy, the late 1970s and early 1980s saw a turning away from humanitarian idealism and solidarity toward more introspective activities. This development occurred not only in Japan but in other advanced nations as well. On the politico-economic plane there was an "almost simultaneous restoration of economic liberalism and traditional conservatism."[26] Around the mid-1970s, popular theories about the so-called national character, which are now known as *Nihonjinron*, appeared in such great numbers that they began to be regarded as a genre per se. This new interest in explanations and definitions of "Japaneseness" was prompted in part by Japan's opening to the world and the need the Japanese suddenly felt to understand themselves and to make themselves understood to the outside world, especially because international criticism tended to satirize the nation as "Japan, Inc." and to characterize its citizens as "economic animals."

Self-explanation as self-defense is, however, only one part of the reason for the new interest in Japaneseness. Growing pride in the nation's economic successes and international standing also provided a new perspective. One important motif in many *Nihonjinron* texts is the refutation of the unconscious or conscious Amero-Eurocentrism in Japanese thinking—or what the authors of popular studies on the origins of the Japanese people, their language, their cultural history, and the "Japanese" brain *held* to be the ethnocentric values of Western nations, which the Japanese had long mistaken for universal ones. Although some of these Japanese criticisms hit the mark, the effect in many cases merely represented a simple exchange of ethnocentric values. If the possibility of universals is denied from the beginning, the task remains only to substitute "genuinely Japanese" attitudes and values for real or supposedly Western ones.

An example of how this attitude has developed since the mid-1970s is the publications of the linguist Suzuki Takao, from his best-selling *Tozasareta gengo: Nihongo no sekai* (*A Closed Language: The World of Japanese*, 1975), down to his most recent *Buki toshite no kotoba* (*Language as a Weapon*, 1985). Suzuki starts with a critique of the history of his discipline and the unconscious Eurocentrism in subject matter and methodology, and then widens his scope to include statements about how to improve the Japanese standing on the international stage. His public influence has grown considerably over the years, as his tone has grown more and more militaristic.[27]

Suzuki is, however, only one prominent spokesman in the chorus of authors dealing with the Japanese language in the form of a *Nihonjinron*. The language is commonly regarded as the core of Japanese culture, symbolizing and representing the essence of Japanese history and race (note the contamination of all these different entities!). Therefore the degree to which the language issue, including the recent discussion about Japanese as a foreign language, dominates public discourse should not surprise us. Roy A. Miller has rightly identified this preoccupation with language as embodying the Japanese essence as a central "modern myth."[28]

As for the issue of World War II, since the mid-1970s a series of publications that document the war experience from the perspective of average citizens have appeared. Tsurumi Shunsuke lists sixteen of them between 1974 and 1983.[29] To this list should be added the series of fifty-six volumes compiled by the youth division of the Buddhist lay organization *Sōka gakkai*, which appeared between 1974 and 1979 under the title *Sensō o shiranai sedai e* (*To the Generation Which Does Not Know War*). The aim of the latter and many other documentary collections is not to deal with the question of how the war could have happened, but to record the sufferings of the ordinary Japanese in order to show the "inhuman nature of war, with honest appeals that the folly must not be repeated."[30]

Wartime sufferings of ordinary people are also a popular subject for TV dramas. Thus, the serialized TV version of the novel *Oshin* centering on the life of a woman called Oshin and a deserter from the Japanese army in the supporting role for the portion of the story that takes place in the "Fifteen-Year War" (between 1930 and 1945), achieved an unprecedented popularity rating of more than 58 percent in 1983.[31] Although these and other popular dramas of the period intended no critical investigation or enlightenment but were aimed at a sentimental identification, Tsurumi points out that there have been consistent (although unsuccessful) efforts on the side of the ruling party and the government to keep the Fifteen-Year War from being treated as the subject of TV plays.[32]

THE GENERATIONAL MODEL FOR POSTWAR LITERATURE

Japanese literary histories resort to the generational model when classifying postwar literature. They also maintain this division into "generations" when discussing the literary approach to the World War II issue, and the model is extended to include the intellectual scene as a whole. For example, Hashikawa Bunzō identifies four patterns of approach to the issue alongside these generational borders:

1. One group, which would correspond to the generation of already established older writers in presentations of literary history, is the generation that has continued to symbolize authority during and after the war, a group supposedly unaffected by war.[33]

2. The second generation is the one that, according to Hashikawa, had finished its higher education during the war, was critical of the "meaningless" and "pathological" war, eagerly awaited its end, and regarded Japan's defeat as a liberation.

3. A slightly younger age group, called the *war generation* (*senchūha sedai*) by Hashikawa, regarded war as a given "natural" fact and as an "everyday myth" (*nichijō no shinwa*). Innocent and young as they were, almost all of them became "unconscious nationalists." Defeat at the end of the war deprived them of all their ideals.[34]

4. The next generation in Hashikawa's model had no direct relationship with the war experience whatsoever. No reorientation was necessary for this group, which espoused a "healthy materialism and a contractual pragmatism" (*kenzenna materiarizumu, keiyakuteki gōrishugi*) and took the initiative in the students' movement.[35]

Hashikawa's model reflects the popularity of generational explanation patterns in modern Japanese history[36] while containing the same blind spots that I have noted elsewhere.[37] (Note, for example, that his model has no room for a "generation" of convinced supporters of the war.)

Despite the obvious biases of the generational model in literary and intellectual history, and despite the fact that it is not an age group model in the strict sense, I suggest a modified version for classifying the literary response to the World War II experience, because it appears useful—and the frequency with which this model is employed seems to back me up. The fact that within modern Japanese culture the war issue is approached predominantly on an individual level, with personal experience being the most important factor, speaks for itself. I propose the following "generations":

1. The older generation of established writers, who are, according to popular opinion, aloof, untouched, and unaffected by the war. Among them, however, we can distinguish between the ones who refused to cooperate (Nagai Kafū and possibly Tanizaki Jun'ichirō)[38] and the rest, who engaged in cooperation to different degrees, such as Kawabata Yasunari, Takamura Kōtarō, and Masamune Hakuchō. A strategy of this generation in coping with postwar reality was, as it had been with many of them during the war years, an escape into aestheticism and an idealized picture of a "purer" or premodern Japan. To give only one example: Kawabata reports himself to have been completely absorbed by his reading of the *Genji monogatari* when the war ended and, not without an element of self-stylization, he writes, "I might well be surprised at the disharmony between me and the train, loaded with the baggage of refugees and victims of the bombings, making its way irregularly through the charred ruins, in terror of another bombing; but I was even more surprised at the harmony between me and a work a thousand years old."[39]

2. The generation of the activists, an age group old enough to be recruited for "patriotic services." We could distinguish several subgroups, such as straightforward supporters, like the "Romantic School" (*Nihon Romān-ha*); former Marxists who underwent conversion (*tenkō*); and a group of writers who started their literary career after the war but were old enough to have taken an active part in the war (whether "voluntarily" or forcibly). This third subgroup makes up the bulk of what is usually subsumed under the heading of the *Postwar Group* (*sengo-ha*), and for them, the war experience forms the central concern in their literature. The best-known names in this group are Noma Hiroshi, Takeda Taijun, Haniya Yutaka, Ōoka Shōhei, Umezaki Haruo, Nakamura Shin'ichirō, and Shimao Toshio.

3. What is—slightly misleadingly—termed the *War Generation* (*senchū-ha*) is the next younger age group of writers who grew up during the war and were indoctrinated by the militarist thought and value system but were not yet in position to play an active adult part in the war. This group includes writers such as Mishima Yukio, Abe Kōbō, or the so-called *third generation* of new writers, to whom, as Matsubara Shin'ichi contends, war was not of such a big concern, as they showed that "even during war, daily life continued without being directly affected by the idea of war" and as they "got through war as a simple individual."[40]

4. The generation of writers who at the end of the war were still children includes those who are occasionally called "engagés" such as Ōe Kenzaburō or Kaikō Ken. Some of this generation began to publish

at the end of the 1950s, but as a whole, the times when they started their literary careers and their motifs and approach in dealing with World War II vary to an even greater degree than in the case of the older generations. Writers such as Kōno Taeko, Kaga Otohiko, or Morimura Sei'ichi fall into this category.

5. The generation born after the war does not figure at all in Japanese generational models dealing with writers' attitudes toward World War II. It is presupposed that, for this generation, the war is of no immediate concern and interest. In fact, Japanese literature appears to contain no works of this generation in which they question their fathers about what they did during the war or about "how it all could happen," as is common in the German context. Writers of this generation, such as Murakami Ryū, treat the topic of war abstractly, as in his *Umi no mukō de sensō ga hajimaru* (*Across the Sea, a War Begins*, 1977).

The generations demonstrate different motivations for dealing with war. The highest degree of relative uniformity, notwithstanding individual differences in ideological outlook, appears to be in the second generation group, where the prevailing motif is the immediately felt necessity to explain, to oneself and to others, and self-justification. At the same time, the period in which these authors have written about their war experiences is relatively short, limited mainly to the immediately postwar years.

The third group deals with the subject over a longer time and across a wider spectrum of accents, their contributions on the topic concentrating on the 1950s and 1960s. The fourth generation shows an even wider variety in time of writing—from the late 1950s to the 1980s—motivation, and topicality.[41]

THREE MORE PARADIGMS

The second paradigm I propose is a topical one, differentiating the writings according to subject matter, such as:

1. War, especially battlefield experience overseas and in Japan;
2. Civilian life during the same period overseas and at home;
3. The end of the war and the capitulation with the large subgroup of so-called A-bomb literature (*genbaku bungaku*);
4. The aftermath of war in postwar everyday life as experienced in physical hardship and value reorientation, generational conflicts because of the war, and the war crimes trials, among other things. Needless to say, this paradigm can be further differentiated.

The third paradigm distinguishes the degree to which the writing focused on the war experience. There are three main categories:

1. War as the central topic;
2. War as a secondary or side aspect; and
3. War as omission or ellipsis (*Ausblendung*).

The second group of works is a large one, containing, for example, many works of the first generation of writers. Kawabata could serve as a convenient example again. In many of his works wartime memories enter into the stories of the characters, frequently and significantly enough to make the reader realize that they constitute a secondary topic.[42] (Again, a certain discrepancy can be noted between a writer's statements about his personal attitude and his literary creation.) This pattern also appears frequently in the works of a writer like Mishima. In the novel *Kinkakuji* (*The Temple of the Golden Pavilion*, 1956), the author's systematic and deeply meaningful allusions to the war in the story, which deals with a young acolyte who burned down the temple in Kyoto in 1950, are so convincing that a Japanese critic classifies the novel as one dealing with the war experience. Nevertheless, *Kinkakuji* belongs to the second category according to our paradigm.

The third group should not escape our attention, especially because although this group is probably substantial in number, the Japanese usually do not take it into consideration when dealing with this topic. Many works that deal with the time of war without referring to war, shutting out this reality, can be found in the narrowly personal genre of *shishōsetsu*. Katō Shūichi, in commenting on two famous examples, finds a relationship to the time: "They are of course solely concerned with the author's personal life, not with the fate of the Japanese Empire. However, Dazai did write *Setting Sun* at the time that the sun of the empire was setting and 'unfit to be human' when Japan was found to be unfit to be an independent nation."[43]

The last paradigm I propose differentiates the (prose) genre. Whereas the interest in literary studies clearly lies in the realm of so-called pure literature, in the case of literature dealing with the World War II experience, Japanese critics tend to be more flexible than usual and to include other genres. Therefore it is important to take into account the following groups:

1. "*Junbungaku*" (pure literature, or literature proper). This group is by far the largest one.

2. "*Taishū bungakū*" (mass literature). Famous examples are the popular novels *Ningen no jōken* (*Human Conditions*), a work in six volumes by Gomikawa Junpei,[44] and *Senkan Yamato no saigo* (*The End of the Battleship Yamato*, 1952) by Yoshida Mitsuru.

3. Personal records (collections of letters, diaries), which, by their publication, gain a status similar to that of literature. Thus the famous

collection of letters by student-soldiers who died in the war, *Kike, wadatsumi no koe* (*Listen, Voice of the Sea*, 1949) is treated as a piece of "antiwar literature" in Odagiri's article on "Sensō bungaku."[45]

4. Documentary accounts, occasionally fictionalized, also have to be taken into account such as Morimura Seiichi's three-volume novel *Akuma no hōshoku* (*A Devil's Feast*, 1982), dealing with Japanese war crimes of a secret special unit using prisoners of war and civilians in Manchuria as guinea pigs for cruel medical experiments, crimes that have not been brought to court. The book clearly was intended to enlighten and was well researched, but according to Katō Shūichi, many may have read it out of a cruel voyeurism comparable to the "outlet" function ascribed to SM comics in Japan.[46]

The last example reminds us that it is important to note carefully the possible gaps between an author's intention and the work's intention, the critic's interpretation of the work (which may be a projection of the declared author's intention) and the critic's own bias, or countless other factors besides it, and the actual impact the work leaves with the typical reader or several representative groups of readers. Or, to give another example: Ōe Kenzaburō's early short stories dealing with war and occupation experiences from the perspective of a boy are usually regarded in Japanese scholarship as fine examples of a decidedly critical stance, the author being known as a representative of a consciously political and anti–A-bomb group of intellectuals. A closer look at the works in question, however, reveals that a far stronger element is his veneration of vitality and power—in fact, the story could well be set in a time other than in the war or occupation.[47]

PATTERNS OF CONTINUITY

The literary work and its reception form the two focuses of the most meaningful approach to the subject of "World War II and Its Legacy in Literature"—at the micro level of one or a group of works, analyzed according to their textual strategies, their "philosophy" and value system, and their effects. Of course, it is vital not to lose sight of the macro level, for even an intratextual analysis necessitates relating elements of a work to inter- or extratextual contexts. Only careful microanalysis will prevent us from producing the stereotypical views that are prevalent in much of the research on the subject so far.[48] There are, however, promising new approaches that dig below surface opinions. In a recent contribution on A-bomb literature, John Whittier Treat shows that Hara Tamiki, a writer famous for his story "Natsu no hana" ("Summer Flowers," 1947), had already developed certain topics, above all, the theme of death, in his writing at an earlier stage, so that he was able to adapt his patterns of description and interpretive schemes to the subject of the atomic holocaust.[49]

It is beyond the scope of this chapter to present practical analyses, but I want to draw attention to some patterns of description and interpretation that can be found in so many examples—regardless of their possible classification within the paradigms presented earlier—that they appear typical for the large corpus of pertinent literature as a whole. I sketch them under the following headings:

- Sentimentalization;
- Strategies of fatalism: depersonalization and derealization (*Entwirklichung*);
- Aestheticizing; and
- Transforming history into nature.

Anyone familiar with modern Japanese literature will also know its sentimental traits, which are particularly characteristic of its central genre: the autobiographical *shishōsetsu*, which concentrates on a phase in the private life of a person, a "focus figure" that the reader identifies with the author.[50] An autobiographical approach, and a basically sentimental mood, is also typical for most Japanese fiction dealing with the war experience. This mood is also evident in the personal accounts of ordinary citizens collected as documentaries on the war. Reliving one's sufferings by telling them, savoring one's past pains, and expressing quiet resignation add up to a basically affective, emotional attitude that leaves no room for reflection. The result is therefore a purely individual description of an instant of personal suffering, from which the historical dimension is shut out. The strictly apolitical stance of even those texts written to document war as history is symbolized by an example from the two-volume *Waga ko ni nokosu—Senchū, sengo boshi no kiroku* (*To Leave Behind to My Child—Records of the Lives of Mothers and Children in War and Postwar Times,* Tokyo, 1978). The reports of the forty mothers include photographs of the author, in one of which the author is shown posing in front of the Imperial Palace, an obviously inadvertent irony, considering the suffering reported in the story.[51]

The prevailing personal approach to war being emotive and sentimental, the reaction to disaster is one of accepting it as fate. This reaction is not only implied in the attitude but sometimes put into words directly. In the story "Sayōnara," by Tanaka Hidemitsu, for example, the author displays a clear consciousness—and thus a degree of detachment and self-criticism—toward this fatalism: Originally published in November 1949, "Sayōnara" features an autobiographical account of events when the author was a soldier fighting against the Chinese. The title is explained right in the beginning as being symbolic of the Japanese attitude, for, whereas in most European and other languages, salutations at parting imply a positive attitude, as in "au revoir" and "auf Wiedersehen," the Japanese "sayōnara—if things are like this, (we will have to part)" has a resigned, "defeatist" coloring.

The protagonist himself demonstrates this attitude in an incident involving an attractive young Chinese soldier, the only one not killed by the Japanese, who usually did not make prisoners of the Chinese. They used the fourteen- or fifteen-year-old boy as a porter. One day when the soldiers marched on a cliff, the boy, as the only act of revenge possible to him, threw his load into the depth and jumped after it, thus committing suicide. The protagonist witnessing this scene likens the dark spot disappearing to a young eagle and shouts, "Sayōnara," behind him, "I only shouted 'sayōnara.' (This is fate. Young man, it cannot be helped. If this is so, I am sorry.)"[52]

Having become a "fatalist by necessity" (*yamu o enu unmeironja ni natte ita*), the protagonist reacts to the sudden death of thirty young girls hit by a bomb in a factory with the same, "extremely simple" (*kiwamete assari*) "sayōnara" ("I only felt this was their fate").[53]

The narrator is a double fatalist, so to speak, for he attributes this fatalism to a mental attitude deeply ingrained in the Japanese, which becomes clear as he further reflects on the deaths of four young Chinese whom he has just killed by himself: "It was not my hands who have killed these young men, it was fate called war that felled these youngsters." And he continues with a comparison of nations:

> The French, who can say "au revoir" or "bon voyage" at parting and who do not believe in war as an inescapable natural calamity, could continue their resistance unbroken under the Nazi occupation, but the miserable people of Japan, who even when parting from a lover, can only say "sayōnara," could not put up any resistance against the takeover of power of the military clique.[54]

This remarkable statement shows that even the slightly ironical reference to his own fatalism is combined with self-justification.

Instead of depersonalization, as in the foregoing example ("It was not my hands . . ."), we may encounter "translation" into the sphere of unreality to cope with reality. Tamiya Torahiko's story "Ashizuri misaki" ("Cape Ashizuri"), first published in October 1949, ends with a scene in which the narrator witnesses a drunken man, a former member of a suicide squad called *Ryūkichi*, stumble through the streets at night shouting his rage against his superiors, the emperor, and all those who told him to die. On hearing the voice gradually fade again as the man disappears in the darkness, the narrator muses, "I suddenly thought that in this voice, I heard the voice of the old pilgrim. It was a dream—everything was a dream. Where is truth which is not a dream? I tried once more to follow the voice of Ryūkichi which could not be heard any more but then the street lights which had flickered weakly, suddenly went out."[55]

Aestheticizing is another widespread strategy, for which numerous examples offer themselves. As a conscious attitude it is practiced by Kawabata Yasunari, of whom Nakamura Mitsuo writes that the more Japan "is made to take the position of a loser" (*makeinu no tachiba ni tatasarereba sareru hodo*), the more he feels driven to stress the beauty of "Japan's soul," and this beauty, according to Nakamura, is embodied in the figure of Kikuko in Kawabata's first postwar novel *Yama no oto*.[56]

In literary practice, there are many examples of the "beauty in destruction" pattern of description—with Mishima Yukio, in a series of novels down to *Akatsuki no tera* (*The Temple of Dawn*, 1970),[57] and in the A-bomb literature. Ōta Yōko, in her *Kaitei no yō na hikari* (*A Light as if at the Bottom of the Sea*), the first literary text to be published about the A-bomb, which appeared on 30 August 1945, writes of the "beauty" of the sacrifice with which Hiroshima was decorated at the end of the war.[58] The "horrible beauty" of an air-raid scene is evoked by Kaga Otohiko in his *Kaerazaru natsu*: in consonance with Japanese conventions, he contrasts the sight with cherry trees in full blossom.[59]

Transformation into aesthetic and erotic categories can go to extremes, as in the case of Mishima Yukio, who imagines the relationship between a Kamikaze plane and the ship to be destroyed as penis and vagina.[60] But other writers show this fascination with destruction as well. Sakaguchi Ango, for instance, has repeatedly written of the "beauty of people submitting to fate."[61]

The fourth pattern of description—transforming history into nature—amounts to an extension of the others: The attitude of regarding war as a category of nature is also characteristic of many descriptions of war. For example, Tanaka Hidemitsu's protagonist called war an "inescapable fate resembling calamity" (*tensai ni nita fukahi no unmei*). A resigned aestheticism has marked the Japanese attitude toward natural catastrophes. Shimizu Ikutarō recalls the sight of those inhabitants of Tokyo who, after the Great Earthquake of 1923, sat within the ruins. Even those who had lost their houses and families felt an indescribable inner calm as they watched how the setting sun colored the sky over the horizon of destruction.[62]

It is interesting to note that similar photographs, showing families sitting in the ruins regarding a newly discovered nature with a wide horizon after the bombings of the capital can be found in documentaries of Shōwa history, suggesting that the attitude was very similar. The attitude is often likened to the aesthetic resignation, informed by the escapist and pessimistic medieval Buddhist outlook of Kamo no Chōmei, who, in his *Hōjōki* (*An Account of My Hut*, 1212), enumerates natural calamities like fire, earthquakes, typhoons, and famines, wonders about the ephemerality of the world, and finds peace in the heart of nature in his lonely hut.[63]

It must be more than mere coincidence that I recently came across a comment on Ibuse Masuji's famous A-bomb novel *Kuroi ame* (*Black Rain*, 1966), which states:

> The ancient Greek notion of Fate pervades the atmosphere of the novel. At the same time, we feel that the reason why Ibuse was able to draw this hellish picture of sufferings of people after the atomic explosion without losing his composure, was partly because he viewed it with the same passive resignation he has shown towards unusual calamities beyond human control in *Aogashima Taigaiki* (*Aogashima Tragedy*, 1934) and *Gojinka* (*The Sacred Fire*, 1944). Therefore, it is possible that his attitude towards the atomic bomb calamity, expressed in *Kuroi ame* (*Black Rain*), *is not fundamentally different from his attitude towards natural calamities*. The novel may be an angry one: the inhumanity of using an atomic bomb seems to be amply revealed through the sheer weight of the facts recorded; however, these facts may have been produced with the *resignation to fate characteristic of Japanese sensibility*. If so, what Ibuse Masuji has presented in this novel . . . is the view of a nihilist observer who reacts with the traditional Japanese resignation to fate. In this sense Ibuse is *a spiritual descendant of Kamo no Chōmei* . . . , who had a traditional penetrating understanding of the transience of the world.[64]

Certainly, there are other attitudes and literary approaches to the subject of war and its aftermath in contemporary Japanese literature,[65] but the cluster of attitudes just sketched is undoubtedly a widespread pattern to be found over the whole four decades. I believe that it corresponds to a number of basic patterns in Japanese intellectual life, which can only be hinted at here.

NOTES

1. Donald Keene, *Dawn to the West: Japanese Literature in the Modern Era—Fiction* (New York: Holt, Rinehart & Winston, Inc., 1984), 773 and 969.
2. Ibid., 971.
3. For Tanizaki, see the translation of Tanizaki's "Streetcorner Story," from a collection

commissioned by the Japanese Literature Patriotic Association in 1943, in Jay Rubin, *Injurious to Public Morals. Writers and the Meiji State* (Seattle and London: Washington University Press, 1984), 278.
4. See his short essay "Kunō no nenkan" ("An Almanac of Pain"), published June 1946 in *Shinbungei*, text in *Daizai Osamu zenshū*, vol. 8 (Tokyo: Chikuma shobō, 1976), 242–54.
5. See, for instance, Okuno Takeo, *Nihon bungaku shi. Kindai kara gendai e* (Tokyo: Chūō kōronsha, 1976), 179.
6. Keene, *Dawn to the West*, 965.
7. Ibid., 968.
8. Ibid., 989.
9. Nakamura Mitsuo, *Nihon no gendai shōsetsu* (Tokyo: Iwanami shoten, 1970), 115.
10. See, for instance, Takahashi Shintarō, "Sensō sekinin," *Yōrei ni miru kindai bungakushi yōgo jiten. Kaishaku to kanshō*, special enlarged edition (July 1970): 160.
11. Keene, *Dawn to the West*, 970; and Usui Yoshimi, *Kindai bungaku ronsō*, vol. 2 (Tokyo: Chikuma shobō, 1975), 190ff.
12. "Sensō sekinin o tsuikyū suru hitotachi no taido wa isasakamo bungaku to michi o tsūjite wa inai," Takahashi, *Yōrei ni miru*, 161.
13. Nobuko Miyama Ochner, "A Japanese Writer in Micronesia: Nakajima Atsushi's Experiences of 1941–42," *Journal of the Association of Teachers of Japanese 21*, no. 1 (April 1987): 37–58.
14. Literary historians such as Tsuzuki Hisayoshi obviously sympathize with this pose of Dazai's and even feel they have to defend him, finally evaluating Dazai as one who sided with Japan even though his patriotism was not expressed so noisily (Tsuzuki obviously implies that this would have to be expected), thereby using the terminology of militarist times. See Tsuzuki, "Sensō to Dazai Osamu," *Kokubungaku: Kaishaku to kanshō* (June 1983): 22–29.
15. On Maruyama, there are two recent publications: Maruyama Masao, *Denken in Japan. Hrsg. und übersetzt von Wolfgang Schamoni und Wolfgang Seifert* (Frankfurt/M.: Suhrkamp, 1988), contains translations of three important Maruyama essays and an informative introduction, including a bibliography of translations and secondary works in western languages; and Ōtake Hideo, "Maruyama Masao no chōkokkashugi bunseki," *University Press* (Tokyo), August 1987, 14–18.
16. Keene, *Dawn to the West*, 999.
17. I quote from the first draft of a paper presented to the conference on "The 1955 System in Japanese Politics" at the Hoover Institution, March 1988, by Ōtake Hideo. My telegraphic style of remarks on the politico-economic development are to a large degree inspired by his paper, but I apologize to him for doubtless presenting a distorted picture of his explanation by my condensation.
18. Jay Rubin, "From Wholesomeness to Decadence: The Censorship of Literature Under the Allied Occupation," *Journal of Japanese Studies* 11, no. 1 (Winter 1985): 71–103.
19. A convenient summary of Maruyama's statements concerning these differences can be found in Shūichi Katō, *A History of Japanese Literature, Vol. 3, The Modern Years* (Tenterden: Paul Norbury Publishers, 1983), 274.
20. Shunsuke Tsurumi, *A Cultural History of Postwar Japan, 1945–1980* (London, New York: Routledge and Kegan Paul, 1987), 106.
21. Ibid., 111.
22. Ibid., 22.
23. See John O. Haley's review of the English translation of the play in *Journal of Japanese Studies* 8, no. 1 (Winter 1982): 165–70.
24. According to Keene, the definitive edition of the book was published as late as 1974. See Keene, *Dawn to the West*, 885.
25. Tsurumi, *A Cultural History*, 22.
26. Ōtake, *A Comparative Analysis*.
27. For details, see Irmela Hijiya-Kirschnereit, "Sprache und Nation," *Das Ende der Exotik* (Frankfurt/Main: Suhrkamp, 1988).
28. Roy A. Miller, *Japan's Modern Myth: The Language and Beyond* (New York and Tokyo:

Weatherhill, 1982); and his *Nihongo. In Defence of Japanese* (London: Athlone Press, 1986).
29. Tsumuri, *A Cultural History*, 148.
30. *Sōka Gakkai News* 105 (15 November 1979): 9.
31. Tsumuri, *A Cultural History*, 148.
32. Ibid., 70.
33. Hashikawa presents this group as pattern no. 4; see his article "Sensō taiken," in Shimizu Ikutarō, ed., *Gendai shisō jiten* (Tokyo: Kōdansha, 1980), 411–13.
34. Ibid., 412.
35. Ibid.
36. Even Western scholars cannot resist the fascination of generational models dealing with modern intellectual and literary history. John Whittier Treat, for example, does so in his categorization of A-bomb writers; however, he classifies writers not by age groups but by their "distance" from the experience. John Whittier Treat, "Atomic Bomb Literature and the Documentary Fallacy," *Journal of Japanese Studies* 14, no. 1 (Winter 1988): 27–57.
37. In the original version of this paper, one section was dedicated to the analysis of Japanese literary and intellectual histories, and there I pointed out a systematical— if not necessarily conscious—evasiveness and vagueness concerning issues such as the wartime role of Japanese authors or the conspicuously different treatment of censorship during and after the war.
38. See note 3 above.
39. Quoted and translated by Edward Seidensticker, *This Country, Japan* (Tokyo and New York: Kōdansha International, 1984), 125.
40. Matsubara, "Sengo no bungaku," in *Nihon kindai bungaku daijiten*, vol. 4, 255–60.
41. Kuroi Senji's novel *Nemureru kiri ni* (*In Sleeping Mist*) of 1987 could serve as a recent example. It deals with a group of Japanese who, as students during the war, were evacuated to Hakone and now, after more than four decades, meet again there to exchange reminiscences of the time they spent there together with a group of interned German soldiers. The novel could be characterized as a slightly sentimental antiwar piece.
42. To name only three random examples: his palm-of-the-hand (*tenohira*) story "Sazanka" ("Sasanqua") of 1946, the short story "Fuji no hatsuyuki" ("First Snow on Mount Fuji," 1952), or the "novel" *Yama no oto* (*The Sound of the Mountain*, 1949–54).
43. Katō, *A History of Japanese Literature*, 279.
44. This work, which was enormously popular, was made into an equally successful TV series. It is the story of a young idealist named Kaji, stationed in Manchuria during the war, who bravely fights within an inhumane system for his fellow men and dies before being able to return to Japan. The work is frequently quoted as a model "antiwar novel." Its TV version was also a great success on German television; it has been broadcast three times during the past two decades. Interestingly, the author practices self-criticism concerning the lack of patriotism in his hero and decides that Kaji's "sentimental humanism" should die with him in the end; Kuritsubo Yoshiki, "Gomikawa Junpei 'Ningen no jōken'," in *Kokubungaku—kaishaku to kanshō*, August 1973, 132f. On this novel, see also *Asahi shinbun*, ed., *Besuto serā monogatari, chū* (Tokyo: Asahi shinbun, 1978), 77–86.
45. *Kindai Nihon bungaku daijiten*, vol. 4, 262.
46. Katō Shūichi, "Im Schatten des japanischen Wohlstands. Kritische Überlegungen zu einigen neueren Bestsellern," in *Japan und der Westen*, Band 3 (Frankfurt/M.: Fischer, 1986), 109–15. See also Morimura Seiichi, *Akuma no hōshoku-nōto* (Tokyo: Banseisha, 1982).
47. I developed this view while studying texts such as *Shiiku* (*The Catch*, 1958) and *Fui no oshi* (*Suddenly Deaf*, 1958).
48. In a thought-provoking review of Gō Shizuko's antiwar novel *Rekuiemu* (*Requiem*), which received the Akutagawa Prize in 1973, Phyllis I. Lyons has pointed out the weakness of this piece of literature. "Shared participation in a cultural experience

counted heavily in influencing literary judgment," explains Lyons, and concludes: "This novel is about thirty years too late for its simple characterizations not to seem simplistic, and we end up with fairy tale, not moral challenge." But she also contends, and I agree, "*Requiem* is an important book, to be read as an example of the ambivalence that still invades so much of Japanese public as well as private mythogenic thinking about history and national life and purpose." Lyons, "Cultural Mythos and Comic Book Heroes," *Journal of the Association of Teachers of Japanese* 21, no. 1 (April 1987): 77–84.

Another example of the way in which the conventional, superficial view stands in the way of an appreciation of a work's real qualities is the opinion of some critics about Kaga Otohiko's long novel *Kaerazaru natsu* (*The Summer That Does Not Return*, 1973), depicting the education and indoctrination of a young cadet who commits suicide at the end of the war. From the very fact that the novel plays in the military, the young heroes orient themselves in the direction of the insurgents of the February 26 incident and commit ritual suicide, and because the emperor system is allotted much space in the novel, the critics felt entitled to accuse the work of glorifying the fight. Kaga Otohiko and Miyoshi Tōru, "Kaerazaru natsu no hibi (taiwa)," *Rekishi to jinbutsu* (April 1974): 128–35.

49. Treat, "Atomic Bomb Literature," 36.
50. On sentimentalism in *shishōsetsu*, see Irmela Hijiya-Kirschnercit, *Selbstentblößungsrituale. Zur Theorie und Geschichte der autobiographischen Gattung "Shishōsetsu" in der modernen japanischen Literatur* (Wiesbaden: Steiner, 1981), especially pp. 139f and 179f.
51. The volumes, which are not for sale, were printed by Furusawa Hideo. The photograph is to be found in vol. 1, p. 128.
52. The text in *Gendai tanpen meisakusen*, vol. 2, 1948–50, ed. by Nihon bungeika kyōkai (Tokyo: Kōdansha, 1979), 259–88.
53. Ibid., 274.
54. Ibid., 271.
55. Ibid., 188–217.
56. Nakamura, "Kawabata Yasunari," *Nihon kindai bungaku daijiten*, vol. 1, 449–53.
57. For this aspect, see Hijiya-Kirschnereit, *Mishima Yukios Roman* "Kyōko no ie": Versuch einer intratextuellen Analyse (Weisbaden: Harrassowitz, 1976), 210.
58. The German translation is contained in Itō Narihiko, Siegfried Schaarschmidt, and Wolfgang Schamoni, eds., *Seit jenem Tag. Hiroshima und Nagasaki in der japanischen Literatur* (Frankfurt/M.: Fischer, 1984), 8–13.
59. The German translation is an abridged version of Helmut Erlinghagen, translator, *Die Hand des Riesen* (Stuttgart: Deutsche Verlagsanstalt, 1976), 142.
60. Mishima Yukio, *Ningen to bungaku*, in Hijiya-Kirschnereit, *Mishima Yukios Roman*, 212.
61. The quotations are in Rubin, "From Wholesomeness," 78f.
62. I quote Shimizu from Watanabe, *Nihonjin to kindai kagaku* (Tokyo: Iwanami, 1976), 175f.
63. Ibid., 176.
64. *Introduction to Contemporary Japanese Literature. Synopses of Major Works, 1956–1970* (Tokyo: University of Tokyo Press, 1972), 58 (my italics).
65. A writer who manages to do completely without sentimentalization and the described type of aestheticizing is Kōno Taeko: see, for example, her stories "Michishio" ("The Tide," 1964) or "Tetsu no uo" ("Iron Fish," 1976) in Kōno Taeko, *Knabenjagd. Erzählungen*, translated by Irmela Hijiya-Kirschnereit (Frankfurt/M.: Insel, 1988).

III

LITERATURE UNDER THE OCCUPATION

6

Literature under the Occupation in Germany: Memories of a Contemporary

Peter Demetz

The Allies had specific plans for the advance of their armies in World War II, but their ideas about what to do in Germany once it was subdued were, at times, incoherent, and the Allies often differed even in their interpretations of action on the battlefield. The U.S. declarations were inclined to speak about Germany as a "defeated enemy country," whereas the Soviets preferred to talk about a process of "liberation," quoting Stalin's dictum about how Hitlers come and go but the German nation endures.

The tempo and the stages of building new administrative structures, political or cultural, clearly showed that the Soviets were resolutely prepared to use the political legacies of the Weimar Republic, and, with the help of the returning Communist Party functionaries, to develop broad support in order to realize their aims in their zone of occupation and possibly beyond. The concepts of the U.S. military government developed rather tortuously. Conflict smoldered between the State Department and the War Office, and not until 1944 did Roosevelt reject the Morgenthau plan to turn Germany into a purely agricultural state after the war. The French, admitted to the rank of the occupying powers only in 1945, believed in de-Prussianizing Germany, making it powerless by creating a group of *Kleinstaaten* (small states) again. The British, more pragmatically minded and knowing something about the exigencies of the European economic situation, held fast to an almost old-fashioned idea of a balance of power.

It is not really a paradox but rather an indication of political skill that the Soviets were first to reestablish a system of political parties. Order No. 2 of the Soviet Military Administration of 10 June 1945 encouraged, if not demanded, the formation of political parties. The other Allies, less convinced than the Soviets about a clear division between bad and good Germans, were more hesitant; political parties were readmitted in the U.S. zone in August, in the British zone in September, and in the French zone not until December 1945.

In the beginning, Germany cultural activities, which were developed primarily with the material help of the Allied powers, were operated and controlled by the appropriate branches and the local offices of the military governments—the Office of the Military Government for Germany in Frankfurt, the Control Commission for Germany/British Element in Bad Oynhausen, the Conseil de Control pour l'Allemagne in Baden-Baden (occupying powers have predilections for old big hotels), and the *Sowjetische Militäradministration* in Berlin-Karlshorst.

Literary historians will have an uneasy time describing the process and the personalities involved in decisionmaking. The contemporaries, at any rate, more vividly remember the officers in the Soviet and French zones than those in Frankfurt, Munich, or Bad Oynhausen who, for all we know, were far less colorful personalities than their Soviet and French counterparts and had, possibly, an awful time trying to keep up with the frequent changes in the table of organizations and the members of the U.S. Senate and the House of Representatives, eager for headlines at home. Soviet policy was controlled, in Berlin, by Colonel Tulpanov, an energetic, impressive political scientist who was an avid reader of German literature; his colleague, Alexandr Dymshitz, a rather orthodox literary critic; and Ilya Fradkin, who later, at home, risked a great deal to defend Bertolt Brecht against the Stalinist friends of socialist realism. The French cultural proconsul Raymond Schmittlein, *Directeur de l'education publique*, a scholar and *Germaniste* who, according to all accounts, ran his department in the best feudal manner, worked with young Alfred Grosser and old Alfred Döblin; among his other achievements, he single-handedly resuscitated the University of Mainz.

The fundamental function of the cultural branches, East and West, was to censor and to encourage (by hot meals and copyrights), and there is evidence that many Americans, at least, felt rather uneasy carrying out functions that occasionally resembled those of the old *Propaganda Ministerium*. Censorship apparently was more concerned with the past than with the present. There was an "illustrative list of National Socialist and Militarist literature" to be used by U.S. personnel, but there were also a number of white, gray, and black lists of Germans to be employed, or not, in cultural affairs, including the theater and film. And the *Landesverwaltung für Volksbildung* (Regional Administration for the Education of the People), clearly a German rather than a Soviet institution in the Russian zone, published a catalogue of 526 pages listing books to be removed from the libraries (needless to say it was rejected by the U.S. administration). It was certainly easier to remove old books than to publish new ones; the summer of 1945 was not November 1918, and readers and publishers who had hoped for a miraculous avalanche of searing manuscripts began to speak of empty drawers (*leere Schubladen*) of German writing.

The first anthology of poetry published after the war in Munich under the imprimatur of the U.S. Information Control Division shows how difficult it must have been to discover young writers and new manuscripts. Günter Groll, a budding film critic and editor, selected a motto from Brecht that promised sober and concrete truth, but in his introductory remarks he relied more on a Hölderlin-like tone invoking fate and the gods. Moreover, after paying his respects to the émigrés, he distinctly defended the writers who went on writing and, often, publishing in the Nazi Reich. The older generation, including Werner Bergengruen, Hans Carossa, and Gertrud von le Fort, actually prevails in the anthology; but, fortunately, at least Rudolf Hagelstange, Elisabeth Langgässer, and Horst Lange from the middle generation are present.

Not many young writers appeared; one of them was "Sebastian Grill"—none other than the editor himself. Groll also invented two poets, "Friedrich Umbran" and "Gregor Walden," with admirably melodramatic antifascist biographies, for whom he produced surrealist and late-expressionist poetry. It was not the first time that a writer had invented other writers, and Günter Groll, in his historical moment, should be excused on grounds of wishful thinking; he gave the reader what should have been there but, unfortunately, was not.

In politics and in literary life, conflicts among those who had survived abroad and those within the country emerged early. In Soviet territory, the returning party functionaries, often writers of distinction, were preferred in sensitive appointments to those who had barely survived at home. And in the American zone of occupation, between May and October 1945, a discussion about the so-called inner emigration touched raw nerves on all sides. Thomas Mann, in a message from California printed on 18 May 1945 in the *Bayrische Volkszeitung*, declared that "it was not a small number of criminals" who were responsible for what had happened but "hundreds of thousands of the German elite" who perpetrated crimes "in sick lust." Among those who responded was Frank Thiess, whose books had sold well in the Third Reich; in the *Münchner Zeitung* (13 August 1945) he claimed that Germans involved in an inner emigration had gathered far more important experiences within Nazi Germany than those who had looked on "from the dress circle and first row seats abroad." This response made Thomas Mann so irate that in his own answer to Thiess he spared nobody: "It might be superstitious, but in my eyes books that could be printed from 1933 and 1945 in Germany are less than worthless, and they are not good to handle. They should all be destroyed" (*Auzeiger* 12 October 1945).

Tempers ran high, and it was Alfred Andersch who, speaking for the middle generation of returning prisoners of war, in his essay "German Literature in the Moment of Decision" (1948), tried to articulate a fair and calm argument, ultimately rejecting the view of Thomas Mann whom he deeply admired. Andersch made an distinction between true literature that was written at an intellectual distance from the regime and nonliterature that was identified with Nazi interests. He suggested that genuine writers, both abroad and at home, had emancipated themselves from the regime, though in different ways and degrees.

As East-West tensions increased, the discussion subsided, but it had its own paradoxical if not ironic elements. Thomas Mann, who had hesitated somewhat, on the advice of his publisher, to break with the Nazi regime immediately in 1933 and to make common cause with the antifascist exiles in Switzerland and elsewhere, in his rage did not exclude from his verdict persecuted writers like Elisabeth Langgässer or Jochen Klepper, who later committed suicide. Andersch, once head of the Bavarian Communist youth organization and a *Wehrmacht* deserter by ideological decision, was careful to make a case for Weinheber (whenever Weinheber was a poet, Andersch said, he could not have been a Nazi) and for Ernst Jünger (Andersch insisted that Jünger's major books written during the war, including the Paris diaries and the *Marmorklippen* [*On the Marble Cliffs*], constituted a self-purification from guilt and made it possible for many young readers to perceive the true character of the Nazi regime).

Among the first novels to appear after the end of the war, Kasimir Edschmidt's *Das gute Recht* (*My Good Right*) (1946), written during the last three years of the regime and finished in August 1945, deserves particular attention for political and, possibly, documentary reasons. Edschmidt, once a well-known expressionist and later a spritely cultural historian, survived, as a writer, in the gaps between the competing Nazi organizations. Without trying to prove that he belonged to the heroes of the resistance, he described in his novel his own situation and that of his family of four in a rented house in southern Bavarian. While armies clashed and corpses burned, the Rothenhahns lived a rather isolated modest, rustic life. He was not permitted to publish (occasionally, his publisher sold a few copies of his earlier books, half legally, half illegally) and he continued to work on a manuscript about Italian cultural history for the future. The family had few friends; the Nazis kept watch on the outsider and made his life difficult by transferring to the top floor of the house a family of spiteful party members who had allegedly lost their house in an air raid and proceeded to play his piano to make it impossible for him to go on writing.

I must confess that I loathed the novel when I first read it, but I have changed my mind about it, while continuing to have some reservations. Rothenhahn/Edschmidt is aware of his limitations, suspects that terrible murders are committed in the East, listens to foreign broadcasts to learn more, and expresses essential thoughts about German intellectuals under Nazi rule, including the newspaper publisher who yields almost totally to the regime "to save a minimum." The novel is unique—cosmopolitan and provincial at the same time, free from excessive self-pity (the curse of contemporary German writing), and instructive on the ideological nuances of speech, including the revealing use of *Heil Hitler*, *Guten Tag*, and *Grüß Gott*! used as greetings by Nazis, and non-Nazis, respectively.

The discussion about exiles and inner emigration went on for some time, but the third force of returning prisoners of war (POWs) increasingly consolidated and helped determine the shape of literary affairs, at least in the West, for some time to come. There were, in May 1945, more than 400,000 POWs in 425 camps in the United States; toward the end of the war, the U.S. Army began to comb these camps for people to be trained for administrative and other functions in defeated Germany. The writers Alfred Andersch and Hans Werner Richter were selected to edit a camp newspaper. After their return to Munich, they persuaded the U.S. authorities that the camp newspaper should continue, in the shape of a German periodical, to inform and educate young readers.

The German *Der Ruf* (*The Call*) was the most intelligent publication of the immediate postwar period, and although the editors were nearly middle-aged, they were admirably able to identify fully with the younger returning soldiers and prisoners. Andersch and Richter believed in combining a reconstituted liberalism with socialist economic principles in order to build a bridge between the great powers, but they had no illusions about the paradoxical German situation; everybody talked about democracy while actually living in a military dictatorship, and Hans Werner Richter, more pragmatic in political matters than the existentialist Andersch, asked how Germans "living behind a Chinese wall of collective guilt" were to be trained, in their quarantine, "to achieve the highest form of social freedom, self-determination, and the right to self-determination."

Trying to develop ideas about the reform of German universities, the editors were surprisingly pro-American, but, precisely because they believed in rationality and American fairness, they were appalled by the way in which the American military "rented out" German POWs to the French, who used them in the coal mines. The U.S. military government finally withdrew Andersch's and Richter's license to publish when Richter, himself a former Communist expelled from the party for alleged Trotskyism, accused the secretary general of the French Communist Party of being disloyal to the central tenets of Marxism and Leninism by preaching national revenge instead of defending the internationalism of the working classes. The U.S. information division had a momentary victory, but the editor and writers of the old *The Call* went on working together and established the Group 47, which dominated literary life in West Germany for at least twenty years.

It has been said that the Group 47 was born in disillusion, but disillusion was essential to its sober views, and the group changed profoundly when its founders ceased to define its literary interests. Andersch, Richter, and Werner Kolbenhoff had all been members of the Weimar Communist Party who had left the organization or were expelled; and after serving in the army, deserting, or willingly being taken prisoner, they admired Roosevelt and the ideas of the New Deal, and inevitably felt frustrated by the contradictions between American missionary ideas and the realities of trying to live under the U.S. military government.

The literary program of the Group 47, in its initial stage, was clearly anticipated and defined by the writers of *The Call*, who preferred the dry, precise, and paratactic style close to Hemingway's *For Whom the Bell Tolls* (that Bible of all writing POWs) and the new Italian *verismo* in the cinema. They argued against rhetoric, the metaphysical flourish, classical perfection, and, above all and in practice, against Stifter, Hölderlin, and Rilke, those poets of the elegant Nazi lieutenants from good families, and a few other connoisseurs, including young Andersch himself. Richter warned against the older realism of Fontane and Spielhagen (for the middle class had little future, he rashly believed); he preferred American writers like Thomas Wolfe, whose works were available in Germany until December 1941, or William Faulkner. Andersch declared that literature that aspired to be art had to be "socially true," and Wolfgang Weyrauch in a famous essay demanded a linguistic *Kahlschlag* (clearing) to reduce the German vocabulary to something simple, stark, and close to the experience among the ruins. Gustav René Hocke, formerly a German correspondent in Rome, argued in favor of the content and against the *calligrafisti* who, by trying to write too beautifully, merely falsified unrhetorical life.

The truth was, of course, that emerging writers did their own thing and that Kafka was reimported from the United States; in 1951 Heinrich Böll, who could still pass for a realist, received the award of the group, but he was followed by Ilse Aichinger and Ingeborg Bachmann, and critics, often reluctantly, admitted that a "magical realism" began to take hold in new writing. In the later 1950s, Andersch withdrew, disgusted for many reasons, and the meetings of the group turned into a stock exchange for manuscripts, realistic or not, which were eagerly bought by attending publishers.

American, or Western, and Soviet assumptions in running cultural affairs were essentially different with respect to German responsibility for the Nazi crimes. The Americans, for a time at least, held to a belief in collective guilt or at least in shared responsibilities and, consequently, insisted on nonfraternization; hence they kept German intellectuals at a certain distance. Soviet policies, in contrast, were based on a division between bad Germans and good antifascists or Germans who could be educated to join the latter group. The Soviets quickly involved German writers and intellectuals, entire groups of whom were flown in from their exile in Moscow, or emerged from the rubble, to participate in cultural mass organizations or conferences. It would be difficult to separate, at least far into 1947, coercion and spontaneity; and although the Soviet Military Administration and the Communist Party worked from well-prepared blueprints, these were based on the idea of the Popular Front—to gather all good people from the Left to the Right to the middle. Many liberals and conservatives, including Ricarda Huch, Gerhart Hauptmann, and the actor Paul Wegener could see no reason not to work for the new *Kulturbund* and its periodical *Aufbau*, which printed a good deal of Thomas Mann, Hermann Broch, Paul Valéry, and Virginia Woolf. Literature was to be antifascist, humanist, socially engaged, and, possibly, respectful of German tradition (Goethe foremost). The terror policies of socialist realism elsewhere were passed over in silence, and Theodor Plievier's massive novel *Stalingrad*, written in the Soviet Union, ran up a print order of a half-million copies in the Soviet zone alone, and was translated, deservedly so, into twenty languages.

Contemporaries read it as a novel of hope; out of bloodshed and destruction two German soldiers emerged—one a proletarian serving in a penal battalion, the other an aristocrat and officer, and both learned their lesson. *Stalingrad* is a highly ideological novel that does not want to be ideological, at least in a narrow sense; the terms *Communist* and

National Socialist are systematically avoided, and Plievier, who moved to the West in 1947, above all showed Russian people defending their fatherland, regardless of by whom it was run or how. Alfred Andersch rightly said that *Stalingrad* was the most important novel of the immediate postwar period. It worked with an old-fashioned omniscient narrator, with massive syntactic repetition in the mode of the Bible and the fairy tale; and yet it paradoxically fulfilled the literary demands made by the writers of *The Call* and the early Group 47 more substantially than any other novel published at the time in the Western zones.

Many older and younger writers in the Western zones, however, were beginning to show something of the traditional German unwillingness to face German history soberly. In a number of ways they tried to be timely and escapist at the same time, whether taking refuge in metaphysics, a mushy existentialism, or retreating to the realm of nature, or both. In the texts of *Trümmerlyrik* ("rubble" poetry), the ideological assumption that history has, as it were, receded somewhere else combined, at times, with a distinct inclination to self-pity or cheap cliché consolations. Dagmar Nick's poem "Es gibt noch Sterne" ("There are still stars," 1946) provides a good example of the entire genre in which, despite all the material and moral destruction, the traditional stanza of four lines and the alternate rhyme survived unimpaired. There are the ruins, the poem suggests, the burned out windows, the nameless dead buried under stone and steel, but there is consolation in the cosmic order beyond the chaos and the destruction of history. "Es gibt noch Sterne über den Ruinen" (there are still stars above the ruins), and "es gibt noch Träume über jenen Dächern, die eingestürzt sind in das Labyrinth der Stadt" (there are still dreams above those roofs that burst into the city labyrinth). The poem exhorts readers to lift their eyes to the eternal sky rather than to stare transfixed at the rubble, that sign of historical change and moral involvement. The worst thing is, of course, that such a poem falls back on a secondhand, late romantic idiom, as if there had been no modern poetry at all, and only a rudimentary line, "wo sie nun klirren, hart und blechern" (there now they clank harshly and tinny), reveals a faint memory of Hölderlin resuscitated in the expressionist age of Georg Heym.

It was easy to argue against the run-of-the-mill *Trümmerlyrik* and its escape route to the undisturbed natural order, but contemporary critics had a more difficult time with Ernst Wiechert's *Jerominkinder* (*The Jeromin Children*, 1945), actually the first novel to appear in occupied Munich under the authority of the District Information Service. Unlike Gottfried Benn, another adversary of history who was blacklisted by the Allies until 1948, Ernst Wiechert, conservative and Protestant, had an impeccable record of distancing himself from the regime. He had given, under Nazi rule, a speech to German youth in which he had admonished listeners to resist the temptations of blind nationalism, after which he was briefly held in Buchenwald concentration camp, and the Ministry of Propaganda removed his novels, especially popular among the educated middle class, from the market.

Nevertheless, the *Jerominkinder* was, in attitude and idiom, an old rather than a new novel, eager to push aside history (which Wiechert identified with greed, the cities, and the instability of willed exploits); and it praised *das einfache Leben* (the simple life), fully consonant with the seasonal rhythm of the earth. The novel had the additional appeal of having been written as a dirge about eastern regions now lost; and though Wiechert, a master of programmatic fuzziness, did not really wish to say whether his lovable villages and *sympathisch* (likable) feudal landowners actually lived in the Baltic or East Prussian landscapes, he skillfully anticipated elements of Bobrowski's and Siegfried Lenz's mystic "East," with pensive if shrewd peasants, vast forests, and thickets of fragrant lilac. History was somewhere else, somewhere out there, the novel insisted: "They marched, from country to country, from battlefield to battlefield, but the dark earth, sustaining, preserving, eternal, endured. . . . They did not want victories but bread, and the most simple among them, not even bread, but the work of their hands." Wiechert did not say why these arcadian regions were now occupied by the Soviets and the Poles. Once again, Alfred Andersch rightly suggested that, in the case of Wiechert, it was inevitable to admire his personal courage and heartily to dislike what he wrote.

Yet it would be impossible to say that any effort to disqualify history counteracts the analytical importance of literature then or now; and while Wiechert regressed to a forest arcadia of many emotions and little thought, Elisabeth Langgässer (whose daughter, after her mother's divorce, was transported to Auschwitz) had few of these consolations to offer. In her later novels, the mystical impulse, or the drive to ask questions of religious import, clashes with her awareness of the historical moment she experienced; the timeless and the actual are fused in an irresistible language of sibylline fervor. The *Märkische Argonautefahrt* (*The Quest*) was published in 1950 but exactly reflected Berlin experiences in the first month of the occupation. Her chapters on the sufferings of the last Berlin Jews huddled in the *Kleiderkammer* (clothes closet) of the Jewish Center before being sent east, her merciless view of life in a small Brandenburg village after the Soviet Army came, and her concluding story about the black marketeers hidden in the cellars have not been equaled in her time.

Yet, like her seven pilgrims who set out from smoldering Berlin to think about their lives in a Benedictine nunnery, where through its recurrent rituals they could partake of eternity, Langgässer is obsessed by the question of how the historical moment and timeless "being" cohere. Trying to annihilate the sequence of time, she establishes a narrative consciousness and a rhetoric of synchronies in which the words of the Jewish Bible, the New Testament, and Indic and Greek myths coexist and illuminate each other. Gethsemane, Sodom, Hiroshima, and the tents of Achilles before Troy, "everything was simultaneous, of equal importance, and wore before its face a mask which (apart from slight nuance) made one suspect that its lacquered, hastily painted canvas concealed identical features."

We are far too tempted to view the first years of the occupation with later eyes and to project the intensifying U.S.-Soviet conflict, clearly emerging in the fall of 1947, into earlier moments. The first postwar moments were more fluid and more open than we believe today, and yet we should not overlook the most important difference in the emerging literary experience in the occupation zones—in the Soviet zone, the reappearance of a compact generation of some of the most famous and productive writers of the Weimar Left who, after surviving the Stalinist purges in the Soviet Union, by command of the party organization and their own resolve, returned to continue their work in the liberated Germany; in the Western zone of occupation, a far more uncertain situation, and only a few exiles returning with the occupying powers, Alfred Döblin perhaps in the French zone, and for a brief tour of discussions at least, Carl Zuckmayer in Bavaria. In the Soviet zone, a discussion of exile and inner emigration would have been largely meaningless, because the substance of the new writing was created by older authors like Bredel, Uhse, and Seghers. It was only in the Western zone that such a discussion made sense, at least before the third force of returning soldiers and POWs, who were largely unknown as writers, emerged as a dominant force through *The Call* and Group 47. The early Group 47 preferred the Hemingway mode to Kafka, and longed for down-to-earth attention to historical experience—Plievier not Broch or Thomas Mann's *Doktor Faustus*.

Their wishes remained largely unfulfilled, because most writers felt happier in escaping traumatic experience into the less-than-historical realm of the cosmos, of the botanical consolations of plants and leaves of grass, or the timeless creative moment. Elisabeth Langgässer was the rare exception among those who had remained at home who reminded her readers of the murder of the Jews (not a question of prime importance to Group 47) and tried to balance the timeless and historical time. It was only in the mid-1950s, with the emergence of a new generation, that the situation changed, but that is another story entirely.

RECOMMENDED READINGS FOR CHAPTER 6

Aichinger, Ilse. *Herod's Children*. Translated by Cornelia Schaeffer. New York: Atheneum, 1963.
Benn, Gottfried. *Prime Vision: Selected Writings*. Edited by E. B. Ashton. New York: New Directions, 1960.
Böll, Heinrich. *Absent without Leave*. Translated by Leila Vennewitz. London: Calder and Boyars, 1966.
Der Ruf: Unbhängige Blätter der Jungen Generation, 1946–49. Munich.
Edschmidt, Kasimir. *Das gute Recht*. Munich: K. Desch, 1946.
Groll, Günter, ed. *De Profundis*. Munich: K. Desch, 1946.
Jünger, Ernst. *On the Marble Cliffs*. Translated by Stuart Hood. Norfolk, Conn.: New Directions, 1947; also London: J. Lehmann, 1947.
Langgässer, Elisabeth. *The Quest*. Translated by Jane Bannard Greene. New York: Knopf, 1953.
Plievier, Theodor. *Stalingrad*. Translated by Richard and Clara Winston. New York: Appleton-Century-Crofts, 1948.
Wiechert, Ernst. *Die Jerominkinder*. Munich: K. Desch, 1945.

7

Literary Reorientation in Occupied Japan: Incidents of Civil Censorship

Marlene J. Mayo

From September 1945 to April 1952, political, economic, and psychological reorientation of occupied Japan was a conscious policy of the postwar American government. This included an ambitious program of ideological reprogramming in support of the American rise to globalism. Japan was in effect reconstituted as a giant reeducation camp under the supervision of General Douglas MacArthur, Supreme Commander for the Allied Powers Japan (SCAP). The concrete aims were to end Japan's "feudal" concepts, characterized specifically as class stratification, glorification of the military, and subservience to authority, together with its racial consciousness and belief in divine mission, and to foster new beliefs, labeled as democracy, individual responsibility, and fair dealing.[1] For the first four years, 1945 through 1949, as millions of overseas troops and civilians were repatriated, Japan was largely cut off from the rest of the world and subject to extensive foreign surveillance of its schools, mass media, postal services, and telecommunications. The preferred methods of control were nonviolent and persuasive, but intimidation and coercion were not ruled out. When policy emphases shifted from reform to recovery in 1948 and controls were lessened but not ended, cultural exchange programs were adopted to strengthen Japan's integration with the United States and the European democracies. Because occupied Japan was not split among a number of victorious allies but remained a political entity under a single military bureaucracy, and was, in addition, an island country, reorientation was easier to implement than in Germany. However, Japan's history and culture were far less known to Americans than Germany's and far fewer Americans spoke or read Japanese than German.[2]

As required by Washington and carried out by SCAP, control and reform of Japan's media were as central to the process of reorientation as were changes in Japan's schools. In practice, this task required an intricate mixture of indoctrination and censorship. To carry out the tasks of fostering democratic and peaceful ideas through the mass media while instilling war guilt, MacArthur relied primarily on units in the Information Division of the Civil Education and Information Section (CI&E).[3] To detect and check militaristic and chauvinistic ideas, he turned to the Civil Censorship Detachment (CCD) of the Civil Intelligence Section. Each section had a distinct mission: the propagandists were to insert or prescribe acceptable words, and the censors were to delete or suppress objectionable ones. Frequently, their functions overlapped, but together they were to immunize Japan against the spread of ideologies inimical to American interests, whether lingering militarism or advancing communism.[4] Although SCAP was not particularly interested in literature per se, literary works came under its scrutiny as published works.

On balance, CI&E was far less concerned with the literary world than with the press, theater, films, or radio broadcasting. Its major contribution to reorienting Japan's literary life was in allocating newsprint, expanding the flow of foreign books to Japan, and, above all, in interacting with other SCAP sections to change the intellectual and political atmosphere for the whole population by constantly promoting the concept and practice of peace, democracy, and responsible international life through numerous information programs, campaigns, and exhibits. Inadvertently, it may also have contributed to a growing American appreciation of modern and classical Japanese literature. In order to observe major reorientation activities that *directly* affected Japanese literary life and production during those years, the chief topic of this essay, one must look rather to the work of the occupation's civil censors.[5] It is here too that some answers may be found concerning the charges subsequently made of an undue interference with literary creativity in occupied Japan.

Quickly organized and employing a combined Allied and Japanese staff of over 6,000 at its high point in 1947, CCD had several branches to carry out its overall mission of surveillance of the media and other channels of public communications.[6] Within this large apparatus, the unit responsible for preventing the mass media from carrying materials harmful to the goal of demilitarization and democratization was the Press, Publications, and Broadcasting Division, or PPB, which, in addition to its functional units, was also divided into three operational districts with headquarters in Tokyo, Osaka, and Fukuoka. The taboos designated in SCAP's Press Code, issued in late September 1945, embraced the broad categories of militarist propaganda, inaccurate statements, incitements to unrest or remarks disturbing to public tranquillity, and criticism of the United States, the Allies, the occupation, or General MacArthur. For internal guidance, there were detailed office manuals and elaborate key logs that extended and periodically updated the list of forbidden subjects.[7]

Well-fortified, PPB's senior media censors and supporting staff acted to delete offensive materials from newspapers, wire service copy, films, plays, slides and lantern shows, paintings and cartoons, magazines, and books. The range of strictly literary activity was surprising, since its priorities, like those of CI&E, were political and economic publications. At first PPB's main target was the ultra Right, but it soon added the Communist Left and continued to watch both extremes closely to the end of its official operations in late 1949. This was a delicate matter since PPB was obligated to protect the Soviet Union from criticism. With the heating up of the cold war, and the onset of the Korean War, SCAP was able to combat the Left more openly, culminating in MacArthur's support of Prime Minister Yoshida Shigeru's government in suppression of the Communist organ *Akahata* (*Red Flag*) in 1950 and purge of leftists from the media. During the first two years of PPB operations, the bulk of Japanese books and periodicals were precensored, with a shift in September 1947 to postcensorship of books followed by magazines at the end of the year. Even then, several troublesome magazine and book publishers on both the Right and Left were kept on a precensorship basis, and in this later stage, any "flagrant" violations of the Press Code could bring fines, reprimands, or even suspensions of sales. Strict measures were taken to keep the existence of occupation censorship secret from the Japanese public by banning all written references to the process and proscribing the use of telltale ellipse marks (*fuseji*) for deleted items or passages. Of course, Japanese authors, editors, and publishers were fully aware of the process as were foreign correspondents. During the period of precensorship, publishers had to submit two copies of all galleys to the censors and wait for decisions, just as in the old days of Japanese government controls.

Within PPB, the key figures in making literary decisions were the chief of PPB, the District heads, and senior officers in the Publications Branch (Tokyo), in particular the book and magazine unit. On occasion the chief censor of CCD became involved, and in highly delicate issues, such as atomic bomb literature, the chief of MacArthur's intelligence operations, General Charles Willoughby, joined the deliberations. For most of the period, 1945–49, the head of PPB was John Costello, a former St. Louis newsman with wartime training in a Japanese language and area program specially created for civil censors at the University of Michigan. The District One Censor in Tokyo was Richard Kunzman, a journalist by trade, who was succeeded in 1948 by Patrick J. Malloy, followed by Robert M. Spaulding, a young graduate at war's end of the Army's intensive Japanese language school. The senior publications officers were American, but the central book and magazine unit in Tokyo also employed European nationals Klaus and Hans Pringsheim (who were residents of Japan from the interwar years and relatives by marriage of the German writer, Thomas Mann), together with hundreds of Japanese nationals at lower levels as scanners, examiners, and translators.[8] As individuals, the American senior censors tended to be well educated, professional people from civilian backgrounds with a modicum of training in things Japanese. Their overseers, however, were career Army officers who tended to look at issues as military or security questions and were careful to protect MacArthur's image.[9]

Almost immediately, foreign journalists began raising questions about press censorship in their home publications, where they were free to exercise their First Amendment rights, and consistently condemned its continued existence as contrary to guarantees of free discourse under the new Constitution of 1947.[10] Systematic study of literary censorship in occupied Japan, however, has been slow to develop. In the aftermath of occupation, Matsuura Sōzō, former editor of the journal *Kaizō*, offered a judicious overview in 1971: Occupation censorship was "more democratic" than the homegrown version but had its "biting edge." Literary historians, such as Honda Shūgo, seconded by Donald Keene and Jay Rubin, posited a postwar literary renaissance, giving much more credit to occupation freedoms and the inner history of the literary circles or *bundan* in shaping the literary scene than to SCAP controls in dampening creativity.[11] A far more negative view, condemning occupation censorship as interventionist and harmful to postwar Japanese literature, owes much to the outrage of author and social critic Etō Jun, whose first articles were written in the late 1970s and based on research in American archives.[12] Since one of his chief concerns was to document a racially motivated SCAP attack on traditional Japanese culture and the Japanese language, his findings, though valuable, were not placed within the larger framework of Japan's long history of literary censorship reaching back into the Tokugawa era. This need has been well addressed by others, among them Jay Rubin, Richard Mitchell, and Ben-Ami Shilloney in their studies of prewar and wartime press and literary controls of the Japanese state, but work on the actual hermeneutics of censorship is not yet very advanced.[13] For truly comparative analysis, moreover, additional research is needed on Japan's exercise of literary censorship and guidance in colonial Korea, 1910–45, including attempts to suppress the Korean language, and in the occupied areas of the Greater East Asia Co-Prosperity Sphere, 1937–45. Nevertheless, Etō's arguments have raised necessary questions and stimulated detailed research. Even if SCAP censorship was less pervasive and different in the selection of banned topics from that of the Japanese state, it did exist, it was intrusive, and it posed a threat to freedom of expression. However altered the conditions in the aftermath of war and defeat, Japanese authors and publishers continued to live with the problem of external censorship and self-censorship to ensure publication. For a critical period, Japanese readers were deprived of certain works in whole or in part.

The record of American and Allied civil censorship in Japan, including strictly literary censorship, is ironically probably the best documented case in history. The bulk of the evidence is contained in the Prange Collection, McKeldin Library, University of Maryland at College Park, and in the SCAP archives housed at the Washington National Records Center in Suitland, Maryland. Both collections are vast, and both must be utilized to arrive at an overview. Together they contain working papers, galleys, original manuscripts, statistics, and internal correspondence. The Prange Collection, in addition, contains reprints of literary classics and new works of fiction in book and magazine format, all in the form in which they were actually published and made available to Japanese readers, 1945 to 1949.

Finding answers in these and supplementary archives is an enormous task. What follows is impressionistic, though based on a systematic search through selected magazine and book files, and owes much to prior researchers. In common with previous case studies, it surveys censorship of reprints and newly written works. The ultimate assessment of Allied literary censorship is part of the larger question of reorientation, and it awaits, not only quantification, but, more important, mastery and textual studies of the literature itself, in addition to examination of memoirs and reminiscences of literary figures and their literary debates.

At the heart of the matter is the question of what the censors actually deleted or suppressed, and why, in serious and popular literature. Here, the work was in two parts—scanning reprints of classics and modern standards and also reviewing new works by established and beginning writers. This was an awesome task at the beginning. Despite forced wartime consolidations and paper shortages and the loss of equipment in fire bomb raids, a good part of Japan's publications industry was still in business. Moreover, the Japanese were a nation of readers.[14]

In the first instance, Yoshiko Yokochi Samuel, citing the interference of censors with reprints of classical and modern masterpieces, contends along with Etō Jun that Japanese readers were alienated "from their own unique cultural heritage, from their inner selves, and from their society."[15] It is true that PPB book censors, who incidentally were keen to destroy Japanese perceptions of uniqueness, closely examined ancient works for signs of ultranationalism, checking for example the poetry of the *Man'yōshū* (compiled in 760 A.D.) and the myth cycles in Japan's first extant historical work, the *Kojiki* (compiled in 712 A.D.). But the evidence indicates mixed reactions and sensitive handling, including consultation with Japanese nationals. By late 1946, the policy, devised by PPB and announced by Richard Kunzman, was to permit reprints of the ancient classics but to suppress "interpretations of these works which misuse them for militaristic or for ultranationalistic purposes" or conveyed anything faintly resembling ideas of a divine emperor. Accordingly, while Yamaguchi Takao's *Kojiki Kōwa* (*Lectures on the Kojiki*) was suppressed in 1947, publication of the *Kojiki* itself was not.[16]

For the medieval and early modern ages, publications censors displayed zeal equal to that of their drama counterparts in checking samurai literature for tales of revenge and martial values. In July 1947, PPB excised a passage from a critical study of Japanese plays for lamenting the recent prohibition of sixty-nine Kabuki plays (in addition to the twenty-nine already banned) "as a great loss to the theatrical world." Also scrapped was the author's question as to why these banned plays were still so popular and retained the "power to charm" present day Japanese. Was it because they were militaristic, he had asked, or because they were "sensitive to beauty which appeals to the human sense of sight or hearing."[17] The following November, PPB suppressed an entire article in the magazine *Dokusho tembō*, for asserting, among other violations, that an English translation in 1879 of the tale of the forty-seven rōnin was one of President Theodore Roosevelt's favorite books. Drama censor Faubion Bowers agreed with the publications unit that this item was "nationalistic propaganda."[18] Attitudes had relaxed somewhat by the fall when SCAP permitted the first postwar performance of *Chūshingura*, the famous version of the forty-seven rōnin story, with a stunning all star cast. Nevertheless a year later in September 1948, a time of postcensorship, PPB applauded the publication of a new book, which it approvingly described as "a disparaging analysis of this most popular story." The author was praised for characterizing the rōnin as a dissipated lot, who instead of sacrificing themselves for their lord's honor were really hoping by their dramatic act to win reinstatement as samurai in order to live idle lives and exploit the people. They were merely using the lord, just as the militarists who started the Pacific War had used the emperor, to attain their own "sinister ambition."[19] Perhaps another reason for relaxation was a growing sense, reinforced by Japanese examiners, that samurai literature was a relatively harmless and perhaps even necessary form of popular entertainment and a deepened understanding of the largely nonmilitary role and values of Tokugawa samurai.

The contention that Japanese readers were cut off from their prewar heritage is much better supported by the record of PPB's actions on reprints of modern literary classics dating from the Meiji period to the 1930s. Samuel's work is especially helpful in identifying instances of such book censorship in the Prange Collection.[20] For example, she discovered that book censors had cut several passages as offensive from a conversation about going off to the Russo-Japanese war in Natsume Sōseki's 1906 novel *Kusamakura* (*Pillow of Grass*, literally, but translated as *Three Cornered World*).[21] By her count, over 100 lines were deleted from Mushakōji Saneatsu's 1918 play, "Aru seinen no yume" ("The Dream of a Young Man"). Prewar installments of Yokomitsu Riichi's novel, *Ryoshū* (*Lonely Journey*), which he had begun writing in 1937 and would complete in 1946, were suppressed. The reasons are unclear, but, since Yokomitsu had been prevailed upon to produce his share of patriotic literature, possibly it was because of criticism of China or Shinto nationalism. A reference to British exploitation of Singapore was removed as criticism of the Allies in a 1946 reprint of Serizawa Kōjirō's *Paris ni shisu* (*Death in Paris*), originally serialized in a woman's magazine in 1942.[22] Also cut were prewar works by proletarian writers, such as a few lines referring to Russia in Kobayashi Takiji's 1929 novel, *Kanikōsen* (*The Cannery Boat*),[23] and a portion of Miyamoto Yuriko's 1931 work, *Sangatsu no dai-yon nichiyobi* (*The Last Sunday in March*), in which she described a crowd waving flags and shouting "banzai" after a fireworks demonstration. The Prange book files further reveal that a passage in a 1928 short story by Kawabata Yasunari, "Shisha no sho" ("Book of the Dead"), which was included in a postcensored seven-volume anthology published in 1948, was blue-penciled and marked "disapproved," evidently for derogatory remarks about Koreans in a conversation between two of the characters.

From the SCAP records come additional examples. In November 1946, PPB was displeased with a proposed reprint of Dazai Osamu's *Shinshaku shokoku banashi* (*New Tales from the Provinces*), a refashioning of late seventeenth-century stories by Saikaku, which the author had finished in 1944 and published at war's end. Several passages were cut as "divine propaganda, incitement to unrest, and justification of revenge."[24] As late as April 1949, Kikuchi Kan's rendition of the "Tale of Chushingura," denounced by the censor as a "violent revenge story," was disapproved as rightist propaganda. Natsume Sōseki's work, too, was still giving the censors problems. In July 1949, a publisher was forced to apologize in writing for his "carelessness" in violating the press code by including "Joining the Colors," an allegedly nationalistic poem from the late Meiji period, in a complete edition of Natsume.[25]

Since the works of most of the affected writers were soon published as originally intended, some as early as 1949, it is questionable how adversely this limited period of censorship affected the literary world or reading habits in Japan. An unintended result may have been greater freedom to indulge in socialist interpretations of the classics as people's literature or a lingering impression of American aversion to Japanese culture. Certainly, there was no permanent reorientation of Japanese from pleasure and pride in these works. A PPB report on book trends, July 1947, noted that "general readers," besides buying "cheap novels and third rate detective stories" were also "craving Japanese classics," such as works by Natsume and Akutagawa Ryūnosuke. Such was the spell of Akutagawa that Hokuseido Press published a new translation of *Hell Screen and Other Stories* in 1948 and reprinted *Kappa* (*Water Sprite*) for English readers in 1949.[26]

Next in question is the fate of new literature written under the occupation by established writers and newer artists in the immediate postwar era, and whether or not authors deliberately left out questionable passages or chose to remain passive in order to guarantee publication. This issue is at the center of the argument over literary renaissance versus literary suppression and of greatest concern to those who wonder how creative artists dealt with problems of war, defeat, and occupation. Here it is possible to use and add to the many individual instances already uncovered by Etō, Matsuura, Keene, Rubin, Samuel, and others, while also challenging and modifying some of their conclusions.

PPB magazine files clearly demonstrate that no Japanese writer, no matter how distinguished or obscure, and no type of literature, whether serious or sensational, was immune from censorship.[27] Among precensorship was Kawabata's very short or palm-of-the-hand story, "Kako" ("The Past"). It appeared in the June 1946 issue of *Bungei shunjū* but suffered two deletions for unacceptable references to fraternization (a taboo listed in the key logs but not in the Press Code). Kawabata's character Yūzō, for example, was in violation for speculating about two Japanese women who were accompanying senior American officers. From their behavior, which did not seem sufficiently "bashful or sophisticated" for proper Japanese ladies, Yūzō concluded that they had probably lived for a long time in foreign countries.[28]

In the precensored September 1946 issue of *Shinchō*, another writer, Nagayo Yoshirō, not as famous as Kawabata but a leading member of the prewar Shirakaba (White Birch Society), lost two passages, one quite long, again for improper references to fraternization. In "Ichijikan no hanashi" ("A Story for an Hour and a Half"), he had not only referred to a GI walking arm in arm with a Japanese girl near Asakusa Station but to the unpleasant feelings the sight generated in the viewer. "Detestable, eh. Of course, many of them are forced to do so. Perhaps just about the time when we get the new rice this fall, lots of blue-eyed babies will come out one after another."[29] Additional examples of PPB deletions for fraternization occur in the Prange files, but it would be precipitate to conclude, as does Rubin, that this is the single greatest reason for deletions. Statistics compiled by PPB for the category of literature, 1946–48, show that the chief offense by far, as in other types of publications, was militarist and nationalist propaganda.[30] PPB sensitivity to the fraternization issue, however, such as deleted references to GI's holding hands with Japanese women or to blue-eyed Japanese babies, not only distorted social reality in the fiction but helped reveal the opposite side of the coin, Japanese racism and sexism, or simply envy of occupation soldiers as male power figures.

The most startling example of precensorship of the famous is the total suppression of a short story, "A fujin no tegami" ("Letters from Mrs. A"), by probably the most distinguished writer of the time, Tanizaki Jun'ichirō, from publication in the August 1946 issue of *Chūō Kōron*. In the view of the original examiner, a Japanese national, the piece, "presumably written before the Surrender," gave an overall impression of militarist propaganda, "although it may not have been the writer's immediate design." Keene calls this Tanizaki's first postwar story, an inferior one at that, and though conceding the author's probable disappointment, almost dismisses this particular act of censorship as a trivial matter. The complete story was subsequently printed in the January 1950 issue of *Chūō Kōron*, not because the censors had changed their minds about the supposed militarism of Mrs. A's infatuation with an unknown Japanese pilot, as Keene indicates, but because censorship had just ended and Tanizaki presumably had pride of authorship. Moreover, the story had been singled out in the first instance, as in the cases of Kawabata and others, by Japanese examiners and brought to the attention of American supervisors. In February 1947, Tanizaki was again a victim. A few phrases were deleted from an entry in his wartime diary prior to publication in *Shinchō* for criticism of the United States. By quoting a speech, he had seemed to accuse President Roosevelt of ordering the bombing of Tokyo merely to gain votes in the 1944 election. In a third instance, Tanizaki's recollections of taking English lessons during his childhood days (submitted to *Shinbungaku*, June 1947), censors cut a passage for implying that the attractive Western women living on the second floor of the foreign style manor housing the classes were high-grade prostitutes catering to rich and famous Japanese.[31]

Nagai Kafū's return to publication after a long silence during which he had refused to write patriotic literature was marred by a deletion for alleged militarism from an installment of his serialized 1941 diary for the new magazine, *Shinsei*, November 1946. Offensive remarks about Americans were also removed from his early postwar diaries, which were published in book format, 1947, as *Risai nichiroku* (*Days of Suffering*).[32] In the June 1946 issue of *Shinchō*, Takami Jun was accused of rightist propaganda in his serialized story, "Waga mune no soko no koko ni" ("The Bottom of My Heart"). He was not allowed, when referring to older school textbooks on Japanese literature, to cite passages praising the Great Empire of Japan or the purity of the nation. Portions of his diary for the spring of 1945, published in *Bungaku kikan* (August 1946), were censored as militaristic.[33] Other famous writers who suffered indignities from the American censors were Ishikawa Jun and Sakaguchi Ango. Ishikawa's short story, "Ogon densetsu" ("Golden Legend"), was cut for magazine publication in *Chūō kōron*, March 1946, and subsequently deleted in full, apparently by his publisher, from a book by the same title at the end of the year. Sakaguchi's story, "Sensō to nitori no fujin" ("The War and One Woman"), submitted to a special issue of *Shinsei* in September 1946, was slashed on almost every page for alleged propaganda and love of war propaganda.[34] In 1947, he published *Niryū no hito* (*The Mediocre Man*) after making minor modifications in lines crossed out by the censors and never bothered in later years, according to Samuel, to restore the original version.[35]

Among these writers, the case of Tanizaki, the best known and most financially successful, is particularly interesting since he had experienced periodic difficulties with Japanese censors going back to his debut as a young writer in 1910. His most recent bouts were in the late 1930s when portions of his translation into modern Japanese of the *Tale of Genji* were cut under duress (a domestic example of selective severance from tradition) and during the war when *Chūō kōron*, in an ultimately unsuccessful effort to stay alive, decided in 1943 to stop serializing *Sasameyuki* (translated as *The Makioka Sisters*) after two installments. Was the earlier Japanese censorship system "little more than an occasional annoyance" to him, as Rubin believes, requiring only "small compromises" in the pre-1937 period, or was it and the subsequent PPB version troubling to his conscience? Tanizaki waited to restore his expurgated translation of *Genji* until October 1949 (the end of postcensorship) when he offered portions of previously deleted materials to readers of *Chūō kōron*. How did other writers feel? A long time before, in 1909, Nagai

Kafu had declared that "The authorities don't read our stories and novels as literature or art: they treat them strictly as 'printed matter.'" How did he judge the situation under foreign authorities after 1945? An entry in a restored edition of his diary, alluding to misconduct by occupation troops in September 1945, reads: "There were a number of dead and wounded [Japanese], it is said, but because of American censorship, there was nothing about the indictment in the papers. The Americans talk about freedom, but they conceal what is to their disadvantage. How very laughable."[36] Textual studies and a search through reminiscences and *zadankai* may yield further clues about the cultural impact of external controls and self-censorship upon Japanese literary creativity.

Among newcomers, one whose aspirations for a literary career may have been thwarted by censorship is Yoshida Mitsuru, in a case made famous by Etō Jun. Yoshida's 1946 epic prose poem, "Senkan Yamato no saigo" ("The Sinking of Battleship Yamato"), in essence a lament of his dead comrades and their fighting spirit, was severely cut prior to publication in the magazine, *Sōgen*, edited by an important critic, Kobayashi Hideo. Even then, it was a close call, for the literary quality and dramatic power of the work were immediately recognized by the first Japanese examiner. A second opinion by a re-examiner undoubtedly helped doom the work: "The simple attitude and the vivid style, as well as the extremely impressive contents themselves, [will arouse] something like deep regret for the lost great battleship, and who can be sure that the warlike portion of the Japanese do not yearn after another war in which they may give another *Yamato* a better chance?" Colonel Rufus Bratton of counter-intelligence, asked to comment, "realized that a renaissance of the spirit is desirable" but in the end did not overrule PPB's finding that Yoshida's poem was militaristic propaganda, "inimical to the development of a peaceful Japan." Visits to headquarters by the author's powerful friends and angry charges that the poem was "fine literature" but the "censors were too dumb to get it" were unavailing.

In June 1949, Yoshida published a reworded and enlarged prose version with the objectionable parts omitted in a popular magazine. To a Japanese examiner in CCD, it was passable as "just another dirge on the end of the Japanese Imperial Navy." When Yoshida next tried to publish the original poem in a book of his collected pieces on the battleship, confessing to his "extraordinary attachment to the original," CCD reprimanded him for taking suppressed material to a publisher. It not only flatly refused permission to print the poem but objected to other passages in the book as rightist and militarist propaganda "that would create nostalgia in the minds of the Japanese audience." A handwritten note by one of the censors said that "whatever the intent of the author," the work "plays into the hands of those who want to see a rallying point for nationalism." By the time Yoshida published still another version in 1952, he had apparently lost all motivation for the life of a writer. The requiem did not appear in its original form until 1981, thirty-five years after its creation. Though unusual, the case was important and not an isolated one.[37]

A more experienced writer who faced similar hurdles but persisted in his career was Ōoka Shōhei. Following repatriation from the Philippines in December 1946, Ōoka began writing, also with Kobayashi's encouragement, a fictionalized account of his experiences as a soldier and as a captive of the Americans. Kobayashi's plan to publish it in the second issue of *Sōgen* was dropped, however, after the crisis over "Battleship Yamato." Subsequently, in early 1948, Ōoka published to much praise and attention a thoroughly reworked version of the prelude to capture, called "Furyoki" ("Record of a POW"), in a recently revived anti-Marxist journal, *Bungakkai*, but apparently had to change "enemy" to "opponent" and omit certain passages describing his treatment by American soldiers. In other ways, Ōoka's case reminds one of Yoshida's plight. He continued to write fiction, in time producing a great war novel, but in his later years became increasingly obsessed with memorializing the Japanese war dead of the Philippines.[38]

In reviewing important new literary journals on the Left, censors marked two items for deletion in the first issue of *Shin Nippon bungaku*, March 1946. They dropped an entire story, "Asahan" ("Breakfast"), by Fujimori Seiichi, once again for violating the taboo against fraternization. The work's leading characters had gone to Tokyo to participate in renewed Communist activities under a certain Mr. S, one of the political prisoners released from jail in October 1945 following SCAP's Civil Liberties Directive. The Japanese examiner did not think the piece was objectionable in itself and simply recommended suppression of references to the eating of K-rations for breakfast since their possession was illegal and implied improper transactions between Japanese. Higher ups disagreed and took more drastic measures. In the same issue, one line was removed from Nuyama Hiroshi's verse collection, "The Braided Hat," for disturbing public tranquillity: "the body of a starving man, who lies prostrate from weakness, falls prey to the cold north wind and becomes its fodder." It is difficult to determine whether the journal's openly leftist slant made it more vulnerable to literary and political censorship, since the Prange files are incomplete for 1946–47, a time of lively debate and quarrel within the group and with supporters of its even more important rival *Kindai bungaku*, for which unfortunately evidence is also limited.[39]

In the postcensorship year of 1949, several literary essays in *Shin Nippon bungaku* were disapproved as leftist propaganda as was a book of collected essays on proletariat literature edited by Nakano Shigeharu and sponsored by the society. The magazine's fiction apparently occasioned no comment. Miyamoto Yuriko, a leading member of the group and like Nakano a Communist, was closely watched through the occupation in all of her activities including postal correspondence. A civil censorship mail intercept of her letter to fellow writer Sata Ineko in July 1949 revealed disappointment at the people's lack of understanding of Communist literature. Creative ability alone was not sufficient, she said. There must be a supportive national movement of the party. Miyamoto exhorted Sata not to worry, however, and to keep on with her writing.[40] Their colleague Nakano, who had experienced confiscation of his poetry by the Japanese police in 1928 and endured a temporary ban on his writing in the late 1930s, was also under constant surveillance. In the January 1947 issue of *Tembō*, his satirical novella of the postwar scene, *Goshaku no sake* (*Five Cups of Sake*), was cut for implying, as the examiner put it, "sarcasm and almighty US influence":

> On the morning the draft constitution was to be presented to the Diet, or the previous day, the presses carried GHQ's statement stressing that the draft was worked out by the Japanese. It is a wonder that the Japanese should permit their government to commit a shameless act in asking a third party country for confirmation of its originality when they make the constitution of the state for none but themselves.

PPB was supposed to censor writers for what they said and not for their political affiliation, as Robert Spaulding reminded his staff in 1948, but censors undercut remarks by leftist figures whenever possible.[41]

Poetry was carefully followed by PPB, since, like wartime *tanka*, it seemed to be a perfect vehicle for rightist and nativist sentiments. Two poetry magazines, in particular, were closely watched as ultranationalistic, *Fuji* and *Musashino* (a network of small magazines of the same name). A principal figure of *Fuji* was suspect for believing that "as long as the Emperor exists in Japan, we must revere him heart and soul." Kageyama Masaharu, one of the magazine's leading contributors and later named in the media purge, was viewed as a fanatic who wished to restore the spirit of the gods to Japan. He kept PPB busy under his own and other names. One of his sample poems, "Song of the Braves," scheduled for publication in August 1947, was totally suppressed as nationalist propaganda. It began

> Though this be a dark age,
> Remindful of the Sun-Goddess' withdrawal,
> Behold the divine image of Mt. Fuji,
> Standing pure and clean in the clouds!

And on it ran for another eight unacceptable stanzas. *Fuji* was retained on the precensorship list in 1948–49. Its poems were regularly cut for rightist propaganda even as SCAP, in line with Washington's shift of emphasis, turned from preoccupation with democratization to economic recovery and heightened concern with leftist propaganda. Still another ode to Mt. Fuji was banned as late as August 1949.[42] Meanwhile, in Saitama prefecture, the editor of *Musashino*, representing only a tiny part of the poetry world with a circulation of fifty, was reprimanded for publishing a poem entitled "Will Die for My Country." The reach of PPB was so great that in June 1948 it had even disapproved of a poem in the initial issue of a magazine called *Classroom of Flowers*, the project of a girls' school in Nagano prefecture. Characterized as derogatory of Christ, this poem was cited as a flagrant violation. The records do not indicate who got into trouble for this piece, the teenage author or the editor; the poem was ignorant and tasteless, but there was no taboo in the key logs against anti-Christianity.[43]

Established poets, like famous novelists, received the same, sometimes harsh, treatment. In the November 1947 issue of *Ningen*, a magazine with a much larger circulation than *Fuji*, two poems of Shaku no Chōkū (pen name of Origuchi Nobuo), were found to be in violation for rightist propaganda and for criticism of occupation forces. One of these was "Airplane," from his "Collection of Modern Elegies":

> Even during the days of war,
> With what a breathless ecstacy of yearning
> I viewed their passing.
> Now I see again the white wings
> Pass roaring, row on row,
> And feel the same yearning anew—
> Even today when our remorse is so deep. . . .[44]

Censors were equally alert to the danger of leftist poetry. To heighten awareness, a special report by PPB in 1949 on "Poetry, Popular Songs, Communist Propaganda Media," carried the warning that leftist poets were promoting proletarian verse to protest tyranny and inculcate a revolutionary spirit.[45] This was hardly a startling charge since SCAP itself used songs and poems as vehicles for democratic propaganda.

The American crusade against literary expressions on the Right did not diminish even as leftist literature became a growing concern. New war stories in 1947–49 by Japanese veterans about their battlefield or POW experiences in the Asian and the Pacific theaters were scrutinized as carefully for nationalistic sentiments as were tales of repatriation by soldiers and civilians from Siberian labor camps for leftist indoctrination. Thus, a prose version of "Senkan Yamato" ("The Battleship Yamato") by Hosokawa Sōkichi, not to be confused with Yoshida's more famous poem, was subjected to heavy cuts in the October 1947 issue of *Kaizō* for rightist propaganda. A sample offensive passage said: "The heavy shameful feeling that we survived while many of our brothers sacrificed their lives as the special attack corps made us feel miserable. This was just the appropriate feeling for the defeated returning home." In the summer of 1948, when the popular wartime writer Hino Ashihei published a new collection of short stories (*Four Hundred Shaku above Sea Level*) through a Fukuoka publisher, the watchful censors in District Three pounced on it as unacceptable rightist propaganda. "Defeat," lamented one of his characters in a marked passage, "would be ruin and the last of Japan. Everything would come to naught. Defeat was too sad even to imagine." It is unclear what action CCD took, if any—fines, reprimands, or confiscation.[46] For other reasons, war-related materials sometimes suffered delay in publication. Dr. Gordon Prange, civil historian in General Willoughby's Historical Section, G-2, attempted to protect the official history he was writing of MacArthur's campaigns by controlling all possible Japanese source materials, even to the extent of keeping them out of the hands of censors and CI&E. It was "most essential," he said in July 1949, "that no publication either in Japanese or English reach the reading public either in Japan or America which may scoop some of the excellent points we shall make in our own studies." Prange had in mind primarily documents and factual materials but may have held up some of the fictionalized accounts of fighting, especially in the Philippines.[47]

As this small sampling indicates, Japanese writers were overwhelmed by their own misery and sorrow or were adrift in postwar chaos, though many were struggling with domestic social issues. Since PPB was not apt to ban expressions of war guilt or remorse, a survey of early postwar fiction in the form it was published should reveal to what extent Japanese authors felt compelled to address larger questions of militarism, aggression, and exploitation of conquered peoples. Clearly, throughout this period, SCAP censors contributed to an inaccurate picture in Japanese literature, as in nonfiction, of Western imperialism and created a distorted image of well-behaved occupiers and of a wholesome United States devoid of social and racial or ethnic problems. The evidence also shows that, generally, in dealing with literature, occupation censors were satisfied with deletion of offensive passages and only infrequently ordered total suppression of a work. Atomic-bomb literature presented a more difficult problem.

As a counterpart to SCAP's quick destruction of Japan's only cyclotron and confiscation of scientific notes and newsreels of atomic damage, PPB suppressed, or as it preferred to say, temporarily suspended, publication of nonfiction accounts by survivors (*hibakusha*) and heavily monitored scientific articles. The main concern of censors was to prevent criticism of the United States or the spread of technical information. In the realm of fiction, it permitted the publication in full of Agawa Hiroyuki's short story about a fictional family, "August 6th," in the December 1947 issue of *Shinchō*, but a year and a half earlier had deleted as untrue and disturbing to public tranquillity a reference to radiation in a piece he submitted to *Sekai* (September 1946), "Nennen saisei" ("Year after Year"): "They say that they [survivors] took refuge in Higiyama Hill. Arriving there, many vomited something green and passed away. By the way, if you marry with a Hiroshima girl, they say she may give birth to a three-legged or one-eyed baby. That can't be. It's true I can tell you! We find for example many deformed plants."[48] Hara Tamiki's prize-winning story, "Summer Flowers," which the editors of *Kindai bungaku* had declined to carry in 1946, apparently after checking with CCD, appeared in Keiō University's *Mita bungaku*, a postcensored magazine, June 1947, precut either by the editor or with the advice of censors.[49] In Fukuoka, 1946, censors in District Three deleted four poems before allowing Kurihara Sadao to publish her anthology of free verse and *tanka* called *Kuroi tamago* (*Black Eggs*). Her 1942 antiwar poem ("War Nears") was totally suppressed, along with a new one addressed to Americans ("Let's Shake Hands"); yet her explicit atomic-bomb poems ("Let Us Be Midwives," "The City Ravaged by Flames," and "The Day They Dropped the Atomic Bomb") inexplicably passed, though portions of explanatory material were omitted. Another survivor, Shōda Shinoe, warned by friends of the occupation's hostility, surreptitiously published and distributed a collection of poems in 1947, *Sange* (*Penitence* or *Scattered Petals*), which she limited to 150 copies.[50] Otherwise, little atomic-bomb literature appeared until late 1948 and 1949; even then, the bulk of such writing, both in titles and numbers of copies, came after the occupation had ended.

Much good work has already been done on the painful experiences of Ōta Yōko, a survivor of Hiroshima, in publishing her novel *Shikabane no Machi* (*The City of Corpses*), originally written in 1945 and first published in 1948 after a struggle and with significant deletions. After its full publication in 1950, following the end of censorship, Ōta herself provided an account in May 1953 of a visit from an occupation investigator in 1946–47, whose chief concern seemed to be disclosures of scientific secrets.[51] The dilemma of PPB censors is better revealed in their disagreement, 1947–48, over a famous work of nonfiction, *Nagasaki no kane* (*The Bells of Nagasaki*), a graphic eyewitness account of the atomic aftermath in Nagasaki by a Catholic medical doctor, Nagai Takashi. Richard Kunzman, to whom the book was submitted in 1947, passed it, only to receive a tongue-lashing from John Costello for failing to see the damage such a litany of horrors would do to the American image in Japan. Lt. Colonel Nugent was brought into the case and agreed with Costello. Quarrels and repeated reviews within PPB, followed by submission of the case in early 1948 to General Willoughby, resulted in a six-month suspension of publication for inviting resentment and disturbing public tranquillity. Willoughby, at a time when PPB was moving into postcensorship of the media, sensed that it might be better to go ahead with publication while the United States was in a position to "neutralize an adverse effect." His idea of neutralization was to insist on inclusion in the book's appendix of an American account of Japanese atrocities in the Philippines, one which his own officers had prepared. Dr. Nagai, who was harassed by counterintelligence officers sent to make sure he was really ill and dying, agreed to compromise, but in thanking GHQ in print for providing the account, he left no doubt in the minds of Japanese readers as to the origins of the appendix. By then, the public had been saturated with media coverage of the war crimes trials, 1946–48, and attendant publicity to Japanese atrocities in the Pacific War and in the China theater. In this instance, as in the case of the poem, "The Sinking of the Battleship Yamato," Yoshida Kenichi, the Cambridge-educated son of Prime Minister Yoshida Shigeru, became involved, helping Dr. Nagai to translate the book into English while arranging publication in Japanese. The Minister of Communications in the Yoshida Cabinet also visited PPB on behalf of Dr. Nagai.[52]

Astonished to find the book in print in early 1949, Robert Spaulding, deputy chief of PPB, made the trenchant comment that linking the two, the bombs and the atrocities, would have an opposite effect to that intended—a "direct demonstration of what the Japanese mean when they claim that Nagasaki-Hiroshima was just as bad as, if not worse than, the Japanese atrocities in Manila and Nanking, and our action cancels out their guilt."[53] *The Bells of Nagasaki* was instantly a best seller in 1949, and soon inspired a film, while a number of suppressed descriptive and literary pieces were at last published. Although the short period of civil censorship had delayed but not stopped publication of the earliest atomic-bomb writings, the difficulties experienced in publicly expressing the anguish had taken a severe psychological toll on the authors.[54]

Censors, incidentally, also read for information as well as for violations of censorship guidelines and forwarded requested items to intelligence officers for analysis of trends or for further investigation. Occasionally, items on the literary Left and Right were reported. An examiner thought he had spotted a valuable piece in the August 1949 issue of *Ningen*, a serialization of Katō Shūichi's novel, *Aru hareta hi ni* (*On a Fine Day*): One of the characters, a painter, had expressed resentment "against the Tenno system with very severe language." Senior censors did not pass it on, but the recommendation shows SCAP's continuing interest in expressions of opinion about the emperor and throne.[55]

In this brief listing of individual instances, the deletions did make a difference in what the author was saying and how the author chose to say it.[56] The evidence, moreover, shows the censors to be overworked but thorough, fairly consistent, and operating closely within prescribed guidelines. The categories may have been arbitrary, but the censors usually were not.[57]

Before reaching final conclusions about the balance of liberation versus interference in literary creativity during the first four years of the Allied occupation of Japan, there is the related question for future evaluation of what got through the censors—what was *not* suppressed or deleted.[58] For the present, however, firsthand research in CCD censorship files yields extensive and sobering evidence of slashed and altered manuscripts. For Japan's literary world, censorship remained very much a fact of life as did thought surveillance. It affected words and themes, the internal flow of ideas and emotions, and overall conceptualization. Although the range of acceptable subject matter was broad, reflection on the war and debate over war responsibility was heavily compromised by the victors' version of the truth. Expression of patriotic sentiment, not merely ultranationalism, was artificially checked, perhaps to the point of ensuring a reactionary return of nativism. Realistic depictions of the experience of living under foreign occupation were handicapped by numerous taboos. As conditions of reading and writing, the Japanese, moreover, had to contend with idealized views of the values and historical experiences of the conquerors.

Even if foreign controls were in fact lighter than earlier home-grown ones or if indeed the inner dynamics of Japan's literary world ultimately were more important in shaping postwar literary life than external guidance, censorship in occupied Japan was dangerous. Freedom of expression was severely compromised. However necessary ideological reorientation may have seemed in the aftermath of total war and in the conduct of a military occupation, there was potential harm in the process to the victorious as well as to the defeated. The large and efficient civil censorship apparatus established by the victors in Japan, the long-term planning they represented, and the alacrity with which the senior American censors took to their jobs of prying into Japanese life and the Japanese psyche reflected the rise of the American national security state. American authorities in occupied Japan rationalized interference with Japanese civil liberties in their own national interests. This was an attitude that could be and was reproduced at home in subsequent years. America's continuing war of words in Japan was thus, in part, a war against its own ideals. SCAP's fear of criticism by foreign correspondents in Japan and the persistent questioning of censorship by Japanese editors, publishers, and writers were an important brake on even more stringent action. The occupiers did not yield their controls happily in 1949 and found ways to perpetuate them in supporting the red purge. There is evidence that in 1950–51, with the outbreak of the Korean War, that SCAP was leaning toward the reestablishment of censorship both of the Japanese media and the foreign press in Japan.[59] In the decades since 1952, many Japanese writers have actively opposed interference with civil liberties and have been vocal on domestic and foreign issues. Their vigilance, including their help in unmasking American censorship, has been a return gift to the universal cause of freedom of expression.

NOTES

1. See SWNCC 162/D, 19 July 1945, "Positive Policy for Reorientation of the Japanese," National Archives, Record Group (RG) 165, ABC 014 Japan (13 April 1944), section 4-2; followed by SFE series 116, early August to December 1945 (National Archives, Microfilm Publication, T 1205); and revised version forwarded to General MacArthur by the Joint Chiefs of Staff as SWNCC 162/2, January 1946, published in *Foreign Relations of the United States, 1946*, vol. 8 (Washington, D.C.: Government Printing Office, 1971), 105–9.
2. Sources for comparative study of reorientation policies in occupied Germany and Japan include James F. Tent, *Watch on the Rhine, Reeducation and Denazification in American Occupied Germany* (Chicago: University of Chicago Press, 1982); Nicholas Pronay and Keith Wilson, eds., *The Political Re-Education of Germany and Her Allies After World War II* (London: Croom Helm, 1985); and Harold Hurwitz, "Comparing Reform Efforts in Germany: Mass Media and the School System," *Americans as Pro-*

consuls, ed. Robert Wolfe (Carbondale: Southern Illinois University Press, 1994), 322–41, 516–23. The terms, "reeducation" and "reorientation," tended to be used interchangeably by postwar policy planners within the American government. In Japan's case, it would be inaccurate to speak of a shift in philosophy from reeducation (1945) to reorientation (1947) or to view reorientation as "a gentler term," as does Tent in discussing occupied Germany (254).
3. Since the Japanese government remained intact and the occupation of Japan was technically indirect, MacArthur set up several special staff sections in his General Headquarters, in early October 1945, to maintain liaison with Japanese officials. Unlike Clay in Germany, he combined educational and informational control in one staff operation (CI&E); also, censorship policies for the two defeated enemies were drastically different—licensing of publishers in Germany, direct censorship by Allied authorities in Japan.
4. I have traced the evolution in wartime Washington, D.C., of the policies of reeducation and of civil censorship and information control for occupied Japan in two essays, "Planning for the Education and Re-Education of Defeated Japan, 1943–45," in *The Occupation of Japan: Education and Social Reform*, edited by Thomas W. Burkman (Norfolk: MacArthur Memorial, 1982), 21–127; and "Civil Censorship and Media Control in Early Occupied Japan: From Minimum to Stringent Surveillance," in *Americans as Proconsuls*, edited by Robert Wolfe, 263–320; 498–515.
5. This essay is part of a larger study that includes CI&E activities in literary guidance, book banning and confiscation by SCAP authorities, and the dilemmas of Japanese nationals in enforcing literary censorship.
6. CCD statistics are misleading and often indicate authorized strength rather than actual employment, such as the frequently used figure of 8,763 in mid-1947 (435 of whom were in fact charged to censorship in District IV, Korea). A CCD Monthly Report for November 1947 indicates that the actual strength was about 5,500 (4,974 of whom were Japanese nationals), that is 742 understrength. In Tokyo, the center of Japan's publications industry, PPB grew from a staff of 131 in November 1945 to over 600 in late 1947. For relevant reports, budget requests, and office correspondence, see National Archives, Record Group 59, 740.0019 Control (Japan)/1-748; and Washington National Records Center (Suitland, Maryland), RG 331, Boxes 8537, 8568, and 8585.
7. For overviews of media censorship in practice, see Monica Braw, *The Atomic Bomb Suppressed: American Censorship in Japan, 1945–1949* (Lund Studies in International History; printed in Tokyo, 1986), pp. 61–96; Mayo, "Civil Censorship and Media Control in Early Occupied Japan"; Matsuura Sōzō, *Senryō-ka no genron dan'atsu* [*Suppression of Speech under the Occupation*] (Tokyo: Gendai janarizumu shuppankai, 1977), together with his earlier book, *Senryōka no gengo dan'atsu* [*Suppression of Written and Verbal Communication under the Occupation*] (Tokyo: Gendai janarizumu shuppankai, 1969). The official history is contained in General Headquarters, Far East Command, Military Intelligence Section, *The Intelligence Series*, X, *Operation of Military and Civil Censorship USAFFE/SWPA/AFPAC/FEC* (Tokyo, 1950); and Documentary Appendices (copies at the Washington National Records Center and at the MacArthur Memorial Archives, Norfolk, Virginia).
8. In the low hundreds, not many thousands, as sometimes implied. Although approximately 5,000–5,500 Japanese nationals worked for CCD, the majority were engaged in postal and telecommunications operations rather than publications work. Moreover, within PPB itself, a larger number of Japanese and foreign nationals worked in press and news agency censorship than in book and magazine processing. For example, in a total staff of about 600 in PPB, Tokyo (November 1947), 458 were Japanese nationals; fewer than 200 worked in press and publications as examiner-translators, associate and junior translators, or clerk typists; 26 employees were foreign nationals, mainly European, Korean, or Chinese in origin (RG 331; Box 8537). Large numbers of Japanese nationals, of course, were also employed in publications work in Districts Two and Three.

9. Background of senior CCD personnel in Mayo, "From Minimum to Stringent Surveillance," 291–92; 299–300; entry for Hans Pringsheim in *Japan Biographical Encyclopedia* (Tokyo: Rengo Press, 1958); see also Robert M. Spaulding's keynote remarks, "CCD's Censorship of Japan's Daily Press," in Thomas W. Burkman, ed., *The Occupation of Japan: Arts and Culture*, 1–16 (Spaulding ultimately succeeded Costello as head of PPB).
10. An early critique of newspaper censorship is William Coughlin, *Conquered Press: The MacArthur Era in Japanese Journalism* (Palo Alto: Pacific Books, 1952).
11. Matsuura, *Senryō-ka no genron dan'atsu*, 100. In placing emphasis on the postwar liberation of Japanese writers and their outburst of creative energy, Keene argues that occupation controls were "in no way comparable to the wartime or even prewar censorship"; despite "adverse circumstances, publication flourished as rarely before in Japan"; see his *Dawn to the West: Japanese Literature of the Modern Era, Fiction* (New York: Holt, Rinehart and Winston, 1984), 963, 967–68. Jay Rubin arrives at similar conclusions in "From Wholesomeness to Decadence: The Censorship of Literature under Allied Occupation," in *Journal of Japanese Studies*, 11: 1 (Winter, 1985): 71–103.
12. Etō Jun provoked overdue examination of occupation literary censorship in 1979 with scholarly presentations at the Woodrow Wilson Center, where he was a resident scholar, and a series of lectures at various American universities. This was followed by publication of Part One of "Tozasareta gengo kukan: Senryōgun no ken'etsu to sengo Nihon," ("Sealed Linguistic Space: The Occupation Army's Censorship and Postwar Japan"), in *Shokun*, 14, no. 2 (Feb 1982), 34–109, with succeeding parts appearing in 1982 and 1984; translated by Jay Rubin in *Hikaku bunka zasshi*, vol. 2/ 1984; vol. 3/1988 (Etō's "sealed linguistic space" is an inspired metaphor, compared with "hot house," "cage," "huge prison," employed by other writers, or my prosaic "reorientation camp"). For amplification of Etō's views and supporting evidence, see his book, *Ochiba no hakiyose: haisen, senryō, ken'etsu to bungaku [Gathering Fallen Leaves: Defeat, Occupation, Censorship, and Literature]* (Tokyo: Bungei shunjūsha, 1981). Brett DeBary provides a succinct review of the debate and of distinctions between literature written under the occupation and early postwar literature in "Comments," Burkman, ed., *Arts and Culture*, 181–82.
13. Rubin, *Injurious to Public Morals: Writers and the Meiji State* (Seattle: University of Washington Press, 1984); complemented by sections on literary censorship in Mitchell, *Censorship in Imperial Japan* (Princeton: Princeton University Press, 1983); and Shilloney, *Politics and Culture in Wartime Japan* (Oxford: Clarendon Press, 1981). No study of imperial Japan is complete, argues Mitchell, "that does not take into account the ubiquitous censor" (337).
14. CI&E and CCD media researchers were quick to note in 1946 the popularity of literature in Japan both in total number of books or magazines sold and in percent of total circulation. In April 1949, literature was still at the top (see, for example, SCAP, *Summation of Non-Military Activities in Japan and Korea*, No. 20, 20 May 1947, MacArthur Memorial Archives, and CI&E Publications Analysis, No. 286, 9 August 1949, RG 331, Box 5116).
15. Samuel, "Momotarō Condemned: Literary Censorship in Occupied Japan," unpublished paper presented to the New England Conference/Association for Asian Studies (Fall, 1982), 15. See also her published remarks in rejoinder to Jay Rubin, "Discussion," Burkman, ed., *Arts and Culture*, 176–80. Samuel expedited book and reprint research for this essay by graciously sharing her photocopies of materials from the censored book galley files of the Prange Collection.
16. Kunzman, Memo for the Record, 10 December 1946 (RG 331, Box 8630); Samuel also notes PPB's suppression of Takeuchi Katsuya's *Kodaishi no mondai: Shinwa to rekishi (Issues in Ancient History: Mythology and History)*; no date), in "Momotarō Condemned," pp. 7, 18. The full extent of PPB censorship of reprints of classical literature remains unclear and would be an excellent topic for additional research.
17. PPB, Action Sheet, 18 July 1947, recording deletion in *Nippon no engeki (Japanese Plays)*, published in Osaka (RG 331, Box 8655).

18. PPB, Action Sheet, 20 January 1948 (RG 331, Box 8632).
19. PPB, District I, Memo for the Record, 22 September 1948, hailing Tamura Eitarō's "The Other Side of the Forty Seven Rōnin" as a "landmark in Japanese publishing history" (RG 331, Box 8631).
20. For book galleys and published books in the Prange Collection, blue pencil marks only rarely indicate the reasons for deletions or disapproval, necessitating research for additional clues in RG 331, SCAP archives, Suitland. Assistant Curator Murakami Hisayo also warns that, in most cases, catalogued books from the period, 1945–1949, represent second, unmarked CCD file copies; it is not known what happened to all of the first copies, presumably bearing postcensorship markings (conversation, August 1989). In short, CCD censorship of new books as well as reprints was probably greater than the Prange evidence at first seems to indicate.
21. Rubin clarifies that there were twelve occupation editions of Sōseki's "Three Cornered World" in the period 1947–49, only three of which were expurgated ("From Wholesomeness to Decadence," 91).
22. For Yokomitsu, this is speculation based on censored passages translated by Samuel, who compared the 1937 and 1946 editions and noted that Yokomitsu replaced the deleted parts in 1946 with revisions. Samuel also uncovered Serizawa's none too smooth rewrites in 1946 of offensive passages in *Death in Paris* ("Momotarō Condemned," 9–10, 14).
23. George Shea discloses earlier forced deletions from Kobayashi's 1929 story, "March 15, 1928," which remained incomplete in a 1946 reprint (the story was first published in English in 1933, with police torture scenes omitted, together with a partial translation of the author's *Cannery Boat*, and selected stories by other proletarian writers); see *Left Wing Literature in Japan* (Tokyo: Hosei University Press, 1964), 314–15.
24. PPB/I, Report on Book Deletions for the Period from 16 November to 25 November 1946 (RG 331, Box 8655). Phyllis Lyons discusses this work in *The Saga of Dazai Osamu: A Critical Study with Translations* (Stanford University Press, 1985), 45–47, 149; as does James O'Brien, *Dazai Osamu* (Boston: Twayne Publishers, 1975), 110–18.
25. Kikuchi example in Daily Operational Report, Publications Section, 29 April 1949 (Box 8648); Natsume example in Memo for the Record, 25 July 1949 (Box 8619). Reminiscent of the Serizawa case, a reprint of Kon Hidemi, *Oinaru bara* (*A Great Rose*), a prewar novel set in Paris, was disapproved during a postcensorship review in August 1949 for a critical reference to French colonial Indo-China; PPB, Action Sheet, 2 August 1948 (Box 8585).
26. PPB Monthly Report, Book Trends, July 1947 (RG 331, Box 8585).
27. Magazine galley files in the Prange Collection that were examined for this essay and a larger study under way include: *Ashai hyōron, Bungakkai, Bungaku jihyō, Bungaku kikan, Bungei shunju, Chōryū, Chūō kōron, Fuji, Fujin kōron, Fujin sekai, Fusetsu, Geijutsu, Gunzo, Hataraku fujin, Hikari, Hyōron, Jōsei Kaizō, Kaizō, Kibachi, Kindai bungaku, Kokoro, Mita bungaku, Nihon shōsetsu, Ningen, Saron, Sekai, Sekai bunka, Shakai, Shichō, Shin bunka, Shinbungaku, Shin Nihon bungaku, Shincho, Shinsei, Shin shōsetsu, Shisō, Sōgen,* and *Tembō.* For a full listing of magazine titles in the collection, see Okuizumi Eizaburō, ed., *Senrōygun ken'etsu zasshi mokuroku* (*Catalogue of Censored Magazines from the Occupation Period*) (Tokyo: Yushodo Shoten, 1982). Some of these files are disappointingly slim, amounting to coverage of only a few issues; others provide extensive data. Although the Prange Collection also has an excellent run of magazines as actually published in the period, there are significant gaps here too. It was therefore not possible to trace the process of censorship for a number of key stories. As a nonspecialist in Japanese literature, I have omitted questions of content, style, and structure. There is, in short, much more work for future scholars in matters of textual comparisons, archival research, literary criticism, and types of literature.
28. It is not clear when "Kako" was fully restored; unless otherwise noted, all citations in this and the next section are from the censored magazine files in the Prange Collec-

tion. Here and there, I have made minor changes for readability in the English renditions of the Japanese examiners.
29. Other pieces by Nagayo ran into trouble, either for militarism or general criticism of the Allies. For example, "Gaen" ("The Feast"), the story of a couple whose only son had died in the war, lost a line describing the mother's grief "for the loss of her only and precious son, who died an honorable death in the Battle of the Solomon Seas" (*Kaizō*, August 1948).
30. Rubin, "From Wholesomeness to Decadence," 92. For book and magazine statistics from the period 1945–49, including categories of deletions, see various PPB/I reports in RG 331, Box 8585. Rubin is, however, right to suggest that self-censorship came to be exercised in making references to American troops or the presence of GI occupiers. An especially interesting example that might have served as a warning to writers is censored remarks about foreigners and Japanese women in an exchange between Hayashi Fumiko and Sakaguchi Ango during the course of a roundtable discussion, "Degeneration and Others," carried by the magazine *Fujin kōron* (*Women's Review*), October 1946.
31. Keene on "Mrs. A," *Dawn to the West*, 967. The restored passages in Tanizaki's recollection appear in Paul McCarthy's translation of *Junichirō Tanizaki: Childhood Years, A Memoir* (Tokyo: Kodansha International, 1988), 168.
32. On diary deletions, self-imposed and externally coerced, see Edward Seidensticker, *Kafū the Scribbler, The Life and Writings of Nagai Kafū, 1879–1959* (Stanford, 1965), 174. Samuel also cites a twelve-line deletion from Nagai's postwar diary, Days of Suffering, for September 1945 ("Momotarō Condemned," 12). His expurgated diary for the wartime years, 1941–44, was published in 1947 as *Kafū nichireki* (*A Diary Written by Kafū*).
33. Ironically, Takami had celebrated the arrival of free speech and publication in diary entries for August and September 1945; see Donald Keene, *Dawn to the West*, 967–69.
34. According to Keene, Ishikawa's "Golden Legend" made it into print, unscathed, but was omitted from the November anthology when the censors subsequently decided it was derogatory to the occupation (*Dawn to the West*, 967). Rubin says that lines at the end, which depicted a Japanese woman running down the street toward a tall, black soldier, were chopped off; he also attributes the later omission of the entire story from the anthology to a decision made by the publishers, possibly in protest against the previous censorship ("From Wholesomeness to Decadence," 92). The Prange censored magazines files lack the relevant issue for verification or reasons.
35. For *Mediocre Man*, see Samuel ("Momotarō Condemned," 13). Sakaguchi's "War and One Woman," told of a wife who was sexually aroused by American bombing raids and otherwise bored with her husband, the narrator of the tale. Rubin adds that Sakaguchi had to change enemy (*teki*) planes and enemy guns into American (*Bei*) planes and guns in his famous story, "The Idiot"; the file copy in the Prange Collection, however, has no markings. Perhaps his editors, wise to the ways of the occupation censors, had already made the revision for him. Others besides Sakaguchi were affected in *Shinsei*'s heavily censored special issue of fiction, September 1946, among them Murō Saisei for "Mother"; Kitahara Takeo for a piece called "Nausea"; Inoue Tomoichirō for "Marco Polo Bridge"; and Shibukawa Gyō for "Evening Glory."
36. Views of Tanizaki and Nagai on Japanese censors in Rubin, *Injurious to Public Morals*, 120, 137–42, 258–60, 263–65; details of his modern language translation of *Genji*, also in ibid., 258–59; and Keene, *Dawn to the West*, pp. 772–73. Translation of Nagai's original diary entry for September 1945 by Seidensticker in *Kafū the Scribbler*, 174. Nagai nevertheless managed to convey a broad hint about the existence of occupation censorship in the published preface to the expurgated 1947 version, *Days of Suffering*, by stating, "The reason for the deletion [verb, *sakujo suri*] of some passages and the names of some people is that, under circumstances today, I am unable to do otherwise" (cited by Samuel, "Momotarō Condemned," 12–13).

37. Based on PPB files, "The Last of the Battleship Yamato" (RG 331, Boxes 8572, 8604); also, *Sōgen* and *Saron* censored magazine files (Prange Collection). Etō Jun tells the story in considerable detail, utilizing interviews and additional materials, in "Shishu to no kizuna" ("Battleship Yamato"), *Shinchō*, February 1980. See also Richard Minear's introduction and translation, *Requiem for Battleship Yamato* (Seattle: University of Washington Press, 1985).
38. The Prange CCD files do not contain this particular issue of *Bungakkai*; for details of writing and censorship, 1946–48, see Sakuko Matsui, introduction to translation of "Prisoner of War, The Prelude to Capture," *Solidarity*, February 1967, 56. Ōoka's various POW stories were published in book format in 1952. An earlier POW story set in Wisconsin, Ohinata Aoi's "Makkoi byōin" ("McCoy Hospital"), published in *Shinchō*, August 1946, was also censored. However, Umezaki Haruo's highly regarded "Sakurajima," a war story with a homefront setting, dating from the same period, seems to have evaded the censors (appeared in *Sunao*, September 1946; no copy in the Prange files).
39. Shea reviews the critical essays and fiction published by *Shin Nihon bungaku* during the occupation (including serialized novels by Miyamoto Yuriko and Tokunaga Sunao) but barely touches on its arguments with the critics of *Kindai bungaku* (see Chapter 12, "The Democratic Literary Movement," *Left Wing Literature in Japan*). Other examples of censorship for this magazine include Uemura Tai's poem, "Angel in Rags" (August 1948) for general criticism of the Allies and Eguchi Kiyoshi's novel *A Bride and One Horse* (January 1949 installment) for criticism of land reforms and leftist propaganda. The few extant examples for *Kindai bungaku* include literary essays by Ara Masahito (June 1946) and Katō Shūichi (September 1946) and a short story by Shinjō Munetoshi (January 1947) for reasons of criticism of the Allies or of American forces. In Shinjō's case, a battlefield story set in the Philippines ("Kuchiba," or "Fallen Leaves"), Rubin argues with reference to the removal of descriptive material that "the *fact* is retained, only the more graphic details having been eliminated" ("From Decadence to Wholesomeness," 87). Such detail, however, is vital to the writer's art and craft in conveying meaning and nuance.
40. Mail intercepts (this one dated 20 July 1949) in RG 331, Box 8703. Miyamoto's experience with SCAP is one of the most puzzling from the occupation period. Although she had a wide following and was able to publish a considerable amount of autobiographical fiction, such as *Banshū heiya* (*The Plains of Banshu*) and *Fuchisō* (*The Weathervane Plant*), without much difficulty both in her own literary organ and in leading magazines, there are at least six or seven instances in the Prange and Suitland archives of censored essays or roundtable remarks by Miyamoto, for example her denunciation of the exploitation of working women in Java and Japan in "For Whose Sake—Women's Life," *Hataraku fujin* (October 1948). Even assessments of her fiction by literary critics and historians were censored. In another form of censorship closer to home, the revived Japan PEN Club in 1947–48 was contemplating an eight-volume edition in English of major modern Japanese works that excluded Miyamoto and fellow Communists Nakano Shigeharu and Tokunaga Sunao (RG 331, Box 8576).
41. Brett de Bary's translation of "Five Cups of Sake," which utilizes a later complete edition of Nakano's works, shows that the passage was restored; *Three Works by Nakano Shigeharu* (Cornell University East Asia Papers, 1979), 97. Spaulding's reminder (as District One Censor), is in Operational Memorandum 106, 15 August 1948 (Box 8568).
42. Suppressed poem cited in PPB/I, Memo, 3 August 1947 (RG 331, Box 8632); information about "ultrarightist" Kageyama Masaharu (Box 8593); special CCD report on the magazine and its editor, 2 October 1946 (Box 8537). The *Fuji* file in the Prange Collection is voluminous.
43. Special Report, *Musashino*, 25 August 1947 (RG 331, Box 8634); Memo for the Record, "Musahino" magazines, 10 December 1948; reprimand of editor of *Musashi*, Memo, 10 May 1949 (Box 8634); Spaulding, Memo for the Record, recording dis-

approval of strongly anti-Christian poem, 17 June 1948, and preparation of flagrant violation report for forwarding to CI&E (Box 8632).
44. In another example of established poets, censors apparently nervous about the expression of Shintō sentiments, first shortened the title of one of Kawaji Ryūkō's poems from "Kaeru tamashiii" (Soul Returning) to "Kaeru" (Returning Home), and then proceeded to eliminate several moving verses about the emotions of coming back from war, defeated and uncelebrated; *Gendai Nihon shishū* (*Modern Japanese Poems*), book galley (date not indicated), Prange Collection.
45. Action Sheet, 13 September 1948 (RG 331, Box 8585); special PPB report on Communist propaganda in the media, 1949 (Box 8648). There are numerous examples of censorship of leftist or proletarian poetry in the Prange Collection and at the Suitland Archives, ranging from works by amateur poets in obscure pamphlets to those by the distinguished writer and poet Tsuboi Sakae.
46. District III, Memo, 15 April 1948, RG 331, Boxes 8585 and 8576. Hino, who managed to publish a great deal though he was labeled a literary war criminal, complained in a speech at the Saga Girls' High School in February 1948 that true war literature could not be created either during the war or under the occupation (reported to Tokyo by the Fukuoka censors in Check Sheet, confidential, 4 October 1948, PPB, District III, RG 331, Box 8576).
47. See various CIS, G-2 check sheets and memoranda, Prange to Willoughby and others, July–August 1949 (quotation from 19 July 1949, RG 331, Box 8519).
48. Agawa, who was repatriated from internment in China to Hiroshima in March 1946, was an important contributor to atomic-bomb fiction but not technically a *hibakusha* author. The Prange Collection does not contain the December 1947 issue of *Shinchō*. For an overview of censorship of mainly nonfiction atomic bomb writings, see Braw, *Atomic Bomb Suppressed*.
49. Rubin describes three cuts in "Summer Flower" (also translated as "Summer Flowers"), in fact the central story in a triptych ("From Decadence to Wholesomeness," 89); the Prange files do not contain the issue. The story of *Kindai bungaku*'s negative decision in 1946 is repeated by Brett de Bary (who confirmed it in an interview with Haniya Yutaka, then a member of the editorial board), in "After the Apocalypse: Hara Tamiki's Writing on the Bombing of Hiroshima," *Journal of the Association of Teachers of Japanese*, 15/2 (November 1980), 150–69.
50. Both a marked galley of Kurihara's *Black Eggs* and a published copy (Fukuoka, August 1946) are in the Prange Collection. Her poem, "War Close Up," translated by Richard Minear in a recent issue of *Bulletin of Concerned Asian Scholars*, did not in fact appear in 1946, as the accompanying remarks assume; "Four Poems (1941–45) by the Hiroshima Poet Kurihara Sadako" (vol. 21, no. 1, January–March 1989, 46–49). Samuel has translated "Let Us Shake Hands" in Burkman, ed., *Arts and Culture*, 177. For publication details of Shōda's *Penitence*, see citation in Wayne Lammers and Osamu Masaoka (comps.), *Japanese A-Bomb Literature, An Annotated Bibliography* (Wilmington, Ohio: Wilmington College Peace Resource Center, 1977), 70.
51. Rubin indicates that "Town of Corpses" was "significantly cut" in 1948, either by Ōta or her *Chūō kōron* editors, although the altered book nevertheless contained "gruesome descriptions" and "criticism of America," along with criticisms of Japanese military leaders ("From Wholesomeness to Decadence," 88–91). Princeton University Press has published Richard Minear's translation of Ōta's complete novel, together with Hara's entire triptych and Tōge Sankichi's famous 1951 poem collection, *Genbaku shishū* (*Atomic Bomb Poems*), in 1990 under the title, *Hiroshima: Three Witnesses*.
52. Based on memos and check sheets in RG 331, Boxes 8519, 8655, and 8630; see also Braw, *The Atomic Bomb Suppressed*, 99–103; and preface and translation, *Bells of Nagasaki*, by William Johnston (Tokyo: Kōdansha, 1984). Internal evidence in RG 331, CCD files, indicates there are missing endorsements for 17 and 18 January 1948; these may show MacArthur's position and clarify the origin of the "Sack of Manila" compromise (perhaps in an exchange with the Department of Defense).

53. Spaulding, note to TJH, 10 February 1949 (RG 331, Box 8630). The CCD file copy of the Nagai published volume in the Prange Collection does indeed contain the account, "Japanese Atrocities in Manila." It carries twice as many photographs of the Manila atrocities as of the Nagasaki bombing.
54. For the frustration and pain caused by delayed publication, see Robert J. Lifton, "Creative Response: A-Bomb Literature," 397–450, in his *Death in Life: Survivors of Hiroshima* (New York: Random House, 1967).
55. Both the Prange files and the CCD records at Suitland contain numerous information sheets (not to be confused with violation sheets).
56. Further examples of CCD literary censorship in my larger study are listed here, since they bolster the argument of extensive tampering with early postwar Japanese literature. In chronological order, these include minor to major deletions from fiction or essays by Mushakōji Saneatsu, "To General MacArthur" (*Shinsei*, January 1946); Abe Tomoji, "Flowers of Death" (*Sekai*, July 1946); Hino Ashihei, "Raging Billows" (*Kaizo*, October 1946); Ōi Hirosuke, "Yoshinaka" (*Kindai bungaku*, October 1946); Ozaki Shirō, "Thoughts of a Gambler," Fukada Hisaya, "Hot Water in the Mountain," and Ishizaka Yōjirō, "Autumn Wind" (all three in *Shinchō*, December 1946, a special anniversary issue that also carried pieces uncut by several famous authors, including Kawabata and Tanizaki); Serizawa Kōjirō, "Destiny" (*Gunzō*, December 1946); Tanaka Hidemitsu, "In Town" (*Shinshosetsu*, December 1946); Dazai Osamu, "Hammering" (also in *Gunzō*, January 1947); Satomi Ton, "A Splendid Scandal" (*Kaizō*, January 1947); Eguchi Kiyoshi, *Black Flag of Death* (*Asahi Hyōron*, February 1947 installment); Niwa Fumio, "Tributary of a River" (*Bunmei*, September 1947); Nagayo Yoshirō, "Restoration of a Lost Object" (*Gunzō*, November 1947); Satomi Ton, "Spiritual Undernourishment" (*Hikari*, January 1948); Tanaka Hidemitsu again, "Brothers" (*Sekai*, July 1948). Also, total suppression of pieces by Komiya Toyotaka, "Unprinted Manuscripts" (*Ningen*, January 1946); Niwa Fumio, "Anti-Human" (*Shinchō*, March 1946); Ishikawa Tatsuzo, "Incarnation of War" (*Shakai*, September 1946); and Tamura Taijirō, "Story of a Prostitute" (*Nihon no shōsetsu*, May 1947).
57. As an example of the standard view, Colonel Walter B. Putnam, Chief Censor, justified civil censorship as "one of the limitations of civil liberties which are unavoidable in the occupation of an enemy country, defeated in war, when the occupying forces are infinitely inferior numerically to the population and charged with a mission which runs counter to the ways of life and patterns of thought wrought in the people by their leaders during hundreds of years of regimentation" (Memo to General Willoughby, 26 November 1947, RG 331, Box 8537).
58. For example, Kawabata's third revised version of *Snow Country* (1948) comes quickly to mind, as do Tanizaki's completion of *The Makioka Sisters* (1947) and many early postwar stories by Nagai Kafū (1946–48). Other well-known writers who published prolifically but not freely were Dazai (a large number of short stories and the novels, *Setting Sun* and *No Longer Human*) and Sakaguchi (his series of famous essays "On Decadence," passed unscathed). Noma Hiroshi was able to serialize his complicated novel *Kurai e* (*Dark Pictures*), and Haniya Yutaka published twenty installments of *Shiryō* (*Ghosts*) by the end of censorship in 1949. Newcomer to the literary scene Mishima Yukio seems not to have caught the attention of censors, and Shiina Rinzō's debut stories were untouched. Veteran writers Hayashi Fumiko, Sata Ineko, and Hirabayashi Taiko were extremely active from the beginning of the postwar era and were widely read. Hayashi serialized popular novels in newspapers as well as magazines, and published numerous stories. Ironically, critic Odagiri Hideo, who was listed in CCD watch files as a "radical communist," was able to publish in September 1948 *Hakin sakuhin shū* (*Collection of Banned Publications*), a miscellany of reviews, articles, poems, dramas, and synopses of books banned by Japanese authorities in the Meiji era; the expanded version would later serve as a major source for Jay Rubin's study of the Meiji state and censorship.
59. Chief of Information, GHQ, FEC, to Chief Censor, 26 July 1951, requesting contin-

gency plans for complete censorship in event of a great emergency, including "details and the necessary organization for the censorship of our own media, newspaper, magazine, radio, telephone, mail and comparable Japanese media, which would in effect clamp full scale censorship on all activities in this theater" (RG 331, Top Secret Boxes, Chief of Information).

8

The Japan Communist Party and the Debate over Literary Strategy under the Allied Occupation of Japan

J. Victor Koschmann

Everything that happened *under* the Allied occupation of Japan (1945–52) was not, of course, necessarily determined *by* the occupation. The Communist-led "democratic literature" movement, for example, drew its early postwar agendas for action directly from earlier paradigms of proletarian literature that had been suspended because of government oppression in the mid-1930s. Liberal modernists, such as Maruyama Masao, saw in the postwar era another opening (*kaikoku*) of Japan to outside influence after a recent period of isolationism, and found the precedent for a postwar Enlightenment in the late-nineteenth-century Meiji period. Still others, such as the novelists Masamune Hakuchō, Tanizaki Jun'ichirō, and Nagai Kafū, more or less continued the same work that had absorbed them during the war. In cases such as these, the occupation was residually important as the guarantor of an environment of peace and liberalization in which various agendas could be pursued, but it certainly did not determine the content of the activities themselves.

Of course, through some of its operational mechanisms, such as censorship, the occupation did directly affect the content of culture. Indeed, literary critic Etō Jun has recently argued that occupation censorship exerted a profoundly negative influence on the development of postwar Japanese literature.[1] Others, including Jay Rubin, have attempted to show that the effect was generally minimal.[2] It must be recognized that at least one type of expression was directly and significantly distorted by censorship—that which dealt with atomic destruction in Hiroshima and Nagasaki.³ Regarding most other types of writing, including the type focused on here, however, it appears that Rubin is correct in concluding that "the predominant influence of the Occupation on postwar writers . . . came not from the imposition of this alien censorship system. Rather it came from the liberation of writers from the native prewar censorship."⁴

This chapter focuses on a coterie of writers that formed for the first time in the early postwar era and is widely considered to be representative of major tendencies in postwar Japanese literature (*sengo bungaku*). Largely through their journal *Kindai bungaku* (*Modern Literature*), the young critics and writers who belonged to this group either touched off or participated actively in virtually all the major intellectual controversies of the early postwar period, such as those dealing with politics and literature, the problem of subjective autonomy (*shutaisei*), writers' war responsibility, modernism, and national literature (*kokumin bungaku*).⁵ All these debates spread beyond literature per se to engage philosophers, behavioral scientists, religionists, and political activists in the wide-ranging controversies on fundamental human issues that so typified the early postwar period. Therefore, the *Kindai bungaku* group offers a focal point for a consideration of Japanese literature and culture under the Allied occupation.⁶

This chapter shows that the postwar policies of the Allied occupation and the Japan Communist Party (JCP) converged on a program of democratic revolution, and that this convergence powerfully determined the parameters of literary and political discourse in the early postwar period. At the same time, ambiguity in the party's definition of democratic revolution was partly responsible for conflict between the party-led literary movement and the *Kindai bungaku* group.

The focal point of this controversy was the revolutionary role to be played by introspective petit bourgeois writers who chafed under party injunctions that they should efface their own subjective viewpoint in favor of an "objective," mass perspective. The *Kindai bungaku* group challenged the party's literary hegemony, and was largely responsible for focusing the attention of postwar intellectuals on the practical ideals of individual autonomy, humanism, and modernity as components of the democratic revolutionary process. Critics in the group, such as Ara Masato, developed a dialectical style of thought and expression and an affinity for imagery related to the body, the ego, and the void that resonated with major themes in postwar fiction. They also appealed to European ideals of autonomous selfhood in their self-critical attempts to come to terms with the war responsibility and the postwar emperor system. Broadly speaking, their priorities and preoccupations can be taken as representative of a peculiarly early postwar literary world view.

THE ALLIED DEMOCRATIZATION POLICY

The occupation played a positive role in creating the environment for a postwar literary renaissance and, in thought, a veritable "age of philosophy."[7] The Allies' most important positive contribution may also have been the least specific, that is, the formation, commencing long before Japan's defeat, of an ideological framework for Japan's postwar reconstruction that emphasized the values of humanism, democracy, and liberalism. These were potent political symbols in the Japanese intellectual environment, although, of course, Marxists, democratic socialists, liberals, and conservative nationalists each understood them somewhat differently. The forceful enunciation of such principles by the Allies beginning as early as the Atlantic Charter contributed powerfully to a shared vision of intellectual priorities for the postwar era. *Democracy*, *humanity*, and *freedom*, along with *history* and *class*, were commonly accepted as the appropriate terms of discourse across a broad political spectrum during the first few years of occupation.

From the perspective of Japanese intellectuals, particularly those on the Left, the most significant general outline of Allied objectives was the July 1945 Potsdam Declaration, which provided the basis for Japan's surrender. Its tough statements of intent regarding the elimination of Japanese militarism appealed to all those Japanese who had come to feel themselves its victims rather than beneficiaries, and broadly paralleled the analyses prepared by Japanese Communists. The document also deployed in a powerful way the symbols of democracy, freedom, and human rights, suggesting that these factors were already latent in the Japanese environment and would emerge if given an opportunity as is evident in paragraph 10: "The Japanese Government shall remove all obstacles to the revival and strengthening of democratic tendencies among the Japanese people. Freedom of speech, of religion, and of thought, as well as respect for the fundamental human rights shall be established."

Moreover, when the Potsdam Declaration was succeeded in early September 1945 by the U.S. government's "Basic Initial Post-Surrender Directive," it began to seem that the Allies were committed to an assault on Japanese monopoly capitalism (although not necessarily to the establishment of socialism): "Encouragement shall be given and favor shown to the development of organizations in labor, industry, and agriculture, organized on a democratic basis. Policies shall be favored which permit a wide distribution of income and of the ownership of the means of production and trade."[8]

Of course, the convergence between the objectives of the occupation and those of left-leaning Japanese intellectuals and parties was not always so close in practice as it seemed in theory. Nevertheless, the feeling was widely shared in early postwar Japan that the march of history had brought Japan to a time of democratization and that the Allied occupation would play an important role in cooperation with progressive Japanese groups in bring this historical opportunity to fruition.

THE JAPAN COMMUNIST PARTY AND DEMOCRATIC REVOLUTION

The apparent convergence of agendas with respect to postwar reconstruction emerges most dramatically in the policy of democratic revolution pursued between 1945 and 1948 by the Japan Communist Party. The defeat of Japanese militarism by a coalition of Allies including the Soviet Union vindicated prewar Communist predictions and, by extension, the cogency of the historical materialist sciences of history and society. Marxism was immediately credited with a kind of superior gnosis that even its severest liberal critics tended to treat with respect. Moreover, a few Communist leaders emerged from prison or exile as national heroes after (in some cases) almost two decades of resistance. They were, it seemed, the only ones who had successfully resisted the appeals of ultranationalism, and in the early postwar period they were revered by elites and ordinary people alike who were in no way connected with the Communist Party.

As a result, at least at the level of stated policy and popular image, the ideological environment for postwar literature was formed by a powerful, historically overdetermined convergence on the project of democratization. Of course, profound differences lurked just under the surface: Occupation New Dealers, democratic socialists, Communists, workers, small farmers, and managers were all lying side by side in the same king-size bed, but as they fitfully began to awake in 1947 and 1948, it became increasingly clear (to those who didn't know it already) that they had been dreaming rather different dreams.

Nevertheless, postwar literary debates must be understood against the background not only of the occupation but of Communist organization and policy. Planning for a postwar Communist program had apparently begun months before Japan's defeat in several locations, one of which was the Fuchū penitentiary near Tokyo. Fuchū housed a number of prewar Communist Party members, including the important leaders Tokuda Kyūichi and Shiga Yoshio. In his memoir of those years, Tokuda says he and Shiga "studied and planned in the greatest possible concreteness and detail," especially after they moved to Fuchū, where "they finally let us read newspapers, and we had more opportunities to meet face to face." According to Tokuda, they also wrote several documents in prison, including "An Appeal to the People," which was issued after their release on 10 October 1945.⁹

"Appeal" was one of the first postsurrender documents issued by the party, and it is particularly important in retrospect because its principal author, Tokuda Kyūichi, emerged from his prison ordeal to become the party's secretary general and probably the most powerful Communist leader in postwar Japan.¹⁰ The document outlined a lasting orientation to postwar politics and society, whose major elements are as follows.

First, support for the Allied forces, which had "advanced into Japan for the purpose of liberating the world from fascism and militarism," and acceptance of the Potsdam Declaration as the operative program for "democratic liberation and world peace." It appears that the jailed Communists had argued as they drafted the "appeal" over whether or not to define the Allied forces as a "liberation army." The issue was to become even more contentious later on. Shiga claims to have told Tokuda that "MacArthur will later suppress us, and it would be best, therefore, to omit that point." However, another Communist imprisoned in Fuchū, Yamabe Kentarō, implies there were at least three different reasons for the decision to welcome the occupation:

> Our reply was yes, we of course realize that . . . but for the time being we will make use of the Occupation forces. . . . We took the "Allied" element in the Allied forces very seriously. Since Soviet forces were involved, we considered it an international antifascist front and didn't know yet about the internal contradictions of the Allied forces. . . .
>
> Once we were finally released and were on the outside, the world had changed. And I believe that this too had the effect of encouraging the "theory of peaceful revolution under the Occupation." We didn't think much about substantial matters. After all, it was "the prime of our youth."¹¹

Second, the appeal welcomed Japan's democratic revolution, which had begun as a result of the Allied advance, and warned that it would be necessary to destroy the emperor system completely before democratization could be carried out. That system consisted of "a union of the emperor and court, the military, administrative bureaucracy, the peerage, parasitic landlords, and monopoly capitalists." The notion that democratic revolution was a necessary stage in Japan's historical agenda, prior to any transition to socialism, was inherited from prewar Comintern directives, particularly the so-called 1932 Theses, and from the analyses of Japanese history and society that had been provided in the late 1920s by the Lectures Faction (*kōza-ha*) of Japanese Marxist scholars. The 1932 Theses had defined the forthcoming revolution in Japan as a "bourgeois-democratic revolution with a tendency to grow rapidly into a socialist revolution."[12]

Third, the document called for establishing a "people's republic government" on the basis of the popular will. The people's republic seems to have been a distinctly postwar innovation, because the 1932 Theses had called for a "workers' and peasants' Soviet government."[13] Fourth, it called for the confiscation and distribution to peasants of all land held by idle capitalists and landlords, establishment of workers' freedom to unionize and bargain collectively, and formation of a "united front with all organizations and forces which share these goals."[14]

The Fourth Party Congress held by year's end extended this position in a leftward direction by providing not only for labor unions but also for "workers' control over essential enterprises."[15] Apparently Tokuda had expected direct action by workers to form a united front from below and eventually something like Soviets. He and Shiga claim they had planned for workers' direct action while still incarcerated.[16] But although workers in some enterprises did succeed in seizing control of management and carrying out "production control" (*seisan kanri*) in the early postwar period, the Communist Party did not initiate those movements and was soon left behind by this and other forms of grass-roots radicalism.[17]

A decisive role in the moderation of Communist policy as it developed in the months following the release of Tokuda and other political prisoners was played by another Communist leader who had spent the war years in the Soviet Union and China rather than in jail. Nosaka Sanzō had been in Yenan since 1940 and had already formulated a plan for postwar democratization.[18] He returned to Japan on 12 January 1946 and very quickly became active in Communist Party affairs.[19] Nosaka seems to have been strongly influenced by Chinese communism and to have absorbed ideas about Japan's democratic revolution that diverged in some ways from the 1932 Theses.[20] It seems that he particularly opposed the dimension of Tokuda's program that still called for workers' direct action leading to socialist revolution.[21] Indeed, soon after he arrived in Japan, Nosaka remarked that "we must become a lovable Communist Party."[22] The phrase caught on immediately as journalistic shorthand for Communist policy in the early postwar years.

During the first couple of years after defeat, Nosaka actively disseminated the image of a Communist Party that was willing to defer its socialist goals in order to focus on a broad democratic front. He called for "a democracy . . . in which workers, farmers, *the working intellectual class, and small and medium-sized commercial and industrial businessmen* will take the leading role [emphasis added]."[23] Similar to the "new democracy" that Mao Tse-tung had advocated in early 1940, Nosaka's conception is noteworthy for its inclusiveness, extending even to certain kinds of small- and medium-scale capitalists and, implicitly, small landlords.[24]

Nosaka's vision of a lovable Communist Party was codified in the declaration issued on 25 February 1946 at the party's Fifth National Congress. On the basis of this declaration, Joe Moore has concluded that in the early postwar period, "A greatly lengthened two-stage revolution became the orthodox line, and committed the party to the gradual attainment of socialism by parliamentary means. On the surface, at least, the new policy foreclosed the possibilities implicit in the Tokuda-Shiga approach, which had left the way open for an early and to some extent violent socialist revolution."[25] Implicitly, that is, the party had moved backward toward a policy appropriate to a slightly earlier historical stage—a stage closer to pure democratic revolution than what had been prescribed for Japan by the 1932 Theses.

The sense of ambiguity, or uncertainty, suggested by early postwar party policy was heightened by Communist literary initiatives that reflected, but in some ways also diverged from, Nosaka's orientation.

COMPETING AGENDAS FOR POSTWAR LITERATURE

In early November 1945, a mere two months after MacArthur's arrival in war-torn Japan, the eminent Communist literary critic Kurahara Korehito wrote a short, two-part piece for a major newspaper, *Tokyo shinbun*.[26] Although inconspicuous, the article was to become known as the initial announcement of a Communist literary agenda for postwar Japan. Kurahara had been a central figure in Communist Party efforts to organize writers and other artists in the late 1920s and early 1930s, and he had played a leading role in prewar Marxist debates on the revolutionary role of art and culture.[27] In postwar Japan, he was to head the party's cultural section and serve as a member of its central committee.

Clearly evident in Kurahara's essay are the elation over Japan's defeat by the Allied powers, which was shared across a broad spectrum of the resurgent Japanese Left, and a hint of real confidence that the Allied military occupation would carry out its promises to demilitarize and democratize Japanese society. At least on the surface, these factors were very important in the formation of Communist literary policy in the early months after Japan's surrender.

Also obvious is the tone of the manifesto. When situated against the background of Kurahara's eminence in the prewar proletarian literature movement and his high status in the postwar Communist Party, Kurahara's short article was clearly designed to preempt a position of authority in the literary milieu. It announced the beginning of the party's bid to set forth and control the terms of postwar literary discourse:

> First of all, writers must recover the element of reality that has been missing from literature, and reproduce within literary works the true circumstances and voice of the masses.... Of course, portraying the true form of reality and, what is more, portraying it artistically, are hardly easy tasks. To accomplish them, it is first necessary that our writers should know reality, and in order to know reality they must live, fight, and share happiness and misery with the masses.[28]

Moreover, it was time not only for writers to describe the masses "without deceit or contrivance," but also to show them "the way out of their predicament"—that is, to "instruct" them in "life." The individuality of the writer was not entirely irrelevant to such a task, but had to be considered secondary to the priority need for objective "research on social life" and the literary reconstruction of that life.

Kurahara's insistence on the need for writers to write from the perspective of the masses would have surprised no one who was familiar with the theoretical essays he had written in the latter stages of the prewar proletarian literary movement. Kurahara had once argued for the viability of artistic, as opposed to purely political, criteria in judging a work's value, and had shown some sensitivity to the problems faced by petit bourgeois writers as they attempted to follow the party's political agenda.[29] After several months in the Soviet Union in late 1930, however, he had contributed an influential essay to the Marxist cultural journal *Senki* (*Battle Flag*), in which he called for the bolshevization of literature. Contrary to his earlier toleration of artistic license, this essay proposed making left-wing art into a didactic instrument for political indoctrination. Just before *Senki* was forced to cease publication, he added a final essay on method in which he called for a uniform approach to writing based on exhaustive study of dialectical materialism. According to Kurahara, the main criterion of literary value should be faithful adherence to Marxist-Leninist epistemology.[30]

The end of the war and the revival of democratic revolution signified to Kurahara an opportunity to take up with new vigor and optimism an agenda that had been prematurely suspended through the interference of militaristic state power. Social realism in literature had been aborted along with Japan's bourgeois-democratic revolution in the early 1930s, but now Kurahara expected that both could reach full fruition concurrently. He assumed that as the Allied occupation went about transforming the social base, writers and other artists could devote themselves to the construction of an appropriate cultural superstructure.

And yet, despite—or, rather, because of—the obeisance Kurahara and other prewar Communists had paid to reductive models of economic determinism, in the early postwar era they put culture in the van and assigned it a revolutionary function that seemed to go some distance beyond party political policy as it was developing under Nosaka's influence. Kurahara seems to have placed such confidence in the radicality and thoroughness of the socioeconomic reforms promulgated by the Supreme Commander for the Allied Powers Japan (SCAP) that he believed culture could now pass rapidly through the bourgeois-democratic stage and begin actively to prepare the way for the construction of socialism.

In sum, despite the party's apparent move in early 1946 toward a political strategy of parliamentary gradualism and indefinite deferral of the socialist revolution, the party's policy under Kurahura seems to have continued to expect an early transition to socialism. In contrast to Nosaka's new democracy, which would be led not only by workers and farmers but by "the working intellectual class, and small and medium-sized commercial and industrial businessmen," the democracy Kurahara described would require that these bourgeois elements defer to the working class, which would lead the democratic revolution.

Rather than indicating a belief on Kurahara's part that culture could advance beyond the institutional base, this suggests that Nosaka and Kurahara each drew his own conclusions from an optimistic view of the SCAP reforms. For Nosaka, the radical political reforms promised by SCAP provided a golden opportunity for the party to present a "lovable" image and attract broad-based support while leaving the occupation to grapple with the difficult and controversial measures that were necessary to revolutionize institutions. Conversely, for Kurahara, SCAP's reform of the economic base promised to fulfill the objective conditions for a type of cultural production that could move with unprecedented speed toward the promotion of socialist consciousness and the world outlook of the laboring masses. At the same time, Nosaka and Kurahara embraced conceptions of the relationship between the party and other groups in society that were equally hierarchical and control-oriented.

In the early postwar era of democratic revolution, therefore, the meaning of democracy in politics and culture fluctuates between associations with the institutions and processes of liberal parliamentarism that were being established by the occupation, on the one hand, and the strongly pejorative associations the Leninist tradition assigned to the term *bourgeois democracy*, on the other. Nosaka and his supporters do seem to have taken democratic revolution seriously, and it does seem genuinely to have constituted the main focal point of party policy. And yet, Kurahara and others continued to disparage liberal democracy in its classical sense, and to enjoin writers toward a more clearly proletarian perspective.

The differences in nuance between Nosaka's clear, if perhaps only tactical, espousal of bourgeois democracy and Kurahara's focus on the need for an early cultural transition to socialism created a double bind for writers whose experience with the prewar proletarian literature movement predisposed them, as soon as the war ended, to question party control over literature. As petit bourgeois intellectuals, these writers were encouraged by the party's political emphasis on a broad democratic front and its support for parliamentary democracy to think that they could play a progressive cultural as well as political role. Yet Kurahara's opening salvos on culture had admonished them to join a centralized writers' organization and dedicate themselves to "living and fighting with the masses" and writing with the "true voice of the masses." Their reaction was negative and immediate.

Shortly after the publication of Kurahara's two-part piece in *Tokyo shinbun*, Honda Shūgo wrote an essay that would become a manifesto of sorts for a small group of left-wing writers, some of them Communist Party members, who mounted a rebellion against party orthodoxy. He published the piece in the inaugural issue of the group's new journal, *Kindai bungaku* (*Modern Literature*).

Honda's differences with Kurahara were evident from his first sentence: " For the artist," Honda wrote, "that is art which most perfectly satisfies the promptings of the heart."[31] For Honda and his collaborators on the new journal, literature had primarily to give expression to the self, the *watakushi* ("I"), of the writer. For an author like Honda, there seemed "no way other than to be true to the inner necessity of our bourgeois selves. . . ." To Kurahara's directives Honda retorted, "Except by being the best petit bourgeois writers they can be, there is no literary way for them to live and fight with the masses."[32]

Among a variety of other issues, Honda introduced generational difference in relation to the experience of war and the collapse of the proletarian literary movement. All but one of the seven founding members of *Kindai bungaku* (there were thirty-two members by January 1949) were in their thirties at the end of the war: Yamamuro Shizuka (thirty-nine), Honda Shūgo (thirty-seven), Hirano Ken (thirty-seven), Haniya Yutaka (thirty-five), Ara Masato (thirty-five), Sasaki Kiichi (thirty-one), and Odagiri Hideo (twenty-nine).[33] Honda points out that, whereas the leaders of the prewar socialist movement had been at least twenty-five years old (Kurahara was twenty-nine) at the time of the Manchurian Incident, and thus were generally in their forties as they reemerged to take charge of the postwar Left, most members of the *Kindai bungaku* generation had not turned twenty-five until about the time of the Marco Polo Bridge incident of 1937, and thus had been able to serve only as the "rear guard" of the prewar movement.

According to Honda, they had naively witnessed a complete historical cycle from the era of democracy and Westernization after World War I, to the insular militarism and oppression of the 1930s, and back again to the reauthorization of democracy and infatuation with the West that were occurring in the early postwar era. They had been beset with nagging doubts about the validity of unilinear historical materialism. They had also watched with dismay in 1933 as top party leaders such as Nabeyama Sadachika and Sano Manabu recanted Communist activity (*tenkō*) and became supporters of Japanese expansionism. As a result, most of these younger men eventually also became disillusioned and followed their elders in various forms of recantation.

In the postwar era, therefore, the *Kindai bungaku* generation were often self-consciously emotional, suspicious of the party line, and preoccupied with the inner need to confront and articulate artistically the meaning of their own prewar and wartime experiences. This time, they refused to deny the "egoistic" forces that welled up from inside. They believed that the party's prewar policy on art, particularly in its more or less final prewar form as articulated by Kurahara in 1931, had been too preoccupied with dialectical materialism and insufficiently sensitive to the human, subjective, and individual dimensions of history and art. The party had paid obeisance to external necessity without devoting enough attention to the "irrepressible necessity within." Now, in the postwar era of democratic revolution, that lack would have to be made up and the self (*watakushi*) of the writer given its due.[34]

All the issues broached by Honda were explored further in another section of the journal's first issue, this time in a face-to-face discussion between Kurahara and journal members. Ara Masato raised the topic that he would explore further in a series of essays: how a writer could relate to the masses. Kurahara had said that a writer must "strive always to make the standpoint of the masses his own, try to be close to them, and be keenly aware of their suffering and joy." But most writers were not of working-class or peasant backgrounds. For such writers, the political injunction to "be with" the masses seemed to imply an artificial, even hypocritical, quest for the masses "from a position somewhere outside them." Wasn't it possible to "be with the masses" in a strictly literary sense without actually trying to enter among them physically or psychologically? Kurahara, however, continued to insist that "there is nothing better for a writer than to go regularly to farms or factories and work together with the masses."

For Ara, this argument was unconvincing: "As petit bourgeois intelligentsia, we [can only] portray ourselves. To investigate oneself thoroughly—this should be the starting point of literature from this moment forward, and ultimately it is this endeavor which will connect us in a literary sense with the masses."[35] To begin from one's own position and one's own outlook on life need not mean abandoning all social relevance or concern. Ara argued that the self provided a *literary* route to the masses.

It is clear that the party's program of democratic revolution created confusion in the realm of culture. Although Nosaka's "new democracy" and the logic of democratic reform demanded that bourgeois and petit bourgeois elements should play an active, often leading, role in reconstruction, Kurahara and other Communist writers of his generation, whose ideas were formed in the prewar proletarian movement, found it very difficult to admit to the legitimacy of a petit bourgeois writer's own perspective of the world as the starting point for artistic engagement. Whereas Kurahara demanded that writers present a relatively direct and unmediated literary representation from the viewpoint of the working masses, the *Kindai bungaku* writers insisted on the priority of their own mediating presence.

HUMANIST DIALECTICS IN POSTWAR WRITING

Ara, Hirano Ken, Odagiri Hideo, and other writers affiliated with *Kindai bungaku* proceeded to fill its pages with a variety of polemical essays that elaborated and made more precise the arguments suggested in their initial exchanges with Kurahara. One of the first to publish was Ara. His "Daini no seishun" (Second Youth) was a long and laboriously crafted piece that gave full vent to its author's dramatic, flamboyant style. The essay began by evoking the end of the war:

> Soon after I began reading literature I learned of Dostoyevsky's rare experience in which, having been implicated in the Petrachevsky Incident, he was condemned to death; and then, just before the sentence was to be carried out, he was miraculously pardoned by a new directive.... I could hardly suppress a feeling of envy that approached despair; envy not of his genius but of a life-experience of the sort that visits only one person in a million....
>
> But when we reflect on our recent defeat and compare it to the momentous experience of the 19th century Russian writer, we find that our own ordeal is in no way inferior. Good men and women ... remained committed to collective suicide right up to the moment at which unconditional surrender was announced. They had consecrated their precious lives during the air raids, in the corners of bomb shelters which were less inviting than garbage pits.[36]

Ara's is perhaps the most powerful and evocative statement of a tendency that appears frequently in early postwar writing, that of a sublime experience of negativism—death, pain, degradation—which leads dialectically to heightened subjective awareness and vitality.[37] For Ara, as for Dostoyevsky, the sentence of death provided a necessary, dialectical prelude to meaningful life.

But the new negativism in postwar Japanese literature emerges not only in dialectical process but also in the tense immobility of irony, or oxymoron, as suggested by the title of Ara's essay. This variant evokes the existentialist Dostoyevsky, for whom individuality was "wretched and revolting, and yet, for all its misery, the highest good."[38] Ara's essay links naïveté with cynicism, illusions with disillusionment, youth with maturity, humanism with egoism, heaven with hell:

> In passing through the era of left-wing movements, by way of fascism and war and democratic revolution to reach yesterday and today, through hopes, despair, and hopes again, in the eras of brightness, dark, and light again, if I have discovered anything it is the beautifully ignoble—ignobly beautiful—human being. I learned to expect pettiness in the midst of greatness, and to find greatness in the midst of squalor.

For Ara, not even in the context of the postwar liberation could one hope for a return to simple humanism. On the contrary, "in this, our second youth, we can by no means resurrect the innocent feelings of the first."[39] It was now abundantly clear that true humanism could only emerge dialectically from utter negativism. Those "who don't know despair, have not felt the abyss, and have never seen hell" were "false humanists," hypocrites, or worse.

> Let's pursue the thought of our own flesh; let's extend it over the abyss—through the limitless realm of negation that wells up from that abyss—all the way to the cosmological limit . . . ! We can then return to the cares of daily life girded with a thorough sense of negativity. Human beings are egoistic, ugly, despicable, and human conduct is submerged in nothingness—let us feel this keenly, and all else will follow![40]

This attitude led to a new skepticism toward the party's authority: "We once made the mistake of enshrining the party leaders as gods, but such behavior is no less primitive than that of the emperor system's slaves, who blindly worshiped the child of the sun." In terms of Ara's new skepticism, political activity could occur only as an extension of self-centeredness, never at its expense: "Instead of those humanist gladiators who served selflessly, it is rather the greedy, ambitious disciples of egoism who are the purest followers of humanism."[41]

Ara followed "Daini no seishun" a month later, in the April issue of *Kindai bungaku*, with an essay titled "Minshū to wa dare ka" ("Who Are the Masses?").[42] Here, irony and skepticism are transformed into biting sarcasm. Left-wing intellectuals were deluding themselves when they allowed their paternalistic pretensions to draw them toward factories, farms, and settlement houses: "They sometimes . . . forget they are not workers themselves and start hallucinating that an increase in wages is actually connected somehow to their own petit bourgeois life. Eventually, they can be heard to say things like, 'We workers . . . , etc.' But an honest petit bourgeois writer will look for the masses only in his own heart: 'In short, the masses are not they, you or us. They are myself, the solitary I.' "[43]

As Ara had argued in "Daini no seishun," naive humanism had to be utterly denied. The new, tougher humanism could only be an "affirmation through negation, the plenitude at the very extremity of nothingness, and the pristine humanism that is the extension of our egoism."[44] The ego marked the unavoidable, the irreducible, pole of the dialectical process, a topos that had to be fully occupied before humanism would emerge as a possibility. Only when one was able to rest unambivalently in the negativism of egocentricity could one tentatively reach out in a gesture of humanistic affirmation.

Against the background of wartime devastation and postwar deprivation, Ara's evocation of the darkness that encloses (and makes possible) light, and of the descent into nothingness that must precede or accompany the affirmation of meaning, made logical and compelling sense. So did his argument that any authentic, productive, and artistically valuable portrayal of the plight of others must be premised on an honest, searching look into the self.

Ara's theme of dialectical negation and paradox was common to a broad cross section of early postwar writing, and is no doubt at some level grounded in the wartime experience of the populace at large. As cultural critic Tsurumi Shunsuke observed, the postwar generation "witnessed the values they had believed in fade to the point of transparency." They concluded that "only when the self hurls forth passion will the world respond with meaning."[45] This loss of faith in values, philosophies, and ideologies often correlated with new concern about defining and differentiating humanity from other forms of life. For many writers, it was only in the lowest common denominator of human existence that some glimmer of hope for the future of mankind could be perceived, and this often meant emphasizing the flesh rather than the spirit. Just as for Ara humanism could be based only in the ego, for the popular writer Tamura Taijirō the only possible bedrock was physical desire.

Tamura was demobilized in 1946 after six years as a soldier in China, and almost immediately began to write. One of his stories, published in early 1947, was to become a landmark in postwar popular culture. Titled "Nikutai no mon" (Gateway to the Flesh), the work deals with a group of teenage girls surviving as prostitutes in the rubble of bombed-out Tokyo.[46] The work illustrates three principles:

First, survival is the ultimate value and goal of human life. Questions of the meaning of life inevitably appear specious in light of constant threats to human survival.

Second, behavior is governed by instinct rather than conceptual reasoning, and animal life provides the most compelling similes with which to describe it. Social order is merely the tenuous product of instinctive, unarticulated attractions and repulsions. Tamura portrays human life without a guiding Logos.

Third, the motif of *nikutai* (flesh) emphasizes surface, texture, and opacity. This is exemplified in a discussion of tattoos. One of the girls, Asada Sen, who calls herself "Komasa no sen," is having the four ideographs (*Kantō Komasa*) tattooed on her shoulder. She goes every other day to a well-known tattoo artist, who caters to petty thieves, gangsters, gamblers, and "working girls" like herself:

> For Sen it was fascinating that all kinds of pictures and writing could be sculpted into the human skin. . . . But that was not all. Just as primitives have to turn themselves into something superhuman in order to stand up against tigers, alligators, or bears, in Sen's life of daily struggle she had an instinctual desire for a mystical, robust power beyond her natural strength. When she thought about the fancy Pan-pans from Yamanote who sometimes invaded her turf, and how she would now be able to pull one into an alley and startle her by baring the "Kanto Komasa" tattoo in the light of the moon and neon signs, Sen's breast tingled with fighting spirit.[47]

Here the flesh generates a form of active subjectivity as the will to fight, but only as a dependent variable, an extension of the biological need to survive. Indeed, it seems that the source of vitality is not in the will per se, but in the material marks—the writing itself. Thus power resides in the inscription which, when etched onto the body's surface, gives it the capacity to signify a magical threat quite alien to human will and understanding. The story allows for transcendence only if that is defined as a transition from numbness to sensation: it consists entirely in a form of carnal knowledge.

Tamura gave an ironically humanistic twist to his preoccupation with the flesh in an essay published in 1947. There he argues that philosophy (*shisō*) of all kinds must remain intimately bound to flesh and blood if it is to be potent enough to respond to problems of war, poverty, and dislocation: "During the war I learned that no 'philosophy' which ignored the flesh could offer any resistance against national actions which overran normal boundaries. Moreover, after a long time in the field I saw Japanese, who claimed to revere high-sounding philosophy, become transformed into beasts. I myself was among them."[48] Since the war, therefore, philosophy had lost its persuasiveness: "The flesh is now an outlaw, rebelling against everything. Is it not true that today the flesh is raising up banners and placards, beating the gong, and waging a frontal attack on 'philosophy'?" In the postwar world, where "only the flesh is true," it was impossible to conceive of a humanism that was not deeply rooted in the flesh: "What power could there be in a form of humanity that is not premised on the flesh? To know the meaning of the flesh is to know the meaning of the human being."[49] If there is to be any meaning at all, it must be materially constructed and always conditional rather than absolute; never cut off from sensuous needs, it is rather their extension.

Another exploration of the body as the basis for life and struggle in early postwar literature is provided by Dazai Osamu's *Shayō* (*Setting Sun*, 1946), a work more familiar to Westerners than Tamura's.[50] There, from his drug-induced delirium, one of the main characters assures us that all manifestations of the spirit are unreliable. He writes in his journal, "Philosophy? Lies. Principles? Lies. Ideals? Lies. Order? Lies. Sincerity? Truth? Purity? All lies."[51]

A problem the novel addresses is whether it is possible for former aristocrats to go on living after the war at a very basic, biological level. Naoji decides that it is not, and chooses death by suicide, while his sister Kazuko perseveres. In order to survive, however, she must confront the selfishness of life: "I can't escape the feeling that it is by sucking the lifebreath out of Mother than I am fattening."[52] Also inescapable is life's ugliness: "The dying are beautiful, but to live, to survive—those things somehow seem hideous and contaminated with blood."[53] Yet once negated as a means to any external ideal or purpose, life can be reaffirmed as an end in itself and thus, paradoxically, provide the basis for a form of engagement: "There was something to which I could not resign myself. Call it low-minded of me, if you will, I must survive and struggle with the world in order to accomplish my desires."[54] Then, in a letter to her former lover, she discovers the final rationale for life in the biological capacity to give new life: "Recently I have come to understand why such things as war, peace, unions, trade, politics exist in the world. I'll tell you why—it is so that women will give birth to healthy babies."[55]

Meaning in life and active engagement with the world do not result automatically from the removal of feudal or fascist constraints. They are not the natural outgrowth of liberation, but the children of renunciation, desperation, and pain.

Related to the literary discourse on the flesh is the theme of cannibalism. Few forms of negation are so provocative as this, because of its capacity to call radically into question conventional forms of humanism. That is, the theme allows the exploration of a major dilemma of human existence, where survival as a human being requires participation in the inhuman act of consuming the flesh of another. It also allows the body to emerge quite literally as a source of life. The theme of cannibalism is used in a powerful way in Ooka Shōhei's *Nobi* (*Fires on the Plain*, 1951), where all positive actions are preceded by violence and death, and Christian imagery relating to death and resurrection is used to dramatic effect.[56]

As these examples (and many more could be cited)[57] suggest, Ara's critical thematic of dialectical irony was by no means an isolated phenomenon. In the early postwar period, truth, sincerity, and humanity were simultaneously termed essential and called into question; meaning, like existence itself, always seemed both essential and tenuous. In light of the tragic, even nihilistic, atmosphere these literary figures represented, it is not surprising that the party's call for self-abnegating homage to the masses was sometimes greeted with rebellious self-centeredness.

WAR RESPONSIBILITY, EMPEROR SYSTEM, EUROPEAN EGO

In a roundtable discussion early in 1946, a group of *Kindai bungaku* writers discussed the emperor system and writers' war responsibility. There, in a manner consistent with the journal's emphasis on the subjective dimension, Odagiri Hideo suggested that writers should see the emperor system not as an external structure but as a set of unconscious emotions that predisposed them toward feudal behavior: "Feudalism penetrates even the small corners of our sensibility in daily life. Therefore, we can fight against it only by conquering what is feudalistic within ourselves . . . ." Ara then connected the problem of the emperor system to war responsibility:

> *Ara*: . . . The emperor system must share responsibility for the war, but the emperor has not admitted that. When confronted with this [anomaly], writers tend either to put up a front of ignorance, on the pretext that as writers they know nothing of politics, or just leave the pursuit of the emperor's war guilt to the Communist Party. But these evasions leave them impotent to take up the war responsibility of writers. If, as writers, we are to pursue the emperor's war responsibility in a literary way, we will have to struggle with the semi-feudal sensibilities, emotions, and desires that are rooted in our own internal "emperor system." That is the only way we can negate the emperor system per se, and the only way that is conducive to the formation of a modern man. . . .
>
> We were unable to oppose the war. . . . Why . . . ? Because we did not have within us a modern ego.

Notions of a modern man and a modern ego were always premised ultimately on the contrast between an intransigently premodern Japan and a modern Europe. Europeans had achieved a universal, "human" belief system and a sense of equality before God, whereas in Japan people still defined themselves according to hierarchical social roles with no autonomous identity as human beings. According to Haniya Yutaka,

> *Haniya*: . . . If we think of Europe, there has always been a kind of authority—for example, until the last century there was God . . . the God of all mankind. Europeans were always standing before a kind of court. . . . And even when this God was transformed, to be replaced by society, or humankind, people always faced a judge, and harbored the internal imperative of a "should" (*sollen*), a notion of how the individual should be as a human being. . . .

In Japan, conversely, the private individual was virtually absent, subsisting merely as a dependent locus of needs and desires that required the encompassing support of communal bonds:

> We [Japanese] have been able to gain self-awareness as human beings only as the result of passive evasion. Our awareness has been penetrated by the Eastern way of thinking, that only by escaping or retreating can one hope to occupy a purely human standpoint. We have understood how to be Japanese nationals (*kokumin*) but not how to be human beings. Humanism has been nothing but an empty world.

It was logical, therefore, that if there was to be a renaissance in the postwar era, it would occur only when the Japanese self was transformed in a modern, which is to say European, direction:

> *Ara*: We have to liberate the Japanese ego. It should become like European individualism.
> *Hirano*: Can it be raised to the level of the European ego? I wonder. It's just not possible to wipe out a tradition overnight, and although one might prefer to replace it with another tradition, that is impossible.
> *Ara*: Not necessarily. You are free to determine whether your own ego will be elevated or not. That is the freedom of our generation. We have to give life to that freedom. I feel a powerful sense of urgency in that regard. Isn't that why we are struggling to publish *Kindai bungaku*?

And yet, their commitments to the West and to the panacea of modernity were not entirely unambivalent:

> *Ara*: We have had no feeling of equality. As a result, we were not modern enough to oppose the war. . . .
> *Honda*: If you mean the reason that we were unable to resist effectively was that modernity was not established within us, I think in

the broad sense you are right. But I really don't quite understand the meaning of modernity. . . .
Sasaki: I know, because the Europeans themselves were unable to avoid the war. But you can say this, I think: In Japan where the modern ego has not been established no one keenly feels war responsibility as his own personal problem . . . . Writers just say, "It couldn't be helped" . . . .
Honda: I think it is true that the lack of consciousness regarding war responsibility is the result of our failure to establish a modern ego. But now that we are at the stage of wondering how to think about war responsibility and what to do about it, it doesn't help much to say that the remedy is a modern ego and a modern literature . . . .[58]

Although they could reach no consensus on how to rectify the situation, the *Kindai bungaku* writers seemed to agree that tasks such as rooting out the emperor system through democratic revolution and fully airing the problem of war responsibility had to be carried out internally, in the minds of individuals, as well as externally in the political arena. This conviction led them to the ideal of modernity, which was intimately associated with the development of autonomous subjectivity, and also to a conception of European culture as the exemplar of that modernity. Finally, their preoccupation as writers with self-clarification and expression set them at odds with the Communist Party's literary ideals of objectivity and realism, and its traditional assumption that politics should lead culture.

NATIONALISM AND THE CRITIQUE OF MODERNISM

As literary critic Watanabe Kazutami has pointed out, while *Kindai bungaku* with its dialectical modernism was occupying center stage during the early postwar years, a contrasting perspective on the relationship among modernity, Japan, and the West was waiting quietly backstage. This perspective, which still harbored vestiges of the wartime suspicion of modernity, a firm resistance against Westernization, and a keen sense of the tragedy that had befallen Japan in the modern era, manifested itself most concretely in the literary journal *Bungakukai* (*Literary Circle*), which resumed publication in June 1947 after a three-year hiatus.[59]

This culturally and historically nationalistic stream of thought was submerged in the early postwar period but, according to Watanabe, began to surface as early as January 1947 with the publication in the journal *Shinchō* (*New Tide*) of the first installment of "Tsumi no ishiki" (Guilt Consciousness) by Kamei Katsuichirō. Kamei was associated with the Japan Romantic faction, and during the war had debated the ways in which Japan could "overcome modernity" (*kindai no chōkoku*). He had also extolled aspects of the war as balm for the wounds inflicted by modernity on the Japanese body politic. In his postwar essays, Kamei emphasized the torments that Japan experienced in its attempts to modernize, and lamented the weakening of national energy and spread of moral corruption. He was one of the first to bring into postwar literary and political discourse the wartime disillusionment with modernity.

Kamei was followed by others, most notably the critic and scholar of Chinese literature Takeuchi Yoshimi. In a 1951 essay titled "Kindaishugi to minzoku no mondai" ("Modernism and the Problem of the Japanese Nation"),[60] he severely criticized the kind of modernist thought that located modernity outside Japan, in European or other models. He further argued that unless this kind of modernism were overcome, Japan would never genuinely be able to modernize, by which he meant to become "truly itself" (*jiko jishin to naru*). This autonomous modernity could only be borne by a national literature (*kokumin bungaku*) that paid special attention to the Japanese people and their achievement of cultural independence.

It is important to note that by this time the Communist Party had also modified its accommodating stance toward the occupation and proposed a "democratic Japanese people's front" (*minshu minzoku sensen*) whose main slogan would be "complete independence."[61] This proposal signified the party's increased willingness to use the term *minzoku*, with its nationalistic connotations, a tendency that was reinforced in the wake of the Cominform's criticism of the party in January 1949, when national independence from American imperialism became the main plank in the party platform.[62]

Kindai bungaku suspended publication for four months in 1950, and reappeared as a less ambitious magazine that lacked its former luster.[63] In the meantime, of course, the Korean War had broken out and occupation censors and purge officials were targeting Communists instead of ultranationalists. A new era had begun, and some would say that the "postwar period" was ending.

NOTES

1. Etō Jun, "Sengo bungaku wa hasan no kiki," *Mainichi shinbun*, 24 January 1978. Also *Ochiba no hakiyose* (Tokyo: Bungei Shunjūsha, 1981).
2. Jay Rubin, "From Wholesomeness to Decadence: The Censorship of Literature under the Allied Occupation," *Journal of Japanese Studies* 11, no. 1 (1985): 71–103.

3. See Monica Braw, *The Atomic Bomb Suppressed: American Censorship in Japan 1945–1949*, Lund Studies in International History 23 (Lund, Sweden: University of Lund, 1986); and Matsuuru Sōzō, *Zōho ketteiban senryōka no genron tan'atsu* (Tokyo: Gendai Janarizumu Shuppansha, 1969).
4. Rubin, "From Wholesomeness," 72.
5. See Usui Yoshimi, *Sengo bungaku ronsō*, vols. 1 and 2 (Tokyo: Banchō, 1972). For an account of the debate on subjective autonomy, see J. Victor Koschmann, "The Debate on Subjectivity in Postwar Japan: Foundations of Modernism as a Political Critique," *Pacific Affairs* 54, no. 4 (Winter 1981–82): 609–31.
6. For discussion of a German group that is perhaps comparable to the *Kindai bungaku* writers, see Siegfried Mandel, *Group 47: The Reflected Intellect* (Carbondale: Southern Illinois University Press, 1973); and Peter Demetz, *After the Fires: Recent Writing in the Germanies, Austria, and Switzerland* (New York: Harcourt Brace Jovanovich Inc., 1986), chapter 1.
7. Rubin notes that "between 1946 and 1949, some 110 magazines carrying serious works of literature were established or reestablished, excluding the many entertainment magazines that flourished briefly. Book publishing, too, favored literature, with 28 percent of all new trade books and 22.5 percent of reprints for 1946 comprised of literature, criticism, and literary theory." See Rubin, "From Wholesomeness," 74–75.
8. *Political Reorientation of Japan, September 1945 to September 1948* (Washington, D.C.: U.S. Government Printing Office, 1949), 78–79.
9. Tokuda Kyūichi, "Gokuchū jūhachinen (shō)" [1947], in Haniya Yukata, ed., *Kakumei no shisō*, Sengo Nihon shisō taikei 6 (Tokyo: Chikuma Shobō, 1969), 44.
10. See the biographical sketch in Rodger Swearingen and Paul Langer, *Red Flag in Japan: International Communism in Action 1919–1951* (Cambridge, Mass.: Harvard University Press, 1952), 107–11.
11. Quoted in Masumi Junnosuke, *Postwar Politics in Japan, 1945–1955*, translated by Lonny E. Carlile (Berkeley: University of California, Institute of East Asian Studies Japan Research Monograph 6, 1985), 89. On early relations between SCAP and the JCP, also see Takemae Eiji, "Early Postwar Reformist Parties," in Robert E. Ward and Sakamoto Yoshikazu, eds., *Democratizing Japan: The Allied Occupation* (Honolulu: University of Hawaii Press, 1987), 339–65.
12. George M. Beckmann and Okubo Genji, *The Japanese Communist Party 1922–1945* (Stanford, Calif.: Stanford University Press, 1969), Appendix F ("Theses on the Situation in Japan and the Tasks of the Communist Party, May 1932"), 339.
13. Pointed out by Joe Moore, *Japanese Workers and the Struggle for Power, 1945–1947* (Madison: University of Wisconsin Press, 1983), 113.
14. Nihon Kyōsantō Shutsugoku Dōshikai, "Jinmin ni uttau," in Hidaka Rokurō, ed., *Sengo shisō no shuppatsu*, Sengo Nihon shisō taikei 1 (Tokyo: Chikuma Shobō, 1968), 245–46.
15. Moore, *Japanese Workers*, 117–18.
16. Tokuda, "Gokuchū jūhachinen (shō)," 44.
17. Moore, *Japanese Workers*, 173–77.
18. See especially Nosaka, "Minshuteki Nihon no kensetsu," a speech at the Seventh National Congress of the Chinese Communist Party, in *Nosaka Sanzō senshū*, vol. 1 [Senjihen, 1933–45] (Tokyo: Nihon Kyōsantō Chūōiinkai Shuppanbu, 1964), 419–68. For background, see Sewaringen and Langer, *Red Flag in Japan*, 73–83.
19. See biographical sketch in Swearingen and Langer, *Red Flag in Japan*, 111–15.
20. See John K. Emmerson quote in Masumi, *Postwar Politics*, 91.
21. See Nosaka's criticism of Tokuda and Shiga during an interrogation at Supreme Commander for the Allied Powers Japan (SCAP), reported by Moore, *Japanese Workers*, 125.
22. Ibid., 92.
23. Nosaka Sanzō, "Minshu sensen ni yotte sokoku no kiki o sukue," in Hidaka, ed., *Sengo shisō no shuppatsu*, 247–58.

24. Mao Tse-tung, "On New Democracy," *Selected Works of Mao Tse-tung*, vol. 2 (Beijing: Foreign Language Press, 1965), 339–84.
25. Moore, *Japanese Workers*, 124.
26. Kurahara Korehito, "Atarashii bungaku e no shuppatsu," *Kurahara Korehito hyōronshū*, vol. 3 (Tokyo: Shin Nihon Shuppansha, 1967), 3–7.
27. On Kurahara's prewar activities, see G. T. Shea, *Leftwing Literature in Japan* (Tokyo: Hōsei University Press, 1964); Tatsuo Arima, *The Failure of Freedom: A Portrait of Modern Japanese Intellectuals* (Cambridge, Mass.: Harvard University Press, 1969), 173–213; and Yoshio Iwamoto, "Aspects of the Proletarian Literary Movement in Japan," in Bernard S. Silberman and H. D. Harootunian, eds., *Japan in Crisis: Essays on Taishō Democracy* (Princeton, N.J.: Princeton University Press, 1974), 156–82.
28. Kurahara, "Atarashii bungaku e no Shuppatsu," 5.
29. Arima, *The Failure of Freedom*, 198–203.
30. Ibid., 212. See Furukawa Sōichirō (pseud.), "Proletaria undō no soshiki mondai," and Tanikawa Kiyoshi (pseud.), "Geijutsuteki hōhō ni tsuite no kansō," parts I and II, in *Kurahara Korehito hyōronshū* 2 (Tokyo: Shin Nihon Shuppansha, 1968), 109–36, 180–261.
31. Honda Shūgo, "Geijutsu, rekishi, ningen," *Kindai bungaku* 1 (February 1946): 2.
32. Ibid., 7.
33. Tsurumi Shunsuke, "*Kindai bungaku* ni tsuite," in Kuno Osamu, Tsurumi Shunsuke, and Fujita Shōzō, *Sengo Nihon no shisō* (Tokyo: Chikuma Shobō, 1966), 2.
34. Honda, "Geijutsu," 9.
35. Ara Masato et. al., "Bungaku to genjitsu: Kurahara Korehito o kakonde," *Kindai bungaku* 1 (February 1946): 25–26.
36. Ara Masato, "Daini no seishun," *Kindai bungaku* 2 (March 1946): 3.
37. Kurrik reminds us that Kant's notion of the sublime includes "a new consciousness of negativity, put in the service of subjectivity." See Maire Kurrik, *Literature and Negation* (New York: Columbia University Press, 1979), 51.
38. Walter Kaufmann, *Existentialism from Dostoyevsky to Sartre* (New York: New American Library, 1975), 12.
39. Ara, "Daini no seishun," 4.
40. Ibid., 12.
41. Ibid., 14.
42. Ara Masato, "Minshū to wa dare ka," *Kindai bungaku* 3 (April 1946): 8–9.
43. Ibid., 17–18.
44. Ara, "Daini no seishun," 13.
45. Tsurumi Shunsuke, "Nihon no jitsuzonshugi—sengo no sesō," in Kuno Osamu and Tsurumi Shunsuke, *Gendai Nihon no shisō* (Tokyo: Iwanami Shinsho, 1956), 198.
46. Tamura Taijirō, "Nikutai no mon," in Itō Sei et al., eds., *Kitahara Takeo, Inoue Tomoichirō, Tamura Taijirō shū*, Nihon gendai bungaku zenshū 94 (Tokyo: Kōdansha, 1968).
47. Ibid., 318.
48. Tamura Taijirō, "Nikutai wa ningen de aru." *Gunzō* (May 1947): 11.
49. Ibid., 12.
50. Tamura's story is discussed briefly by Rubin, "From Wholesomeness," 82–83.
51. Osamu Dazai, *The Setting Sun*, translated by Donald Keene (New York: New Directions Publishing Corporation, 1956), 62.
52. Ibid., 42.
53. Ibid., 124-25.
54. Ibid., 125.
55. Ibid., 172.
56. Ooka Shohei, *Fires on the Plain*, translated by Ivan Morris (New York: Alfred A. Knopf, 1957).
57. Obvious, although diverse, examples would include Noma Hiroshi's *Kurai e* (*Dark Picture*, 1946), Shiina Rinzō's *Shinya no shūen* (*Midnight Feast*, 1947), and Sakaguchi Ango's *Hakuchi* (*The Idiot*, 1945).

58. Ara Masato et al., "Zadankai: bungakusha no sekimu," reprint in Usui Yoshimi, ed., *Sengo bungaku ronsō* 1 (Tokyo: Banchō Shobō, 1972), 65–67.
59. Watanabe Kazutami, "Sengo shisō no mitorizu," in Tetsuo Najita, Maeda Ai, and Kamishima Jirō, eds., *Sengo Nihon no seishinshi: sono saikentō* (Tokyo: Iwanami Shoten, 1988), 105. Also see his *Nashonarizumu no ryōgisei: wakai hito e no tegami* (Tokyo: Jinbun Shoin, 1984), 203–21.
60. Takeuchi Yoshimi, "Kindaishugi to minzoku no mondai," *Takeuchi Yoshimi zenshū* 7 (1981): 28–37; also see Takeuchi, "Kindai to wa nani ka," *Zenshū* 4: 128–71.
61. Miyakawa Tōru, Nakamura Yūjirō, and Furuta Hikaru, *Kindai Nihon shiso ronsō* (Tokyo: Aoki Shoten, 1963), 221.
62. Hidaka Rokurō, "Kaisetsu: sengo no 'kindaishugi'," in Hidaka, ed., *Kindaishugi*, Sengo Nihon shisō taikei 34 (Tokyo: Chikuma Shobō, 1964), 42.
63. Watanabe, "Sengo shisō no mitorizu," 111.

IV

POSTOCCUPATION LITERARY TRENDS

9
Postoccupation Literary Movements and Developments in West Germany

Judith Ryan

No other participant of a major war—whether winner or loser—has been so often regarded as a kind of hospital patient as postwar Germany. Although the diagnosis has mostly been psychoanalytical (the Germans are widely said not to have "done the work of mourning"[1]), I propose to look at some of the physical symptoms of this supposed illness and convalescence: to take the patient's pulse, as it were, or perhaps more accurately, chart the encephalogram throughout a period of some thirty-five years, 1949 to 1985. This approach has the advantage of not presupposing any particular illness, or indeed ill health at all. Conceiving the results as a kind of graph has another advantage as well: it moves us away from the conventional literary historical approach of more or less unified periods that succeed one another in a relatively orderly way. This is not to say that the notion of periods should be entirely abolished; but of greatest importance for the retrospective on nazism are those moments when the chart peaks and a new intensity of activity is clearly discernible.

Since the end of the occupation there have been two major peaks—around 1959 and again around 1968—along with a minor peak around 1985. The two major peaks mark high points in a distinctive movement of literature in West Germany that attempted to look at the Third Reich from an entirely new angle of vision, a phase that lasted throughout most of the 1960s and 1970s.

The literature of this movement attempts not only to recall the events of the Third Reich, but also to suggest, by mapping out alternative scenarios, that these events were not inevitable, that even in difficult circumstances we often have more choices than we think. Framing this important literary movement are, on the one hand, the somewhat hesitant literature of the early postoccupation years, a period that liked to think of itself as a fresh start but that was actually an attempt to reestablish continuity with the high modernism[2] of the early twentieth century, and, on the other, a new vein of generational conflict literature that begins in the 1970s but does not establish itself as the dominant mode until the 1980s.

As readers familiar with postwar West German developments know, our patient at first appears to be comatose. Perhaps what we see are actually the results of a rather heavy dose of sedative. Doctor-prescribed or self-administered? The question has been hotly debated whether the passivity of early postwar West Germany stemmed from psychological repression of memory or from suppression imposed by Allied censorship. But the cultural depression of the immediate postwar phase, known to the writers themselves as the "zero hour,"[3] was not so negative as it is often presented. The occupying Allies not only cut West Germans off from their recent past, they also brought with them the beginning of a whole new way to think about the relationship between writing and the world. By founding a new type of journalism along American lines, the Allies set out to demonstrate that it was important to distinguish between fact and opinion, and that it was vital to hear a variety of opinions about any given set of facts. From now on, news reporting and commentary were to be clearly demarcated. At the same time, Allied censorship of all kinds of writing during the occupation reinforced a sense (already part of the German tradition since Schiller) that writing was significant. These early lessons were of crucial importance for the development of West German literature throughout the whole period to be considered here; indeed, this notion that literature bears profound political and social significance continues to distinguish contemporary West German literature from its counterpart in the United States, where fiction is more commonly seen as a diversion and entertainment. Unless we grasp this crucial distinction, the course of recent West German literature will remain relatively opaque.

In a number of ways the new attempt to reestablish links with the rest of modern Western literature, from which Nazi literature had deliberately isolated itself, meshed well with these two concerns. The new interest in opinion versus fact could readily be translated into the point-of-view techniques that had been developed by writers like Faulkner; the concern for the social impact of literature was able to find models in Hemingway, on the one hand, and Sartre, on the other. Disparate as they are, these three writers became the most important influences on West German literature of the 1950s, which thus presented a complex and quite disunified picture, hovering uneasily between socially concerned realism and twentieth-century modernism. Not having participated in the debates of the exile writers about realism versus modernism, West German writers of the early postoccupation years were not fully aware of the often radical internal contradictions their writings presented.[4] It remained for a later generation to debate all over again, in a new context, the relative merits of these two basic literary techniques.

Thus 1950 and 1951, for example, saw the appearance of such heterogeneous works as Elisabeth Langgässer's *Märkische Argonautenfahrt* (*The Quest*, 1950), an adaptation of the story of the argonauts to postwar Germany, reminiscent in its basic intent of Joyce's novel *Ulysses*; Heinrich Böll's *Wanderer, Kommst Du nach Spa* (*Traveler, If You Come to Spa*, 1950), a realistic depiction of the early postwar years; and Wolfgang Koeppen's *Tauben im Gras* (*Pigeons in the Grass*, 1951), which applies the interior monologue technique to a social analysis of the same period. The sheer variety of different approaches makes it difficult to assign a clear label to this early period of literary development in West Germany.

Most critics are agreed that the early 1950s were a highly unsatisfactory phase. Just as there was no characteristic literary technique in this phase, neither was there an agreed-on analysis of how nazism had come about, who was actually guilty, what this guilt involved, and what its precise implications were for postwar German society. But despite the frustrating slowness of any useful consensus about the Nazi past to emerge, much else was brewing that was to give rise to the first peak to appear on our chart.

RESISTANCE IN RETROSPECT

In 1959 a group of novels that had clearly reached a new level of mastery burst on the scene. Heinrich Böll's *Billard um halb zehn* (*Billiards at Half-Past Nine*), Günter Grass's *Die Blechtrommel* (*The Tin Drum*), and Uwe Johnson's *Mutmaßungen über Jakob* (*Speculations about Jakob*) were the expression of a widespread dissatisfaction about literature in the early 1950s. Profiting from their predecessors in terms of theme and technique, they were able to attack the large questions about the Nazi past with greater energy and more analytic subtlety. At the same time, they continued the two major tenets of the early postwar years: that literature was of necessity political, even when it might not seem to be, and that truth was to be found through an exploration of many different opinions rather than from statement of a single point of view.

These three novels set the stage for a whole spate of works that continued until around 1963. The three writers themselves produced new masterpieces in rapid succession: Grass's *Katz und Maus* (*Cat and*

Mouse, 1961); Johnson's *Das dritte Buch über Achim* (*The Third Book about Achim*, 1961); Böll's *Ansichten eines Clowns* (*The Clown*, 1963); Grass's *Hundejahre* (*Dog Years*, 1963). Others joined in, notably Martin Walser with his novel *Halbzeit* (*Half-Time*, 1960); Peter Weiss with *Abschied von den Eltern* (*The Leave-taking*, 1961) and *Fluchtpunkt* (*Vanishing Point*, 1962); Alfred Andersch, who had made a noteworthy start in 1957 with his novel *Sansibar oder der letzte Grund* (*Zanzibar*), with *Die Rote* (*The Redhead*, 1961); and, somewhat later, Alexander Kluge with *Schlachtbeschreibung* (*The Battle*, 1964) and Wolfgang Hildescheimer, with his fascinating novel *Tynset* (1965). Generally speaking, then, the first peak of our chart occurs between 1959 and 1963.

Almost all these "first peak" novels have three characteristics in common: an interest in perspectivism, an attempt to analyze the "suppression of memory" phenomenon, and a concern for the relationship between the Nazi past and the postwar present. If we look at the three novels that mark the inception of this phase, we find in *Billiards at Half-Past Nine* a Faulknerian multiple point-of-view technique, in *The Tin Drum* an unreliable narrator, and in *Speculations about Jacob* a combination of interior monologue and narration through group discussions. The three authors posit very different theories about the so-called suppression of memory: Böll sees it in terms of individual psychology, Grass in terms of a combination of psychological repression and government-instigated suppression, and Johnson (whose novel focuses on East Germany) in terms of officially promoted suppression. All three, however, are at great pains to explore the phenomenon and to propose theories about its origins. All three, finally, are deeply concerned about the relation of past and present, especially about the possible continuation of Nazi attitudes in contemporary society.

The timing of this new literary activity is, of course, no accident. The new Federal Republic would soon have lasted as long as the Nazi regime: but had it really freed itself from its tainted past? The continued presence of former Nazi Party members in political office was already the subject of open debate. The efficacy of the West German government was under attack: in particular, it was widely claimed that the two-party system that had been set in place by the Allies was not really functioning. By 1961, a number of these issues came to a head in what came to be known as the *Spiegel* affair, when a piece of investigative journalism published in the magazine claimed that the nation's defense system was inadequate and chaotic. In the furor that ensued, the minister for defense, Franz Josef Strauss, was forced to resign, and the *Spiegel* declared itself to be the only true parliamentary opposition in West Germany. This affair gave extraordinary weight to writing as a means of changing society. The gulf between journalists and creative writers diminished as the two began to espouse a common cause.

The *Spiegel* was undoubtedly a major factor in the political and cultural climate of the 1959–63 peak. Indeed, had it not been for the *Spiegel*, with its use of irony, satire, allusion, and insinuation, the reading public in West Germany might have been ill-prepared for the complex works of literature that were now being written.[5] To understand the new novels of 1959 one had to be skilled in two-track reading, looking simultaneously at the surface and at the implied depths. The provocative style of the magazine had educated a readership that could be activated in entirely new ways.

Just as the *Spiegel* saw itself as the opposition party in West Germany, so the writers of the 1959–63 period saw themselves as a kind of opposition force. Insofar as the new literature attempted a new look at the Nazi past, it could thus be described as one of resistance in retrospect. The principal writers of this movement aimed to develop a sense of the possibilities for resistance that could have been deployed during the Nazi era and to inculcate a new spirit of resistance that could be deployed to break the political apathy that had dominated the early Federal Republic.

Günter Grass's *Cat and Mouse* (1961) is perhaps the best example of the new method at work. Narrated by an earnest young man self-righteously but anxiously looking back at his childhood, this novella seems at first glance to tell the story of the author's classmate who foolishly falls prey to Nazi propaganda and ends by committing suicide when he sees the error of his ways. The narrator's obvious hesitancies, his tendency to shy away from certain topics, and his final indirect admission that he is at least partly responsible for his friend's death ultimately lead the reader to a different interpretation, however. We begin to surmise that the apparent Nazi is in fact a covert resister—or, at least, a would-be resister. The story of his involvement with nazism forces us to rethink a whole gamut of different possibilities, from acquiescence and collaboration through collaboration as a front for resistance, to open opposition. Adopting an essentially Brechtian technique, this tale, like much of the other fiction of the 1959–63 period, tries to make its readers imagine what should have been done while enacting in fictional form the sort of thing that actually was done. The Brechtian technique of forcing the audience to invert the action it observes is the hallmark of the basically leftist literature that forms this first peak on our graph.

Despite its adoption of quasi-Brechtian methods, the first peak is mainly characterized by novels. Closely linked with this first peak, however, is a group of dramas, largely motivated by the war crimes trials of

Gestapo official Adolf Eichmann in 1961 and of the Auschwitz concentration camp guards in 1963 to 1965. With the exception of plays like Siegfried Lenz's *Zeit der Schuldlosen/Zeit der Schuldigen* (*Time of the Innocent/Time of the Guilty*, 1961), German-language drama in the period around 1960 was primarily a product of the Swiss writers, of whom Dürrenmatt in particular had worked out his own rather complex response to Brechtian theory. Perhaps it was the reports from the courtroom that led to the new upsurge of drama in the Federal Republic; in any event the young writers now seemed eager to appropriate the form for themselves.

Certainly the news reports from the courtroom led to a move away from Brecht (except for Grass's *Die Plebejer proben den Aufstand*) (*The Plebians Rehearse the Uprising*, 1966) and toward the development of documentary drama. Although one important novel of this period, Alexander Kluge's *The Battle* (1964) experiments with the documentary method, the form is used primarily in the theater. Rolf Hochhuth's *Der Stellvertreter* (*The Deputy*, 1963), Peter Weiss's *Marat/Sade* (1964) and *Die Ermittlung* (*The Investigation*, 1965), and Rolf Schneider's *Prozeß in Nürnberg* (*Trial in Nuremberg*, 1967) are the main examples of the genre.[6] But despite this lack of overt Brechtianism during this subpeak of the mid-1960s, the prime concern of all these dramas is to activate their audiences. By a skillful arrangement of the various documents they draw on, the plays reveal the moral scandal while retaining an apparently flat tone. Left to "speak for itself" in this form, the evidence is particularly forceful, and it is not surprising that these dramas were successful on the international stage as well as in West Germany itself.

AFTER THE STUDENT REVOLUTION

The new movement might well have relapsed into apathy once again had it not been for the student revolution of 1967–68, which gave the impetus for a second major literary peak. Initiated by Siegfried Lenz with his novel *Deutschstunde* (*The German Lesson*, 1968), the second literary peak was a response to a renewed call for resistance to authority in all forms. The war in Vietnam and the spread of American influence were among the immediate causes of the new movement for antiauthoritarianism, but as *The German Lesson* made clear, these enemies were also ways of projecting continuing problems of German society itself onto other objects. The leftist novels of the 1959 phase had suggested what effective resistance to Hitler might have been like; but although they also took care to indicate that resistance was still needed, they had not really been successful in changing public attitudes. The student movement, despite the heavy backlash from conservative quarters, which set in immediately—and despite the fact that it rapidly lost the sympathy of many senior professors and thus split up the traditional intellectual camp—ended by achieving a much more widespread and permanent influence than may at first appear to have been the case.

One of the principal reasons for this influence was the fact that the movement was no longer limited to highbrow publications. On the literary front, it mobilized forces that had been active since the creation of the workers' literary movement Group 61 (named after the year of its founding), and spread right down into children's literature, where its influence on a whole generation was quite profound. Store-front nursery schools; the protests against broadcasts of the American children's TV program *Sesame Street*, and the ultimate insertion of "antiauthoritarian" episodes into the series; the emergence of a generation of permissive parents and schoolteachers—all these were part of a sweeping attempt to remodel West German society entirely. The focus was now very much on the young. If older people continued to practice a kind of psychological "denial" of the Nazi period or at best to engage in lip service about what should have been done to change it, perhaps the attitudes of children and adolescents could be more effectively molded. To achieve this ideal, they would, as Lenz's title clearly implies, have to "learn the lesson of history." Questionnaires revealed, however, that the younger generation knew practically nothing about the Nazi period. A new phase of education would have to begin.

Although 1968 is thus clearly a turning point in German social history, it would be an exaggeration to claim this for German literature. Here literary history and social history, linked though they inevitably are, run somewhat different courses. In essence, the literary peak of 1968 and after was a continuation of the "resistance in retrospect" movement of 1959. Irony, open-endedness, provocation of the reader— in short, the "two-track reading" effects inculcated by the *Spiegel* and supported by the Brechtian theories that dominated the 1959 literary turning point—continued to mark the works spawned by the student revolution of 1968.

Lenz's novel *The German Lesson* was not, technically speaking, a radical departure. Its importance lay primarily in its articulation of the theme suggested by its title: the notion that Germans still had to learn the lesson of history. Lenz's novel raised the question to what extent the past could really shed light on the present and made this relatively complicated issue accessible to a broad range of novel readers. Was there really a lesson to be learned from history? Through the mouth of his young protagonist, interned in a reform school on an island in the River

Elbe, Lenz showed in his novel that the answer is highly complex. Young Siggi is right to oppose his father for continuing Nazi practices (confiscating modernist paintings) long after the Nazis have been defeated, but is it really proper for Siggi to take right into his own hands? By having his juvenile delinquent turn an assigned essay on "The Joys of Duty" into a several-hundred-page novel, Lenz simultaneously questioned the role of writing in the confrontation with the past. To be sure, the idea of writing as a kind of therapy, a means to free oneself of guilt, had already been put into question by Grass in *The Tin Drum* and *Cat and Mouse*. But by introducing an almost caricatured psychologist as one of Siggi's interlocutors, Lenz went even further in his questioning of psychoanalysis and the therapeutic method. Writing, furthermore, imposes its own patterns, as Siggi had earlier discovered when asked to write a school composition on "My Hero." Lenz's next novel, *Das Vorbild* (*An Exemplary Life*, 1973), continued some of these same themes and problems.

The "lesson of history" is the central theme of a number of plays from the student revolution phase, which, although not directly exploring the Nazi past, manifestly comment on it by implication: Peter Weiss's *Vietnam Diskurs* (*Vietnam Discourse*, 1968), Tankred Dorst's *Toller* (also 1968), and Dieter Forte's *Luther/Münzer* (1970).[7] The "lesson of history" is also a major theme in Günter Grass's two novels from the 1968 peak: *Örtlich betäubt* (*Local Anaesthetic*, 1969), which contrasts a schoolboy's planned act of protest against Vietnam (setting fire to a living dog on the streets of Berlin) with an older narrator's recollections of the Nazi past, and *Aus dem Tagebuch einer Schnecke* (*Diary of a Snail*, 1972), in which Grass's own political engagement—his support for Willy Brandt's 1969 election campaign—is played off against a fictive tale about Nazi Germany. One characteristic of both Lenz's and Grass's novels of the turn into the 1970s is the clear emergence of an autobiographical streak. Increasingly, authors around this time seem willing to question themselves and their own moral position.

Perhaps the most significant works of this period are two vast novel projects that question the lesson of history and the value of writing in a quite radical way. Bringing together techniques derived from the first novel peak—perspectivized narration, the problem of fact versus fiction, the relation of present to past—and adapting them to the more openly leftist atmosphere of the 1970s, these projects attempted to survey the whole panoply of issues that had been raised in the reflection of nazism over a decade or more. The first to start appearing was Uwe Johnson's *Jahrestage* (*Anniversaries*, 1970–83) that, by interspersing sections of his protagonist's interior monologues about the past with excerpts from *The*

New York Times, which she reads in the present, makes clear the extent to which even seemingly "objective" newspaper reporting is, in fact, merely a representation of opinions. Here is the beginning of a new turning, described more fully later, in which the journalist has ceased to be the good guy; the newspaper, although constantly referred to as "Auntie Times," is in fact not always a benevolent relative.

The second vast novel project, Peter Weiss's novel *Die Ästhetik des Widerstands* (*The Aesthetics of Resistance*, 1975–81), which clearly bears the imprint of the early 1970s despite the fact that it did not begin to appear until somewhat later, attempts to relativize the great works of art, literature, and philosophy by showing how they become assimilated to the minds of a group of youngsters engaged in the resistance against Hitler. Weiss's novel mimics the form of a theoretical work: the style is that of expository prose rather than fiction, the sentences and paragraphs are long, and intellectual concerns dominate over external events. Unwieldy though it appears, it soon exerts its own peculiar spell on the reader. The fascination is caused largely by the slow but striking process of metamorphosis the great works undergo as they are appropriated by the boys, hungry for guidance in their self-education toward resistance. Underneath the apparent status of the classical works they study and discuss together, models of resistance reveal themselves, brought to life by the boys' creative imaginations.

Works we had thought familiar reveal unsuspected aspects, and with the young resisters we find new impulses and new intensities of engagement in them. In many ways *The Aesthetics of Resistance* is a panoramic exemplar of the two-track reading method initiated by the novels of 1959, recast in a more explicitly neo-Marxist mode.[8] The student revolution and the protests against Vietnam clearly underlie Weiss's ambitious novel sequence, just as the new tendency to personalization led him to describe it as the autobiography he wished he had. But Weiss's novel is by no means an exercise in wishful thinking. Like the great German novels of the 1959 phase, *The Aesthetics of Resistance* is a highly effective polemic: an attempt to show, in the most forceful intellectual terms, what the resistance should have been. Forced to project imaginatively into the young protagonist and his friends, the reader reconstructs a possible mode of resistance to nazism while undergoing a thorough education in neo-Marxist theory. It is a striking appeal to the contemporary intellect with its fascination for theories and its interest in the relation between art and ideology.

In many ways more typical of the whole turn into the 1970s, however, is Heinrich Böll's novel *Die verlorene Ehre der Katharina Blum* (*The Lost Honor of Katharina Blum*, 1974). In contrast to the broad canvas of his

Gruppenbild mit Dame (*Group Portrait with Lady*, 1971), the more compact *Katharina Blum* may at first appear less significant. Instead of looking at the past through a large cast of characters, as he had done in *Group Portrait*, Böll turns his attention to the present and focuses on a restricted set of figures. Yet in its exploration of repressive mechanisms which he saw still at work in contemporary West German society, *Katharina Blum* also comments on the relation between the postwar state and its claims to have broken completely with the controlling practices of the Nazi dictatorship.

This story of a solitary and puritanical young woman who aids a terrorist and kills a newspaperman almost against her will was widely read when it appeared and further popularized by being made into a film,[9] but it has never been thoroughly examined in the critical literature. On the surface, the novel attacks the sensationalist press, in particular the tabloid *Bild*, with its distortions of reality and its invasions of privacy. Many readers understood it at the time merely as Böll's revenge against the Springer press for its invasions of his own privacy as he began to take the side of the young Marxist revolutionaries and to propose a sympathetic explanation of the rise of terrorism in West German society. But there is another level to *Katharina Blum* that has been little examined: the insinuating voice of the narrator, who insists that he will just tell us the facts but who recognizes from the outset that in dredging them up he is also, in some sense, silting up his narrative system. Where have we heard this insinuating voice before, these ironic allusions, these parenthetical insertions, these mocking aspirations cast in a tone of justified moral outrage? In the *Spiegel*, of course. Böll does a wonderful job in imitating the well-known style. But our unease with this narrator calls the whole method into question. The *Spiegel* has become no longer the only justified, "good" opposition to the status quo; it has become merely another questionable voice among many. Here, even more markedly than in Johnson's *Anniversaries*, novelists and journalists have begun to part company. The spell of the *Spiegel* affair has finally been broken.

THE NOSTALGIA WAVE AND THE GENERATIONAL CONFLICT

But the "lesson of history" novels that peaked around 1970 were accompanied by at least two other significant movements: the "nostalgia wave" and the generational conflict mode. German literature of the early 1970s is one of those cases in which periodization of the simplified kind begins to break down. Indeed, for German postwar literature it is in many ways less important when a work was written than when its author was born. Generational differences account in large measure for the three-way split that characterizes the 1970s. The student revolution had dramatized these differences and made it clear that people who had lived through the Third Reich as adults, people who had been children during that period, and people who were born during or after the war had fundamentally different perspectives both on the Nazi past and on the social problems of the present.

As people who had grown up during the Third Reich reached middle age, they became increasingly disturbed by the need to cast a veil over their childhoods as if they had never happened. A new effort to reclaim personal memories of the Nazi period set in. At the vanguard of this moment was Walter Kempowski with his *Tadellöser & Wolff* series (1971–75), which soon began to be shown in a television adaptation. While educational children's television of the same period was trying to show young people the hard facts about nazism and provoke questions about resistance, middle-aged adults were being kept spellbound by the nostalgic evocation of their youth as a time of social and family security. With a sort of bittersweet smile, Kempowski's narrator depicts the closeness and comfort of life during the 1930s, even though he also clearly knows that it is not proper to portray the Nazi period in a positive light. The title of one of the novels, *Uns geht es noch gold* (*We're Still Doing Fine*), indicates the slightly apologetic tone in which the series is cast.

Hermann Lenz's semiautobiographical novel *Neue Zeit* (*New Times*, 1975) is a little more careful to employ a note of mild irony when describing the young protagonist; but this ironic surface is relatively thin. Horst Bienek's series of personalized novels about Upper Silesia (1975–82) also belongs in certain ways to this group: personal experience is openly evoked, the protagonists are seen as more sinned against than sinning, and emotional identification is called for rather than the thinking through of complex moral and political issues.

Is this attempt to recapture personal memories and reclaim individual dignity synonymous with what was called the New Subjectivism? Despite their emphasis on a return to the self of actual experience and the domain of private life, the novels of this movement, which extends more or less throughout the 1970s, are very different from the lyric poetry whose simultaneous upsurge caused journalists and literary critics to invent the new name. The poetry of the New Subjectivism was written primarily by erstwhile student revolutionaries who were disappointed with the fading of the protest movement after the early part of the decade. These poets were basically on the political Left, and although they spoke tenderly of home life, it was communal apartments with provisional furniture, old cigarette butts, and dried-out tea bags that formed the backdrop of their rather languid, almost prosaic verses. Their nostalgia was for the 1968–71 period—the high point of the student demonstrations, the group excitement, and the marches. Novelists of the Kempowski school were politically more to the right; their nostalgia was for orderliness and security; and they wanted to reclaim what they saw as the good parts of their childhood, which they hoped could be separated from the curse that had been cast over the 1930s as a whole. By and large they were of an older generation than the poets, most of whom had not been born until the war years. Although the critics tended to castigate both groups equally, it is important to distinguish between the leftist poets and the more conservative novelists in the new trend towards subjectivism.

Partially overlapping and ultimately succeeding the older novelists who were attempting to reclaim their childhoods was a group of novelists drawn from various age groups who were becoming spokesmen for the younger generation. At the turn into the 1980s, Germans born after the war were beginning to confront, with very mixed emotions, the idea that their parents may have been involved in criminal actions during the Third Reich. Could guilt really be inherited, and, if so, were the heirs obliged to accept this unwanted burden? The novelists who now began to articulate these questions range from Alfred Andersch, born in 1914, to Peter Schneider, born in 1940. In contrast to the novels of the "nostalgia wave," the novels of generational conflict are less frequently an account of the author's personal experience than imaginative projections into the mind of someone whose parents were Nazis.

Peter Schneider's brilliant story *Vati* (*Daddy*, 1986) marks a high point in this movement. The narrator, a successful Freiburg lawyer, recounts his painful encounter with a father he has known only through letters, photographs, and the stories told about him by other relatives. A former member of the S.S., the father (a character modeled on the Nazi doctor Josef Mengele) has fled to South America to escape trial for his Nazi crimes; only the closest family members know his whereabouts. The son's confrontation with his father unleashes complex thoughts and emotions that can only partially be accommodated in the narrative— thoughts that the reader, who is specifically addressed at the beginning and the end, is not even expected to understand or believe. When the narrator travels to South America a second time to visit his father's grave, he fully accepts the possibility that readers may think that he is merely inventing the story of his father's death as a deceitful maneuver intended to help the old man remain in hiding. The narrator finds himself in an ambiguous position. Unlike the novels of the "nostalgia wave," this tale not only expects our empathy, but also requires us to retain a certain distance.

In a similar vein, Alfred Andersch's story *Der Vater eines Mörders* (*The Father of a Murderer*, 1980) recounts a Greek lesson inspected by the high school principal, who happens to be the father of Heinrich Himmler. The narrative revolves around the conflict between the older Himmler and his son, humanism and nazism, Karl May and Greek grammar. The complex continuities between the terms of these seeming dichotomies are dramatized in the narrator's final discovery that, dry as they may seem, the facts of Greek grammar have memorably poetic names. The uneasy shifts of this story—what side does the narrator take in the conflict between Himmler senior and junior?—are characteristic of a tendency to raise new, more complex, and less easily answered questions about the older and younger generations and their response to nazism. Other literature in this mode includes Hartling's *Felix Güttmann* (1985), an attempt to reconstruct the life of a kind of adoptive grandfather to the narrator who was also a Jew who had to emigrate from Nazi Germany; and Gert Hofmann's *Veilchenfeld* (1986), which uses the story of Hansel and Gretel to allegorize the relationship between the guilty father and the abandoned children. The German attempt to work through the past is cast in these texts as a search for the father, a search that inevitably ends in ambiguity and frustration.[10] Although I have named examples mainly from the 1980s, it should not be forgotten that the generational conflict mode reaches back into the 1970s; indeed, *Deutschstunde* (*The German Lesson*), that paradigmatic novel of 1968, is one of the earliest explorations of this problem.

Despite the extensive overlaps among the three main movements of the 1970s and 1980s—the last phases of "resistance in retrospect," the "nostalgia wave," and the generational conflict genre—two events mark important caesuras in this period. The first was the broadcast of the American television series "Holocaust" in 1979; the second was the historians' debate of 1986.

THE "HOLOCAUST" BROADCAST

Did "Holocaust" dramatically change the German reflections on the Nazi past? Certainly the series, viewed by unusual numbers, unleashed extraordinarily emotional reactions. A quarter-million viewers requested the additional documentary material offered by the government; thousands of telephone calls were made to the television stations in response to the broadcast. Sophisticated critics were astonished that "black and white, realism and totally un-Brechtian empathy"[11] had moved a German audience to unheard-of reflections on their Nazi past.

These overwhelming reactions took even the Germans themselves by surprise. What Fest's documentary and Syberberg's modernist Hitler films had failed to do, "Holocaust" achieved: widespread response, considerable discussion, and—despite everything—an astonishing agreement about its significance. No one could deny that this program was the most banal of kitsch, but neither could anyone deny that he or she had been moved. It is no mystery why this program succeeded in affecting a broad public where more ambitious films and the prize-winning novels of 1959 and after had not. The nostalgia wave had already shown that Germans were crying out for realism and for a chance to empathize with what they read in books or saw on stage or screen. But realism and empathy with those who had shared the Nazi perspective—even when, as in the case of Kempowski and his followers, the empathy was only for selected, possibly salvageable portions of that experience—was not something with which the Germans could be entirely comfortable. But here at last was permissible realism and empathy, since the audience was asked to identify with the Jewish victims of nazism. Pity and fear, adapted for an audience more used to soap opera than to classical tragedy, had the desired cathartic effects: many of the people who called the television stations were openly weeping. Tired of the highly cerebral, two-track mode of the 1959 and 1968 "resistance in retrospect" fictions, the public turned with relief to a film that let them empathize with the victims of nazism and understand for the first time something of the suffering that Hitler's "final solution" had caused.

The showing of the "Holocaust" film in West Germany not only mobilized a new and widespread response to the Nazi past, but also gave rise to a number of films that put contemporary Germany into the international limelight and involved a broad section of the German public in more sophisticated reflections on the Nazi past.[12] To a large extent, these films can be said to have taken over a task previously performed by literature. Ranging from Alexander Kluge's "The Patriot" (1979) through Helma Sanders-Brahm's "Germany, Pale Mother" (1980) to Edgar Reitz's television series "Heimat" ("Homeland") (1984), the new German films displayed considerable technical variation from modernist innovation to conventional realism. Despite these formal differences, however, they were all conceived in opposition to Hollywood models, in certain cases quite specifically as attempts to counter "Holocaust." Kluge's "The Patriot," for example, although begun in 1977 and clearly related to Kluge's experiments with montage effects in the novel, developed into an explicit response to the American television series. In its demand for complex and intellectually sophisticated viewing techniques, it was certainly the equivalent of the great innovative novels of the 1959–63 phase.

Edgar Reitz's "Heimat," by contrast, returned to straightforward realism while nonetheless presenting an image of recent German history radically different from that portrayed in "Holocaust." Set in the Hunsrück area, its emphasis is on regionalism and everyday life. Except in certain episodes, nazism tends to be viewed as peripheral to the real events and concerns of people's lives. Although there has been some debate among critics about whether this marginalization of nazism may have been critical in intent, there can be no doubt that the vast majority of the viewing public saw the film as an affectionate tribute to a particular landscape and a particular way of life. Nostalgia is certainly an important element in the series, linking it with Kempowski's *Tadellöser & Wolff* novels of over a decade before (televised in 1974 and 1975, the Kempowski sequence was also a highly popular cultural event). Yet despite these very evident shortcomings, "Heimat" made a broad segment of the German public see themselves as part of history and reflect, however inadequately, on the relation between present and past.

In contrast to the film wave of the late 1970s and early 1980s, the publications during this period by the great novelists of 1959 and 1968 were more the coda of an old than the beginning of a new phase: there were Günter Grass's *Der Butt* (*The Flounder*) in 1977 and *Kopfgeburten* (*Head Births*) in 1980, Siegfried Lenz's *Exerzierplatz* (*Exercise Yard*) and Heinrich Böll's posthumous *Frauen vor Flußlandschaft* (*Women against River Landscape*) in 1985, and Grass's *Die Rättin* (*The She-Rat*) in 1986. But the immediate appearance of an ingenious parody of *The She-Rat* titled *The Grass* by one "Günter Ratte" suggests that the public was less inclined to take this kind of writing seriously than it had fifteen or twenty years before. It is presumably significant that the blockbuster novels of the Grass-Böll era have been superseded by the slighter forms of novella and short story, but what this new trend may indicate can only be surmised. Certainly the younger writers no longer have any pretension to present a complete account of what happened during the Nazi era.

THE HISTORIANS' DEBATE

Has the Nazi past been exorcised? Have the West Germans become less politically passive? Has the lesson of history been learned? There are many indications in modern German society to suggest that these aims of literature in the 1960s and 1970s have still not fully been realized.

Social problems that seemed at first quite unrelated—the emergence of feminism, the difficulties of integrating foreign workers—gradually revealed themselves as issues of majority and minorities, periphery and center, that might have been viewed very differently had the Nazi past been more completely debated in the early years of the Federal Republic. Nonetheless, the West German state is clearly no longer inclined to regard itself as a convalescent in need of therapy. The patient is up and around, well enough, indeed, to be even at times a little mean and snappish (to its foreign workers, for example).

This historians' debate,[13] a heated scholarly exchange over the extent to which Nazi Germany could be regarded as a unique historical development, was the first hint that this new phase might merely be a temporary remission. From the point of view of literary history, to be sure, the historians' debate seemed remarkably belated. These questions had all been dealt with, on a fictional level, by the major writers of 1959 and 1968. But the reemergence of the controversy on a more abstract and theoretical level once again seemed to prove the impotence of sophisticated fiction to change the way people think. Once again, as in the case of the "Holocaust" television series, the assumptions of the 1960s and 1970s that sophisticated literature could provide a powerful impulse for ideological change were to prove misguided. This time it was not the broader public but the academics who needed to think basic issues through once again. What "Holocaust" had done for the masses, the historians' debate did for the academy.

The implications of this most recent development for literature may at first seem rather bleak. Is literature powerless to do what it seems expressly designed for: to change fundamentally the way people think and feel? It would be distressing for those of us concerned with literary studies if this were the conclusion that had to be drawn from postwar German literature. I hope, however, that this conclusion is premature. In evaluating the effects of literary production, we must take into account an almost inevitable lag between literature and reflection on literature. The great authors of 1959, Grass and Böll, were not at first fully understood; by the same token, it is too early yet to see what the fiction of the 1980s really portends.

More important, however, it may be time to break with the illness metaphor entirely. The Nazi past has had profound and continuing psychological ramifications, but it is not a pathology that can somehow be cured once and for all. It is, rather, a historical event that needs to be analyzed from a new angle of vision by each succeeding generation. In articulating at one and the same time resentment over the burden of the past and shock at confronting it once again, as does the narrator of Peter Schneider's *Vati*, the new German literature of the 1980s may be part of a transition towards a new, more historical understanding of the Third Reich.[14] It is doubtless salutary that the old aim of "mastering" the past is gradually coming to seem more questionable, a desire to erase history rather than to analyze it.

NOTES

1. It is more important to understand what was meant by Alexander and Margarete Mitscherlich in their book *Die Unfähigkeit zu trauen* (1967) (*The Inability to Mourn*, 1975). What the Germans were unable to mourn was not—as Walter Hinderer claimed in the discussion at the conference at the Woodrow Wilson Center in Washington, D.C., on which this volume is based—the loss of the führer, but their own complicity in the Holocaust. For a sensitive treatment of this problem, see Andreas Huyssen, *After the Great Divide* (Bloomington: Indiana University Press, 1986), 97–99.
2. For a detailed account of the modernism debate, see Eugene Lunn, *Marxism and Modernism: A Historical Study of Lukacs, Brecht, Benjamin and Adorno* (Berkeley: University of California Press, 1982), chapter 3, 75–90.
3. On the "zero hour" see Peter Demetz, *Postwar German Literature: A Critical Introduction* (New York: Pegasus, 1970), 46–52; and *After the Fires: Recent Writing in the Germanies, Austria and Switzerland* (San Diego: Harcourt, Brace, Jovanovich, 1986), 1–17.
4. Hildegard Emmel, *History of the German Novel* (Detroit: Wayne State University Press, 1984), points out some of these contradictions in her chapter 8, especially p. 320.
5. Günter Grass directly engages with the *Spiegel* in his *Cat and Mouse*; see Judith Ryan, *The Uncompleted Past: Postwar German Novels and the Third Reich* (Detroit: Wayne State University Press, 1983), 95–111.
6. Hamida Bosmajian gives an extended analysis of *The Investigation* and *The Deputy* in *Metaphors of Evil: Contemporary German Literature and the Shadow of Nazism* (Iowa City: University of Iowa Press, 1979), 147–82.
7. Treating the different genres separately, as Demetz did in his first book on this topic, *Postwar German Literature*, and as does Lowell A. Bangerter in his more sketchy *German Writing Since 1945: A Critical Survey* (New York: Continuum, 1988), does not really work because in terms of literary history and social impact the genres are not hermetically sealed off from each other. Significantly, in *After the Fires*, Demetz no longer separates the genres, although he does note in his postscript that "the most remarkable genre of the 1950s was poetry, that of the 1960s drama, and that of the 1970s and 1980s the prose narrative" (p. 391).
8. On *The Aesthetics of Resistance*, see Huyssen, *After the Great Divide*, 115–38.
9. Film is a topic that cannot really be excluded from any detailed account of postwar German literary developments. The reader is referred to Anton Kaes's *From Hitler to Heimat: The Return of History as Film* (Cambridge, Mass.: Harvard University Press, 1989), which gives a fine description of the attempts by West German film members to deal with the Nazi past.
10. I am indebted to Paul Michael Lützeler for his contributions to the discussion at the conference and for a number of valuable suggestions concerning this phase of postwar West German literature.
11. Demetz, *After the Fires*, 29.
12. Kaes, *From Hitler to Heimat*, gives a close analysis of five of the most important West German films that treat this problem: *The Patriot; The Marriage of Maria Braun; Germany, Pale Mother; Hitler: A Film from Germany*; and *Heimat*.

13. On the historians' debate, see Charles Maier, *The Unmasterable Past: History, Holocaust and German National Identity* (Cambridge, Mass.: Harvard University Press, 1988).
14. In the historians' debate, the term *historicize* came to be used primarily in connection with those who claimed that the Holocaust was not a unique event in history. I do not use the word in this narrow sense.

10

Postoccupation Literary Movements and Developments in Japan

Van C. Gessel

Japanese fiction after the occupation is in many ways an extension as well as a rethinking of the two major types of writing that dominated prewar composition—specifically, the works by the socially and ideologically committed proletarian authors (*Puroretaria bungaku sakka*) and the predominantly asocial, semiautobiographical personal narratives (the infamous *shi-shōsetsu*). There was little cross-pollenization between these two rival factions; the proletarian writers considered the *shi-shōsetsu* writers to be needlessly parochial, overweeningly narcissistic, and dangerously removed from the political and social concerns that were already tearing apart the fabric of experimental democracy in the Taishō period (1911–26). For their part, the creators of autobiographical fiction, with some justification, looked upon the leftist writers as novice artists who were sincere enough in their convictions but inadequately trained in literary technique to be able to present their social messages in anything other than an embarrassing framework.

The polarization between committed social activism and equally sincere artistic purism carries over into the postwar era. The past forty years or so of Japanese literary developments can be described in terms of the constant interplay between the reconstituted versions of these two camps. The postwar Marxist writers represent what might be styled the "social trend" in postwar literature. These are authors who initially highlighted the moral horrors of the war that had just ended and then went on to define a positive path of involvement for the writer in the creation of a new Japanese society. They came to the task of writing with a vision of the potential for social change through imaginative art. These writers, known in Japanese literary jargon as the *Sengoha* (après-guerre faction) were displaced for a time—significantly just as the occupation ends, around 1952—by young writers who were clearly cut off from social and intellectual activism, and who represent what might be called the "private" trend in Japanese fiction. These writers, the first wave of whom are labeled the *Daisan no shinjin* (the third generation of new writers), produced a literature of anxious tension: a placid, well-constructed, modernized surface undercut by a negative vision of internal collapse and despair. As writers, they functioned outside the borders of society, restoring Japanese artists to their traditional relationship with the majority; in their withdrawal, they also returned to—although later I suggest ways in which they simultaneously made significant modifications in—the autobiographical mode of writing.

Even though the third generation of new writers is loosely fashioned here as a group, it is important to observe that literary groupism in Japan—which, in one form or another, was one of its most consistent features in the classical and medieval periods and a mainstay in the development of modern literature from the 1880s through the occupation years—had largely collapsed as a governing influence in the creation and discussion of literature by the early 1950s. The *Sengoha*, the Marxist writers who made their debut shortly after the defeat in 1945 with their own literary journal, *Kindai bungaku (Modern Literature)*, established and maintained a mutually consistent set of literary goals for themselves, however they may have interpreted and modified those goals individually.[1]

In the third generation, however—the writers who were brought together essentially at random less than a year after the end of the Allied occupation—the sense of unity, shared purpose, and even shared intellectual experience that had characterized the *Sengoha* was gone. Just as their writings began to call into question the spiritual and emotional foundations of the resurgent Japanese social system, their lack of cohesion as a literary group echoed the anxiety they felt just at the time their nation began the march toward economic domination in Asia.

The question of how the war and the defeat were reflected and interpreted in Japanese fiction of the postwar period becomes a complex one, then, because the initial response to those devastating incidents came almost immediately (*Kindai bungaku* published its first issue in January 1946) from the *Sengoha* writers, primarily men in their thirties who had a tantalizing brush with leftist philosophy and existentialism before they were eradicated from Japan by ideological censorship of the 1930s. The war had come between the *Sengoha* and their moral idealism, but the interruption had been temporary, and once the shackles on free speech were removed with the coming of the occupation, they swiftly and easily turned back to their intellectual roots and wrote literary critiques of the war in an attempt to point out the error of militarism and the hope that awaited Japan through a socialist revolution. The first interpretation of the war that was offered to the postwar Japanese reading public was one filled with revulsion for the immediate past, but one necessarily dripping with mea culpa toward the question of war responsibility: although the Japanese readily embraced the belief that they had been too easily duped by militarist propaganda, they resisted grappling with the larger questions of national guilt. But that initial interpretation was also filled with anticipation for the political phoenix that could be resurrected from the ashes of defeat.

THE EARLY POSTWAR SETTING

It is important to recall, however, that this message of optimism was being broadcast to a nation that was largely in ruins. By the time the war ended, more than 3 million Japanese had been killed, almost a third of the population had lost their homes, and industry was operating at one-quarter its previous level of productivity. There were 5.5 million soldiers to be demobilized and another 3.25 million civilians to be repatriated from abroad. And it was no simple matter for Japan to cope psychologically with the first defeat and foreign occupation that their nation had experienced in recorded history. It is understandable that the Japanese populace did not immediately rise to its feet to respond to the call to Marxist revolution: there were so many people too weary and underfed to have the energy to get to their feet, either figuratively or literally.

It is similarly necessary to factor in the style with which General MacArthur administered the occupation: the imperial manner in which he forced democratic reforms on the Japanese government had a certain appeal for the Japanese. MacArthur easily fit into the mold of surrogate rulers who governed in the name of the emperor (the occupation planners wisely decided to keep Hirohito in place to provide legitimacy for their reforms), and the general's popularity in Japan reached such a peak that there was widespread shock and mourning when he was dismissed by Truman. Finally, by 1950 the policies of the occupation had considerably improved the overall quality of life in Japan; hence the extra economic punch provided by the outbreak of war in Korea that summer proved to be mere icing on the cake. It must have seemed to many in the early 1950s that the goals of the Marxist writers were being reached, not through proletarian revolution but through the firm but benign administrative orders that emerged from MacArthur's GHQ.

Because the Japanese occupation was carried out under American direction and thus avoided the carving out of zones of influence that divided Germany, a mood of quiet optimism was evident among the people. When the occupation formally ended in 1952, many in Japan could easily have felt that they had emerged the better for what had transpired over the past seven years. The financial shot-in-the-arm provided by the Korean War, along with the occupational institutions put into place, set the stage for what would be the beginnings of the Japanese "economic miracle" by the late 1960s.

THE EARLY POSTOCCUPATION LITERATURE

It would be natural, then, to expect that the literature that appeared in the wake of the occupation would capture this mood of exhilaration, or at least of hope. But we are accustomed to finding that literature betrays such facile expectations, and the Japanese case is no exception. Most of the writers who began their literary careers at just about the time the occupation troops were withdrawing and the economy was starting to build up steam were young men who had been born a few years on either side of 1920. Few of them had been old enough to absorb Marxist or any alternative philosophical response to the growing militarism of their country, and many had been plucked out of college to serve in the war effort before they had developed any solid concepts of selfhood. In essence, they gave their youth to the war. Almost without exception, those who returned from the battlefield to become the writers known in the 1950s as the third generation of new writers went through utterly bizarre experiences in the war.

Kojima Nobuo (born in 1917), for instance, received his teaching credentials to become an instructor of the English language just six months before Pearl Harbor. When the bombs fell on Honolulu, English became a proscribed subject in Japan, and Kojima fell victim to the draft. He was shipped off to northern China, where his commanding officer ordered him to forget every word of English he had ever learned. In the spring of 1944, however, he was transferred to Beijing to decode transmissions intercepted from American units in the Pacific; when it became evident that Japan would be defeated, Kojima's new commanding officer ordered him to remember all his English, so he could teach his superiors useful English phrases such as "I am not a war criminal." Meanwhile, Kojima's original unit was shipped off to the Philippines, where every single man was killed in the fighting at Leyte.

Kojima's experience was by no means extreme for his age; Shimao Toshio (1917–86), another writer who is sometimes linked with the third generation, was made commander of a suicide torpedo boat squadron stationed on an island north of Okinawa. He spent almost a year there, training under cover of darkness for his mission of death. But that entire year consisted of nothing more taxing than the simple act of waiting. Orders to prepare for launch finally came—on 14 August 1945. The men donned their battle gear, armed their torpedoes, and waited for the final order to launch. That order, of course, never came and Shimao was charged with the duty of reporting to his men that the imperial broadcast, which none of them heard, had ordered unconditional surrender rather than a fight to the death. It comes as no surprise that the engines of war continue to race beneath the surface of Shimao's fiction, whether he is writing about his kamikaze experience or about his wife's going insane after the war.

Armed (or disarmed) with such experiences of war, the new writers of the 1950s could only feel bewildered about the meaning of the war, uncertain about the import of the occupation, and decidedly unconvinced about the desirability of bowing down to the newfound gods of capitalism, democracy, or communism. One writer from this generation, Yoshiyuki Junnosuke, has written about the hesitance that he and his contemporaries felt toward all the new ideas that were being bandied about in Japan:

> The [*Sengoha*] writers spent their youth in league with communism, but mine was spent very differently. As a result, my concerns are unlike theirs. During the war, I couldn't bring myself to sacrifice my life for the sake of any single philosophy, even if its ideals might be realized at some point in the future. Many willingly made that sacrifice, but the very thought repelled me. The idea of becoming a sacrifice gave me no pleasure. I considered myself an "individualist"—not an egotist, certainly, but something more refined. In those days, the word "individualist" was considered equivalent to "traitor," but I bravely used it to describe myself anyway. . . .
>
> Communism enjoyed a great wave of popularity shortly after the war. . . . But the innate resistance I felt toward that philosophy was the same resistance I had felt toward the militarism of the war years. I could not bear the thought of putting on another uniform when I had just taken off the previous one and thereby liberated my individuality. Neither did I care for the thought of martyring myself for the sake of some ideal that might possibly be realized in some distant future.[2]

Because of the ambivalence born of their experience and the mistrust they felt toward any new direction Japan might take, a gulf opened between these writers and their society. The nation embarked on an aggressive, single-minded pursuit of economic expansion; but the authors whose careers commenced contemporaneously with the period of growth were "plagued by an inability to act purposively.... For them, the postwar period—which should have been an age of liberation—was instead a time to which they were ill-suited.... They could not believe in the outer world, in lofty, absolute philosophies, or even in the pull of their own emotions."[3]

THE IRONIC SHI-SHŌSETSU

The literary form that was appropriated by this third generation of postwar writers was, understandably enough, the comfortable, experientially centered *shi-shōsetsu* (the autobiographical "I"-novel). But there is a significant difference in the perspective that they bring to a recounting of their private lives. Partly because of the absurdity of their wartime experiences, partly because of their philosophical naïveté, and thanks also to their perception of the gap of incongruity that was opening up between themselves and their society, the third-generation writers brought to the *shi-shōsetsu* a vital element that it had been lacking in the prewar period: irony. So while the popular media journals began extolling Japan as a nation efficiently rebuilding in the wake of war, the fiction in the literary magazines turned to describing the process of destruction that was perceived to be taking place within the genteel walls of middle-class civilization. The immediate benefit for literature is that the narrating persona of fiction has become schizophrenic: he or she can relate personal experience with the same degree of sincerity and rhetorical flourish as the prewar writers, but a narrational doppelgänger lurks somewhere in the text, functioning as a second set of eyes to view events from a separate perspective, or as a mocking voice uttering contradictory opinions from between the lines of the discourse. It is no coincidence that *Sukyandaru* (*Scandal*, 1986; translated 1988), the most recent novel by Endō Shūsaku (born 1923), a leading member of the third generation, has as its central subject the question of split personality, of evil doppelgängers who mockingly challenge the sincerity of people who are striving to live a moral life.

This ironic, split narrational perspective is most obvious in the novella *Kaihen no kōkei* (*A View by the Sea*, 1959; translated 1984), by Yasuoka Shōtarō (born 1920). The narrator is a young man whose father has returned from the war with no skills and apparently no desire to provide a livelihood for his fractured family. This pathetic man's wife is finally driven to insanity and death by the bleak circumstances of postwar Japan (and, more specifically, by her son's willful destruction of the bond that links him to her). Through the eyes of the accusing son who blames his father for all this collapse, we see a portrait of a failed patriarch who can no longer guide and sustain his family. But even as we are given that view, Yasuoka subtly provides us with another perspective on this family, and we are able to discern the faint outlines of a father who has struggled desperately to find means to feed an unappreciative wife and son, and who nurses his wife with the utmost solicitude and tenderness once she has passed beyond the boundaries of sanity. The voice of the son in the text condemns the emotionally crippled father, but a second voice beneath the surface of the narrative implicates every member of the family for the severing of the ties that once held them together.

Another novel that makes use of an architectural metaphor to bring the internal collapse of postoccupation Japan into ironic focus is Kojima Nobuo's *Hōyō kazoku* (*Embracing Family*, 1966). The work centers on a physical structure—a house that belongs to the Miwa family. The husband, Shunsuke, is a scholar steeped in the ways of Western civilization, and on the surface he appears to have all the enlightened knowledge he needs to govern his life. But as a human being, he is very much like his trouble-plagued house. That structure is the dominant image throughout the novel; in fact, although one prominent Japanese critic has described *Embracing Family* as the most "anthropocentric" Japanese novel of the modern period,[4] I am inclined to argue that the house is the true protagonist of the work, and that it has taken over as the central "consciousness" because Shunsuke has, in his "enlightened" way, abrogated his responsibilities as master.

The main action of the novel involves several attempts by Shunsuke to rebuild the family house, always at the instigation of his wife, Tokiko. Equal weight is given to the act of "housecleaning." But, tellingly, all the energies of this family are focused on the external concerns of building and cleaning, while inside their whited sepulchre there is an extraordinary amount of moral decay. Shunsuke, caught up in lecturing on contemporary Western family mores and building a house that is described as resembling "a country villa in the highlands of California" (even though it ends up a creaking nightmare of leaking roofs and malfunctioning "foreign" appliances), is not even aware of the fact that his wife has been having an affair with an American marine who remained in Japan after the occupation. Even after the housekeeper tells him of the affair, he does not know how to respond. "What should he say? What should he do? The answers to these questions had not appeared in any book he had read, and no one had ever taught them to him."[5]

The ironic chasm that Kojima gouges into this text suggests an extreme reticence on the part of the narrator. Shunsuke, as in the quotation, is perpetually asking the crucial questions; but Kojima's narrator stubbornly refuses to provide any answers. This third-person narrator essentially mocks Shunsuke's inability to make moral judgments; as a result readers find him ridiculous, frustrating, and pathetic. At the same time, Kojima forces us to fill in ourselves the answers to the questions that Shunsuke poses, or to declare the novel morally vacuous. And observing our struggles alongside Shunsuke's stands the house, solid on the outside but crumbling within.

THE THIRD GENERATION'S INTERPRETATIONS OF THE WAR

The interpretations of the war afforded by the authors of the third generation are naturally far more cynical and personalized than those of the *Sengoha*. If the prototypical *Sengoha* treatment of the war—say, Noma Hiroshi's *Shinkū chitai* (*Zone of Emptiness*, 1951)—had as its aim "to analyze the responsibility of the intellectual and the revolutionary . . . to depict the Japanese people as a whole during the war,"[6] the standard third-generation novel about the same war made no claims to universalization of experience. The soldiers of their war novels are confused, isolated individuals whose response to the call to arms is neither political nor intellectual; it is, in fact, difficult even to call it "emotional." The reaction is essentially physiological, with chronic diarrhea appearing as a recurrent motif.

The ambivalence of these unwilling warriors can be seen in Kojima's writings, especially in the short story "Hoshi" ("Stars," 1954; translated 1984) and the novel *Bohimei* (*Epitaph*, 1960). The protagonist in both these works is a Japanese-American who has the misfortune of being in Japan when the war breaks out and ends up being drafted to serve in the Japanese army. Perhaps the most effective literary moment in the two works comes at the very end of *Epitaph*: the soldier Tomio (Tom), who looks very much like an American, is sent with his battalion to fight in the Philippines. There, his commander dresses him up in an American uniform and sends him out as a decoy to lure enemy soldiers into ambushes. Tom naturally has mixed feelings about engaging in this bizarre activity and being exploited in this way (much the same way, in fact, that Kojima's English-language talents were exploited by his military superiors). After it becomes evident that the Japanese resistance has failed, the battalion is dispersed and Tom wanders alone through the jungle. He strips off the American uniform, then removes his Japanese uniform. He stops short when he sees a rifle pointed at him from the undergrowth. He cannot see whether the hands holding the weapon belong to an American or a Japanese, and at this stage he is not sure which to consider as enemy and which as ally. He shouts, "Don't shoot! I'm not Japanese! And I'm not American, either!" Then he reaches up to rip off his uniform, but finds himself naked, left with only the noncommittal skin he was born with. That scene epitomizes much of the confusion and anxiety that beset a generation of Japanese during the war, and represents the postwar response to that experience.

OTHER RESPONSES TO THE WAR EXPERIENCE

Let us turn now from the private, visceral reactions to the war experience evident in the writings of the third generation to two other categories of response: (1) the eulogistic and chroniclelike attempts to capture certain key moments of the war and (2) the abstract Marxist-influenced philosophical fiction of the *Sengoha* group mentioned earlier. The categories are less distinct than this breakdown implies, however, because even when works in the first category deal with major battle incidents, such as the sinking of the great warship *Yamato*, they tend to be either very personal records of loss, as in Yoshida Mitsuru's *Senkan Yamato no saigo* (*Requiem for Battleship Yamato*, 1952; translated 1985),[7] or detailed, sensitive portraits of military figures as important for their private doubts about the war as for their heroism. The prime examples of this latter category are the three lengthy, moving biographies of admirals written by Agawa Hiroyuki (who is sometimes classed with the third generation), *Yamamoto Isoroku* (1969; translated as *The Reluctant Admiral* in 1979), *Yonai Mitsumasa* (1978), and the highly acclaimed *Inoue Seibi* (1986).

The most important pieces of war literature in the second category include Noma Hiroshi's *Zone of Emptiness* and many works by Ōoka Shōhei (1909–87), a student of French poetry and fiction who was drafted to fight in the Philippines and spent nearly a year in an American prisoner-of-war camp. His literary recreation of that experience, *Furyoki* (*A Prisoner's Story*, 1948), is a work of remarkable philosophical detachment. But his most harrowing portrait of the war is in the novel *Nobi* (*Fires on the Plain*, 1952; translated 1969), an unsparing portrait of the manner in which war destroys the last vestiges of individual humanity. Like Kojima's *Epitaph*, this novel deals with a solitary soldier who wanders the jungles of the Philippines at the end of the conflict, but his withdrawal from the human race as a result of his experience is so extreme that he decides he can only unite himself with his fellowmen once again by participating in an act of cannibalism, which is described in imagery that links it to the Catholic communion. Ōoka suggests, in a literary transformation of his war experience that makes considerable demands on the Japanese reader,[8] that it would require some extraordinary spiritual transmutation to reintegrate a soldier into peacetime society, but the horrifying form that this metamorphosis assumes drives his protagonist mad, and he writes his war reminiscences from an insane asylum.

THE QUESTION OF WAR GUILT

Few of the works in any of the three categories of war writings from the postwar perspective treat Japanese war atrocities, either to deny or defend them or to reflect on their meaning. In fact, the bulk of the war literature with which I am familiar has precious little to do with the confrontation between Japanese and non-Japanese within the framework of war. The great majority of writings deal with the internal conflicts, whether they be among members of the same battalion or within an individual. That tendency, of course, can to some extent be attributed to the long-standing tradition in Japanese prose to focus tightly on the narrow, introspective moment and the individual confessions, but in isolation from their social contexts.

I do not wish to suggest here that Japanese writers have avoided the question of war guilt. Rather, I do not see much consideration of national culpability; instead, there is considerable retrospection about individual responsibility. In fact, I believe that the intellectual responses to war that emerged from the Marxist *Sengoha* writings are something of a cultural aberration, whereas the gut-level, personalized, and even trivialized reactions from the third generation are more in keeping with the traditions of Japanese literature—and, more important, in keeping with the rhetorical potentialities and limitations of the language—in the twentieth century.

THE RETREAT FROM MARXISM IN POSTOCCUPATION JAPANESE LITERATURE

It is, then, somewhat ironic that Marxist criticism has dominated the postwar discussions of the war while the literature itself has focused primarily on private responses to that event. Some of the chief tensions within the Japanese literary establishment have arisen from the disproportionate influence that Marxist critics have exercised in the literary journals. As Donald Keene notes,

Postwar literary critics were largely Marxists, and they tended to exaggerate the importance of writers of their own persuasion. One is likely therefore to obtain the impression that left-wing writers were much more significant at this time than any of the older generation. . . . In general the literary world of the immediate postwar period, and even much later, was sympathetic to left-wing causes. This was partly because of the opprobrium attached to the right wing, partly by way of reaction to the popularity of the American way of life among ordinary, nonintellectual Japanese. The *Asahi shimbun* (the newspaper most widely read by intellectuals), the government-owned radio and television stations, the leading intellectual magazines—all, to a greater or lesser degree, espoused left-wing causes.[9]

It is a simple matter to identify writers and intellectuals of the past forty years who have been sincerely sympathetic for left-wing causes. It is far more difficult, however, to isolate those who have not become disillusioned with the extraordinary factionalism of the progressive political parties in Japan, or who have sought some philosophy other than dialectical materialism to guide their thinking after an initial flirtation with Marxism. As I noted earlier, virtually all the writers of the *Sengoha* generation were proclaimed Marxists when they began their literary careers. A number, including Noma Hiroshi and Abe Kōbō, became members of the Communist Party. One must struggle, however, to find a writer who has not been expelled at least once from the party, while many others withdrew either formally or informally. Most were also closely in sympathy with the wave of existential philosophy that was sweeping the postwar world. Yet within a decade or so, many of these young activists had cooled toward leftist philosophy, and some of the more important of them began looking for some way to reintegrate themselves into their Japanese spiritual heritage through a study of Buddhism, or into the revitalized Western tradition through conversion to Christianity.

Initially, the jarring and tearing and soul-crunching of their war experience had put them on the offensive, turning them against native tradition in all its forms and placing into their hands convenient, foreign weapons of intellectual battle at a time when it seemed likely that the Japanese past had been obliterated. Once the occupation had run its course, however, and Japan appeared to have put its pieces back together again, many of these writers searched for some means to plug themselves back into a tradition that had proved strong enough to survive all the blasts of war. Noma Hiroshi, whose earliest postwar stories, including "Kao no naka no akai tsuki" (Red Moon in Her Face, 1947; translated 1962), argue that the war and defeat had made it impossible to form satisfying relationships with any other human being, by 1960 was absorbed in the writing of a novel, *Waga tō wa soko ni tatsu* (*There My Pagoda Will Stand*), which he described as an attempt to "accurately analyze the Buddhism which even now lives and throbs deep within the hearts of Japanese." Without that study, he maintained, "I would be unable to understand most Japanese or to obtain a clear insight into what controls their actions."[10] And Shiina Rinzō (1911–73), a Communist as well as the most Sartre-like writer in Japan in the late 1940s, converted to Christianity at the end of 1950.

The same process can be seen in the second generation of leftist writers, most prominently represented by Ōe Kenzaburō (born 1935). Ōe's political and social commitment is evident in works such as "Sebuntiin" ("Seventeen," 1961) and the documentary essay collection *Hiroshima nōto* (*Hiroshima Notes*, 1964; translated 1981). Disappointed by petty factional conflicts both in the leftist political movement and the Hiroshima peace movement, Ōe in 1964 abandoned the overt political methodology of his earlier writings after his first child was born with significant brain damage. In his novel *Kojin-teki na taiken* (*A Personal Matter*, 1964; translated 1969), Ōe adopted the autobiographical mode of fiction and transformed it into a medium of social and moral drama. In virtually all Ōe's fiction since that time, he presents the very private image of a deformed baby, born with a brain tumor that makes him look as though he has two heads. But Ōe's staunch social commitment will not allow him to let the image remain a personal, autobiographical one. It is as though he sees an image of the Hiroshima mushroom cloud superimposed over the grotesque tumor on his baby's head, and his child is transformed into an innocent victim, whose torment Ōe has described in the following words: "Could any conscious state be so full of fright and hurt as perceiving pain and not its cause, and perceiving pain only, because an idiot infant's murky brain was apparently to go unsoothed?"[11] The child, unaware of the sources of its own agony, can only open its mouth and form the shapes of a silent cry (one of the images in Ōe's 1967 novel, *Man'en gannen no futtobōru*, translated in 1974 as *The Silent Cry*).

In the cavern of that wordless moan echo the tormented voices of those who suffered and perished at Hiroshima, and in his own original way Ōe is presenting his readers with a moral choice. We have the memory of Hiroshima placed before us, in the same way that the baby's father has to confront his deformed infant. Do we embrace that memory and accept responsibility for our guilt, as the father does in Ōe's *A*

Personal Matter, or do we attempt to obliterate the memory altogether, as the father does in "Sora no kaibutsu Aguii" ("Aghwee the Sky Monster," 1964; translated 1977) by conspiring with the doctors to kill his baby?

By equating the personal and the social and making our choice one of global life or death, Ōe breathes a new and profound significance into the I-novel. In his best writing, Ōe can be movingly intimate and personal in the stories that derive from his own experience, and at the same time publicly and politically forceful in delineating the implications that his private experience has for all of us in the wake of the A-bomb. Here again, for the Japanese writer at least, Marxism appears to have limited value as a literary tool until it is transmuted through personal experience that renders it palpable in the Japanese context.

THE VIETNAM WAR

I can only briefly treat the manner in which the Vietnam War makes its appearance in Japanese literature, and that view will be oblique. The most important artistic treatments of that war, which certainly aroused important debate and controversy in Japanese intellectual circles,[12] may come not from the mainland but from the writings of Okinawan novelists who debuted in the late 1960s. The Akutagawa Prize, the most important new-author award in Japan, was first given to an Okinawan author in 1967: the recipient was Ōshiro Tatsuhiro, whose short story "Kakuteru pāti" ("Cocktail Party," translated 1989) examines the frustrating relations between Okinawans and the American troops stationed there. A second Okinawan author, Higashi Mineo, received the prize in 1971 for "Okinawa no shōnen" ("A Boy from Okinawa," translated 1989), which concerns a young boy who decides to steal a boat and leave Okinawa for the open sea when he can no longer stand being evicted from his bedroom so that the neighborhood prostitutes (for whom his parents pimp) can service American soldiers. Neither story overtly protests the Vietnam War, but both are sensitive depictions of the way in which the American military presence in Japan, of mounting strategic importance to the U.S. effort in Southeast Asia, erodes the moral fabric of the community and renders life on Okinawa unbearable for some.

REVIVAL OF THE CLASSICAL LITERARY TRADITION

Another key feature of postwar literature in Japan is the manner in which the classical heritage has been resuscitated and perpetuated through the efforts of some of the finest writers of the century. Here again, there was some initial speculation after the war that perhaps the defeat and occupation had been sufficiently traumatic to sever all ties with classical culture. One prominent critic of the 1950s, Kuwabara Takeo, wrote, "I do not think much effort should be spent maintaining traditions that have been transmitted without any relation to modernization. The beauties of old Japan that early foreign residents admired will gradually disappear."[13] Although it may be foolhardy to try to give full credit to one person for turning the tide and reestablishing a link with traditional literature, it is tempting to single out Tanizaki Jun'ichirō (1886–1965) for that distinction, and to select his long novel, *Sasameyuki* (*The Makioka Sisters*, 1942–48; translated 1957), as the crucial work in that process of revitalization.

What Tanizaki achieves in *The Makioka Sisters* is a denunciation of the very concept of history by forging a link between postwar literature and the aesthetic heritage that stretches back a thousand years to *The Tale of Genji*. The points of convergence between Tanizaki's novel and the *Genji* have almost nothing to do with plot; it is rather in the sense of time, the perception of the seasons, the centrality of aesthetic values, and the importance of annual observances as a measure of who the family is and how they get along that these two works are joined. And it should be borne in mind that Tanizaki began work on *The Makioka Sisters* shortly after he completed his own translation of *Genji* into modern Japanese, a labor of love in which he engaged three times in his career (twice after the war).

The subsumption of literary tradition in the postwar period can be divided into three large categories. First are the modern translations of classical works by prominent authors. Included here are Tanizaki's *Genji* and another significant version of that tale by the leading woman writer of the postwar age, Enchi Fumiko (1905–86). A score of other major novelists have produced their own modern translations of the classical text that reverberates most persuasively for them; some examples are Yoshiyuki Junnosuke's renditions of Ihara Saikaku's seventeenth-century erotic masterpieces, *Kōshoku ichidai otoko* (*The Life of an Amorous Man*) and *Kōshoku ichidai onna* (*The Life of an Amorous Woman*).

A second category includes modern, often cynical, adaptations of traditional works, including Mishima Yukio's modern Nō plays, Dazai Osamu's retelling of Saikaku's stories about the merchant class, and the reshaping of traditional myths by Ōe Kenzaburō, Nakagami Kenji, and others.

Third are the independent creative works that clearly owe a measure of their inspiration to specific classical works, but go far beyond the bounds of simple retelling or adaptation. Tanizaki's *Makioka Sisters* belongs to this category, as does the informal trilogy of novels by Enchi

Fumiko, which demonstrates a clear indebtedness to *Genji*. Her *Onnazaka* (*The Waiting Years*, 1957; translated 1971) adopts the male-centered power structure that lies at the heart of *Genji* and examines the ways in which the perpetuation of such a structure in the modern period affects her female protagonist. *Onnamen* (*Masks*, 1958; translated 1983) explores the vengeful spirits of wronged women and the ways in which they have their revenge. And *Namamiko monogatari* (*Tale of a False Shamaness*, 1965) is itself set in the tenth-century court of Heian, recreating an idyllic love relationship between the emperor and his chief consort, but surrounding that pure association with so many layers of falsehood, betrayal, and political manipulation that it becomes clear that Enchi believes such tales can no longer exist in our contemporary, cynical age.

The "new subjectivism" that became the hallmark of Western fiction in the late 1970s actually developed somewhat earlier in Japan, when a second-phase reaction against the sociopolitical concerns of such writers as Ōe and Kaikō Takeshi produced what has been labeled a "generation of introverts" (Naikō no sedai), writers who once again, in the manner of the third generation, strip politics and ideology from literature and restore focus to the home, the workplace, and the individual leading a life of "quiet desperation" in various complex social institutions. These authors, virtually none of whose work has been translated into English at this point,[14] include Furui Yoshikichi, Abe Akira, Kuroi Senji, and Sakagami Hiroshi. Like their direct predecessor from the third generation, Shōno Junzō, the "introverts" focus on the apparently placid surface of everyday life, while hinting at a gnawing pit widening its circumference beneath. Thus, in their reaction against the overt social consciousness of Ōe's generation, these writers calmly depict the solidity of society's structures, while simultaneously, and with great subtlety, probing the hollowness that lies at the core. Abe Akira's "Hibi no tomo" ("Friends," 1970; translated 1985) is a prime example of this: "friendships" among co-workers at a television station are described as healthy, normal, and perhaps a bit distant, but the best one can expect with the hectic pace of contemporary life. Yet as the story unfolds, it becomes evident that these relationships are worse than fragile; they cannot keep several from the brink of madness or even suicide. Even though I emphasize the return to the elements of everyday life in the "introvert" generation, however, it is important to note that these writers demonstrate a more mature sense of outrage, a more indignant belief that alternatives are possible, than can be discerned from the fiction of the third generation.

I want to mention also the existence of an intriguing new subgenre in Japanese fiction that may well be a reaction against the ineffectual activism of the late 1970s. Several prominent writers in recent years have composed novels of "secession," of small communities on the fringes of Japan that quite literally declare their independence from the mother country and launch out on their own. The implicit social criticism is obvious, but the humor and linguistic playfulness introduced into these works suggest that something of a new direction is being carved out here. I have in mind such works as Ōe's *Dōjidai gēmu* (*Contemporary Games*, 1980), Inoue Hisashi's *Kirikirijin* (*The People of Kirikiri*, 1981), and Abe Kōbō's bleak *Hakobune Sakuramaru* (*The Ark Sakura*, 1984; translated 1988). One might even expand the collection with Kurahashi Yumiko's *Amanonkoku ōkanki* (*A Record of Intercourse with the State of Amanon*, 1986), which creates fantasy kingdoms of men and women after the nuclear holocaust.

CONCLUSION

Most of the writers who clung to classical tradition as their means to endure the postwar trauma are now dead, whereas most of the writers associated with the *Sengoha* and the third generation now jostle with one another for positions of leadership in the closed literary establishment of Japan. And yet a moralistic Catholic writer such as Endō Shūsaku is now studying Buddhism and Jung and writing about sadomasochism (as a metaphor for unredeemable evil) in an attempt to cope with war atrocities, while some of those who seemed to be the most staunchly humanistic, even materialistic, critics and writers are, in their later years, being baptized as Christians. The legacy of ideological conversion from the prewar years survives. It is this unpredictability within the confines of convention that makes the Japanese literary scene fascinating to observe.

NOTES

1. For a description of the literary and social goals of the *Sengoha*, see Donald Keene, *Dawn to the West: Japanese Literature in the Modern Era/Fiction* (New York: Holt, Rinehart & Winston, 1984), 970–71.
2. Yoshiyuki Junnosuke, *Watakushi no bungaku hōrō* (Tokyo: Kōdansha, Kōdansha Bunko, 1976), 26–27.
3. Hattori Tatsu, *Warera ni totte bi wa sonzai suru ka*, compiled by Yasuoka Shōtarō, Endō Shūsaku, and Muramatsu Takeshi (Tokyo: Shimbisha, 1968), 348–49, 364.
4. Etō Jun, *Seijuku to sōshitsu: "Haha" no hōkai* (Tokyo: Kawade Shobō Shinsha, Kawade Bungei Sensho, 1975), 125.
5. Kojima Nobuo, *Hōyō kazoku*, in *Kojima Nobuo zenshū*, 6 vols. (Tokyo: Kōdansha, 1971), 3: 12–13.
6. Keene, *Dawn to the West*, 980.

7. Yoshida's *Requiem* has a complicated publishing history, involving two instances of censorship by officials of the Civil Censorship Detachment of the American occupation. That history is detailed in Yoshida, *Requiem for Battleship Yamato*, translated by Richard H. Minear (Seattle: University of Washington Press, 1985), xxxix–xlii. See also the citations of articles by Etō Jun on the censorship.
8. "The status of Christianity in Japan is remarkably similar to that of Marxism. Both have been taken up to a certain extent, particularly among intellectuals, but most people find it difficult to relate to either one. Both are held at arm's length by the establishment." See *Japanese Religion: A Survey by the Agency for Cultural Affairs* (Tokyo: Kōdansha International, Ltd., 1972), 72–73.
9. Keene, *Dawn to the West*, 999 and 1005.
10. Quoted in Keene, *Dawn to the West*, 983–84.
11. Ōe Kenzaburō, *Teach Us to Outgrow Our Madness*, translated by John Nathan (New York: Grove Press, 1977).
12. In November 1965, for instance, Kaikō Takeshi, an important writer who worked in Vietnam as a war correspondent for several years, spearheaded a protest that culminated in a full-page anti–Vietnam War statement published in *The New York Times*.
13. Kuwabara Takeo, "Tradition versus Modernization," in *Japan and Western Civilization: Essays in Comparative Culture*, translated by Kano Tsutomu and Patricia Murray (Tokyo: University of Tokyo Press, 1983), 62.
14. There is a translation of Abe Akira's "Friends" ("Hibi no Tomo") in the second volume of *The Shōwa Anthology: Modern Japanese Short Stories*, edited by Van C. Gessel and Tomone Matsumoto, 2 vols. (Tokyo: Kōdansha International, Ltd., 1985). Howard Hibbett's anthology, *Contemporary Japanese Literature* (New York: Knopf, 1977), contains a short story by Furui Yoshikichi.

V

THE CRITIC AND CRITICAL INSTITUTIONS IN THE POSTWAR ERA

11

Opening and Closing the Past in Postwar German Literature: Time, Guilt, Memory, and the Critics

Dagmar Barnouw

Before we start exploring the different ways in which the question of an "uncompleted past" has been posed in West German literature, and the critical responses elicited by these texts, we have to consider briefly certain important features of fictional discourse. The fictional mode, in contrast to, for instance, the historiographical mode, is responsible for a text-world that is less grounded in the situations of the life-world, even if it clearly refers to them. It therefore draws attention to the constructed character of cultural reality. Statements of truth have a different status in fiction, which is therefore a nonassertive model and which grants the author a degree of interpretative choice in relation to a life-world shared, to a degree, with the reader. Fictional discourse, too, gives the reader considerably more freedom in negotiating the connection between text-world and life-world than a historiographical text does; by its nature fictional discourse is relational and pluralistic, and therefore multivalent.

In the case of literary texts that deal explicitly with the question of the recent past, a question both central and repressed in West German culture, such interpretative elasticity on the part of the author and of the reader is checked in certain important ways. The text's context as a complex of cultural issues asserts itself as a complex of references, including values—in this case, the cultural experience of temporality, guilt, and memory. The author who is responsible for constituting and mapping the text-world must be prepared for the direct questioning of this experience—outside, that is, of the protective boundaries of the text-world. The author must also be self-consciously focused on conceptual strategies that control important narrative decisions to which the reader responds. The cultural historian who asks postwar German literature about its treatment of the cultural issue of the recent past has to keep in mind both that the literary medium is epistemologically distinct from other kinds of discourse *and* that its status as fictional discourse has to be reconsidered if certain kinds of thematic questions are put to it. This situation becomes even more complicated with the issue of critical reception, that is, the question of the critic's mediating activity. For this reason, I have restricted to two authors my investigation of the critical mediation between literary texts that deal with the cultural meaning of the recent past and West German reading audiences. I chose Wolfgang Koeppen and Ernst Jünger because they are on opposite ends of a spectrum of possible understandings of that meaning which have resulted in either opening—and keeping open—or closing the past.

KOEPPEN AND HIS CRITICS

Between 1951 and 1954, Wolfgang Koeppen published three novels that forcefully insisted on the importance of cultural witnessing and anamnesis, the undoing of forgetting. These novels immediately established him as one of the most noteworthy postwar novelists—in spite of many critics' reservations regarding his singleminded preoccupation with the themes of time, guilt, and memory and his decidedly modernist narrative intentions and strategies, which emphasized both the importance of contingency and responsibility in human affairs. He has not published another novel since. In a short 1959 autobiographical sketch,[1] he stated that he had started writing again after the war at his publisher's prompting: "Then I, too, asked myself what I have been waiting for all these years and why I had been a witness and stayed alive." In the late 1950s and early 1960s he published several travel books; since then he has worked on an autobiographical novel, parts of which were published in journals and in the much acclaimed 1976 volume of short prose texts, *Jugend* (*Youth*).

Koeppen's relatively small output since the mid-1950s, and above all the fact that he wrote no more novels, has been regarded by critics as an "event of silence," which they have interpreted and evaluated in a variety of ways. Peter Demetz in his 1970 *Postwar German Literature* sees Koeppen in self-imposed exile from his contemporary reality. Reinhard Baumgart, too, holds this view, if more ambiguously so because he explicitly admires Koeppen's qualities as a writer and emphasizes the importance of the travel books. In his 1986 essay "Nachkrieg und Postrevolte" ("Postwar and Post-revolt"), Baumgart limits the full pathos of the German catastrophe and of the missed opportunities for a new beginning as an important topic for literary texts more or less to the immediate postwar years.[2] In his most recent overview of German-language literature, the 1986 *After the Fires,* Demetz links Koeppen's falling silent for so many years to his being "exhausted by these explosive novels." Referring to *Youth* as a "tense and exhilarating volume of memories," he also rightly notes that it was "welcomed by nearly everybody as a sign that more important novels were perhaps waiting for publication"—a sentiment which he seems to share.[3]

When Koeppen won the Büchner Prize in 1962, Walter Jens in his *laudatio* ranked him as perhaps the greatest prose writer in postwar Germany and praised him as a perceptive, sophisticated verbal gourmet of sounds, tastes, smells, shapes, and shadows of the past in the present.[4] Helmut Heissenbüttel, in a 1968 *Merkur* essay, "Wolfgang Koeppen—Kommentar," proclaimed him at the frontiers of language, wrestling, in Wittgensteinian fashion, with that which cannot be (fully) articulated, the complexities of the self, the real reality.

None of these critics seems to have been concerned about the relatively slight impact on the general German reading audience of an undoubtedly talented writer dealing with undoubtedly important questions. In contrast, Marcel Reich-Ranicki, in reviews published first in *Die Zeit* and *Der Monat* in the 1960s and republished repeatedly in different collective volumes, characterized Koeppen as enchanted by the riches and complications of experience, but profoundly discouraged by a lack of adequate response to his novelistic explorations of what he thought central to postwar German culture, namely the unfinished past.[5]

Now the editor of Koeppen's works in six volumes, Reich-Ranicki has consistently emphasized the cultural value of Koeppen's passionate and level-headed critique of a German sociopolitical reality. Writing about the Auschwitz trial, which took place in Frankfurt from 1963 to 1965, Reich-Ranicki mentions Koeppen as one of the few writers who would be able to deal with such an experience meaningfully.[6] And in his 1976 review of *Youth,* "Wahrheit weil Dichtung" ("Truth because Fiction"), he praised the small volume of prose fragments as an important cultural event: thoroughly poetic and thoroughly concrete, he said, these texts constitute the clearest possible answer to all questions about the use and uses of literature. He quoted—and accepted—Koeppen's description of all his work as "the experiment of a monologue against the world," arguing that in its passionate and precise eloquence it has turned out to be a monologue *for* the world, which Koeppen experienced too richly to withdraw from it. As always, Reich-Ranicki accused the general German reading audience (and German book-dealers) of being insensitive to the unique achievement of Koeppen's work, which, for Reich-Ranicki, signifies its clearly accessible political dimension.[7]

All these reactions are arguable, though Reich-Ranicki's seems the most useful and perceptive with regard to the complex potential of Koeppen's texts. They do, of course, reflect the critics' priorities of interest and involvement that might change over time. But on the whole there has been little change through the decades in the critics' views of Koeppen's importance as a writer. The question is, then, why has this critical esteem never translated into larger numbers of readers, even during periods of general cultural interest in the significance of the uncompleted past for the present?

Some critics have changed their minds about the timeliness of Koeppen's novels. Hans Schwab-Felisch, in a 1952 essay in *Der Monat*, attacked *Tauben im Gras* (*Pigeons in the Grass*, 1951) for its inexorable pessimism, which in his view lacked "substantial greatness." Fourteen years later Schwab-Felisch published a revision of his judgment in the same journal, explaining that he had come to understand Koeppen's need to show what he perceived as the dark, threatening aspects of German postwar society. The elaborately structured narrative strategies (calling up both the patterns of the great tradition, the myths of the past, and the confused dailiness of the present), the use of collage, and of juxtaposition and confrontation, now seemed to Schwab-Felisch to be a successful attempt to direct the reader's experience of apprehension and shock.[8]

In the mid-1960s, Koeppen's disruptive insistence on anamnesis appeared to this and other critics as less disturbingly singleminded and more appropriate in view of German and international cultural developments. It was a period of increasing interest, especially among the young, in opening up the past, which, in their view, had been stored away by their fathers like dangerous waste—a period that was promptly followed by the privatization of the generational conflict in the children's *Väterbücher* (books about fathers) of the 1970s.[9] Schwab-Felisch's articulated change in critical response, although quite rare and admirable in its honesty, reflects, too, the elusive power of the "spirit of the times," that most tantalizing challenge to the cultural historian. By the mid–1960s, it had become acceptable, even in vogue, to emphasize the political role and function of literary texts that included important questions about the uncompleted past.

KOEPPEN'S DYSTOPIAN NOVELS

Even a substantial change in attitude did not mean that a majority of professional and general readers would now be able to respond more thoughtfully to the posing of such questions in literary texts. Schwab-Felisch's second review of *Pigeons in the Grass* essentially neglects the political dimension of the novel: that is, it focuses too much on a general modern loss of intersubjective contact, communication, and meaning. Pointing to the compelling reflection of the restless and uncanny aspects of our world, Schwab-Felisch declared that the novel's pessimism is not shallow, as he had thought before, but rooted in its author's profound, inexorable sadness. Significant, too, was Schwab-Felisch's choice of a quote from the novel for the conclusion of his argument, a sentence that speaks of the world as perhaps "a cruel stupid divine accident" and links the scattering of birds to human motion through time and space. Consequently, Schwab-Felisch now sees the "stark beauty" and the "darkness" of the novel in the poetic power of Koeppen's deeply melancholic uncertainty. But this interpretation constitutes yet another misleading and incomplete reading of the text—which may be both characteristic of readers' responses and responsible for their absence. Koeppen has indeed been preoccupied with the frightening centrality of accident in human affairs. He has, however, advanced this view in political rather than existential terms, and he has stressed the dangers inherent in forgetting the cultural meanings of contingency. Such a warning does not signify a tolerance for chaos and randomness in the sociopolitical sphere; moreover, it emphasizes the importance for this sphere of the connection between the present and the past.

The statement about the world as a cruel divine accident—very much in tune with postwar existentialism—is a sentence in a novel. It has been filtered through a fictional temperament and context and thus presents rather than re-presents a particular view of human affairs, and it represents one perspective among others on the Munich of 1951. The city is still the setting for deeply ambiguous pantomines of power-relations between the German "have-nots" and the American "haves," driven by the oral desires born of emptiness and anxiety: cigarettes, liquor, chocolate, coffee. Need in its most naked black-market form is already a memory, but one that is right underneath the surface of the present, not yet transfigured: a level of memory easily accessible to the characters acting in the now of the text-world.

All three novels employ an explicit interplay between an immediate postwar past and present, and it is repeated in the relationship between the time of the novel and the time of its contemporary reader: *Tauben im Gras* (*Pigeons in the Grass*), published in the summer of 1951, analyzes one day in Munich in the early spring of 1951; *Das Treibhaus* (*The Hothouse*), published in the fall of 1953, describes two days and two nights in Bonn in the spring of 1953; *Der Tod in Rom* (*Death in Rome*), published in the fall of 1954, takes the reader through two and a half days in May of 1954. This relationship between different strata of time and memory serves as a focusing structure for the act of anamnesis. In the preface to the second edition of *Pigeons in the Grass* (1956), Koeppen explains his intention to show the anarchy and chaos of the immediate postwar years as the "Urgrund unseres Heute" (the source and basis for our today), the restorative, affirmative 1950s. But looking back in 1990, "today" could be the acquiescent early 1960s, the disruptive, questioning late 1960s and early 1970s, or finally the *Tendenzwende* (the political and cultural turn toward conservatism) connecting the 1970s and the 1980s. A growing cultural tolerance for economic corruption and inequality, for sociopolitical ruthlessness and forgetfulness, is traced back to missed opportunities for German renewal after the end of the fires of war and persecution.

"Undoing the forgetting" of these difficult years might contribute to changing what Koeppen sees as the savage cultural-political shortsightedness in West Germany. But quite clearly, in the texture of his three novels and later texts like *Youth*, the need for anamnesis is rooted at greater temporal depth, in a period both more remote from the reader's present and more entangled with it, the past reality of war and persecution. When Fritz Raddatz remarks that Koeppen, having returned from Holland to Nazi Germany in order to be a witness, "did not write one line about the period of his witnessing," he neglects to consider this orchestration of temporal connections.[10] Koeppen's disturbingly acute critique of postwar developments in West Germany had its point of reference in Hitler who, repressed or domesticated, has remained with us.[11]

None of Koeppen's characters is able to use this insight constructively. They are either stunted or destroyed by it. In *Pigeons in the Grass*, Philipp, a writer and observer like his author, remains helplessly caught up in the confusions of his present that he cannot really relate to the past.[12] The results are silence and noise: he cannot find a language in which he could tell others what he sees and in which he could clarify his perceptions for himself; nor can the sons of *Death in Rome* in their too easily aborted confrontation with their fathers, who either murdered or condoned murder. Terrified by the past, the sons reject it so totally as to do themselves harm, without helping their fathers who seem still untouched by the meanings of their past acts. Committing suicide, the politician Keentenheuve in *The Hothouse* withdraws into the ultimate silence, desperately intent on escaping from the corruption and complications of the politics of rearmament.

The search for a connecting language, a shared system of reference, is both the subtext to *Pigeons in the Grass* and the author's comment on the characters' despair of meaning. Men and women in their social relations and actions appear like pigeons in the grass; if there are patterns they do not reveal their meaning. The young American soldier Richard is struck by the fact that he cannot fathom the people he meets in Munich. They appear to him in some inexplicable way distorted, caught in a sick lack of balance between hustling and inertia. The reader sees the confusion with the outsider's eyes, but he also sees the inside through Philipp, the author's own witness. His perspective is contrasted with that of the "great" poet Edwin, a combination of Thomas Mann and T. S. Eliot. Celebrating European *Geist* (spirit) as the future of freedom, Edwin is successful, dignified, and futile. He quotes Gertrude Stein—"Pigeons on the grass alas"—and dismisses her and other mere *Zivilisationsgeister* (lacking in cultural profundity) with their emphasis on man's accidentality, that is, lack of connection with a divine origin and meaningful order in which Edwin believes. Every pigeon knows its home in the hands of God, he declares, while his audience has gone to sleep.

Koeppen is not like Edwin; he *is* in some important ways close to Philipp, who shares Edwin's futility; to Keetenheuve, who is too imaginatively apprehensive to be a credible politician; to the young composer Siegfried Pfaffrath, son of the fellow traveler Friedrich Wilhelm and nephew of the murderous S.S. general Judejahn, who decides to respond to the beauties of the world rather than go on being hurt by the challenge to remember. In his 1962 acceptance speech for the Büchner Prize, Koeppen spoke of the writer as involved in the struggle against misused power, violence, the coercions of mass culture—a struggle that would naturally make him an outsider. All art is responsible to society, but society can defeat the artist: Koeppen, born in 1906, sees his generation of writers as the truly defeated, the lost generation that has suffered too intensely through too many speechless years. Yet, admitting these doubts and reservations, he insists on the enduring importance of the artist's sociopolitical role and function.[13] "Who but the writer should play the role of Cassandra in our society?" he had asked in a 1961 interview, and in 1971 he referred to his books as manifestoes against war and oppression: "As a human being I feel powerless; not so as a writer." But on this occasion he also spoke of the difficulties of "communicating" the disturbing implications of a West German postwar reality in a period of rapid technological development and mass communication: "In the ocean of unheard-of events author and reader are drowned. The writer has to seek his own truth, the reality of his perception, to hope against reason that he might make his readers see."[14]

Koeppen may have succeeded in making his readers see, but he has not reached many of them, though from his first postwar novel on, he has found a comparatively large number of sympathetic reviewers—even from the conservative camp[15]—among them respected highbrow journalists, academics, and fellow writers of primary texts. Almost all of them more or less assumed that his novels would have difficulties with educated general readers. Rudolf Kraemer-Badoni gave his perceptive 1952 review of *Pigeons in the Grass* the title "They Will Cry 'Crucify Him!'"[16]—both for the novel's relentlessly critical attitude toward the shiny illusions of a German *Wiedergeburt* or *Restauration* and for its consistently modernist narrative strategies.

In actuality, "they" neglected rather than crucified him. *Pigeons in the Grass* had two editions and sold 6,500 copies when it came out in 1951—a figure that, given the circumstances of that time and the fact that Koeppen was an unknown author, was not all that low. However, paperback editions in 1956 and 1966 did not do much better. When the novel was included in the highly successful *Bibliothek Suhrkamp* in 1974, at a time of heightened sensitivity to the issue of cultural anamnesis regarding the "uncompleted past," it did not sell more than 5,000 copies, though it was acclaimed as Koeppen's most considerable achievement and one of the most important postwar novels. In contrast, Koeppen's first travel book on Russia (1958), *Nach Russland und anderswohin. Empfindsame Reisen* (*To Russia and Somewhere Else: Sentimental Journeys*), went through four editions and sold 16,000 copies in a short time. The 1953 novel *The Hothouse*, thought to be a *roman à clef* about the world of Bonn, expectedly did better, selling 12,000 copies; but the 1954 *Death in Rome*, which dealt most explicitly with the problem of cultural memory and generational conflict, sold only 6,000.[17]

CULTURE, HISTORY, AND POETRY: THE WRITER AS CASSANDRA

What, then, have been the reasons for Koeppen's enduring position as an outsider that he himself, despite his unambiguous affirmation of the social responsibility of the writer, seems to have accepted as a given on a personal and general cultural level? In the 1976 *Youth,* a sensuous, lucid evocation of the spaces of youth and their meaning for the child born out of wedlock in Pomeranian Greifswald in 1906, his sharp-sighted melancholy and the grown-ups' quiet despair dominate all relationships. He senses his grandmother's hopelessness, "a deadly growth feeding on the sight of me, for it was my birth she saw as the last and final seal pressed on the decline of the kin."[18]

Koeppen has extended such traumatic experience of decline to his generation of writers with implications of the writer's status as social outsider who sees things too clearly for his reader's comfort. Remembrance in *Youth* seems to add urgency to the difficulties of that position, which has been most sharply defined in the postwar situation with its profoundly ruptured cultural tradition (*Zivilisationsbruch*). And the claims on the reader to engage, with the author's help, in the disturbing reflections on time, guilt, and memory are therefore particularly pressing.[19]

What is the role of critics in this situation? What is the meaning of their mediation between culturally significant, if highly demanding texts, and what Dr. Johnson called "the common reader"? By temperament and background some critics will be more sensitive than others to the questions posed by these texts. Is that degree of sensitivity significantly influenced by a persuasive power of the literary texts themselves? Or is the general cultural climate, the "spirit of the times," more important for the formation of a critic's position? How much influence does such a cultural trend have on the relationship between critic and text—that is, on the reading of the text by the critic in his presentation to a general reading audience that is also following that trend?

Then there is the added complication that a periodically greater frequency of literary texts dealing with the "uncompleted past" reflects not only shifts in the general cultural attitude—to which some of these texts may have contributed—but also, and increasingly so, publishers' marketing decisions regarding such shifts. Will the critic, confronted with a larger number of such texts, be more sensitive to the degree of thoughtfulness with which a difficult, if timely topic, is treated?

This brings us to the most important question underlying any inquiry of this kind: how to account—in the attempt at evaluating critical reception of complex, demanding, literary texts according to their thematic focus—for the individual critic's more or less developed literary sensitivity to precisely that multivalent tension created by language usage as artifact? Overviews of critical reception of postwar texts dealing explicitly with the "uncompleted past" can indicate lesser or greater interest in this specific theme in literary production, but they cannot say anything about the specific role of literary production in general cultural developments.

Who else but the poets will take on the role of Cassandra in high-living postwar Germany? asked Koeppen. Koeppen meant to draw attention to the specific potential of the "literariness" of fictional discourse. It concerns not only the way in which an author presents a culturally significant issue to the reader. Rather, the literary mode has informed the manner in which the author first approached and understood the issue. Engaged in the presentation of reality, some poets have seen it more clearly in its sociopolitical constructedness and temporal relationism. This "enriched" understanding may enable multiple access to reality for the critic as well as the general reader—as has long been claimed by the defenders of literary discourse. The mediating process is once more enriched, that is, complicated, in the responses of imaginative and subtle literary critics who tend to collapse, more flamboyantly than most academic critics dare to, the distance between primary and secondary texts. Yet, this distance can be synonymous with the distance of historically reflected perspective, which, in turn, ideally counteracts the problem of hindsight.

Koeppen's novels—and this is their real political dimension—have succeeded in at least partly controlling their critical reception precisely with respect to this perspective. Critics have praised them, attacked them, neglected them. Praising them, they have distilled their own texts out of his—Schwab-Felisch, Jens, and Heissenbüttel more than Reich-Ranicki, Korn, and Kraemer-Badoni;[20] Lothar Baier more than Alfred Andersch.[21] Yet even then they could not help reacting to the way in which the novels presented the past as a key problem of the present. Koeppen's highly subjective *and* historically reflected perspective, as it has been integrated into his conceptual and narrative strategies, has left no doubt about the nature of his doubts regarding the completion of the German past and the finding of a meaningful order in history. But Koeppen has also made it clear that such order—if possible at all, and then only tentatively, fragmentarily so—cannot preexist the historiographical activities of the poet, nor can it be the poet's task to establish it. That task is, rather, to argue for considering history as a cultural challenge and not to accept it as a given. Here is the locus of the most formidable obstacle to a fuller understanding of Koeppen's novels even for sympathetic critics who frequently have been too impressed by their dark beauty of loss, resignation, elegiacal withdrawal, despair, negation, silence.[22] Koeppen may have allowed his characters to indulge in such beauty of futility—to show the quality of their failure. But the meaning of his texts has been to warn of its temptations, because it would sap the energy needed to keep the past open for the present.

When *Death in Rome* was published in English translation in 1961, a lonely reviewer wrote in *Library Journal* that "this modern *Goetterdaemmerung* . . . should have been published in this country much sooner: however, its appearance during the Eichmann trial does seem timely."[23] In contrast to Siegfried Lenz's *The German Lesson* (1968), a best-seller in West Germany and successful with American audiences, *Death In Rome* found few readers in Germany and fewer in the United States, precisely because it was so timely. The ghosts from the past which Koeppen visits on his readers are not the colorful domesticated ones of *The German Lesson*; their meaning is threatening and their claims to be heeded are unambiguous.

The German Lesson was published right into a lively cultural debate over the issues of memory and guilt, which had begun in the mid-1960s as a political disruption of the status quo by the sons against the generation of the economically successful fathers. Not unexpectedly,[24] the political energy of this disruption soon dissipated. It appeared transformed in the *Väterbücher* (books about fathers) of the 1970s,[25] with their increasingly sterile obsession to distance the sons, young intellectuals, from their fathers whose criminality was now more clearly located in their fellow-traveling, in mass consumption and authoritarian Christian-Democratic order rather than in fascism. But the success of *The German Lesson* in 1968 had to do precisely with the fact that Lenz was much less clear about the meaning of the past for the present than Koeppen, and that readers were much freer to read into or out of his text positions with which they agreed or disagreed. Such ambiguity, of course, could be and has been presented as indicative of the text's richness, its interpretative potential. But this ambiguity has also supported Lenz's efforts at superimposing in the novel a "somehow" meaningful pattern on history, and reinforced his readers' eagerness to accept it.[26]

The preoccupation with the German past emerged again in the mid-1980s, almost a half-century after the end of the war, as an intergenerational, rather than generational, conflict concerning the singularity of the recent German past. The issues brought up in the *Historikerstreit* (historians' debate)[27]—stunningly emotional for the outsider—are of great interest to the cultural historian because they throw into sharp relief the historian's historicality. The fact that historical understanding is positional constitutes perhaps the most important problem in historiography generally, and especially in the historiography of the German past. The conflict between peers, as irreconcilable as that between sons and fathers, has been fueled by the inability to reflect on the motivations for and conditions of one's own position and the positions of others. The bitterness of the past, unresolved and enduring, has surged up powerfully in the bitterness of the confrontation that seems to bear out the urgency of Koeppen's warning. In *Pigeons in the Grass* and *Death in Rome* the question of the singularity of the German past has been asked and then deferred in a manner that might suggest, almost four decades later, a way to circumvent the stalemate of many debates of this question today. Koeppen's lucid analyses of memory as the complex interaction of the experience of time and guilt have insisted on the singularity of the German past mainly in terms of its potential for the future—"Hitler, der bleibt uns" (Hitler remains with us)—perhaps also because Germans will finally be able to choose so, accepting, into their present, the challenge of his meaning in the past.

JÜNGER'S UTOPIAN NOVELS

With their provocatively singleminded focus on witnessing and "unforgetting" as cultural tasks, Koeppen's texts have had, on the whole, a rather critical positive reception. But because they preceded, by more than a decade, a more general cultural awareness of "unforgetting," they have had no demonstrable effect on general reading audiences. With his agnostic melancholy moralism supporting the clearly disturbing political dimension of his novels, Koeppen has remained an involuntary outsider in the pluralistic, multifaceted business of West German culture.[28] Ernst Jünger, in contrast, has not only voluntarily assumed the position of outsider, but has given it a specific cultural significance—despite the fact that his numerous general readers and his critics, even when they might be expected to disagree sharply with the radically conservative implications of his texts, have been very receptive to their "literariness." What liberal critics have called "the Jünger case,"[29] a curious mix of admiration and repulsion, raises questions about the relationship between literary production and political-cultural attitudes that are instructively complementary to those raised by the Koeppen reception.

When in the fall of 1939 Jünger published *Auf den Marmorklippen* (*On the Marble Cliffs*), built on the narrative model of the autobiographical diaristic fiction to which all his texts conform, it quickly sold 35,000 copies before the authorities stopped further printing.[30] Jünger had intrigued critics and larger audiences since the 1928 republication of his *In Stahlgewittern* (*The Storm of Steel*, 1920), a highly stylized celebration of World War I as the modern experience,[31] and his *Der Arbeiter* (*The*

Worker, 1932), a tract on the worker-warrior's heroic achievement of perfection through renunciation of self and happiness for the higher good of the collective as *Volk*.[32]

After World War II, the critics hailed *On the Marble Cliffs* as an effective political fable about the power games of the Hitler regime[33]—a reading that Jünger at first denied but in 1973 explicitly affirmed in an interview with *Le Monde*, where he stated that his position against Hitler had always been entirely clear.[34] In all his work, however, Jünger has focused on the value for the individual of existentially extreme situations rather than of political behavior.

Such a focus has in itself proved an important cultural influence on Jünger's critical and general reception in the postwar period, including, importantly, *On the Marble Cliffs*, which, with the 1929 and 1938 versions of the diary collection *Das abenteuerliche Herz* (*The Adventurous Heart*), can be seen as the primary text underlying all his postwar writing. In their conceptual and narrative strategies these texts have reflected Jünger's unchanging, "timeless" preoccupation with the preservation and continuity of the significant individual in a period of mass demotechnocracy. Since the 1920s he has held to an eclectic German- and French-centered, elitist, bio-cultural nationalism, with highly stylized military leanings that are clearly expressed in the all-pervasive images of hunting and war. The Nazi regime appears in *Marble Cliffs* as yet another cultural rupture imposed on his alter ego protagonist and his peers by fate, that is, the fault of the low breeding of modern mass man rather than a general political failure for which the elites, too, would be responsible.

The voluminous *Strahlungen* (*Radiations*, 1949), a collection of Jünger's diaries from the spring of 1939 to the end of 1948, went through five editions amounting to 57,000 copies during the first year. The 1949 *Heliopolis*, a postdisaster science fantasy with high-cultural pretensions, went through several editions between 1949 and 1956 when it was taken up by the German book club.[35] The politico-historical fantasies offered did not originate in one intelligent and sensitive person, but by what Jünger habitually referred to as a "hoher Geist" (literally: high-ranking spirit) or "Geister hoher Rasse" (spirits of high breeding). Like *The Adventurous Heart*, *Radiations* presents a highly mannered precious still life composed of surrealistically distinct, dreamily beautiful battle, bombing, and torture scenes,[36] of minute descriptions of objects, plants, and insects, and occasionally of stunning landscape imagery. This still life is framed in sententious affirmations of a mysterious "order of spiritual configurations" just behind the great conflagrations, which in Jünger's rendition become silently magnificent, fastidiously recorded spectacles in blood red: no sounds of explosion or crashing buildings, no stench of burning flesh. Pain, if mentioned, is celebrated as heroic initiation to that higher order of being.

If there is any insight into the methods of the totalitarian regime—for instance, its "high-level cannibalism," which Jünger finds fascinating[37]—it is diffused by a formulaic linkage of modern barbaric behavior patterns to images from a high-cultural tradition: "Thus strange demons divide and cut up with their instruments men, their naked prey, in the great paintings of Bosch."[38] The reference to Bosch as to other "great" painters or poets or philosophers does not so much draw attention to the imaginative potential of art, but rather fits the modern event into the unquestionably meaningful pattern of a Great Tradition.[39] Accident is eliminated; all events are fated; what is more, fate conforms to the structures of art: "vast, powerful symphonies of fate."[40] As the battles of World War II and of totalitarian politics were recent memory for the postwar reader, and the devastation they left behind still omnipresent, the appeal of this totally artificial presentation, with its brilliantly enameled surfaces achieved by remote control of a chaotic, extremely difficult lifeworld, is a culturally significant phenomenon.

The point of observation of the diarist persona is characterized by remoteness to the point of transcendence.[41] Inviolate, the diarist observes and speaks from a higher level of reflection that has always been his—as has, since *The Storm of Steel*, Jünger's obsession with his own, and only his own, physical inviolateness.[42] The reader is firmly taken out of the time and space of his postwar everyday life. The same escape is offered in *Heliopolis* of 1949, set in some indefinite post-conflagration future, and in its later version, *Eumeswil* (1977). Variations of the model of *On the Marble Cliffs*, both utopian fictions present references to power constellations in the Nazi regime, which Jünger understood to be archetypical for the modern period: the battle between a highly disciplined, *ritterlich* (knightly) military elite and the decadent leaders of the plebeian masses. There are reflections on the meanings of totalitarian rule and persecution,[43] but in their sententious abstraction they are also clearly removed from the reality of the reader's past as bewildering, chaotic coincidence of accident and wrong choices. The tendency of these reflections to neutralize, indeed close, this disturbing past is reinforced by the constant references to higher levels of meaning, higher ranks, more significant orders of being, even where the use of violence is concerned.[44]

Such removal is all the more effective, because the references and reflections are part of the "time after our time" presence of the warrior-intellectual protagonists, Kommandant Lucius de Geer in *Heliopolis* and the "Anarch"-historian Venator in *Eumeswil*, both of them alter egos of their author in their observer position of "contemplative activism."[45] Both are connoisseurs of power, arrested in their fascination with extreme conflicts rather than engaged in attempts at understanding them. Venator, the historian as observer, has direct (that is, unreflected) access to the brutal power-games both of his present (in his position as night steward to the Junta general Condor) and of the past (in the "Luminar," a sort of temporal television that can penetrate and call up every corner of the past). The lack of reflection on his own historicity and historiographical perspective is not intended as a reflection on his cultural irrelevance[46] as historian. Rather, it points to the dark contemporary cultural situation *after* a meaningful—in Jünger's terms, meaningfully continuous—history. It is the present that has violated and corrupted the past. De Geer, in the more hopeful context of the earlier *Heliopolis*, seems to develop toward greater sociopolitical involvement when he finally acts against characters affiliated with the evil rule of the plebeians like the Nazi doctor Mertens: de Geer blows up Mertens's institute and rescues one of his victims.[47] But with this mission, too, de Geer is above all interested in the ecstatic experience of observing the beauty of the annihilating flames and feeling connected with the "field of force of enormous power."[48]

Significant, too, is the antimodern figure of the transworldly Regent, who decides the terrestrial battle between good and evil and whose services de Geer will join in the end, leaving behind the time and space of Heliopolis for some vaster, higher realm. Most repulsive to the Regent, even more so than the "intelligent bestiality" of the decadent leader of the plebeians, a Göring figure,[49] is the coldly calculating technological rationality of the Mauretanians, an order of warrior intellectuals reminiscent of Goebbels, who, already in *Marble Cliffs*, are in conflict with an older, more rooted elite of landed lords like de Geer. In these utopian fables there is no place for the experience of modernity and no time for memory and guilt.

JÜNGER AND HIS CRITICS

In 1973, Jünger published *Die Zwille* (*The Barge*), which, according to Heissenbüttel,[50] is a mythologizing account of a group of adolescents around 1920, the future perpetrators and victims of the Nazi regime. The book was respectfully received, though it met with some severe criticism, from among others, Siegfried Lenz (*Spiegel*), Michael Rutschky and Klaus Prange (both in *Frankfurter Hefte*), and Wolfgang Kämpfer (*Die Zeit*). They criticized both Jünger's failure to establish a viable historical perspective through credible characters and his inability to change his elitist position of observation.[51] Yet, this same year, critical reception was beginning to focus exclusively on the literary dimension of Jünger's texts: their literary dimension was seen as either clearly separable from their reactionary political implications or itself a progressive political energy. This tendency climaxed in Karl-Heinz Bohrer's voluminous 1978 study of Jünger's prewar texts, *Die Ästhetik des Schreckens* (*The Esthetics of Terror*).

In his celebratory 1973 "Ernst Jünger vor Augen" ("Looking at Ernst Jünger"), François Bondy referred to the left-liberal Alfred Andersch's praise of Jünger, just published by the leftist *Frankfurter Rundschau*, as a "provocative document," and declared 1973 a milestone in the Jünger reception. Bondy stressed the critics' reactions of fascination by and objection to Jünger's texts, linking *The Worker* as "an early structuralist book" with Foucault, and finding in Jünger an experimental attitude similar to that of Diderot.[52] Such sweeping comparisons are meant to emphasize Jünger's European contemporaneity—an idea that before 1973 was limited largely to the conservative wing of Jünger criticism. The critics' evaluation of Jünger's change to a more mellow humanism in his postwar texts[53]—important, for instance, to Andersch—is no longer an issue; the general opinion now seems to be that there was no need for such change. An increasing number of critics in the liberal-left camp, too, now see Jünger's prewar texts as diagnostically contemporaneous then as now, by virtue of their literary qualities. They thus imply that his early work in the 1930s and 1940s is the really important, significantly subversive contribution to the culture of the 1970s and 1980s.

This interpretation had already been offered by the conservative critic Karl A. Horst in a 1961 *Merkur* essay that praised Jünger's "thought style" (*Denkstil*) as both being subjected to the discipline of rationality and transcending it in powerful imagery, as both penetrating the modern experience in diagnosis and prognosis and searching for the deeper transhistorical reality behind it.[54] Curt Hohoff had celebrated, in several essays in the 1960s,[55] Jünger's enduring literary and intellectual contemporaneity, especially his stance against the systemic pressures of the technological world. When he elaborated on the truly modern, dual "Optik" of Jünger's texts in a 1965 interview with him, Jünger eagerly agreed: In the centrally important *The Worker*, he had anticipated, he stated, the "consequences of a new age" rather than merely propagated political tendencies. Significantly, too, Jünger praised in this context the cultural situation in France with its critical distinction between literary quality and political opinion.[56]

Such a view of the deeper vision of Jünger as an artist penetrating mere history and politics—the exact opposite of Koeppen's view of the writer as natural Cassandra—predominated the reception in 1965, the year of his seventieth birthday,[57] which is well represented in the Jünger Festschrift *Wandlung und Wiederkehr (Transformation and Return)*.[58] There were some critical voices among liberals—for instance, Michael Hamburger in *Neue Rundschau*. Yet he, too, was more irritated by the heavy sententiousness of Jünger's postwar texts—in contrast to the more spontaneous prewar texts—than by the cultural-political implications of his enduring aggressive cultural conservatism with its militant elitism and forceful closing of the past.[59] Rarely were there any unambiguously critical views, as in Franz Baumer's 1967 analysis of Jünger's centrally passive, apolitical stance—repulsion but no active resistance—before, during, and after the war, and of the sameness of an ornate imagery reflecting both an eclectic high-cultural fastidiousness and fascination with barbarous cruelty.[60]

The appreciation of Jünger's texts, then, has not changed in substance since the end of the war. It has widened to include larger numbers of left-liberal critics, reflecting the cultural shift since the early seventies. Misleadingly termed "postmodernism," that shift signifies just another aspect of the troubled cultural experience of modernity for which Jünger's work, pre- and postwar, is indeed a prime example. This widening trend has found its clearest expression in Bohrer's 1978 study, which was enthusiastically received by critics like Rutschky (who had voiced reservations about Jünger's mythologizing five years earlier) and Wolf Lepenies, both of whom were particularly impressed by Bohrer's "radical" emphasis on the highly self-conscious literary qualities of Jünger's texts. Both accepted, too, Bohrer's thesis of a "post-histoire" cultural progressivity of Jünger's strategic cultural anachronism.[61]

This reading was shared by Jürgen Habermas, who, in a long preface to the *Observations on "The Spiritual Situation of the Age"* (1979), presented the mass society of the thirty-year-old Federal Republic as a system that had devastated the communicative capacities of the life-world, praising, for contrast, Bohrer's and Jünger's neoromantic, diagnostically subversive intelligence.[62] Reacting with the greatest sensitivity to verbal nuances in the professional historiography of the uncompleted past—those of Klaus Hildebrand, Michael Stuermer, Andreas Hillgruber, Ernst Nolte—in the recent *Historikerstreit* (historians' dispute),[63] Habermas does not read closely where literary texts are concerned. He just generously assumes they exhibit that disruptive power that he thinks so important for the salvation of contemporary West German culture.

The controversy around the award of the 1982 Goethe Prize of the city of Frankfurt brought out, once more, the "Fall Jünger" (the Jünger case), that is, the ability or inability of critics to respond to the political implications of his stylistic self-presentation. Such ability is intimately connected with sensitivity to a German cultural task of "undoing the forgetting" of the past.[64] Thus Golo Mann assaulted the crude attacks on a subtle, fastidious writer, Rutschky wrote about honoring a radical, Jünger himself presented his position as "parteilos" (without party affiliations) and therefore, of course, suspect. A rare exception, Heissenbüttel, a close reader, understood the political implications and titled his commentary "Der Goethe der CDU?" There *was* unanimous official protest against the award by representatives of the Frankfurt Social Democratic and Green factions. Not so easily seduced by the high-cultural sheen of Jünger's enduring militantly elitist, apolitical, transhistorical conservatism, they remembered the message of *Storm of Steel*. But had *they* read Koeppen?

NOTES

1. Wolfgang Koeppen, "Autobiographische Skizze," *New York*, in Marcel Reich-Ranicki, ed., *Gesammelte Werke in sechs Bänden* (Frankfurt: Suhrkamp, 1986), 5:250–52. All references are to this edition; unless otherwise stated all translations are mine.
2. Reinhard Baumgart, "Nachkrieg und Postrevolte: Zwei Momentaufnahmen deutscher Prosa. Böll, Koeppen, Schmidt—diese Drei," *Glücksgeist und Jammerseele Über Leben und Schreiben, Vernunft und Literatur* (Munich: Hanser, 1986), 165–82, 173.
3. Peter Demetz, *Postwar German Literature* (New York: Pegasus, 1970), 168–72; Demetz, *After the Fires: Recent Writing in the Germanies, Austria, and Switzerland* (San Diego: Harcourt Brace Jovanovich, 1986), 316.
4. Walter Jens, "Melancholie und Moral: Rede auf Wolfgang Koeppen," in *Jahrbuch der Deutschen Akademie für Sprache und Dichtung 1962* (Darmstadt: Deutsche Akademie für Sprache und Dichtung, 1963), 93–102.
5. Marcel Reich-Ranicki, "Der Fall Wolfgang Koeppen: Ein Lehrbeispiel dafür, wie man in Deutschland mit Talenten umgeht," *Die Zeit*, 8 September 1961; *Literarisches Leben in Deutschland: Kommentare und Pamphlete* (Munich: Piper, 1965), 26–35; and *Wer schreibt, provoziert. Kommentare und Pamphlete* (Munich: Deutscher Taschenbuch Verlag 384, 1966), 11–18; "Der gierige Zeuge. Über Wolfgang Koeppen," *Der Monat* 15, no. 177 (1963): 65–75; and *Deutsche Literatur in Ost und West: Prosa seit 1945* (Stuttgart: Europäischer Buchklub, 1963), 34–54; "In einer deutschen Angelegenheit," *Wer schreibt, provoziert*, 109–12.
6. See also Koeppen's review, "Hitler, der bleibt uns," of Horst Krueger's 1966 essay collection *Das zerbrochene Haus* (*A Crack in the Wall: Growing Up under Hitler*; New York: Fromm International Publishing Corporation, 1982). For a title Koeppen used part of the concluding sentence of Krueger's essay on the Auschwitz trial, "Gerichtstag" ("Day of Judgment"): "This Hitler, I thought remains with us—all the days of our lives," and he commented: "a deeply disturbing thought; I am afraid, a very obvious truth." Krueger's excellent essay was first published in the May 1964 issue of *Der Monat* and singled out for praise by Reich-Ranicki: "Horst Krueger. Die Wollust der Unbefangenheit (1970)," *Entgegnung Zur deutschen Literatur der siebziger Jahre* (Stuttgart: Deutsche Verlagsanstalt, 1981), 143–49, 147. Reich-Ranicki supports Krueger's insight "that the German past can never be mastered. At most one can describe it and show it. This is exactly what Krueger has done." This is a position which Koeppen shares with Krueger. Despite his much more emphatic descriptive strategies, Koeppen also shares Krueger's ability to both understand the social-psy-

chological phenomenon of *Mitläufer*, the inertia of the silent majority, and not accept it.
7. "Wahrheit weil Dichtung," *Entgegnung*, 60–66, 61, 66. See also Koeppen's reaction to some of the reviews of *Pigeons in the Grass*, "Die elenden Skribenten," *Die Literatur* (Stuttgart) 1 (15 March 1952), now in *Gesammelte Werke* 5:231–35.
8. Hans Schwab-Felisch, "Wolfgang Koeppen: *Tauben im Gras*," *Der Monat* 4 (1952): 427–28, and "Widerruf," *Der Monat* 18 (1966): 89–93.
9. See Reinhard Baumgart, "Das Leben—kein Traum? Vom Nutzen und Nachteil einer autobiographischen Literatur," *Glücksgeist und Jammerseele*, 198–228, 210ff. Marcel Reich-Ranicki, "Anmerkungen zur deutschen Literatur der siebziger Jahre," *Entgegnung*, 17–35.
10. Fritz J. Raddatz, "Wolfgang Koeppen," in *Die Nachgeborenen Leseerfahrungen mit zeitgenössischer Literatur* (Frankfurt: S. Fischer, 1983), 217–27, 219.
11. See note 5 above.
12. Koeppen, notoriously reticent about himself, once described himself as "a spectator, a quiet watcher, a silent man, an observer," in "Kein Merkzettel," in Richard Salis, ed., *Motive: Deutsche Autoren zur Frage: Warum schreiben Sie?* (Tübingen and Basel: Erdmann, 1971), 191.
13. Wolfgang Koeppen, "Rede zur Verleihung des Georg-Büchner-Preises 1962," in *Jahrbuch der deutschen Akademie für Sprache und Dichtung 1962*, 103–10.
14. Koeppen quoted in Horst Bienek, *Werkstattgespräche mit Schriftstellern* (Munich: Deutscher Taschenbuch Verlag, 1965), 55–67, 65; Christian Linder, "Im Übergang zum Untergang Über das Schweigen Wolfgang Koeppens," *Akzente* 19 (1972): 41–63, 60ff and 49. In 1971 and 1972 Linder discussed the meaning of Koeppen's silence in nine interviews and articles in newspapers, journals, and radio programs; see the bibliography in Eckart Öhlenschläger, ed., *Wolfgang Koeppen* (Frankfurt: Suhrkamp, 1987), 390–470, 440f.
15. See the remarkably thoughtful review of *Pigeons in the Grass* by Karl Korn in *Frankfurter Allgemeine*, 13 October 1951, stating that the novel said more about the political situation of the Federal Republic than volumes of political reports and still managed to be a "real novel" with a multitude of milieus, characters, events, levels of consciousness. Ulrich Greiner, ed., *Über Wolfgang Koeppen* (Frankfurt: Suhrkamp, 1976), 25–29.
16. *Neue literarische Welt* (Darmstadt, Zürich), 25 January 1952, now in Greiner, *Über Wolfgang Koeppen*, 30–32.
17. Greiner, *Über Wolfgang Koeppen*, 11ff.
18. *Jugend*, in *Gesammelte Werke* 3: 7–100, 8.
19. Ulrich Greiner, in his survey of the critical responses to Koeppen, does not agree, but Dietrich Erlach does, suggesting that Koeppen should have been satisfied with the critics' responses, because they were, on the whole, positive (*Über Wolfgang Koeppen*, 12f). I do not agree with Greiner's dictum that a positive, but not sufficiently thoughtful, review can be more destructive than an equally thoughtless negative critique. But I also think mistaken the attitude toward this issue in Dietrich Erlach, *Wolfgang Koeppen als zeitkritischer Erzähler* (Uppsala: Studia Neophilologia, 1973).
20. See notes 4, 5, 14, and 15 above.
21. Alfred Andersch, "Choreographie des politischen Augenblicks," *Texte und Zeichen* 1 (1955): 251–56, now in Greiner, *Über Wolfgang Koeppen*, 72–79; Lothar Baier, "Ein nichtgeschriebener Roman: Zu 'Der Tod in Rom,' " Greiner, in *Über Wolfgang Koeppen*, 223–29.
22. It is instructive to glance over the titles of the reviews recorded in the extensive bibliographies of Greiner, *Über Wolfgang Koeppen*, pp. 283–94, in Thomas Richer, *Der Tod in Rom: Eine existential-psychologische Analyse von Wolfgang Koeppens Roman* (Zürich und Munich: Artemis, 1982), 149–53, and, most comprehensively, in Öhlenschläger, *Wolfgang Koeppen*, 444–70.
23. J. R. Blanchard in *Library Journal* 86 (1961), I, 1620.
24. See here the perceptive 1968 analysis by Horst Krüger, "Die schöne Revolution der

68er," in *Zeit ohne Wiederkehr: Gesammelte Feuilletons* (Hamburg: Hoffmann und Campe, 1985), 197–203.
25. See note 9 above.
26. See the useful analysis by Judith Ryan, *The Uncompleted Past: Postwar German Novels and the Third Reich* (Detroit: Wayne State University Press, 1983). In her reading of *The German Lesson*, Ryan draws attention to Lenz's depiction of the position of the painter Nolde who, despite the prohibition of his paintings by the Nazis, held certain opinions important to Nazi ideology: "This perception of Nolde's ambiguity was evidently unfamiliar to those readers of *The German Lesson* who made the book a bestseller. Such readers seem to have identified as the positive features of *The German Lesson* its story of a family divided under Nazism and its evocative descriptions of familiar North German landscapes and of what they take to be re-creations of the spirit of Nolde's vision of this landscape" (115). This is a shrewd assessment of readers' reactions; but I do not agree with Ryan's assessment of Lenz's degree of insight into Nolde's ambiguity, which would "become clear as we look more closely at the novel" (115). Ryan's first chapter "Pattern and Paradigm History as Design" presents an illuminating analysis of the strong impulses toward such design in postwar literature. Ryan did not, so far as I can see, connect these impulses, evident in the narrative patterning of these texts, with conceptual ambiguities regarding a general cultural understanding of the past.
27. *Historikerstreit: Die Dokumentation der Kontroverse um die Einzigartigkeit der nationalsozialistischen Judenvernichtung* (Munich, Zürich: Piper, 1987).
28. See Koeppen's "Nach neun Jahren," *Frankfurter Allgemeine Zeitung*, 205 (5 September 1983), now in *Gesammelte Werke* 5:307–09, remembering the year he spent as "Stadtschreiber" (town scribe) in a small town in Hessen, the writer as active citizen.
29. See Franz Baumer, *Ernst Jünger* (Berlin: Colloquium, 1967), 6.
30. Koeppen's second novel *Die Mauer schwankt*, which attempted to show, under the guise of a foreign setting, the destruction of civil liberties in Germany, had no audience when it was published in 1935.
31. The late 1920s saw a great interest in war novels, pro and con. Curiously, Erich Maria Remarque, author of the enormously successful antiwar novel *All Quiet on the Western Front*, reviewed *Storm of Steel* very positively: see Armin Kerker, *Ernst Jünger–Klaus Mann: Zur Typologie des literarischen Intellektuellen* (Bonn: Bouvier, 1974), 59f. André Gide, too, thought *Storm of Steel* the best war novel he had read: see Hans Egon Holthusen, *Der unbehauste Mensch: Motive und Probleme in der modernen Literatur* (Munich: Piper, 1951), 146.
32. See Dagmar Barnouw, *Weimar Intellectuals and the Threat of Modernity* (Bloomington: Indiana University Press, 1988), chapter 5, sections 2 and 3.
33. Hans Egon Holthusen, "Die Überwindung des Nullpunkts. Aspekte der deutschen Literatur seit 1945," in *Der unbehauste Mensch*, 137–68, 146.
34. "Ernst Jünger s'explique," interview with Jean-Louis de Rambures, *Le Monde*, 22 February 1973, *Le Monde des livres*, 15 and 32. See also Kerker, *Ernst Jünger–Klaus Mann*, 100. For differing interpretations of *Marble Cliffs* see Barnouw, *Weimar Intellectuals*, chapter 5, section 7.
35. In both cases, remarkable in the immediate postwar situation, there were both a small half-leather-bound edition of four hundred numbered copies and a leatherbound edition of one hundred copies signed by the author.
36. The example most often used by critics suspicious of this attitude is an entry of 27 May 1944, which describes a bombardment of Paris: Jünger, on the roof of the Hotel Raphael, observes, as a connoisseur, both the intelligent strategy (deducing a "feinen Kopf") of the attack, the beauty of its destructive results and its higher meaning: "The second time, at sunset, I held in my hand a glass of burgundy in which strawberries floated. The city with its red towers and cupolas lay in its vast beauty like a calyx under deadly fertilization. All this was spectacle, was pure power, affirmed and heightened by pain." (*Strahlungen* II, *Sämtliche Werke* [Stuttgart: Klett-Cotta, 1979] 3:

271. All references hereafter are to *S.W.*, the most recent and complete edition. The text of *Heliopolis*, as all the other texts, underwent continuous revisions). This still life of sunset, formulaic sexual associations, and higher meaning is a clear example of Jünger's inclination to *Edelkitsch* (high-level kitsch).
37. See the character of the "intelligent" cannibal Dr. Mertens in *Heliopolis*, who conducts unethical medical experiments on opponents to the regime (*Heliopolis*, *S.W.* 16:296ff).
38. 15 February 1944, *Strahlungen* II, *S.W.* 3:224f. Jünger had just heard of his teenage son's arrest and sentencing for hostile remarks about the regime, but the few paragraphs concerning this situation could have been written by an observer from another planet (223f). It is true, Jünger has cultivated this pose since *Storm of Steel*, but it is still striking in this context. While his wife is trying desperately to find and make contact with the son, he is deeply touched by the elegant attention to rank (*Rangordnung*) in Saint-Simon's character descriptions. There is also a telling passage in a letter written to General Speidel, Jünger's protector in Paris, after the son was killed in action in Italy in the spring of 1945: the son had always wanted to follow his father and now had gone infinitely beyond him: "unendlich über mich hinaus" (quoted in Baumer, *Ernst Jünger*, 77).
39. See the entry for 14 December 1944: sorting out papers, Jünger finds an old Swiss review of *Marble Cliffs*, which he criticizes for its negligence in drawing attention, in the situation of 1939, to the book's political associations. More important, the reviewer had blamed him for his frequent use of *so* at the beginning of a sentence, referring to Mallarmé's injunction against that word: "This cannot influence me. It (i.e., *so*) plays a role in my feeling of life—as relation to something higher, a governing force within the objects and the connection between them, which becomes concretely visible" (*Strahlungen* II, *S.W.* 3:342).
40. See the entry for 14 March 1944, ibid., 237. References to the higher meaning of it all can be found on almost every page.
41. This is an observation made by several critical readers: see the excellent introduction to Jünger's work by Wolfgang Kämpfer, *Ernst Jünger* (Stuttgart: Metzler, 1981), 98ff.
42. See Barnouw, *Weimar Intellectuals*, chapter 5, section 3.
43. See "Unruhen in der Stadt," *Heliopolis*, *S.W.* 16:64–78, with its explicit parallels to the persecution of Jews.
44. See "In der Kriegsschule," ibid., 188–201.
45. See Rolf Schroers, "Der kontemplative Aktivist: Zu Ernst Jünger," first published in *Merkur* in 1965, now in his *Meine Deutsche Frage: Politische und literarische Vermessungen 1961–1979* (Stuttgart: Deutsche Verlagsanstalt, 1979), 145–61.
46. See here Rolf Schroers's review, "Ernst Jüngers Endspiel," published first in *Merkur* 32, no. 1 (1978), now in his *Meine Deutsche Frage*.
47. "Das Unternehmen auf Castelmarino," *Heliopolis*, *S.W.* 16:289–304.
48. Ibid., 300.
49. *Heliopolis*, 337.
50. See Helmut Heissenbüttel's review of *Die Zwille* in *Buch der Woche*, Hessischer Rundfunk, 3 June 1973.
51. See Siegfried Lenz's Besprechung in *Der Spiegel* 17 (1973), which is especially clear in its rejection of Jünger's "Standort" (position) from which he has obtained so many calm observations of a suffering world; Klaus Prange, "Vollendete Vergangenheit," *Frankfurter Hefte* 28, no. 9 (1973): 667–68; Michael Rutschky, "Ein Jugendbuch," ibid., 668–72; Wolfgang Kämpfer, "Eine Seele für zwei Personen," *Die Zeit* 23 (1973).
52. *Merkur* 27, no. 10 (1973): 968–73.
53. See Wolfgang Kämpfer, "Wandel oder Verwandlungskunst? Anstelle eines Vorworts," in Kämpfer, *Ernst Jünger*, 1–7.
54. Karl A. Horst, "Versuch über Ernst Jüngers Denkstil," *Merkur* 14, no. 10 (1961): 994–98.
55. See especially Curt Hohoff, "Erinnerungen an das 'Abenteuerliche Herz,'" *Gegen die Zeit* (Stuttgart: Klett, 1970), 82–92. Hohoff stresses here Jünger's connection with

European nihilism, placing him next to Nabokov and Borges; he also rightly sees parallels between Jünger's imagery and the imagery of Brecht, Bloch, and Moeller van den Bruck.
56. Curt Hohoff, "Interview Ernst Jünger 1965," ibid., 92–103 (broadcast 21 March 1965, in *Deutschlandfunk*, first printing in *Frankfurter Allgemeine Zeitung*, 7 August 1965).
57. Siegfried Lenz, too, holds this position in his largely praising "Gepäckerleichterung Ernst Jünger zum 70. Geburtstag," in *Beziehungen: Ansichten und Bekenntnisse zur Literatur* (Hamburg: Hoffmann und Campe, 1970), 143–49.
58. Heinz Ludwig Arnold, ed., *Wandlung und Wiederkehr* (Aachen: Text und Kritik, 1965). See especially the essays by Kurt Lothar Tank, editor-in-chief of the cultural section of the Hamburg *Sonntagsblatt*, "Was wird aus dem Menschen? Aspekte des utopischen Romans" (213–30); and Rolf Schroers, "Der Intellektuelle und die Politik," (231–37); both anticipated Bohrer's argumentation. Schroers was to change his position in his review of *Eumeswil*, see note 46 above.
59. Michael Hamburger, "Gedanken zu Ernst Jünger," *Neue Rundschau* 76, no. 2 (1965): 364–68.
60. Franz Baumer, *Ernst Jünger* (Berlin: Colloquium, 1967), especially 60–72ff.
61. Wolf Lepenies, "Gesinnungsästhetik," *Merkur* 32, no. 10 (1978): 1055–60; Michael Rutschky, "Die Ästhetik des Schreckens," *Neue Rundschau* 89 (1978): 457–64. Rutschky (his note 4) refers to Heissenbüttel's and Enzensberger's admiration for Jünger after the war, influenced by Andersch. But in his contribution to the special Jünger issue in the 1968 *Streit-Zeit-Schrift*, Heissenbüttel unambiguously criticizes Jünger's mannerist style. However, Böll's respect for Jünger is well documented; see Raddatz, *Die Nachgeborenen (Later Generations)*, 59. Raddatz gives a separate chapter to Jünger and Sieburg as "Zwei Autoren der Vorkriegszeit, die die Nachkriegsliteratur wesentlich prägten"—an unconvincing proposition. See the excellent critique of Bohrer in Wolfgang Kämpfer, *Ernst Jünger*, 164ff.
62. Jürgen Habermas, ed., *Observations on "The Spiritual Situation of the Age"* (Cambridge, Mass.: MIT Press, 1984), 24ff.
63. Jürgen Habermas, "Eine Art Schadensabwicklung," and "Vom öffentlichen Gebrauch der Historie," *Historikerstreit*, 62–76 and 243–55.
64. See the list of responses in Raddatz, *Die Nachgeborenen*, 463–65.

12

Mechanisms of Ideas: Society, Intellectuals, and Literature in the Postwar Period in Japan

Katō Shūichi

If I may begin with a personal note, I believe that I am perhaps the only contributor to the present volume who has had extended personal experience as a writer and teacher in both Germany and Japan, a fact that provides the challenge and the privilege of examining Japanese postwar intellectual and artistic life on the basis of the sorts of intercultural comparisons that I myself have observed. Indeed, my own experience in Germany was a rather special one, as I was invited in 1969 to the Free University of Berlin by the students themselves, who sought a view of Japan, and of Asia, different from that available to them through the traditions of European Sinology and Japanology, which have always stressed classical literature, language, and religion, particularly Buddhism. The students were interested in the social and historical aspects of modern Japan, and because of the intellectual unrest in Berlin at the time at which I was invited, they were committed as well to an examination of Japan based on a kind of ideological framework that was itself in revolt against the intellectual style of traditional German scholarship, with its emphasis on evidence and learned argument. Such an attitude on the part of those students seemed to be quite exceptional, and, indeed, it has since been replaced by a more traditional set of attitudes.

In any case, the insights I gained during the three years I taught in Berlin helped give me some perspective as to how the Japanese intellectual establishment performs the functions it has assumed for itself. Still, it is difficult to make general statements on the postwar intellectuals because there have been crucial shifts in those self-definitions during the forty-year period since the end of the war.

Until the 1960s, the early postwar period might well have been termed the "age of intellectuals" in Japan. During the early postwar years, an intellectual was seen as a person who could and should embrace any and all issues; intellectuals were considered to be thinkers who were prepared to provide general guidelines to society. Intellectuals were not confined to any particular field but were, in fact, expected to cope with the whole range of important problems of the time. A glance at the newspapers of the period quickly shows the differences in attitude between cultures. In the American newspapers of the period (and now as well) commentaries on events and statements of opinion were provided by specialists on those subjects. On the other hand, in Japanese newspapers, as well as radio and television broadcasts, wide-ranging comments were provided by a group we might class as general intellectuals—writers, social scientists, and sometimes historians. Such people felt comfortable voicing their opinions about the larger issues of society. The model in Japan in the early postwar period, therefore, was closer to that of Europeans than that of the Americans.

Why was this so? Throughout the early postwar period, Japanese society was in a state of transformation. When a society faces radical social change, intellectuals can play a crucial role in addressing the uncertainty that may bring about divisiveness and de-evaluation of historical forces and of tradition.

By the late 1960s, however, the general course for postwar Japan had been set. When the framework for society becomes established and no radical social change is expected soon, the actual problems of society can, indeed must, be discussed from within that generally agreed-upon framework. In such a phase, the role of experts becomes more important than the role of older-style more "general" intellectuals.

Looking at the situation in the United States, for example, since no radical changes took place during the early postwar period, there was a real need to find some means to urge those typically more specialized intellectuals to speak beyond the confines of their expertise, in order to raise and examine important larger questions. In the early postwar period in such countries as Japan, France, and Italy, however, the patterns of society were not yet firmly set. That is why, in those cultures, that period might be justly termed the "age of the intellectuals," when larger issues were freely discussed in general terms.

There are, of course, certain dangers in a wide-ranging approach. Often intellectuals advance an opinion for which they lack a background of sufficient knowledge. Such an impressionistic method of expression, however, does convey ideas and feelings to a larger public, one that might not be willing or able to follow the intricacies of a more technical level of debate. Although Japanese intellectuals are not generally linked with large popular organizations such as trade unions or political parties, they are less isolated than they may appear. They often see themselves as spokesmen for the more ordinary citizens vis-à-vis the power of the government bureaucracy, which, in Japan at least, certainly does not set out to represent popular sentiment.

One example of this sense of representation can be seen in the activities of the intellectuals at the time of the disturbances surrounding the ratification of the Security Treaty in the 1960s. Quite a few intellectuals spoke up against the treaty at a time of large public demonstrations. In doing so, they felt they could truthfully represent the views of the nation. Of course, all such "representations" are more or less arbitrary; even if a million people demonstrated in the Tokyo streets, they represented only 1 percent of the population at large. Nevertheless, the overwhelming majority of respondents to repeated public opinion polls undertaken by different organizations were in accord, in one way or another, with the stance taken by the demonstrators, who opposed the ratification of the renewal of the Security Treaty and demanded the dissolution of the Diet. The intellectuals certainly came closer to representing the views of ordinary citizens than did the government. In that sense, the intellectuals were, and are, not isolated. At a later time, the intellectuals performed the same function with respect to popular protests on pollution and other ecological problems in postwar Japanese society.

The government understands this function of the intellectuals very well. When their protests are really understood as representing popular sentiment, the government reacts, changes policies, and follows with increased prudence its more long-range goals. Such has been the case with nuclear arms issues as well as with problems of pollution.

The response by the public to this "representation" of its views by intellectuals, however, is complex. Certainly the debates of the intellectuals can be found in such widely disseminated publications as *Bungei shunjū* (*Literature and the Times*), *Chūō kōron* (*The Central Review*), *Sekai* (*The World*), and the *Asahi Journal*. Yet it is doubtful that the public pays any more attention to such material than ordinary German citizens do to similarly sophisticated publications in their culture, such as *Der Spiegel* or *Die Zeit*. Nevertheless, in the case of Japan, there has been a change of reading habits paralleling the kind of break in the role of intellectuals during the 1960s I referred to earlier.

During the occupation, many independent magazines for artists, intellectuals, and the like were published. They were widely read by a larger public. There were radio broadcasts, to a certain extent, and daily newspapers available as well, but because of a shortage of newsprint and other economic factors, the number of pages in daily newspapers was limited. Therefore the various magazines that came and went during those years were quite widely read.

After the occupation, from 1952 until about 1960, daily newspapers were able to increase the number of pages and began to supply more objective information concerning internal problems such as labor as well as issues pertaining to international affairs. During the 1960s, the newspapers became the major suppliers of information and were quite widely read. Magazines such as *Sekai*, a magazine of social and political opinion, also achieved wide circulation. Books by authors such as Maruyama Masao, political scientist; Shimizu Ikutarō, a sociologist; Nakano Yoshio, a literary critic; and Noma Hiroshi, a novelist, were intellectually influential. Films directed by Kurosawa Akira, Ozu Yasujirō, and Mizoguchi Kenji were much discussed by a wide public. All these activities were possible because the Japanese economy had recovered from the war, and, perhaps even more fundamentally, because the question of Japan's future course remained open. The 1960s represented a period of transition, a time to be marked by the consequences of accelerated economic growth during a decade: orientation to material consumption, a gradual depoliticization of the public, and extreme stability in political power.

In the 1970s and after, intellectual magazines such as *Sekai* and *Chūōkōron* lost their appeal for the general public and found readers only in a comparatively small circle. And although newspapers continued to supply information and commentary, their role, in terms of a larger public, was effectively taken over by television. The commercialization of ideas has caused ordinary Japanese citizens to abandon high-quality newspapers and magazines for television, comics, and the kind of entertainment provided by automobiles, traveling, fashions, and food.

Even in terms of books, so-called middlebrow authors who, during an earlier period, would never have been taken seriously by the serious reading public, are now extremely popular, men such as Murakami Haruki and even Akagawa Jirō. The middle ground of book readers in Japan has disappeared. Earlier in the postwar period, there was a middle range of perhaps ten thousand readers who took a sustained interest in reading serious material. Now that middle range has declined. The public tends to be polarized into a small reading public of thousands and a large, commercialized mass public of hundreds of thousands. Most readers no longer seek to debate the fundamental development of their society; the basic values no longer appear to need examination. Rather, they seek specific information about their own narrower fields of interest: engineering, economics, the stock market, international currency, or whatever, and they leave aside the larger issues. Not surprisingly, the general public takes no active interest in materials of this specialized nature. Instead, they are interested in information of the "how to" category—how to repair broken-down cars, rear children, fix inexpensive meals, and the like.

This commercialization of culture has put much of the great Japanese tradition out of the reach of the general public. Philosophy and literature are now regarded as material for specialists. Any sense of duty to know the past on the part of the educated public has faded. Literature in particular has suffered. The public is being robbed of any proper literary heritage; even our classics written less than a century ago and so much appreciated by readers well into the postwar period have been replaced in the affections of the public by popular novels. The public can no longer concentrate; readers and theater-goers flit from one experience to another, without commitment and without the chance to deepen their responses. Even the great modern Japanese writers, such as Natsume Sōseki and Mori Ōgai, find few readers now. Instead, it is very difficult to find, in a university classroom setting, *any* Japanese classic or important modern literary text that all students have read.

This phenomenon may not be limited to Japan. When German students made use of Marxist terminology in the late 1960s, they often quoted from the Frankfurt School, authors such as Marcuse, Adorno, and the rest, but few were actually acquainted with any major work of Marx or Engels. Not much more of Goethe or Schiller was common knowledge. Still, such general trends are probably most obvious in Japan today. No Bible, no *Faust*, no Confucian classics, no *Tale of Genji*, no core that can sustain our cultural history exists. This is a crisis of utmost importance.

The publishing industry, which makes the work of writers and intellectuals available to the public, also functions in ways that help bring about these changes rapidly. There are, of course, a number of small presses in Japan that produce books and monographs that make important cultural contributions. Nowadays, these presses tend to employ small and talented staffs of a dozen or more people as editors, often some of them writers themselves, who are self-critical, demanding, and active in producing publications of real quality. Medium-size publishers, such as Iwanami, Chikuma shobō, and Heibonsha have much larger staffs and eventual access to the larger public. Such publishers continue to play an important role in sustaining a cultural role in the Japanese publishing world. The really large publishers, such as Kōdansha and Shōgakkan, manage to produce good books as well, but they also publish comics, and their activities on behalf of culture go hand in hand with a tremendous drive for commercialization. Since the 1970s, it is the medium-size publishers that face the greatest difficulties. Again, two groups develop, a small one for the elite and a huge one to respond to and develop mass taste. It has become more and more difficult to span that crucial middle ground. The medium-size publishers are surviving, but they often find themselves in serious financial difficulties.

Having said this much about the mechanisms of intellectual life in Japan, it may be useful to make some mention of the means particular to Japanese culture by which ideas are conveyed. One technique used most frequently in magazine and journal formats is that of the *zadankai* (roundtable discussions). Although such discussions are sometimes employed in other cultures, in Japan, arguments in the Western sense are seldom put forth in these roundtable discussions. Various conclusions are juxtaposed, without the benefit of real debate; real debate, in fact, would be impossible to achieve without an enumeration of facts within a rational framework of understanding. The effect of such roundtable discussions is more like a conversation, a fact that is related, in turn, to certain basic tenets in the Japanese cultural tradition. In that way of thinking, so long a part of collective psychological response, the society is seen as a large collective; within it, in order to maintain harmony, opinions must not be made too explicit and arguments must not be advanced with too much rigor. Confrontation must be avoided.

Still, a lack of confrontation does not mean that a real consensus has been achieved. The results are often closer to a compromise. To the extent that a minority voice is raised as the discussion continues, the minority *must* be willing to compromise. In Japan, the existence of a minority opinion or dissident voice is looked on as an unhappy accident. Thus the unarticulated purpose of the discussion may well be to force those who hold a minority view to compromise, so that they will conform to at least the outlines of the majority view. The social pressures within a particular group can be very strong indeed, so some apparent consensus is almost always produced.

In modern Western society, it is deemed perfectly acceptable for various people to have differing, even contradictory opinions. Techniques of majority rule, voting, and so forth have been developed to accommodate those differences. All such activities are rooted in the fact that, in those cultures, it is taken for granted that different people will maintain different views. In Japan, however, the ideal is for everyone to have the same opinion. This conviction reveals a fundamental difference between Western and Japanese society. Coping with an unhappy accident is far different from learning to deal with basic differences.

In such a collectively oriented society as Japan, the community as a whole tends to assume responsibility for the actions and behavior of its individual members. A family takes care of an error made by one of its members; a company issues a public apology for the failure of one of its employees; the nation as a whole considers, or is supposed to consider, itself responsible for the misjudgments of its leaders. At the end of the war, the Japanese slogan was *ichioka sōzange*, "ten million repent," meaning that the entire nation should repent the crimes of the war. To hold everyone responsible, however, amounts to saying that no one was responsible. The Tokyo war crimes trials, held by the Allied forces, individualized those war crimes, pinning down a few Japanese leaders. Japanese society has never undertaken on its own initiative any trial of any person on war crimes, a sharp contrast with the German attitudes toward Nazi misconduct. In Germany, the Nuremberg trial was followed by a series of German court cases concerning anti-Semitic atrocities.

At the end of the Pacific War, the Japanese people were indeed fed up with the miseries of the war and with the dictatorship of the military. Their antiwar and prodemocracy sentiments were based on their own sufferings, in other words, on the memory of the Japanese people as victims. Yet there was little mea culpa for Japanese soldiers as victimizers of other Asian nations. No one was accused for the Nanking massacre, the biological experiments on human bodies, or for the deportation of the Koreans to be used as forced labor in the Japanese mines, where many of them died. Ministers of General Tōjō's cabinet, the equivalent of Hitler's, returned to power quietly as political leaders in postwar Japan; ex-officers of the *tokkō* (Special Police), the Japanese counterpart of the Gestapo, came to hold quite influential positions in the administration after the war. These events would have been unthinkable in Germany.

From the early 1960s onward, the government devoted its energies to planning for economic growth. This shift, with its emphasis on materialism and a high standard of living, constituted the basic change in direction, one that has led to the situation as it is today. Now the memory of the war is remote; the younger generation has become complacent; fewer and fewer people reflect on the meaning of the Japanese war experience. Yet some problems lie outside mere economic concern: what other goals can Japan set for itself? Military goals? Social welfare? Pacifism? Apparently no one knows the answer. It is impossible to decide anything important about the future without defining clearly the meaning of the past. The society that has quietly buried its unpleasant memories is incapable of defining a historical context in which goals for the future must be conceived. Hence one of the main tasks for true Japanese intellectuals is to try to maintain the meaning of history as objectively as possible, to keep alive the memory of the war, including the Japanese war crimes.

Some of the early postwar writers wrote movingly about the war, including the atomic bomb. Writers such as Hara Tamiki, Ibuse Masuji, and Ōe Kenzaburō wrote about nuclear arms; others such as Hotta

Yoshie, Noma Hiroshi, and Oda Makoto insisted in their work that the Japanese were victimizers as well as victims. For example, Ooka Shōhei, best known in the West for his novel *Nobi* (*Fires on the Plain*), documented in his monumental work *Leite senki* (*Chronicle of the Battle of Leyte*) the way in which both the Japanese and the American armies devastated the land and destroyed the lives of the people in the Philippines. Morimura Seiichi has written with eloquence about the secret medical experiments performed in Manchuria; Endō Shūsaku has described the atrocities involved in wartime medical experiments. As the commercial media, the government bureaucracies, and the society at large tended to keep silence, however, speaking out became the province of the intellectuals, in novels as well as in the theater. Powerful figures such as Kinoshita Junji and, more recently, Inoue Hisashi have demonstrated explicitly or implicitly by their plays the political and psychological links between Japanese militarism, which produced the Japanese aggressions in the 1930s, and the power of money that came to dominate postwar Japanese society.

The career and attitudes of one writer, famous in Japan but little known in the West, exemplify the courageous role that intellectuals took in these early postwar years. Takeuchi Yoshimi (1910–77) was a literary critic, historian, writer, and specialist in Chinese literature, particularly in contemporary literature. He is perhaps best remembered in Japan as the translator of the complete works of Lu Hsün (1886–1936), the great Chinese novelist and essayist who became a hero for those involved in the Marxist revolution. I knew Takeuchi personally and found him to be a most interesting person. We often disagreed. In various debates, he made three basic points, which he emphasized again and again in one way or another.

First, Takeuchi established a line of argument that equated imperialism as a concept with imperialism of the West. In doing so, he brushed aside all historical complexities and, to my taste, oversimplified his conceptual framework. Nevertheless, his vision was a striking one. For him, China stood for revolution, that is, anti-imperialism. In Takeuchi's view, China's attitudes toward the challenge of the West, and therefore to Western colonialism, represented a confrontation that was ultimately defined on the ideological level. Specific historical conflicts thus represented for China a confrontation over the choice of an ideological system. Takeuchi much admired China for having faced up to such confrontations in the course of its modern historical development. In contrast, Takeuchi believed that the Japanese had, since the Meiji period, avoided confrontation with the West and, instead of boldly changing systems, had merely borrowed bit by bit from Western culture. As a result, Japan has never undergone a revolution; rather, it has kept its older values and has simply taken on desired elements, adding but not replacing. Thus the slogan of Meiji Japan was *wakon yōsai* (Western technology, Eastern ethics).

Those "Eastern ethics," or traditional moral values, however, were often incompatible with democratic ideals. Japan was successful in industrialization; there was little bloodshed and, by the same token, little consciousness of basic human rights as well. This situation stands in sharp contrast, according to Takeuchi, with the Chinese revolution of 1949, which certainly did involve enormous human sacrifice, yet looked so promising, at least at its outset, not only in terms of national independence but for the egalitarianism it appeared to offer as well.

Takeuchi's second point involves the well-known concept of the reciprocal nature of the master-slave relationship. In this view, the Western powers appeared, until the end of World War II, as masters toward the Asian countries. Japan, in its turn, appeared as a master to China in the 1930s. In this historical context, Takeuchi was bent on criticizing not only the masters but also the slaves. He insisted that the master-slave relationship, on the psycho-existential level, corrupts both sides. This was true for China and Japan, France and Algeria, the United States and Vietnam, and many of the other sets of relationships between the dominating and the dominated, the patronizing and the patronized, and even those aid-providing and aid-receiving partners.

Finally, Takeuchi's analysis of Japan during war years remains particularly trenchant. As the master-slave relationship was for him always a condition of Japan's modern history, he saw Japan as playing a dual role, a master in Asia, a slave to the West. In this paradigm, both Japanese leadership and Japanese culture could only become corrupted. Nor, he maintained, had the problem been solved, even in the postwar period, for to him the Japanese-Asian problem remained an ideological problem within.

However one may feel about the details of Takeuchi's argument, his fundamental ideas went to the heart of the contemporary situation: any power relationship, whatever the power involved might be, political, economic, cultural, or even linguistic, sooner or later tends to create serious problems, such as moral corruption (Takeuchi), the impossibility of real communication (Genet), or a crisis in self-identity (Franz Fanon). Takeuchi emphasized the effects of international power relations, while, at a later time, Michel Foucault developed a theory concerning the existence of power relations at different levels in a given society. Although the two men examined different contexts, their views converge in a central theme: that of the generalization of the master-slave relationship in Takeuchi's language, or that of a mechanism of power in Foucault's terminology. This phenomenon has probably existed in every period of history, but a compelling consciousness of this dynamic marks our time.

Takeuchi was a critic who clearly articulated the ideas that concerned him, and he exerted far-reaching influence on Japan's intellectual life. Writers of fiction, however, have more difficult problems in the Japanese tradition, which, in its lyricism, provides little realm for political or ideological discourse. Some artistic problems are very hard for Japanese writers to solve. Writers such as Takeda Taijun, Hotta Yoshie, and Noma Hiroshi, who wrote openly and bravely about the situation immediately after the war, were able to contribute a great deal, but the period in which they did so was short. And the older generation of writers, the Kawabatas and the Tanizakis, said virtually nothing about the war at all. Perhaps the only exception was Ishikawa Jun, who wrote not only fiction but essays in an elaborate style of Edo prose, filled with sharp and critical observations on society during and after the war.

The Japanese literary tradition, particularly in fiction, had focused on daily life rather than on the larger world of society and politics, which so far surpasses our individual perceptions. In order to deal with larger subjects, Japanese writers both before and after the war felt it necessary to go to European writers to see how they dealt with such large-scale subject matter. Thus the continuance of the Japanese tradition, ironically, forced an increased dependence on Western models. After the occupation, when Japan began to enter a phase of economic expansion, writers like Kojima Nobuo and Yasuoka Shōtarō again turned inward. These writers felt an overwhelming need to go back to a sense of daily life, a private existence in a small area more or less separated from larger concerns.

Some writers, of course, continue to take up larger questions. Interestingly enough, some of them were born outside Japan and therefore have been able to look at Japanese society somewhat more objectively. The novelist Abe Kōbō, for example, was born in Manchuria, and Hotta Yoshie once lived in Shanghai. Perhaps even I myself might be included because I have lived so much abroad.

In a sense, such writers may feel themselves on the margins of Japan's society, yet this is a privileged position from which to observe. There is much to see.

Three trends in contemporary Japanese society are of particular concern to me. These problems have already been alluded to, but perhaps they should be mentioned again in closing. The first concerns the changes that the creation of a consumer society has brought to Japan;

the situation implies an illusion of individual freedom, but, in fact, people are being manipulated by the powerful publicity firms. This situation is dangerous because the illusion of individual freedom is accompanied by complacency and a creeping sense of malaise, which indeed might be transformed into some sort of political opposition.

The second change concerns the depoliticization of the citizenry as interest is diverted from political issues to trivial material things. Germany is prey to the same problems. It is perfectly clear that depoliticization of ordinary citizens, and particularly of the young people, actually works for the conservative political forces in the country concerned. Jean-Paul Sartre once said, "Politics is something you may or may not be interested in, but something from which you cannot escape." Silence is a political statement, one that works for the conservative cause.

The third change involves the commercialization of the arts and literature brought about by increased prosperity. In Japan, the situation has reached an extreme. If we as professional writers write the equivalent of, say, 400 words, we may expect to be paid from 3,000 to 10,000 yen. With proper publicity, we may receive twice again as much. Yet certain writers who compromise in the interests of the "establishment" will be invited to deliver some safe and banal lecture to company employees. The fee for a one-hour talk may average 500,000 yen. Accordingly, they can work four hours a month and live comfortably in Tokyo on 2 million yen. The lectures remain the same because the audiences are different. During the war, the Japanese military government organized writers and artists. Now it is big business. There is plenty of money, and so it is an organizing war. Brutal as it may be to say it, business is buying the intellectuals.

Such is the situation we intellectuals have to face, and as the difficulties shift, so must our weapons.

VI

THE WRITER AS
PUBLIC CONSCIENCE?

13
A Writer in the Present World: A Japanese Case History

Oda Makoto

One fine day, I received an invitation from the German Academic Exchange Service offering me an interesting opportunity to spend a year in West Berlin as an "artist in residence." I decided on the spot to accept and left for Europe, taking my family with me; in fact, a daughter was born in that divided city during our stay. I lived in West Berlin for a year and a half, returning to Japan at the beginning of 1987. Even after this experience, I must acknowledge that I neither read nor write German and that I have never properly studied German literature and culture. It was certainly convenient for me that most intellectuals in West Germany speak English, which I have managed to learn to do as well.

I came to know many Germans in Berlin. As a writer and, possibly, as an intellectual, I made friends among writers and intellectuals there. Indeed, some of them became close friends.

When I talked with my German counterparts as we ate and drank together, I often felt an unusual affinity for them, a feeling of closeness that I had never before experienced with writers and intellectuals from other countries. This unusual affinity or feeling of closeness was public as well as personal. Perhaps this closeness to my German associates was, first of all, related to our mutual past, a past of which neither side can be proud and from which neither can be entirely free: the Nazi past on the German side and an expanding, invading Japan on the other. I understood this burden of the past both intellectually and emotionally when I was with my German counterparts.

Perhaps more is involved, too, than mere recognition of the burden. With respect to the Japanese past, for example, I prefer not to employ the usual terms such as *Japanese militarism* or *militaristic Japan*. The use of such terms narrows the scope of the real problem and thus obscures its real core. The past of Japan that I always keep in mind, and am sometimes least determined to face, is the past that began with the Meiji Revolution (I avoid the usual term *Meiji Restoration*) about a hundred years ago—an upheaval that overthrew the feudal regime of the Tokugawa shogunate and thus enabled Japan to embark on the path leading to the status of a modern nation, under the strong and autocratic rule of the *tenno* (emperor) system, a path that led to World War II, and Japan's total defeat. In other words, this past of which I speak is the entire history of modern Japan itself.

In this history, there is much of which we Japanese can be properly proud. I say this with a natural confidence that accompanies pride in one's achievements. Yet when we look more closely at our history, we find many other things of which we can never be proud. Claiming— and essentially, it was an undeniable fact—that "our" East had been under the imperialistic domination of "their" West for many unbearable years, Japan inflicted and imposed, under the name of "our" liberation, a similar kind of domination on the other peoples of Asia through colonization, suppression, discrimination, exploitation. This domination culminated in a war of aggression that spread over all of East Asia and eventually to the land, and lives, of us Japanese ourselves. The war ended with our total defeat. In summary, we first brought tragedy to others in this history, but, within the same arc of time, it returned to us in the form of destruction and misery, particularly in the most horrible example of all, our holocaust—the destruction of Hiroshima and Nagasaki. We first killed, destroyed, and burned; then everything came back to us, forcing us to experience many horrors similar to those experienced by our former victims.

The Germans, of course, have a similar recent history. It is not necessary to say much about this, but I want to point out that, within the fairly recent past, Japan and Germany were for a time strongly united under the name of the Axis powers, which included Italy as well. The Axis alliance was important for both parties: the support of Germany made it easier for Japan to commit itself to aggression and expansion in Asia, while the support of Japan in Asia made German expansion in Europe all that much easier. Many meetings were held in 1986 to commemorate the beginning of the Spanish Civil War fifty years before, but few noticed that 1986 was also the fiftieth anniversary of the anti-Communist pact concluded by Japan, Germany, and Italy, which marked the beginning of activities that would result in the formation of the Axis alliance. That pact was meant, it was said, to provide a means to oppose the worldwide threat of communism, but its final result was the spread of killing and destruction all over Asia and Europe, irrespective of ideology. This fact represents an historical lesson important not only for the Japanese and the Germans but for all peoples throughout the world. History does not usually repeat itself in the same form, but it does repeat itself in different forms and with different faces.

I was born in 1932, the second year of the Japanese military expansion into China and just one year before Hitler seized power. At roughly the same time in Japan too, the military was beginning to have power in politics and other fields. Just before my birth, an abortive military coup, the first of its kind, was staged in Tokyo, and the prime minister was shot. One small example can suggest the close relationship between Japan and Germany during my boyhood: names such as Hitler or Goebbels were the first European names I learned or remembered. My father often mentioned German names of a different kind: Goethe, or Schiller. My father was not a professor of German literature, just a lawyer. From the Meiji era until the end of World War II, the structure of higher education in Japan was under strong German influence. A product of this system of higher education, my father was an ardent admirer of German literature and culture—precisely those elements of German civilization that those Germans with names familiar to the ears of his son tried to destroy in their own country at that time.

So much for my boyhood "German connection." What remains important about my affinity with Germans is not limited to the fact that we Japanese and Germans shared a past. How a Japanese or a German sees the past, and how honestly and thoroughly she or he is determined to face it, even if that past is full of abhorrent matters, is far more important to me.

I do not suppose that every German or Japanese can summon up a sincere determination to face that past. What I write here is not meant to serve as an objective indication of how the Japanese people in general see their past, but rather to explain something about how I myself, both as a Japanese and as a writer, face that past. I do not claim that most Japanese share my view, but there are many who are as determined as I to face it. Anyone who tries to understand present-day Japan and its people must understand that the number of Japanese who have been willing to look back has never been small, and, perhaps more importantly, what they have thought and achieved in various fields has provided the most significant ideological, and at the same time the most realistic, basis for a postwar *democratic* Japan, both as a nation and as a society.

My experience of the war as a young boy can be divided into two parts: first came the brighter part, then the darker one. In the experience of a war, when the darker part comes later, the effect is appalling, miserable, for one tends to think of this latter part as though it represented the entire experience.

The brighter part of my war experience was that of waving a small paper flag of the rising sun at a rally celebrating a great victory of the invincible imperial army or navy. The darker part was quite simply the experience of hunger and air raids, a witness to the destruction caused by repeated bombings. Throughout the final stages of the war I lived in Osaka, the second biggest city in Japan after Tokyo. As one of the most important industrial and commercial centers of Japan at the time, Osaka, where I had been born and brought up, was heavily and repeatedly bombed, and its citizens were starving. War-stricken and hungry, I, along with many others in Japan at that time, was altogether miserable.

Naturally, I began to see the war mainly through the eyes of the victim. Japanese really suffered from the war. Many men had died for nothing at the front, every city had been destroyed and burned, and, of course, there was the fact of Hiroshima and Nagasaki. The sense that "we really suffered" formed a common basis of sentiment not only for postwar peace movements but for the making of postwar society.

After the war, Japan reappeared on the world scene as a small, peace-loving nation rather than as a large and threatening military power. But this small, peace-loving nation was doomed from the beginning, sandwiched as it was between two superpowers beginning to play the dangerous power game of cold-war politics. The United States forced Japan to become its faithful ally and gradually to rearm, ignoring the wishes of many Japanese who opposed the direction that Japan was taking under pressure from America. Such a direction apparently violated the famous "Peace Constitution" which the United States itself had helped to write; and such policies were dangerous not only for peace but for the development of postwar democracy.

Japanese conservative political leaders who had held power since the end of the war, making the most of their close collaboration with the United States as well as the American pressure being brought to bear on Japan, continued to try as best they could to restore the values and the system of the prewar period in postwar Japan. In this effort they were aided by influential conservatives in other fields, such as business and culture. At the time this shift in national policy was referred to as the "Reverse Course." Many Japanese were opposed not only to the extent of U.S. power and influence but in particular to this specific policy, which attempted to place Japan again under the rule of the reactionary politics of the prewar period.

Despite strong opposition in the country, many of these "Reverse Course" policies were implemented and enforced. Many Japanese began to feel that "we really suffered in the past, and we really suffer now." This feeling still fuels our peace movements and indeed any political movements undertaken by the opposition. Such feelings are natural and important, yet something different and more powerful was required to cope with the new situation.

The Vietnam War was an unpopular war in Japan as elsewhere in the world. Public opinion polls unanimously indicated the enormous distaste felt for the war; even the Japanese government appeared to hesitate to give the war its open support. The general reaction among the populace toward the war can best be summarized in one sentence: Why is "America," which we have so far trusted, doing this stupid and unjustifiable thing? Although there had been sudden eruptions of anti-American sentiment and a fairly strong anti-American tradition in the Japanese left-wing camp, America had undoubtedly been the most popular foreign country in postwar Japanese society. This "America" was not just a nation or a state or a military power but a principle or a cause, such as Democracy or Freedom.

The Vietnam War seemed to many to violate everything this lofty principle or cause represented. For the first time since 1945, people began to question America. Yet to question "America" was to question Japan itself, which was collaborating with the United States in such a stupid and unjustifiable war, although Japan was not so much willing as forced into such participation. Still, willing or forced, Japan was apparently an "accomplice," and a grasp of this situation led in turn to a fundamental reexamination of Japan, both past and present. How was it possible for postwar Japan, which claimed to have been established on such important principles as democracy, freedom, and peace— and a strong self-criticism of its past—to participate in this unjustifiable war, which was destroying the land and the lives of a small nation and so violating the principles presumably held dear not only to the United States but to a new democratic Japan as well? These were the sorts of questions faced by those who were concerned about the Vietnam War and Japan's complicity in that conflict.

In the reexamination of postwar Japan, a number of fundamental questions were raised, including not only those matters directly related to Japan but to other nations as well. Is a nation truly democratic when it appears satisfied with the existing situation in politics and society and shows within itself no will to work for change? Is a state democratic when it neglects fundamental questions of discrimination within its own society? How can we dwell on our suffering in Hiroshima and Nagasaki without considering the enormous number of Korean victims of our own holocaust—many of whom were brought to Japan as forced laborers? I will provide some examples of this particular problem later in this essay. In this regard, progressive and left-wing politics in our country also require a radical reexamination. Just as democracy had to be questioned, conscientious Japanese also had to question socialism's lack of regard for fundamental human rights.

At this point, many Japanese began to view their own national past from a new perspective. They began to grasp the significance of World War II in its entirety, not just from a "beginning" at Pearl Harbor in 1941, but as a fifteen-year war of aggression that had begun in 1931 when Japan invaded Manchuria; indeed, all these events began to appear to represent the inevitable extension of modern Japanese history after the Meiji Revolution. Now many Japanese viewed a reexamination of the past and present of Japan as fundamental. In attempting to carry out such a reexamination, many thought it was important to admit the responsibility of ordinary people like themselves for the war, realizing that they must be understood not only as victims but at least as "accomplices," even as they accused the emperor for his unavoidable responsibility for the war.

During the Vietnam War, Japan again became a powerful nation. This change represented not just the beginning of domestic prosperity; it also meant the beginning of Japanese domination over Asia and other parts of the third world, this time not by military action but by economic expansion. This economic power itself was the result of innovative technological and industrial developments made possible by the talents of the hardworking Japanese people. By the same token, that power was strengthened through a series of clever decisions taken by the leaders of the country, who purposely avoided any dependence on military industries and who took full cognizance as well of the enormous imbalance of development between what is sometimes termed the world of the "north" and that of the "south." The economic power that resulted not only stimulated the prosperity of Japan but helped generate as well its domination of postwar Asia. What is more, this rapid progress of the Japanese economy was accomplished by neglecting needed measures for the welfare of the general population, measures that should have been proposed and carried out as a matter of course as the national economy improved. Yet the environment and policies to ensure the social welfare of the Japanese people were neglected. These facts help define our present. Those who were determined to reexamine Japan and her past had to face them. I counted myself as one such person.

Just after the beginning of the U.S. bombings in North Vietnam, I, together with others who were concerned about the war and Japan's complicity in that war, organized an anti-Vietnam War movement, which began with a sizable demonstration in Tokyo in April of 1965 and later developed into a nationwide movement. Initiated by ordinary citizens like myself (our group included writers, professors, workers, students, and housewives), and without any political and ideological affiliation, without any guidance and financial assistance from outside—and "withouts" were rare in Japan at that time—our movement was politically and ideologically free: anyone who was concerned about the war and Japan's part in it could join. Indeed, people joined the movement in great numbers, eventually to make it a national one. This movement, which was called *Beheiren* and officially translated as the Japan "Peace for Vietnam!" Committee—or, more appropriately, the Committee of Citizens Alliance for "Peace for Vietnam!"—later even became known internationally through its various activities.

One of these international activities involved helping American soldiers who opposed the war. There were (and still remain) a variety of American bases in Japan that played a decisive role in the Vietnam War. American soldiers who opposed the war expressed their opposition through a variety of activities ranging from small on-base meetings and the publication of antiwar newspapers to desertion from the front. It was our assistance to those soldiers who had left the front that made us so well known internationally.

We, certainly I personally, were particularly sympathetic toward soldiers who had been sent to Vietnam, for they reminded us of the Japanese soldiers who had been sent to China or other places in Asia during Japan's war of aggression. Both conflicts, the Vietnam War and Japan's war of aggression, were unjustifiable conflicts, in which ordinary American and Japanese citizens were drafted and sent to the front. Many, of course, might have willingly joined the war, naively believing in the stated causes, such as the establishment of peace in Asia or the defense of freedom, without much knowledge of what they were doing and what the consequences would be. The draftees were, in general, the victims of the powers above them, which forced them to join the war and to fight. To join the war and to fight meant, in essence, to kill, and in this action, they also became aggressors. The fact was that these soldiers were aggressors precisely *because* they were victims, not *despite* the fact that they were victims.

This victim-aggressor relationship or mechanism forms the basis of the "war machine" (a word quite popular at that time in the anti-

Vietnam War movement) in any conflict, but particularly so in an unjust war, such as the Vietnam War or Japan's war of aggression. Seen from this standpoint, what these antiwar American GIs were doing could be seen as attempts to dissociate themselves from this victim-aggressor relationship and move toward dismantling the "war machine." We felt a strong affinity with them, because we felt we also were trapped in a victim-aggressor relationship. Although we opposed the war, our country was officially cooperating with the United States in that war, so that collaboration was more or less being forced upon us.

The example of Okinawa was a particularly striking one. Okinawa was then still under U.S. occupation, and U.S. bases on this territory represented one of the most significant territories involved in the American war effort. Because the bases occupied so much of the available land in Okinawa, many Okinawans could find work only on those bases maintained for the American troops and for the war effort, deprived as they were of the land and opportunity to pursue their own economic development. Most in Okinawa at that time longed for liberation from the American occupation and looked for a political reversion to Japan. Thus it was not surprising that the opposition to the war in Vietnam was even stronger in Okinawa than on the Japanese mainland. Workers on the U.S. bases in Okinawa who found themselves forced by economic circumstance to help load the very bombs that were to be dropped on Vietnam represented perhaps the most conspicuous example of this victim-aggressor relationship I have attempted to describe, yet all of us who participated in the movement felt that we were involved at least to some degree with the same problem. In this, our antiwar efforts represented precisely our efforts to dissociate ourselves from those connections.

To see ourselves in such a perspective helped us to reexamine Japan, both its past and its present, in the fundamental ways I have tried to describe. On a more personal basis, it gave me, as a novelist, a new insight into war, society, human life, and many other matters I faced as a human being and a citizen—an insight that I might never have obtained if I had not tried to dissociate myself from this victim-aggressor relationship by my commitment to the anti-Vietnam War movement.

For many years I had felt that I had to write a novel about Hiroshima. Just after the end of the war, just after my own experiences of the air raids and all the misery involved in the bombings and the fires, I heard a rumor: in the holocaust, Japanese victims, themselves heavily wounded, saw some other victims (the rumor did not specify the number) suddenly appear in the fire, others who, although they were also seriously wounded and dying—living ghosts like the Japanese victims themselves—were clearly different from them. The Japanese discovered, to their astonishment, that these "ghosts" were Americans—the American prisoners of war who had been garrisoned somewhere in the city. With this discovery, this realization that these were the soldiers of the very country that had brought such indescribable misery upon them, the Japanese began to attack the Americans, and a battle occurred between the Japanese ghosts and American ones—surely one of the saddest encounters in human history. Neither side had the force necessary to win the battle, and both ghosts fell down together in the black rain.

This rumor continued to persist in my memory for many years after the end of the war, and gradually it was proved true, at least in essence. The existence, and the destruction, of American prisoners of war in the holocaust has been verified through research undertaken by a number of persons, including me.

As this rumor, this truth persisted in my memory, I conceived the idea of writing a novel about Hiroshima. Perhaps this plan was not just an "idea" but represented an inner necessity for a Japanese writer like me who had experienced the miseries of the war. The idea developed into a determination: I had to write it.

For any writer, to take up the subject of Hiroshima is an appallingly difficult job, for the subject is too large to grasp and the scene too unreal to imagine. For many years I could not launch myself into the task. It was only after I began to find commitment in my own way to the antiwar efforts at the time of the Vietnam conflict that I could begin to write the novel, which took me seven years to complete. In this effort, I think that my "discovery" or realization of the victim-aggressor relationship helped me to grasp the meaning of the holocaust, "personalizing" and "universalizing" the entire tragedy. The American prisoners of war who had perished in the holocaust were no doubt victims; yet for the Japanese, especially for the Japanese victims, they apparently represented the aggressors, at least to some extent. In the holocaust, not only those Americans but many other foreigners perished. The majority of the foreign victims were Koreans, who accounted for about 10 percent of all those killed in Hiroshima and an even higher proportion in Nagasaki. Most of those Koreans who perished had been brought from their homes as forced labor, to work and to die. For them, the Japanese, even as victims, were the aggressors. In the holocaust, victims and aggressors alike died together. For the Koreans, the Japanese were the colonizers:

the Japanese always stood above them. On this "ladder" of rule and discrimination, the stronger always stood above the weaker. This hierarchy or "ladder" suddenly collapsed in the holocaust.

My novel, which is titled simply *Hiroshima*, was published in 1981 and has been translated into English (as *The Bomb*)[1], French, Arabic, and Russian. Partial translations have been published in German, Dutch, Vietnamese, and some other languages. In the book, various characters representing various nationalities and national backgrounds appear drawn to the vortex represented by Hiroshima itself: Japanese, Koreans, Americans, American Indians, Malaysians, Japanese-Americans, even a person from the Congo. They come together in different ways and by different means at various times, not to live, but to die, in the same form and in the same way.

Today, I see the contemporary world as a collage formed by five pictures, five images formed in my mind. One of those pictures is that of a nuclear holocaust. I do not have to use many words to express the direct meaning of this picture. What I wish to emphasize here is that this picture not only reveals the present crisis of the world but also suggests the process toward some final end, through an enormous buildup of arms, militarization, and the weakening of democracy in society. The culmination of such trends might well be called a nuclear fascism. And this picture of a nuclear holocaust reveals the possibility of a holocaust caused not only by the use of nuclear weapons but by accidents in nuclear power stations.

The second picture is that of hunger in Africa, Asia, and other parts of the third world. We are by now quite familiar with pictures of hungry children in these areas, but I see not only hunger but also poverty in the third world, the imbalance of development and economy between the "North" and the "South," the inequality between the privileged and the deprived in the third world itself, as well as the continued exploitation in various forms that has created the wealth and power of the "North" and of the privileged in the "South" so perpetuating the poverty and hunger that still prevail in the third world.

Then, two other pictures appear before my eyes. Rather than vague pictures, they are actual scenes. One of the two is that of scattered bones and skulls of the victims who were executed during the terrifying rule of the Pol Pot regime in Kampuchea, a scene I came across when I visited the former execution site in Phnom Penh a few years ago.

After that visit, I went on to Ho Chi Minh City (formerly Saigon). While I was there, I visited a hospital where I saw what the so-called Agent Orange, used by the U.S. troops to kill trees and grasses, had done to human bodies. In a small room of the hospital, I saw a number of babies and small children with deformed bodies who had been forcibly taken from their mothers. The bodies of these babies could hardly be called human, yet what were they? These human fragments remain in my mind as the fourth of the pictures with which I am always confronted.

The scene of the bones and skulls on the ground demonstrates a crude reality that still exists in some socialist countries and in some parts of the third world—a reality that begins from a repression of freedom and a refusal of human rights and extends in extreme cases to concentration camps and even to human slaughter. And the scene of the deformed bodies or human fragments represents one of the many examples of inhumane acts that people on the other side commit in the name of the defense of freedom, believing and claiming that the society in which they live, the country to which they belong, is truly free, democratic; they see themselves as deeply concerned with justice and human rights not only for themselves but for the whole world. The former image reveals the miserable and cruel results of politics that once claimed to be seeking the liberation of oppressed people, while the latter shows an ignorant arrogance on the part of people of self-acclaimed freedom and concern for human rights.

These two scenes or pictures that haunt my mind are depressing enough. More frightening still is the scene in my mind in which refugees coming from that country of bones and skulls, a land of torment and repression, enter into a new land, one that still produces Agent Orange and appears ready to make use of it under various pretexts, such as the defense of freedom or the progress of science. In such instances there appears to be in the minds of policymakers no serious regard for a need to think through the kind of fundamental changes needed in order to shape the future, so as to make decisions based on a true understanding of what has been done in the past, what is now being done, and how the past and the present inevitably can shape what the future holds.

The fifth picture is an actual scene, but of a different kind. It is an actual scene in Nishinomiya, the lovely town in Japan in which I now live with my family, including my daughter, born in West Berlin. Nishinomiya is a typical suburban middle class or upper middle class town, with an air of wealth and liberality, that occupies land between Osaka and Kobe, the kind of suburban town one can easily find elsewhere in Japan as well as in any "advanced" country. Osaka, as an important industrial and commercial center, and Kobe, a large international port city, have both played a decisive role in the development of the Japanese economy; indeed, the kind of "suburbia" represented by Nishinomiya came into being quite early in the prewar period as a result of the economic base that both cities developed. With the development of such a modern suburbia, with its beautiful mansions and houses, modern hotels and restaurants, good golf courses and theaters, plus an atmosphere of liberalism that can now be found in so many towns of this type, modern middle or upper middle class life began to shape itself and to spread in this area long before that kind of life developed elsewhere in Japan. Indeed, the novelist Tanizaki Jun'ichirō used to live in Nishinomiya, about which he wrote his masterpiece *Sasameyuki* (translated as *The Makioka Sisters*), which described the prewar life in this town so well.

Underneath this beautiful suburban spot and the splendid landscape that spreads from the middle of the mountain range that runs behind these communities down to the seacoast, something frightening took place during the war. It was an event that transpired without the knowledge of most of the inhabitants of the area. Because the project undertaken was abandoned because of the defeat of Japan, it remained incomplete and so still escaped the knowledge of many. This awful thing was, in fact, the construction of a series of underground tunnels intended as a place for hidden factories for the production of fighter planes, as well as the hidden headquarters of the Japanese navy in this area; it may even have been intended as a possible hideaway for the emperor. Many Koreans were brought from their homeland by force to work on this construction and, as elsewhere in Japan at the time, the Korean forced laborers had to work under the most difficult conditions, right in the midst, or, more correctly, right *underneath* this middle or upper middle class suburbia, with its affluent and relatively liberal life. All of this was accomplished without the public's knowledge.

After the war, these tunnels, totaling fifty or so, were left to crumble into oblivion. It was only in December 1987, some forty years later, that one of these many tunnels was discovered by a group of Korean citizens doing research into what traces might remain of Korean wartime forced labor in this area. For the first time since the war, these tunnels were entered, the spot where the real site of this forced labor took place. There such phrases as "Korean independence!" were scrawled on the walls. This part of our history, of which we Japanese cannot be proud, had been hidden since the end of the war under the affluent city where I now live with my family.

This discovery shocked me. And it make me think. The long tunnel near Kobe constructed for the famous Japanese "bullet train," the *Shinkansen*, the pride of our advanced technology and history, goes through those same hills. It burrows even deeper underneath those hills of hidden history, beneath all the agony and misery of those poor Korean prisoners. When a "bullet train" runs through this tunnel at enormous speed, the very walls of those beautiful modern mansions and houses standing just above begin to vibrate; everything begins to shake. What will happen, we all say, if a big earthquake comes?

Our apartment is located by the sea. We have a commanding view of the landscape, which is so beautiful in this area. Now, when I look over this beautiful scene from our windows, I sometimes feel that I am facing Japan's past as well as her present.

Such is the world in which I live. I must decide what to write and how to write; this question is a difficult one for me to answer. I would rather say what kind of literature I am determined *not* to write, rather than what I wish to undertake.

As my five pictures suggest, the world can be a depressing place. One course of action is to separate one's world from such pictures and thus not see them at all. Such writers may find it easy to remain aloof, detached from the real world; if they can accomplish this, then they can write pleasant stories and novels. I know that this can be done. But this is not the sort of literature that I will write. I must face those scenes, those pictures. Yet I know too that those who face them also confront the danger of adopting a fatalistic attitude toward all things—wars, revolutions, human error. I will not write in this fashion either.

I am determined as well not to write what I call the "literature of return." There are many such novels written by "progressive" or "concerned" writers living in "advanced" countries. In such accounts, the central character (who might well serve as the alter ego of the author) goes to a "troubled" area in the third world where some sort of fighting may be taking place. This fighting may well be so severe, and the situation so confused, that justice or any righteous cause seems lost, even that of the side that seeks liberation and revolution. What is truly happening, however, is not the central question of such novels; rather, the central character easily becomes disillusioned, often deciding to pack up and go home, saying, "I have seen enough," and "I have seen too much." Once home, the protagonist plunges into normal family life, insisting on "no more politics," because "I have seen enough politics, too much politics, over there." It is at this point that the protagonist begins to write the novel. Such is the "literature of return."

Unfortunately, those who live in such troubled third-world areas, including writers, cannot "go home." They have no other spot to which to "return," however severe the fighting in their area, however confused the justice of the situations they must face. They cannot escape, however much they may wish to do so. They must simply stay and face the situation.

I do not mean to suggest, of course, that "progressive" or "concerned" writers should be forced to visit such areas in order to write, staying on until the end, faithful to some concept of revolutionary justice. Indeed, whether traveling or staying home in our "advanced country," writers must face whatever situation confronts them. Nor must a writer invariably choose social themes. A writer may well compose a love story, facing these questions in life as they are. In fact, one of my short novels is titled *A Love Story*.

On 14 August 1945, about twenty hours before the formal surrender of Japan, Osaka experienced one of the most severe air raids it had known during the war. Many died without knowing that peace was to come soon. I was there at that time. After passing some terrifying hours in a clumsy crude shelter, I went outside, where I found a leaflet on the ground, which had apparently been dropped from one of the planes that bombed the city. It was written in Japanese. I picked it up and began to read. It began, "The war is already over. Your government has proposed to surrender." I could not believe my eyes, but indeed, the next day, Japan surrendered.

After the war, I began to wonder, young as I was, why this bombing of Osaka had taken place. Japan had already told the United States and its allies that it was ready to surrender. So why did the enormous destruction take place in my city? As I studied and reflected, I gradually discovered the truth. Those who ruled Japan, including the emperor himself, decided to capitulate just after the atomic bombings of Hiroshima and Nagasaki because they found it impossible to continue the war. They sent word to the Allies through neutral powers that Japan would surrender on one condition: a guarantee from the Allied powers that the reign of the emperor, the *tenno* system, would continue. Those in power, including the emperor himself, appeared to be seeking to assure the safety of their own lives under this elegant pretext. They already knew the fate of the leaders of Nazi Germany and Fascist Italy, who had been their allies in making war. It must be noted as well that our leaders sought no guarantee for the safety and well-being of the Japanese people.

When receiving word, passed along by channels provided by neutral countries, indicating that Japan wanted to surrender, the United States decided to stop the daily bombings of Japanese cities, which had caused such widespread destruction. Still, despite the fact that the Americans had already decided to keep the emperor system in place, with the expectation that its continuation would be useful for their own political purposes, the U.S. government did not at first provide a clear answer to the Japanese.

Japan wasted precious time waiting for a clear guarantee of support of the emperor system, and it was during this time that many people unnecessarily faced death—people on both sides of the war, plus many people in Asia who belonged to neither side. Impatient with the Japanese attitude, which seemed only to prolong the formal declaration of capitulation, the Americans decided to resume air raids on Japanese cities, in order to force Japan to accept a formal surrender. Several air raids took place during those two or three days just before 15 August. Among those final raids, the largest was aimed at my city, Osaka, on the afternoon of 14 August 1945, that bombing in which many died without knowing the background of their death, or its meaning, which was, quite simply, that their death was just a meaningless death. They died in fire and chaos. Twenty hours or so after the raid on my city, the emperor's recorded voice solemnly, and in a flat tone, announced Japan's surrender. I heard his voice. I did not weep.

As a citizen and a human being, whenever I feel forced to act in the face of injustice, the memory of 14 August returns and drives my thoughts, my deeds. As a writer, I know that this memory constitutes the basis of what I set down—even when I compose a *pure* love story.

NOTE

1. Oda Makoto, *The Bomb* (New York and Tokyo: Kodansha International, 1990).

14

German Postwar Strategies of Coming to Terms with the Past

Peter Schneider

Being neither a historian nor a sociologist, I cannot speak as a specialist on the political debates of my country. I can speak only as a representative of my generation, that is, as a participant in the approaches and hidden escapes of German intellectuals of my age with respect to our past.

I am glad to meet my friend Oda Makoto here, on neutral soil, and to open a debate that we were supposed to have had earlier in Germany and in Japan. I agree with what Oda has been quoted as saying on the issue of our countries' past: that Germany and Japan, geographically so distant, became embarrassingly close under the sign of fascism. When he was asked why he had accepted an invitation to come to Germany last year, Oda answered that he was simply curious to find out how the Germans faced their problems. I am similarly curious about his country, but my curiosity is ambiguous, afflicted with the emotions of suspicion, shame, and unwanted complicity.

Although we are both writers and have written on the issue in both essay and narrative forms, we can hardly claim to speak for our nations. For my part, I seriously doubt that a writer can or should represent his country. One of the main reasons for becoming a writer, in my country at least, is to write yourself away from the silent majority rather than to speak for it.

In the past, democratic societies welcomed a writer's taking on the role of troublemaker: the critical writer was said to function as a public conscience. Besides being a novelist or playwright, the writer appeared to be at the same time a researcher, reporter, psychoanalyst, sociologist, and political activist. All these functions made sense in a society where there was almost nobody else to do the job. And they still are a writer's business in societies where censorship reigns, where there is repression of information, and where dissent cannot be voiced. But democratic societies have largely limited the former monopoly of the writer. That is why so many writers have a residual suspicion of democracy, because democracy tends to cut off many of their former mandates.

In Germany, the last one to play the role of the writer as public conscience was Heinrich Böll. It is no accident that his throne has been left empty and that no pretender is in sight. It can be argued that this is the case because the new writers lack talent and decision, but I think there is a structural reason: the writer as public conscience, as a leader of social dissent and opposition, can prosper only in societies in which everything is shaped by a powerful center. Such conditions form the ideal arena for a confrontation of champions: Gorki against Lenin, Sartre against de Gaulle, Böll against Adenauer. Our "post-something" societies are increasingly marked by centrifugal tendencies; leadership becomes more and more decentralized, despite the fact that many cultural or political leaders are not aware of the process.

As a result, having and expressing opinions is no longer a singular privilege. Especially in West Germany it is evident that the role of the writer as a public conscience has been taken on by groups such as the Greens, Greenpeace, or the Citizens' Initiatives. Although some writers might regard this "socialization" as a personal loss, it certainly is a gain for society. Space does not permit thorough exploration of this topic, but my own conclusion is that the writers now, more than at any other time, are bound to speak for themselves. And only by doing so can they hope to find people who agree or disagree with them.

It is the purpose of this chapter to analyze four different strategies in dealing with the past. To begin with, I am not happy that this project usually has the title *Vergangenheitsbewältigung*. I agree with Mark Twain: such a word is much too long not to arouse suspicion. Not by accident, the word *bewältigen* is hard to translate. In English it would be "to master" the past, which seems to be an impractical project even for professional forgetters. Or you could say "to overcome" the past, which implies pure ignorance. I prefer the German word *umgehen mit*, which means "facing" the past. The four strategies I want to discuss are (1) maintaining silence; (2) evoking the past through artistic and intellectual means; (3) rebelling against the past; and (4) the race for being the victim.

MAINTAINING SILENCE

Let us begin with some autobiographical notes. Born in 1940, I was five years old at the end of the war. Reading Oda, I was struck by the parallels of our respective postwar experiences. The same silence, the same escape to a purely economic rebuilding, the same apologies of our parents about the past: "It was a terrible time," "you will understand when you're older," "you can't judge since you were not there. . . ."

I had the feeling of growing up in a permanent shadow, in some gray, unclear substance that covered memories and feelings, as if I could look at reality only through a tinted glass. Nobody would speak out. I remember those silent lunches, where I heard only the clinking of knives and forks. The absence of speech and laughter were more disturbing to me than anything I might have heard about World War II.

I remember a physician, a friend of our family, who used to come to our house in the evenings to play chamber music. He once told us that he had met his former maid again, sitting in an apple tree waving at him. He reported how grateful she was that he had saved her life back in those terrible years by testifying that she did not qualify for the Nazis' extinction program of *unwertes Leben* (unworthy life). I was about sixteen years old then, and I wanted to ask this man who had worked in the psychiatric clinic in Emmendingen, which had been involved in the *Rassenhygiene* (racial hygiene) project, how many people he had saved in this generous way. But I did not dare ask him this question; rather, I asked it of my father after the doctor had left. "Don't you have other questions at this moment?" was my father's reply to me.

For schoolchildren in the 1950s, our so-called reeducation amounted to only two hours on the history of Nazi fascism during our nine years of history classes. Our teacher explained his reluctance; he had once taught at one of the *Führerschulen* that had indoctrinated young activists in the Nazi philosophy. He somehow felt inhibited and incompetent to give a historical evaluation of this period.

I myself was not very eager to find out about the past. It was more or less sheer rebellion that urged me to look for somebody who would explain to me what I found inconceivable: fascism had been so fascinating. I wanted an expert, a believing Nazi, someone who could still remember that he had once believed. Given the fact that the Nazi Party had 6 million members, I estimated that there should be at least one in my town who had been a true, straightforward Nazi who could satisfy my curiosity. I still think that this was not an absurd proposition. I never found this one man or woman; perhaps I gave up too soon. All that I did find were secret opponents, inner emigrants, the ever-skeptical persons; indeed, everyone I asked had somehow been against Hitler. Believing them, one could come to the conclusion that the Nazi Party had been an enormous organization for undercover resistance fighters.

I should mention here another element about the German way of coming to terms with the past: the most suspicious things in postwar

Germany seemed to be feelings. Security was found only in what one could grasp and consume, in the famous "material values." A generation whose beliefs and ideals had failed so completely now tried to survive by renouncing any values but material ones. As a result, the children of this generation were to grow up in an emotional vacuum. Twenty years later, when the reconstruction was over, Germans began to understand that it takes more time to rebuild an identity than to build houses and towns. The rejection by our parents' generation of any but materialistic values was one of the reasons for the overproduction of ideologies and moral absoluteness on the part of the 1968 movement.

EVOKING THE PAST THROUGH ARTISTIC AND INTELLECTUAL MEANS

In the reconstruction period, writers had an almost complete, unwanted monopoly on facing the past. Although the writers of Group 47 never had a common platform or program, they were united in an unwritten antifascist consensus. Some of the most famous writers of that period— Heinrich Böll, Günter Grass, Martin Walser, Wolfgang Koeppen, Alfred Andersch, Siegfried Lenz, and Hans Magnus Enzensberger— invested their very different individual skills in a common project: to find out what the immediate German past meant for the creation of a new society. This was also true for writers who focused their efforts on a new way of writing that would reflect the historical break of 1945 in the literary form itself, among them Arno Schmidt, Werner Heissenbüttel, and Peter Weiss. In this period we find the writer assuming the role of public conscience precisely because neither politicians nor academics seemed eager to challenge their unwanted monopoly.

I cannot go into the merits and contradictions of that literature, except to say that literature alone, left with such a task, is always overburdened. However, I want to address one of the characteristic features of that postwar literature, which is that the preferred hero is, if anything, the typical Nazi, the man of the street, who appears simultaneously as victim and victimizer. The fiction makes almost no attempt to approach the horror of the camps, the killers and bureaucrats of the Holocaust, the "monsters," as if they were not part of our history. Another omission also is painfully evident: the absence of the historical victims of the Holocaust. These issues were left to the so-called documentary literature, as written by, for example, Peter Weiss or Heinar Kipphardt. There is good reason to question whether fiction can address what was called the "final solution." But regardless of the answer, what Alexander and Margarete Mitscherlich stated in their *Inability to Mourn* remains true:

"The Germans still have no emotional perception of the real people whom they were ready to sacrifice to their dream of being a master race: as people, they have remained part of the de-realized reality."[1] Moreover, I also find no emotional perception of the murderers in the literature.

In contrast, in the history of literature, evil and evil-doer, far from being omitted, have been preferred subjects. Shakespeare, Schiller, the Schlegel brothers, and E. T. A. Hoffmann all had a weird interest in the extreme villain. Some of these authors discussed at length the question of how and for what purpose literature should represent such a villain. Schiller considered the fictional representation of evil as an educational duty of literature. He wanted to break down the easy contempt of the lawful citizen toward the criminal by exploring the psychology of the criminal; only by recognizing the troublesome similarity between the criminal and the normal citizen would the latter find the moral strength to reject the seduction to do wrong. In other words, Schiller did not trust the myth of the monster as belonging to a different species. He thought that even the most horrible human "monsters" are human after all and that therefore human beings can become "monsters."

Hannah Arendt has pointed out that the Nazi criminal represents a completely new type of evil, hitherto unknown not only to literature, but to history: "Eichmann was no Richard III, no Iago and no Macbeth, and nothing would have been more alien to him than to decide with Richard III to become a villain. The upsetting thing about Eichmann's personality was that he was alike to many a man and that those many have been neither perverse nor sadistic, but terribly and terrifyingly normal."[2]

The nearly complete absence of fictional representation of the Nazi criminal in the German postwar literature presents us with a dilemma: Does this fact mean that fiction is altogether unable to approach the Holocaust, and that only the documentary is able to do so? Or does this fact indicate that the German writers, along with their compatriots, escaped the German atrocities by leaving them to a purely documentary approach, suggesting that the crimes were committed by alien monsters who came from another planet?

Karl Heinz Bohrer, a German essayist, suggests that the embodiment of evil as Hitler-fascism has disconnected evil from the imagination. Far from solving this dilemma, I can only emphasize here how current this dilemma remains, for the same problem had to be faced by the author of the recently published book *The Nazi Doctors*, Robert Jay Lifton, of which I happened to read a review in the *New York Times*, written by Lifton's friend Bruno Bettelheim.[3] Bettelheim outlined Robert Jay Lifton's dilemma in the following way: by investigating so singlemindedly the psychology, motives, and their apologies of the Nazi doctors, the investigator had finally failed to maintain the distinction between understanding and forgiving. Interestingly enough, the same objection was made, some weeks ago, in a German left-wing paper, the *taz*. For me, as a German, there remains a suspicion: what does it mean when today's young Germans, in their need to prove their antifascism, are prepared to warn Robert Jay Lifton of playing down the atrocities of the Nazi doctors?

REBELLING AGAINST THE PAST

If German literature of the postwar period was marked by a need to face the past, this no longer holds true for writers of my generation. One reason might be that we know Nazi fascism not through direct experience but through the accounts or nonaccounts of our parents. Another reason certainly is that many of us believed that a literary approach was not enough. The 1968 movement in Germany had a precise motive underlying it: to be antiauthoritarian meant to question not only the so-called superfluous forms of authority, but also the authority of the specific generation that was responsible for Nazi fascism. Although no other denunciation was more popular than the deadly word *fascist* (or *fascism*), it was very rarely used to pinpoint the historical period to which it refers. As early as the Adenauer era, the word served mainly the purpose of denouncing the political enemy. In a kind of "reflex insult" response, the 1968 movement imitated this bad example. Anyone who opposed the "revolutionary" order of the day was sent to the corner as a fascist. Thus the most popular insult in postwar Germany mysteriously was never used to refer to the infamous twelve years in which it entered the vocabulary of international language. For the 1968 activists, this abuse seemed to be justified by the theory of "structural fascism." In retrospect, it is glaringly obvious that this theory had, apart from its instructive value, an unburdening function. As long as we could see our parents as victims of "the conspiracy of the ruling classes" and of capitalism, which "necessarily ends up as fascism," there was no need to debate the personal guilt of our daddies and mommies.

This debate started only in the late 1970s, in what is called "the father literature." Significantly, such autobiographical stories have a common point of departure: they begin with the sickness or death of a parent and develop into what one might call a posthumous confrontation. Only the death of a parent, it seems, made it possible for people of my generation to admit their emotional wounds—wounds opened by a recognition of our complicity.

DEFINING ONESELF AS A VICTIM

It seems unbelievable that the first nationwide discussion on the Holocaust that I can remember started in the late 1970s, as a result of a television show imported from the United States: the "Holocaust" series of CBS television. Although I share the doubts of many friends as to whether an incomparable historical crime could be expressed by means of an American fictional television series, the aesthetic criticism betrays elitist biases. In West Germany at least, reference to the "unspeakable" has too often served the purpose of not speaking at all. Purely aesthetic criticism misses the point if it does not refer to the unquestionable result of the series: that this fictional approach to the Holocaust finally broke through, to use the Mitscherlichs' term, the "sluggishness of reaction" in West Germany, which numerous documentary films had failed to do.

Is this result to be explained by the hypothesis that this highly debated series managed to make the notoriously "unimaginable" imaginable? That it awoke, to use the Mitscherlichs' term, in the "real people," the victims and the murderers, an "emotional perception?" Does this hypothesis mean that the "work of mourning" remains necessarily unsuccessful so long as the victims are represented only as mountains of bones and ashes, rather than as once-living, individual human beings? Asking these questions, I do not suggest that the documentary approach could or should be replaced by anything else. Given the existence of disbelievers who do not want to know the facts or who choose to regard them as pure myth, as propaganda lies of the enemy, there was and is no alternative to crude evidence. But it is one thing to find the perpetrator guilty, and another to reach his soul.

The "Holocaust" program on television was followed by an embarrassed silence that lasted another five years. In this period, which was anything but healing, new and more subtle instruments were invented to come to terms with the past. These new, sophisticated weapons, which might be called "anti-guilt-missiles," can be viewed as arms in "the race for being the victim." The prominent participants in this race, who have become known through the "historians' debate," have been widely discussed. It is unnecessary to quote Ernst Nolte's attempt to question the uniqueness of the Holocaust. The statement that Chancellor Helmut Kohl issued in Israel, that he is happy to share "the grace of being born too late," backfired and prompted attention instead to the question of when Helmut Kohl was actually born and what kind of education he enjoyed during the period between 1933 to 1945. (By the way, Helmut Kohl, being a politician, refers to the time as a "dark and terrible" period. Günter Grass, being the same age but a writer, insists in his novel *Cat and Mouse* that, for a young German boy, this period was rather exciting and adventurous. I believe that in Germany time seemingly does not heal the wounds—it only kills the sensitivity to pain.)

But let us focus here on the foreseeable losers of the race. Forty years had to go by before the dusty stage of collective memory could be cleared for a forgotten group of my generation: the children of the murderers. With this term I refer not to the typical German child with his fellow-traveler father, but rather to the sons and daughters of prominent Nazis such as Frank, Mengele, Sievers, and Eichmann. It was known that these children existed, but nobody took any particular interest in them, and the children themselves, growing into adults, never spoke out.

This changed in 1985 when Rolf Mengele, the son of the Nazi criminal Josef Mengele, was interviewed by the West German weekly *Bunte Illustrierte*. This publication was followed by Peter Sichrovsky's book *Born Guilty: The Children of Nazi Families* (1987), which can be regarded as a breakthrough. Later in the year came a series of articles on Hans Frank, Hitler's governor in Poland, written by his son Niklas.[4]

Theoretically, the children of Nazi criminals had to handle two, possibly equally strong, feelings: their natural attachment to their fathers and the disgust for their crimes. Sichrovsky's book makes clear that this model of conflict is far too rudimentary.

The cases of Rolf Mengele and of Niklas Frank might appear to be diametrically opposed. Rolf Mengele learned only at the age of fifteen that his father was none other than the so-called death angel of Auschwitz and that he was still alive and living in Latin America. Rolf started an exchange of letters, hoping to learn from his father what he had done and by what motives he had been guided. The startling effect of this attempt at understanding was a reversal of roles. It was the son who seemed to need the justifications and explanations for his father's behavior, because the father never showed the slightest sign of bad conscience. It is all the more surprising that Rolf kept calling a man whom he had never known and whose crimes he detested "daddy." By 1977, Rolf agreed to visit his father, then living in São Paulo. But even in a face-to-face conversation, which sometimes came close to a cross-examination, he never managed to break through his father's defenses. Rather, the father seems to have succeeded in shaking off his son's accusations. As late as 1985, when Rolf Mengele was interviewed, he was not ready to admit that his father had to be called a "murderer" or a "criminal."[5] Obviously he rejected any idea of denouncing his father and having him extradited. During an American TV talk show in June 1986, he said, "Nobody can ask a son to denounce his own father."

It is easy to be indignant about Rolf's attitude. It is more difficult to answer the question of what one would have done in Rolf Mengele's place. There is no doubt that Rolf, facing the dilemma between loyalty and disgust, chose loyalty. But it also has been said that his collaboration with the authors of *Mengele*[6] helped to accomplish the most complete and precise description of his father's crimes so far.

The case of Niklas Frank illustrates the counterexample of a pitiless attempt to even the score with his father. The points of departure of the two sons could hardly be more different. Niklas's father, Hans, was found guilty as a war criminal in the Nuremberg trials. Niklas was seven when his father was hanged. The son's series of articles in *Der Stern* can be read as an attempt to execute his father a second time. From the first line of the series, Niklas Frank betrays his ambition, which is to set a model for his generation. In the beginning he imagines the act of his, Niklas's, procreation. Father Hans is rolling onto his wife, Brigitte, who never enjoys an orgasm because Hans ejaculates within seconds. In the next paragraph Niklas describes a photo of his hanged father "with his broken neck . . . did you actually bite your lips when you were dropping in a free fall?" the son asks.[7] Later on, Niklas claims that this photo has heavily conditioned his early sexual fantasies. He remembers himself becoming aroused in a restroom as he imagines the moment when his father's neck cracked: "That is where I get my orgasm."

The shock and nausea brought on by this introduction were certainly intended. And the cruel attempt of a son, who verbally annihilates his criminal father, has at least the merit of having no predecessors among the Nazi's children. Indeed, Niklas may have been able to accomplish research into the atrocities in which his father took part only because of his desperate repression of any "family feelings." My sense of unease stems from the fact that Niklas's goal—to even the score—ends up too fully accomplished. Niklas has obviously repressed all his inner conflicts. He never seems to be worried about what characteristics he might have inherited from his father. He never comments on the curious fact that it took him forty years to perform this seemingly spontaneous outburst of hatred. In his unquestionable solidarity with the victims of his father, he seems to suggest a hidden personal motive: to depict himself as a pure victim. He certainly is a victim, but there is a difference between being the victim of bad conscience and being the victim of physical extermination.

Niklas Frank, faced with the conflict between loyalty and revulsion, opted for being the toughest prosecutor. He tried to resolve his conflict by denying any feelings of loyalty. The uneasiness the reader feels as a result of both Rolf's and Niklas's attempts to come to terms with their conflicting emotions indicates that there is no clear resolution for such conflict. The only clear suggestions that I can make are these: we must keep the conflict in the open rather than trying to "resolve" it, and no German, of any age, can claim to enjoy the grace of being born too late.

NOTES

1. Alexander and Margarete Mitscherlich, *The Inability to Mourn*, translated by Beverly R. Placzek (New York: Grove Press, 1975).
2. Hannah Arendt, *Eichmann in Jerusalem* (New York: Viking Press, 1964).
3. Robert J. Lifton, *The Nazi Doctors* (New York: Basic Books, 1986); Bruno Bettelheim reviewed Lifton's book in "Their Specialty Was Murder," *New York Times Book Review* (5 October 1986).
4. Rolf Mengele in *Bunte Illustrierte*, nos. 26 to 30 (1985); Peter Sichrovsky, *Born Guilty: The Children of Nazi Families*, translated by Jean Steinberg (New York: Basic Books, 1988); the original German version was published in 1987. Niklas Frank, *Der Stern* (serial in each of the weekly editions from no. 22, 20 May 1987, to no. 28, 2 July 1987). This series of articles has been published as a book by Niklas Frank, *Der Vater* (Munich: C. Bertelsmann, 1987).
5. *Bunte Illustrierte*, no. 27 (1985): 26, translated by Peter Schneider.
6. Gerald L. Posner and John Ware, *Mengele: The Complete Story* (New York: McGraw-Hill, 1986).
7. *Der Stern*, no. 22 (1987): 33, translated by Peter Schneider.

Annotated Bibliography and Suggestions for Further Reading

Preference has been given here to works published in English, but many of the cited works contain extensive bibliographies referring to further publications in the original language.

We owe thanks to Marlene Mayo, Nobuko Sakurai, and Reed Thompson for their help in assembling this bibliography. The speakers and discussants also provided bibliographical information, in addition to the works cited in their footnotes.

SELECTED BIBLIOGRAPHY OF WORKS OF GENERAL AND HISTORICAL BACKGROUND

A. Comparative

Baring, Arnulf, and Masamori Sasse, eds. *Zwei Zaghafte Riesen? Deutschland und Japan seit 1945*. Stuttgart and Zurich: Belser Verlag, 1977. The papers collected in this volume focus, with a comparative approach, on historical, political, and military aspects in the postwar period.

Wolfe, Robert, ed. *Americans as Proconsuls: United States Military Government in Germany and Japan, 1944–1952*. Carbondale: Southern Illinois University Press, 1984.

B. German

Adorno, Theodor W. "What Does Coming to Terms with the Past Mean?" In *Bitburg in Moral and Political Perspective*, Geoffrey H. Hartmann, ed., 115–29. Translated by Timothy Bahti and Geoffrey Hartmann. Bloomington: Indiana University Press, 1986. This is the first

English translation of Adorno's important 1959 essay that addressed, with a foresight of almost three decades, many of the current debates.

Arendt, Hannah. *Eichmann in Jerusalem*. New York: Viking Press, 1964.

Craig, Gordon. *The Germans*. New York: Putman's Sons, 1982. This is a general introduction that takes long glances down the corridors of the past and much interest in German cultural and intellectual life.

Dahrendorf, Ralf. *Society and Democracy in Germany*. Garden City, N.Y.: Doubleday, 1967. A classic.

Evans, Richard J. "The New Nationalism and the Old History: Perspectives on the West German Historikerstreit." *Journal of Modern History* 59 (December 1987): 761–97. This article contains a wealth of information about the recent "historians' debate" and in its ample documentation provides excellent sources for further studies.

Feldman, Lily Gardner. *The Special Relationship between West Germany and Israel*. Boston: George Allen and Unwin, 1984.

Friedländer, Saul. *Reflections on Nazism. An Essay on Kitsch and Death*. New York: Harper and Row, 1984. (French original, 1982).

Gimbel, John. *The American Occupation of Germany: Politics and the Military 1945–1949*. Stanford, Calif.: Stanford University Press, 1968. A classical study and still invaluable.

Habermas, Jürgen, ed. *Observations on "The Spiritual Situation of the Age."* Translated and with an introduction by Andrew Buckwalter. Cambridge, Mass.: MIT Press, 1984. This collection of essays presents a selection from the original German two-volume edition. Despite the omission of some of the original essays, this is still an important document of contemporary German intellectual perspectives on topics such as politics and society, religion and culture, theology, historiography, and terrorism.

Historikerstreit: Die Dokumentation der Kontroverse um die Einzigartigkeit der nationalsozialistischen Judenvernichtung. Munich: Piper Verlag, 1987. In this volume are collected the articles, refutations, and controversies that constitute the core of the recent West German "historians' debate." It is indispensable reading for any understanding of the post-1986 intellectual debates in the Federal Republic about German history and historiography in relation to the mass murder of the Jews.

Hogan, Michael. *The Marshall Plan: America, Britain, and the Reconstruction of Western Europe, 1947–1952*. Cambridge, Eng.: Cambridge University Press, 1987.

Iggers, Georg, ed. *The Social History of Politics: Critical Perspectives in West German Historical Writing Since 1945*. New York: St. Martin's Press, 1985. Iggers's excellent introduction discusses post-1945 German historiography as it reinterprets German history and historiography of the past two centuries.

Jaspers, Karl. *The Future of Germany*. Translated and edited by E. B. Ashton, with a foreword by Hannah Arendt. Chicago: University of Chicago Press, 1967.

———. *The Question of German Guilt*. Translated by E. B. Ashton. New York: Dial Press, 1948, 1978.

Kogon, Eugen. *The Theory and Practice of Hell: The German Concentration Camps and the System Behind Them*. Translated by Heinz Norden. New York: Farrar, Straus, 1950 (German original, 1946).

Maier, Charles S. *The Unmasterable Past: History, Holocaust, and German National Identity*. Cambridge, Mass.: Harvard University Press, 1988.

Mitscherlich, Alexander and Margarete. *The Inability to Mourn*. Translated by Beverly R. Placzek. New York: Grove Press, 1975. One of the earliest and most insightful psychological explorations of the German post-1945 mind (German original, 1967).

Pronay, Nicholas, and Keith Wilson, eds. *The Political Reeducation of Germany and Her Allies After World War II*. London and Sydney: Croom Helm, 1985.

Schneider, Peter. "Hitler's Shadow: On Being a Self-Conscious German." Translated by Leigh Hafrey. *Harper's Magazine* (September 1987): 49–54.

Sichrovsky, Peter. *Born Guilty: Children of Nazi Families*. Translated by Jean Steinberg. New York: Basic Books, 1988.

Tent, James. *Mission on the Rhine: Re-education and Denazification in American-Occupied Germany*. Chicago: University of Chicago Press, 1982.

C. Japanese

Arima, Tatsuo. *The Failure of Freedom: A Portrait of Modern Japanese Intellectuals*. Cambridge, Mass.: Harvard University Press, 1969. An extended treatment of the role of writers and intellectuals, indicating how prewar attitudes caused later wartime attitudes to develop as they did.

Beardsley, W. G., ed. *Modern Japan: Aspects of History, Literature and Society*. Berkeley: University of California Press, 1975.

Beckmann, George M., and Genji Okubo. *The Japanese Communist Party 1922–1945*. Stanford, Calif.: Stanford University Press, 1966.

Brackman, Arnold C. *The Other Nuremberg: The Untold Story of the Tokyo War Crimes Trials*. New York: William Morrow and Company, 1987.

Braw, Monica. *The Atomic Bomb Suppressed: American Censorship in Japan 1945–1949*. Lund Studies in International History 23. Lund: University of Lund, 1986.

Buckley, Roger. *Japan Today*. Cambridge and New York: Cambridge University Press, 1985.

Burkman, Thomas, ed. *The Occupation of Japan: Arts and Culture*. Norfolk: MacArthur Foundation, 1987. An unusual and highly informative compilation of articles about the arts in this complex period.

Calder, Kent E. *Crisis and Compensation: Public Policy and Political Stability in Japan, 1949–1986*. Princeton, N.J.: Princeton University Press, 1988.

Christopher, Robert C. *The Japanese Mind*. New York: Linden Press Simon and Schuster, 1983. A popular treatment of contemporary attitudes that contains some valuable general insights.

Cohen, Theodore. *Remaking Japan: The American Occupation as New Deal*. Edited by Herbert Passin. New York: Free Press, 1988.

Doi, Takeo. *The Anatomy of Dependence*. Translated by John Bester. Tokyo and New York: Kodansha International, 1981. A now classic account of basic contemporary Japanese patterns of behavior.

———. *The Anatomy of Self: The Individual in Japanese Society*. Tokyo and New York: Kōdansha International, 1986. A continuation of themes first stated in Doi's earlier book.

Dower, John W. *Empire and Aftermath: Yoshida Shigeru and the Japanese Experience*. Cambridge, Mass.: Harvard University Council on East Asian Studies, 1979.

———. *War Without Mercy: Race and Power in the Pacific War*. New York: Pantheon Books, 1986. A remarkable new interpretation of attitudes on both sides of the Pacific during the war years.

Eto, Jun. *A Nation Reborn: A Short History of Postwar Japan*. Tokyo: International Society for Educational Information, 1974.

Harries, Meiron and Susie. *Sheathing the Sword: The Demilitarization of Postwar Japan*. New York: McMillan Publishing Company, 1987.

Hasegawa, Michiko. "A Postwar View of the Greater East Asia War." *Japan Echo* 11, special issue (1984): 29–37.

Hata, Ikuhiko. "The Postwar Period in Retrospect." *Japan Echo* 11, special issue (1984): 12–21.

Havens, Thomas R. H. *Artist and Patron in Postwar Japan: Dance, Music, Theater, and the Visual Arts*. Princeton, N.J.: Princeton University Press, 1982. An excellent analysis of the interrelationships between creativity and society in postwar Japan.

Hosoya, Chihiro, et al., eds. *The Tokyo War Crimes Trial*: An International Symposium, Tokyo and New York: Kōdansha International, 1986.

Irie, Takanori. "The Lingering Impact of Misguided Occupation Policies." *Japan Echo* 11, special issue (1984): 22–28

Iriye, Akira, and Warren I. Cohen, eds. *The United States and Japan in the Postwar World*. Lexington: University Press of Kentucky, 1989.

Johnson, Chalmers. *MITI and the Japanese Miracle: The Growth of Industrial Policy, 1925–1975*. Stanford: Stanford University Press, 1982.

Kawai, Kazuo. *Japan's American Interlude*. Chicago: University of Chicago Press, 1960.

Kosaka, Masataka. *100 Million Japanese: The Postwar Experience*. Tokyo and New York: Kōdansha International, 1972.

Koschmann, J. Victor. "The Debate on a Subjectivity in Postwar Japan: Foundations of Modernism as a Political Critique." *Pacific Affairs* 54, no. 4 (Winter 1981–82): 609–31.

Maruyama, Masao. *Thought and Behavior in Modern Japanese Politics*. Edited by Ivan Morris. Oxford: Oxford University Press, 1963. An important study, never superseded, of attitudes toward politics and society in modern Japan.

Masumi Junnosuke. *Postwar Politics in Japan, 1945–1955*. Translated by Lonny E. Carlile. Berkeley: University of California, Institute of East Asian Studies, Japan Research Monograph 6, 1985.

Minear, Richard, H. *Victor's Justice: The Tokyo War Crimes Trial*. Princeton, N.J.: Princeton University Press, 1971. Considered the basic study of the subject.

Moore, Joe. *Japanese Workers and the Struggle for Power, 1945–1947*. Madison: University of Wisconsin Press, 1983.

Murakami, Hyoe. *Japan, the Years of Trial, 1919–1952*. Tokyo and New York: Kōdansha International, 1982.

Packard, George R. *Protest in Tokyo: The Security Treaty Crisis of 1960*. Princeton, N.J.: Princeton University Press, 1966.

Reischauer, Edwin O. *The Japanese*. Cambridge, Mass.: Harvard University Press, 1977.

Schaller, Michael. *The American Occupation of Japan: The Origins of the Cold War*. New York: Oxford University Press, 1985. A recent study that incorporates a good deal of new information.

Shillony, Ben-Ami. *Politics and Culture in Wartime Japan*. Oxford: Oxford University Press, 1981.

———. "Universities and Students in Wartime Japan." *Journal of Asian Studies* XLV, no. 4 (1986): 769–85.

Shimizu, Hayao. "The War and Japan: Revisionist Views." *Japan Echo* 11, special issue (1984):3–11.

Smith, Robert J. *Tradition, Self, and the Social Order*. New York: Cambridge University Press, 1984. A much-acclaimed study of basic modern Japanese patterns of behavior.

Swearingen, Rodger, and Paul Langer. *Red Flag in Japan: International Communism in Action 1919–1951*, 107–11. Cambridge, Mass.: Harvard University Press, 1952.

Takeda, Kiyoko. *The Dual Image of the Japanese Emperor*. New York: New York University Press, 1988.

Thayer, Nathaniel. *How the Conservatives Rule Japan*. Princeton, N.J.: Princeton University Press, 1969.

Tsurumi, Kazuko. *Social Change and the Individual: Japan Before and After Defeat in World War II*. Princeton, N.J.: Princeton University Press, 1970.

Tsurumi, Shunsuke. *A Cultural History of Postwar Japan: 1945–1980*. New York: Kegan Paul International, 1988. An unusual view of the postwar period by a leading Japanese social critic.

———. *An Intellectual History of Wartime Japan*. London and New York: KPL Ltd., distributed by Routledge and Kegan Paul, 1986.

Ward, Robert E., and Yoshikazu Sakamoto, eds. *Democratizing Japan: The Allied Occupation*. Honolulu: University of Hawaii Press, 1987. A now standard account of the period.

Williams, Justin, Sr. *Japan's Political Revolution under MacArthur, a Participant's Account*. Athens: University of Georgia Press, 1979.

Yoshida, Shigeru. *The Yoshida Memoirs*. Boston: Houghton Mifflin, 1962.

Yoshida, Mitsuru. *Requiem for Battleship Yamato*. Translated by Richard H. Minear. Seattle: University of Washington Press, 1985.

SELECTED BIBLIOGRAPHY OF GENERAL WORKS ON LITERATURE

A. German

Demetz, Peter. *After the Fires: Recent Writing in the Germanies, Austria, and Switzerland*. New York: Harcourt Brace Jovanovich, 1986. This volume supplements, expands, and continues the discussions of the author's preceding *Postwar German Literature*. Both books offer indispensable background information and thoughtful, contextual analyses of individual writers. An extensive bibliography emphasizes availability in English.

———. *Postwar German Literature*. New York: Pegasus, 1970. A very useful overview of the continuities, discontinuities, and developments in all German-speaking literatures from 1945 on.

Hamburger, Michael. *After the Second Flood: Essays on Postwar German Literature*. New York: St. Martin's Press, 1986.

Mayer, Hans. *Outsiders: A Study in Life and Letters*. Translated by Denis M. Sweet. Cambridge, Mass.: MIT Press, 1982.

Parkes, K. Stuart. *Writers and Politics in West Germany*. New York: St. Martin's Press, 1986. Part I of the study presents overviews in line with commonly accepted periodizations; part II discusses individual authors such as Grass, Böll, Enzensberger, and Martin Walser. The extensive bibliography, although mostly in German, concentrates on sociocultural issues but also deals selectively with the writers discussed.

Ryan, Judith. *The Uncompleted Past: Postwar German Novels and the Third Reich*. Detroit: Wayne State University, 1983. This very useful and topical discussion deals with a wide arsenal of postwar German novels.

Schneider, Michael. "Fathers and Sons, Retrospectively: The Damaged Relationship Between Two Generations." Translated by Jamie Owen Daniel in *New German Critique* 31 (1984): 3–51. This poignant essay is part of Schneider's *Den Kopf verkehrt aufgesetzt oder die melancholische Linke. Aspekte des Kulturzerfalls in den siebziger Jahren*. Darmstadt and Neuwied: Luchterhand, 1981.

B. Japanese

Allen, Louis. "Japanese Literature of the War and Postwar Years." *Japan Foundation Newsletter* 9, no. 4 (1981): 7–10.

Etō, Jun. "An Undercurrent in Modern Japanese Literature." *Journal of Asian Studies* 23 (May 1964): 433–45. A trenchant description of neo-Romanticism and the Right by a leading Japanese critic.

Fowler, Edward. *The Rhetoric of Confession*. Berkeley: University of California Press, 1988. A first-rate study of the modern Japanese "I" novel and the implications of the form for modern and contemporary Japanese literature.

Hibbett, Howard S. "Tradition and Trauma in the Contemporary Japanese Novel." *Daedalus* 95 (Fall 1966): 925–40.

Isoda, Koichi. "The Historical Context of Postwar Japanese Literature." *Japan Foundation Newsletter* 12, no. 2 (1984): 1–8.

Katō, Shūichi. *A History of Japanese Literature*. 3 vols. Translated by David Chibbett. London: Macmillan, 1979–88. The third volume, dealing with the modern period, contains a number of trenchant observations on the problems of the postwar literary scene.

———. "Japanese Writers and Modernization." *Changing Japanese Attitudes Toward Modernization*. Edited by Marius B. Jansen, 425–45. Princeton, N.J.: Princeton University Press, 1965. A highly useful introduction to the difficulties involved in recasting the traditions of Japanese literature in order to confront shifting social and philosophical problems in the modern and internal climate.

Keene, Donald. "The Barren Years: Japanese War Literature." *Monumenta Nipponica* 23, no. 1 (1978): 67–112. An earlier version of material contained in the longer history, cited below.

———. *Dawn to the West: Japanese Literature of the Modern Era*. 2 vols. New York: Holt, Rinehart & Winston, Inc., 1984. A lengthy and highly evocative study of the entire modern period, with the most complete account yet available in English or Japanese of the postwar period through the 1970s.

Kimball, Arthur G. *Crisis in Identity and Contemporary Japanese Novels.* Tokyo and Rutland, Vt.: C. E. Tuttle Co., 1973.

Kokusai Bunka Shinkokai. *Introduction to Contemporary Japanese Literature. Part II: 1936–1955.* Tokyo: Kokusai Bunka Shinkokai, 1959.

———. *Introduction to Contemporary Japanese Literature, 1956–1970: Synopses of Major Works.* Tokyo: University of Tokyo Press, 1972.

———. *Synopses of Contemporary Japanese Literature.* Tokyo: Kokusai Bunka Shinkokai, 1970.

Kuwabara, Takeo. "Tradition Versus Modernization." *Japan and Western Civilization: Essays in Comparative Culture.* Edited and translated by Kano Tsutomu and Patricia Murray. Tokyo: University of Tokyo Press, 1983. Useful essays on postwar Japanese cultural and intellectual issues.

Ōe, Kenzaburō. "Postwar Japanese Literature and the Contemporary Impasse." *Japan Foundation Newsletter* 14, no. 3 (1986): 1–6.

Rimer, J. Thomas. *Modern Japanese Fiction and its Traditions.* Princeton, N.J.: Princeton University Press, 1979.

Rubin, Jay. "From Wholesomeness to Decadence: The Censorship of Literature Under the Allied Occupation." *Journal of Japanese Studies* 11, no. 1 (1985): 71–103. The most complete account on the subject available in English, before Marlene Mayo's essay (Chapter 7) in this volume.

Shea, G. T. *Left-Wing Literature in Japan.* Tokyo: Hosei University Press, 1964.

Treat, John Whittier. "Atomic Bomb Literature and the Documentary Fallacy." *Journal of Japanese Studies* 14, no. 1 (1988): 27–57

Ueda, Makoto. "Japanese Literature Since World War II." *Literary Review* 6, no. 1 (1962): 5–23.

———. *Literary and Arts Theories in Japan.* Cleveland, Ohio: Western Reserve University Press, 1967. Although not a study of the arts in the modern period, this highly useful book explains many basic Japanese attitudes on the role of art and culture.

———. *Modern Japanese Writers and the Nature of Literature.* Stanford, Calif.: Stanford University Press, 1976.

Yamanouchi, Hisaaki. *The Search for Authenticity in Modern Japanese Literature.* New York: Cambridge University Press, 1978.

SELECTED BIBLIOGRAPHY OF LITERARY WORKS IN ENGLISH TRANSLATION

A. German

This section lists primarily the German authors mentioned in this book, and therefore the focus is on prose literature, as opposed to poetry or drama. For a complementary list of works available in translation, consult Demetz, *After the Fires*, 395 (see section II above).

Andersch, Alfred. *Efraim's Book*. Translated by Ralph Manheim. Garden City, N.Y.: Doubleday, 1970.

——. *Flight to Afar*. Translated by Michael Bullock. Bath: Cedric Chivers, Ltd., 1971.

——. *My Disappearance in Providence, and Other Stories*. Translated by Ralph Manheim. Garden City, N.Y.: Doubleday, 1978.

——. *The Redhead*. Translated by Michael Bullock. New York: Pantheon Books, 1961.

——. *Winterspelt*. Translated by Richard and Clara Winston. Garden City, N.Y.: Doubleday, 1978.

Bauer, Josef Martin. *As Far as My Feet Will Carry Me*. Translated by Lawrence P. R. Wilson. New York: Random House, 1957.

Böll, Heinrich. *Absent Without Leave and Other Stories*. Translated by Leila Vennewitz. London: Weidenfeld and Nicholson, 1967.

——. *And Never Said A Word*. Translated by Leila Vennewitz. New York: McGraw-Hill, 1978.

——. *And Where Were You, Adam?* Translated by Leila Vennewitz. London: Secker and Warburg, 1974.

——. *Billiards at Half Past Nine*. Translated by Leila Vennewitz. New York: McGraw-Hill, 1962.

——. *The Bread of Those Early Years*. Translated by Patrick Bowles. New York: McGraw-Hill, 1976.

——. *The Clown*. Translated by Leila Vennewitz. New York: McGraw-Hill, 1965.

——. *The End of a Mission*. Translated by Leila Vennewitz. New York: McGraw-Hill, 1967.

———. *Group Portrait with Lady*. Translated by Leila Vennewitz. New York: McGraw-Hill, 1973.

———. *The Lost Honor of Katharina Blum*. Translated by Leila Vennewitz. New York: McGraw-Hill, 1975.

———. *The Safety Net*. Translated by Leila Vennewitz. New York: Alfred A. Knopf, 1982.

———. *Tomorrow and Yesterday*. Translated. New York: Criterion Books, 1957.

———. *The Train Was on Time*. Translated by Richard Graves. London: Weidenfeld and Nicholson, 1973.

Born, Nicolas. *The Deception*. Translated by Leila Vennewitz. Boston: Little, Brown, 1983.

Enzensberger, Hans Magnus. *The Havana Inquiry*. Translated by Peter Meyer. New York: Holt, Rinehart & Winston, 1974.

———. *The Sinking of the Titanic*. Translated by the author. Boston: Houghton, Mifflin Co., 1980.

Forte, Dieter. *Luther, Münzer, and the Bookkeepers of the Reformation*. Translated by Christopher Holme. New York: McGraw-Hill, 1973.

Gaiser, Gerd. *The Final Ball*. Translated by Marguerite Waldman. New York: Pantheon Books, 1960.

———. *The Last Squadron*. Translated by Paul Findlay. New York: Pantheon Books, 1956.

Grass, Günter. *Cat and Mouse*. Translated by Ralph Manheim. New York: Harcourt Brace and World, 1963.

———. *Dog Years*. Translated by Ralph Manheim. New York: Harcourt Brace and World, 1965.

———. *The Flounder*. Translated by Ralph Manheim. New York: Harcourt Brace Jovanovich, 1978.

———. *From the Diary of a Snail*. Translated by Ralph Manheim. New York: Harcourt Brace and World, 1973.

———. *Headbirths, or the Germans are Dying Out*. Translated by Ralph Manheim. New York: Harcourt Brace Jovanovich, 1982.

———. *Local Anaesthetic*. Translated by Ralph Manheim. London: Secker and Warburg, 1970.

———. *The Meeting at Telgte*. Translated by Ralph Manheim. New York: Harcourt Brace Jovanovich, 1981.

———. *On Writing and Politics*. Translated by Ralph Manheim. San Diego: Harcourt Brace Jovanovich, 1985.

———. *The Rat*. Translated by Ralph Manheim. San Diego: Harcourt Brace Jovanovich, 1987.

———. *Speak Out*. Translated by Ralph Manheim. New York: Harcourt Brace and World, 1969.

———. *The Tin Drum*. Translated by Ralph Manheim. New York: Pantheon, 1962.

Handke, Peter. *Across*. Translated by Ralph Manheim. New York: Farrar, Straus & Giroux, 1986.

———. *The Goalie's Anxiety at the Penalty Kick*. Translated by Michael Roloff. New York: Farrar, Straus & Giroux, 1972.

———. *The Innerworld of the Outerworld of the Innerworld*. Translated by Michael Roloff. New York: Seabury Press, 1974.

———. *The Left-Handed Woman*. Translated by Ralph Manheim. New York: Farrar, Straus & Giroux, 1978.

———. *A Moment of True Feeling*. Translated by Ralph Manheim. New York: Farrar, Straus & Giroux, 1977.

———. *Nonsense and Happiness*. Translated by Michael Roloff. New York: Urizen Books, 1976.

———. *Repetition*. Translated by Ralph Manheim. New York: Farrar, Straus & Giroux, 1988.

———. *Short Letter, Long Farewell*. Translated by Ralph Manheim. New York: Farrar, Straus & Giroux, 1974.

———. *Slow Homecoming*. Translated by Ralph Manheim. New York: Farrar, Straus & Giroux, 1985.

———. *A Sorrow Beyond Dreams*. Translated by Ralph Manheim. New York: Farrar, Straus & Giroux, 1975.

———. *They Are Dying Out*. Translated by Michael Roloff. London: Eyre Methuen, 1974.

———. *The Weight of the World*. Translated by Ralph Manheim. New York: Farrar, Straus & Giroux, 1984.

Härtling, Peter. *Granny*. Translated by Anthea Bell. London: Andersen Press, 1977.

———. *A Woman*. Translated by Joachim Neugröschel. New York: Holmes and Meier, 1988.

Heinrich, Willi. *The Cross of Iron*. Translated by Richard and Clara Winston. Indianapolis: Bobbs-Merrill, 1956.

Heissenbüttel, Helmut. *Texts*. Translated by Michael Hamburger. London: Calder and Boyars, 1977.

Hildesheimer, Wolfgang. *The Collected Stories of Wolfgang Hildesheimer*. Translated by Joachim Neugröschel. New York: Ecco Press, 1987.

———. *Marbot: A Biography*. Translated by Patricia Crampton. New York: G. Braziller, 1983.

———. *Mozart*. Translated by Marion Faber. New York: Farrar, Straus & Giroux, 1982.

Hochhuth, Rolf. *The Deputy*. Translated by Richard and Clara Winston. New York: Grove Press, 1964.

———. *A German Love Story*. Translated by John Brownjohn. Boston: Little, Brown, 1980.

———. *Soldiers: An Obituary for Geneva*. Translated by Robert David MacDonald. New York: Grove Press, 1968.

Johnson, Uwe. *An Absence*. Translated by Richard and Clara Winston. London: Cape Press, 1969.

———. *Anniversaries I: From the Life of Gesine Cresspahl*. Translated by Leila Vennewitz. New York: Harcourt Brace Jovanovich, 1975 (translation of vol. 1 and part of vol. 2 of *Jahrestage*).

———. *Anniversaries II: From the Life of Gesine Cresspahl*. Translated by Leila Vennewitz and Walter Arndt. San Diego: Harcourt Brace Jovanovich, 1987 (translation of vols. 2–4 of *Jahrestage*).

———. *Speculations About Jacob*. Translated by Ursula Molinaro. New York: Grove Press, 1963.

———. *The Third Book About Achim*. Translated. New York: Harcourt Brace and World, 1967.

———. *Two Views*. Translated by Richard and Clara Winston. New York: Harcourt Brace and World, 1966.

Jünger, Ernst. *Copse 125*. Translated by Basil Creighton. New York: Howard Fertig, 1988.

———. *On the Marble Cliffs*. Translated by Stuart Hood. Harmondsworth: Penguin, 1970.

———. *The Storm of Steel*. Translated by the author. New York: Howard Fertig, 1975.

Kirst, Hans Helmut. *Zero Eight Fifteen: The Gunner Asch Trilogy*. Translated by Robert Kee. Boston: Little, Brown, 1955–57.

Kluge, Alexander. *Attendance List for a Funeral*. Translated by Leila Vennewitz. New York: McGraw-Hill, 1966.

———. *The Battle*. Translated by Leila Vennewitz. New York: McGraw-Hill, 1967.

———. *Case Histories: Stories*. Translated by Leila Vennewitz. New York: Holmes and Meier, 1988.

Koeppen, Wolfgang. *Death in Rome*. Translated by Mervyn Savill. London: Weidenfeld and Nicholson, 1956.

———. *Pigeons on the Grass*. Translated by David Ward. New York: Holmes and Meier, 1988.

Krüger, Horst. *A Crack in the Wall: Growing up Under Hitler*. Translated by Ruth Hein. New York: Fromm International Publishing Corporation, 1982.

Langgässer, Elisabeth. *The Quest*. Translated by Jane Bannard Greene. New York: Alfred A. Knopf, 1953.

Lenz, Siegfried. *An Exemplary Life*. Translated by Douglas Parmee. New York: Hill and Wang, 1976.

———. *The German Lesson*. Translated by Richard and Clara Winston. London: MacDonald, 1971.

———. *The Heritage*. Translated by Krishna Winston. New York: Hill and Wang, 1981.

———. *The Lightship*. Translated by Michael Bullock. New York: Hill and Wang, 1962.

———. *The Survivor*. Translated by Michael Bullock. New York: Hill and Wang: 1965.

Meckel, Christoph. *The Figure on the Boundary Line: Selected Prose*. Edited and translated by Christopher Middleton, Brian Harris, and Margret Woodruff. Manchester: Carcanet Press, 1983.

Plievier, Theodor. *Stalingrad*. Translated by Richard and Clara Winston. New York: Appleton-Century-Crofts, 1948.

Richter, Hans Werner. *Beyond Defeat*. Translated by Robert Kee. New York: Putnam, 1950.

Schmidt, Arno. *The Egghead Republic*. Translated by Michael Horowitz. Boston: Marion Boyars Publishing Inc., 1979.

———. *Evening Edged in Gold*. Translated by John E. Woods. New York: Harcourt Brace Jovanovich, 1980.

———. *Scenes from the Life of a Faun*. Translated by John E. Woods. London: Marion Boyars Ltd., 1983.

Schneider, Peter. *The Wall Jumper*. Translated by Leigh Hafrey. New York: Pantheon Books, 1983.

Stefan, Verena. *Shedding*. Translated by Johanna Moore and Beth Weckmueller. New York: Daughters Publishing Co., 1978.

Strauss, Botho. *Big and Little*. Translated by Anne Cattaneo. New York: Farrar, Straus & Giroux, 1979.

———. *Devotion*. Translated by Sophie Wilkins. New York: Farrar, Straus & Giroux, 1979.

———. *Tumult*. Translated by Michael House. Manchester: Carcanet Press, 1984.

Süsskind, Patrick. *Perfume: The Story of a Murderer*. Translated by John E. Woods. New York: Alfred A. Knopf, 1986.

Walser, Martin. *Breakers*. Translated by Leila Vennewitz. New York: Henry Holt and Co., 1987.

———. *The Inner Man*. Translated by Leila Vennewitz. New York: Holt, Rinehart & Winston Inc., 1984.

———. *Letter to Lord Liszt*. Translated by Leila Vennewitz. New York: Holt, Rinehart & Winston Inc., 1985.

———. *Runaway Horse*. Translated by Leila Vennewitz. New York: Holt, Rinehart & Winston Inc., 1980.

———. *The Swan Villa*. Translated by Leila Vennewitz. New York: Holt, Rinehart & Winston Inc., 1982.

———. *The Unicorn*. Translated by Barrie Ellis-Jones. London: Calder and Boyars, 1971.

Weiss, Peter. *Bodies and Shadows*. Translated by E. B. Garside and Rosemarie Waldrop. New York: Delacorte Press, 1969.

———. *Discourse on Vietnam*. Translated by Geoffrey Skelton. New York: Dell Publishing Co., 1970.

———. *Exile*. Translated by E. B. Garside, Alastair Hamilton, and Christopher Levenson. New York: Delacorte Press, 1968.

———. *The Investigation*. Translated by Jon Swan and Ulu Grosbard. New York: Atheneum, 1966.

———. *The Leavetaking*. Translated by Christopher Levenson. New York: Harcourt Brace and World, 1962.

———. *Marat/Sade*. Translated by Geoffrey Skelton. New York: Atheneum, 1965.

———. *Song of the Lusitania Bogey* in *Two Plays*. Translated by Lee Baxandall. New York: Atheneum, 1970.

———. *Trotsky in Exile*. Translated by Geoffrey Skelton. New York: Atheneum, 1971.

———. *Vanishing Point* in *Leavetaking and Vanishing Point*. Translated by Christopher Levenson. New York: Harcourt Brace Jovanovich, 1962.

Zwerenz, Gerhard. *Little Peter in War and Peace*. Translated by William Whitman. New York: Grove Press, 1970.

———. *Remembrance Day: Thirteen Attempts in Prose to Adopt an Attitude of Respect*. Translated by Eric Mosbacher. London: Hutchinson, 1966.

B. Japanese

(1) Anthologies

Because of a relative scarcity of translators, far fewer full-length prose works from the postwar period have been translated from the Japanese than from the German.

Gessel, Van C., and Tomoe Matsumoto, eds. *The Shōwa Anthology*. 2 vols. Tokyo and New York: Kōdansha International, Ltd., 1985. The most comprehensive anthology of work from this period available.

Gluck, Jay, ed. *Ukiyo, Stories of Postwar Japan*. New York: Grosset and Dunlap, 1964. Difficult to locate, this collection is worth seeking out for the rare material it contains, much of it written during and just after the occupation.

Hibbett, Howard, ed. *Contemporary Japanese Literature: An Anthology of Fiction, Film, and Other Writing Since 1945*. New York: Alfred A. Knopf, 1977. This collection contains a number of the best-known postwar shorter prose works.

Iwamoto, Yoshio, and Yoshiko Samuels, eds. *Japanese Writing, 1974–1984*. Special issue of the *Literary Review* 30, no. 2 (Winter 1987). A useful and stimulating collection of current Japanese writing, the only one of its kind.

Keene, Donald. *Modern Japanese Literature*. New York: Grove Press, 1960. Most of the works contained in the anthology were written before the war, but some major modern texts are provided.

Lippit, Noriko Mizuta, and Kyoko Iriye Selden, translators and editors. *Stories by Contemporary Japanese Women Writers*. New York: M. E. Sharpe, 1982.

Mishima, Yukio, and Geoffrey Bownas, eds. *New Writing in Japan*. Harmondsworth: Penguin Books, 1972. An excellent compilation of postwar works in prose and poetry.

Mitsios, Helen, ed. *New Japanese Voices: The Best Contemporary Fiction from Japan*. New York: Atlantic Monthly Press, 1991.

Morris, Ivan I., ed. *Modern Japanese Stories, An Anthology*. Translated by Edward Seidensticker. Tokyo and Rutland, Vt.: C. E. Tuttle, 1962.

Ōe Kenzaburō. *The Crazy Iris and Other Stories of the Atomic Aftermath*. New York: Grove Press, 1985.

Saeki, Shoichi, ed. *The Shadow of Sunrise: Selected Stories of Japan*. Tokyo: Kōdansha International, Ltd., 1966. Stories reflecting on the war, many of them of high literary quality.

Tanaka, Yukiko, and Elizabeth Hanson, translators and editors. *This Kind of Woman: Ten Stories by Japanese Women Writers, 1960–1976*. Stanford: Stanford University Press, 1972.

———. *To Live and Write, Selections by Japanese Women Writers, 1913–1938.* Seattle: Seal Press, 1987. Although the anthology contains material written before the Pacific war, some of the major modern writers are included here, several of whom continued to write important works in the postwar period.

(2) Individual Works

Only representative works have been included for some of the more widely translated authors.

Abe, Kōbō. *The Ark Sakura.* Translated by Juliet Winters Carpenter. New York: Alfred A. Knopf, 1988.

———. *The Face of Another.* Translated by E. Dale Saunders. New York: Alfred A. Knopf, 1966.

———. *The Man Who Turned into a Stick.* Translated by Donald Keene. Tokyo: University of Tokyo Press, 1986.

———. *The Woman in the Dunes.* Translated by E. Dale Saunders. New York: Alfred A. Knopf, 1964.

Agawa, Hiroyuki. *The Reluctant Admiral.* Translated by John Bester. Tokyo and New York: Kōdansha International, Ltd., 1979.

Ariyoshi, Sawako. *The Doctor's Wife.* Translated by Wakako Hironaka and Ann Siller Kostant. Tokyo and New York: Kōdansha International, Ltd., 1978.

———. *The River Ki.* Translated by Mildred Tahara. Tokyo and New York: Kōdansha International, Ltd., 1980.

———. *The Twilight Years.* Translated by Mildred Tahara. Tokyo and New York: Kōdansha International, Ltd., 1984.

Dazai, Osamu. *No Longer Human.* Norfolk, Conn.: New Direction, 1958.

———. *The Setting Sun.* Translated by Donald Keene. Norfolk, Conn.: J. Laughlin, 1956.

Enchi, Fumiko. *Masks.* Translated by Juliet Winters Carpenter. New York: Alfred A. Knopf, 1983.

———. *The Waiting Years.* Translated by John Bester. Tokyo and New York: Kōdansha International, Ltd., 1971.

Endo, Shusaku. *The Samurai.* Translated by Van C. Gessel. New York: Harper and Row, 1982.

———. *Scandal*. Translated by Van C. Gessel. New York: Dodd, Mead and Company, 1988.

———. *Silence*. Translated by William Johnson. Tokyo: Sophia University in cooperation with C. E. Tuttle, 1969.

Hayashi, Fumiko. *Floating Cloud*. Translated by Y. Koitabashi and Martin C. Collcutt. Tokyo: Hara Shobo, 1965.

Ibuse, Masuji. *Black Rain*. Translated by John Bester. Tokyo and New York: Kōdansha International, Ltd., 1969.

Kawabata, Yasunari. *Beauty and Sadness (The Sleeping Beauty)*. Translated by Howard Hibbett. New York: Alfred A. Knopf, 1975.

———. *Japan the Beautiful and Myself; The 1968 Nobel Prize Acceptance Speech*. Translated by Edward Seidensticker. Tokyo and New York: Kōdansha International, Ltd., 1981.

———. *The Sound of the Mountain*. Translated by Edward Seidensticker. New York: Alfred A. Knopf, 1970.

———. *Thousand Cranes*. Translated by Edward G. Seidensticker. New York: Alfred A. Knopf, 1958.

Kaiko, Takeshi. *Darkness in Summer*. Translated by Cecilia Segawa Seigle. New York: Alfred A. Knopf, 1973.

Kinoshita, Junji. *Between God and Man*. Translated by Eric J. Gangloff. Tokyo: University of Tokyo Press; Seattle: University of Washington Press, 1979.

Kobayashi, Takiji. *The Factory Ship* and *The Absentee Landlord*. Translated by Frank Motofuji. Seattle: University of Washington Press, 1973.

Maruya, Saiichi. *Singular Rebellion*. Translated by Dennis Keene. Tokyo and New York: Kōdansha International, Ltd., 1986.

Mishima, Yukio. *After the Banquet*. Translated by Donald Keene. New York: Alfred A. Knopf, 1963.

———. *Confessions of a Mask*. Translated by Meredith Weatherby. Tokyo and Rutland, Vt.: C. E. Tuttle, 1970.

———. *Madame de Sade*. Translated by Donald Keene. Tokyo and Rutland, Vt.: C. E. Tuttle, 1965.

———. *The Sound of Waves*. Translated by Meredith Weatherby. Tokyo and Rutland, Vt.: C. E. Tuttle, 1956.

———. *The Temple of the Golden Pavilion*. Translated by Ivan Morris. New York: Alfred A. Knopf, 1958.

———. *The Sea of Fertility*, a tetralogy: *Spring Snow, Runaway Horses, The Temple of the Dawn*, and *The Decay of the Angel*. Various translators. New York: Alfred A. Knopf, 1972–74.

Murakami, Ryu. *Almost Transparent Blue*. Translated by Nancy Andrew. Tokyo and New York: Kodansha International, Ltd., 1977.

Noma, Hiroshi. *Zone of Emptiness*. Translated by Bernard Frechtman from the French. Cleveland: World Publishing Press, 1956.

Oda, Makoto. "Making Democracy Our Own." *Japan Interpreter* 6, no. 3 (Autumn 1970).

———. *The Bomb*. Translated by D. H. Whittaker. Tokyo: Kodansha International, 1990.

Ōe, Kenzaburō. *Atomic Aftermath: Short Stories about Hiroshima and Nagasaki*. Tokyo: Shuseisha, 1984.

———. *Hiroshima Notes*. Translated by Toshi Yonezawa. Tokyo: YMCA Press, 1981.

———. *A Personal Matter*. Translated by John Nathan. New York: Grove Press, 1969.

———. *The Silent Cry*. Translated by John Bester. Tokyo and New York: Kōdansha International, Ltd., 1967.

———. *Teach Us to Outgrow Our Madness*. Translated by John Nathan. New York: Grove Press, 1977.

Ōoka, Shōhei. *Fires on the Plain*. Translated by Ivan Morris. New York: Alfred A. Knopf, 1957.

Osaragi, Jirō. *Homecoming*. Translated by Brewster Horwitz. New York: Alfred A. Knopf, 1954.

Takeda, Taijun. *This Outcast Generation; Luminous Moss*. Translated by Sanford Goldstein and Yasaburo Shibuya. Tokyo and Rutland, Vt.: C. E. Tuttle, 1967.

Takeyama, Michio. *Harp of Burma*. Translated by Howard Hibbett. Tokyo and Rutland, Vt.: C. E. Tuttle, 1966.

Tanizaki, Junichirō. *Diary of a Mad Old Man*. Translated by Howard Hibbett. New York: Alfred A. Knopf, 1965.

———. *The Makioka Sisters*. Translated by Edward Seidensticker. New York: Alfred A. Knopf, 1957.

———. *Seven Japanese Tales: A Portrait of Shunkin, The Tattooer, The Thief, Aguri, and A Blind Man's Tale*. Translated by Howard Hibbett. New York: Alfred A. Knopf, 1963.

Tsuboi, Sakae. *Twenty-four Eyes*. Translated by Akira Miura. Tokyo: Kenkyūsha, 1957.

Tsushima, Yūko. *Child of Fortune*. Translated by Geraldine Harcourt. London: Women's Press, 1988.

———. *The Shooting Gallery*. Translated and compiled by Geraldine Harcourt. New York: Pantheon Books, 1988.

Ueda, Makoto, ed. *The Mother of Dreams and Other Short Stories*. Tokyo and New York: Kodansha International, Ltd., 1986.

Yasuoka, Shōtarō. *A View by the Sea*. Translated by Karen Wigen Lewis. New York: Columbia University Press, 1984.

Yoshiyuki, Junnosuke. *The Dark Room*. Tokyo and New York: Kodansha International, Ltd., 1975.

About the Authors

Arnulf Baring, professor of contemporary history at the Freie Universität Berlin, studied law and political science at the universities of Hamburg, Berlin, and Freiburg in Germany, and received an M.A. from Columbia University in New York. In 1958 he was awarded the LL.D. from the Freie Universität Berlin. Baring has been political editor of the West German Broadcasting System, a research fellow of the German Society for Foreign Affairs, and a guest scholar at the Woodrow Wilson International Center for Scholars. From 1976 to 1979 he worked in the office of the President of the Federal Republic of Germany. His publications include *Im Anfang war Adenauer: Die Entstehung der Kanzlerdemokratie* (1969, 1982) and *Machtwechsel: Die Ära Brandt-Scheel* (1982). With Masamori Sase he edited *Zwei zaghafte Riesen? Deutschland und Japan seit 1945* (1977). His latest book is *Unser neuer Grössenwahn. Deutschland zwischen West und Ost* (1988).

Dagmar Barnouw, professor of German and English at the University of Southern California, has published numerous essays on cultural and literary history, as well as books on Eduard Mörike, Thomas Mann, Elias Canetti, and feminist science fiction. Her most recent publications include *Weimar Intellectuals and the Threat of Modernity* (1988) and *Visible Spaces: Hannah Arendt and the German-Jewish Experience* (1990). She received a Ph.D. in German from Yale University and has held several fellowships including a Guggenheim.

Peter Demetz, Sterling Professor of German at Yale University, was born in Prague and earned his doctorate there at Charles University. He received a second doctorate from Yale University and has taught at Yale ever since. He is corresponding member of the Akademie der Künste, Berlin, and member of the PEN Club of the Federal Republic of Germany, of the United States, and of Austria. He served as President of the Modern Language Association of America, and has been the recipient of numerous distinguished fellowships. In 1984, he was awarded the Commander's Cross of the Order of Merit of the Federal Republic of Germany. He is the author of numerous articles on nineteenth- and twentieth-century German literature and literary criticism. His books include studies on R. M. Rilke and Theodor Fontane; *Marx, Engels und die Dichter* (1959) has been translated into English, Spanish, and Japanese and *German Post-War Literature: A Critical In-*

troduction (1970) was also published in German. His most recent book is *After the Fires: Recent Writing in the Germanies, Austria, and Switzerland* (1986).

Van C. Gessel, associate professor in the Department of Asian and Near Eastern Languages, Brigham Young University, received M.A. and Ph.D. degrees in modern Japanese literature from Columbia University, and he has taught at Columbia and Notre Dame universities. He has translated into English four full-length works by Endō Shūsaku, including *The Samurai* and *Scandal*, and he is co-editor of *The Showa Anthology*. He has recently completed a critical study, *The Sting of Life: Four Contemporary Japanese Novelists*, Columbia University Press, 1989.

Carol Gluck, George Sansom Professor of History at Columbia University, received an M.A. and a Ph.D. from Columbia University and has twice been visiting research associate at the Faculty of Law of Tokyo University. Her field of research is modern Japanese intellectual history, including postwar Japan, ideology in modern Japan, and Japanese and comparative historiography. Her publications include *Japan's Modern Myths: Ideology in the Late Meiji Period* (1985), and *Versions of the Past: The Japanese and Their Modern History*.

Irmela Hijaya-Kirschnereit, professor of modern Japanese studies at the University of Trier, received her doctorate from the Ruhr-Universität Bochum where she also wrote her Habilitation. She has been associate professor for modern Japanese literature and the sociology of literature at Hitotsubashi University and has taught at the Ruhr-Universität Bochum and Vienna University. Her field of research is modern Japanese literature, literary criticism in Japan, and Japanese sociolinguistics. Her publications include translations of fiction and scholarly works, as well as a book on Mishima's novel *Kyoko-no ie* (1976), *Selbstentblößungsrituale* (1981), with translations into Japanese (1989) and English (1989), as well as a collection of essays on contemporary Japanese culture and society *Das Ende der Exotik* (1988).

Walter H. Hinderer, professor of German at Princeton University, received a D.Phil. from the Maximiliansuniversität, Munich. He has taught at Pennsylvania State University, the University of Colorado, Stanford University, the University of Maryland, and has held several fellowships. His areas of specialization and research are eighteenth-, nineteenth-, and twentieth-century German literature, especially drama and poetry; literary theory, history of criticism, poetics and aesthetics; and German rhetoric and oratory. His many publications include books on Hermann Broch, George Büchner, literary criticism, Friedrich Schiller's drama *Wallenstein*, and *Über deutsche Literatur und Rede. Historische Interpretationen* (1981). He has edited several books on nineteenth- and twentieth-century literature, including works on Börne, Kleist, Schiller, Goethe, Büchner, and Brecht.

Katō Shūichi, professor of Japanese culture and history at Ritsumeikan University in Kyoto, taught at the University of British Columbia, the Ostasiatische Institut of the Freie Universität Berlin, Sophia University (Tokyo), Yale, Brown, and Cambridge. He is the author of a three-volume *History of Japanese Literature* and of fifteen volumes (in Japanese) of *Selected Works*, including poetry, short stories, and essays on classical and modern Japanese literature, art, and society. He is also coauthor, with Robert Lifton and Michael Reich, of *Six Lives–Six Deaths: Portraits from Modern Japan*.

J. Victor Koschmann, associate professor of Japanese history at Cornell University, worked in Tokyo for several years as a translator and editor with the quarterly journal *The Japan Interpreter* before earning a Ph.D. from the University of Chicago. He has written *The Mito Ideology: Discourse, Reform and Insurrection in Late Tokugawa Japan, 1790–1864* (1987) and edited books on conflict in modern Japanese history, Japanese folklore studies, and political thought in postwar Japan. His current research focuses on intellectual and literary debates in the early post–World War II period.

Marlene Mayo, associate professor of history at the University of Maryland, has also taught at Columbia University, Bucknell University, and Sarah Lawrence College. She is the recipient of many grants and awards including a Fulbright research grant and a Social Science Research Council award, and has served as consultant to a variety of organizations on projects dealing with Japan and the United States. She received her M.A. and Ph.D. from Columbia University, and is the author of many publications on U.S.-Japanese history, including *The Emergence of Imperial Japan: Self Defense or Systematic Aggression?* and a book in preparation on American wartime planning for the occupation and reform of defeated Japan, 1942–45.

Oda Makoto is a novelist and literary critic in Tokyo. As an outspoken critic of the establishment, he was also the founder of the Peace for Vietnam Committee. He received a bachelor's degree in ancient Greek literature from the University of Tokyo, and studied in the United States as a Fulbright scholar. He has written essays for a variety of social and political causes and is the author of the best-selling account of his travels in the United States, *Amerika*, as well as of the novels *Hiroshima*, *D*, and *Berlin Story*. He is also the author of *Gato Island*, *Ethics and Logics of Social Change*, *At the Turning Point of History*, *The Philosophy of Ware Ware (We)*, and a book of criticism of Mao Tsetung.

J. Thomas Rimer, chair of the Department of East Asian Languages and Literatures of the University of Pittsburgh. He served in the same capacity at the University of Maryland, College Park, from 1986 to 1991. Mr. Rimer has also served as chief of the Asian Division at the Library of Congress, as chairman of the Department of Chinese and Japanese at Washington University, and as director of USIA's American Cultural Center in Kobe, Japan. He earned a B.A. from Princeton University and an M.A. and Ph.D. from Columbia University. Mr. Rimer has published many works on Japanese literature and theater, including *Toward a Modern Japanese Theatre: Kishida Kunio* (Princeton N.J.: Princeton University Press, 1974), *Traditions in Modern Japanese Fiction* (Princeton N.J.: Princeton University Press, 1978), *The Way of Acting: The Theatre Writings of Tadashi Suzuki* (New York: Theatre Communications Group, 1986), and *Pilgrimages: Aspects of Japanese Literature and Culture* (Honolulu: University of Hawaii Press, 1988).

Judith Ryan, professor of German and comparative literature at Harvard University, was born and educated in Australia, where she received a B.A. in German at the University of Sydney. She earned a D.Phil. at the University of Münster. She has published numerous articles on twentieth-century literature and is the author of books on R. M. Rilke and postwar German literature, including *Umschlag und Verwandlung. Poetische Struktur und Dichtungstheorie in R. M. Rilkes Lyrik der mittleren Periode (1907–1914)* (1972) and *The Uncompleted Past* (1983). She is currently on the Executive Council of the Modern Languages Association of America.

Ernestine Schlant, professor of German and comparative literature at Montclair State College in New Jersey, received M.A. and Ph.D. degrees in comparative literature from Emory University and has taught at Spelman College and the State University of New York at Stony Brook. She has received several awards and fellowships. Her publications include *Die Philosophie Hermann Brochs* (1971) and *Hermann Broch* (1978) as well as numerous articles on 20th-century German and Austrian literature.

Peter Schneider, a novelist, screenplay writer, essayist, and critic in West Berlin, has written widely on literary, social, and political subjects. His literary works include *Lenz* (1973), *. . . schon bist du ein Verfassungsfeind* (1975), *Der Mauerspringer* (1982) (translated into English as *The Wall Jumper* [1983]), *Die Wette* (1978), and, most recently, *Vati* (1987). Among his critical works are *Atempause. Versuch, meine Gedanken über Literatur und Kunst zu ordnen* (1977), *Die Botschaft des Pferdekopfs und andere Essais aus einem friedlichen Jahrzehnt* (1981), and *Deutsche Ängste* (1988).

Index

Abe Akira, 221
Abe Kōbō, 109, 217, 222, 258
Adenauer, Konrad, 23, 46–48, 52, 53, 55, 57, 87, 88, 93, 94, 284
Adorno, Theodor W., 23, 82–86, 93, 253
Agawa Hiroyuki, 105, 215
Aichinger, Ilse, 91, 129
Akagawa Jirō, 252
Akahata (Red Flag), 66, 137
Akutagawa Ryūnosuke, 142
Allemann, Fritz Rene, 49
Allersweltsparteien ("catch-all" parties), 49
Americanization: of Germany, 43–45; of Japan, 67–68
Andersch, Alfred, 47, 82, 92, 126, 127–31, 192, 200–201, 236, 242, 282
Anouilh, Jean, 91
Anpō protests, 72, 74
Anti-Comintern Pact, 5, 183
Ara Masato, 102, 164, 173, 174–80
Arendt, Hannah, 86, 92, 283
Atlantic Charter, 165
Augstein, Rudolf, 88n
"August 15" records and reminiscences, 65
Auschwitz trial, 15, 53, 92, 194
autobiographical fiction. *See* "I" novel
A-bomb literature (*genbaku bungaku*), 110, 112, 115, 150–51, 271–72

Bachmann, Ingeborg, 129
Baier, Lothar, 236
Baring, Arnulf, 66
Basic Law (*Grundgesetz*), 51
Baumer, Franz, 243
Baumgart, Reinhard, 228–29
Becker, Rolf, 88n
Benjamin, Walter, 93
Benn, Gottfried, 130
Bergengruen, Werner, 125
Bettelheim, Bruno, 284
Bienek, Horst, 199
Bildzeitung (newspaper), 54

Bismarck, Otto von, 4
Bohrer, Karl-Heinz, 242, 283
Böll, Heinrich, 47, 91, 92, 93, 129, 191, 192, 197–98, 203, 280, 282
Bolshevik Revolution (1917), 4
Bondy, François, 242
Bonn republic: development of democracy, 49–51; founding of, 51–52
Borchardt, Knut, 55, 57
Borchert, Wolfgang, 91, 92
Boveri, Margret, 44
Bowers, Faubion, 140
Brandt, Willy, 23, 52, 53, 94, 196
Bratton, Rufus, 145
Brecht, Bertolt, 124, 125, 193–94
Broch, Hermann, 129, 132
Broszat, Martin, 40
Byrnes, James F., 44, 86

Carossa, Hans, 125
CCD. *See* Civil Censorship Detachment
censorship: during occupation of Germany, 124, 190; during occupation of Japan, 135–53, 163–64
Chinese Revolution (1911), 4
Christian Democratic Party (West Germany), 46, 49, 52
Churchill, Winston, 51
CI&E. *See* Civil Information and Education Section
Citizens' Initiatives, 280
Civil Censorship Detachment, 136–37
Civil Information and Education Section, 136, 137
Clay, Lucius D., 51
Club of Rome, 56
cold war, 9–10, 13, 25, 87
Communist Party (China), 4–5
Communist Party (Japan), 66, 164, 166–70, 217
Constitution: of Germany, 51; of Japan, 14, 65–66, 138, 266
Control Commission for Germany, 124
Costello, John, 137, 151

317

critics and criticism, 27–28; of Jünger, 238–44; of Koeppen, 228–38
cultural homogeneity, 19, 50

Dahrendorf, Ralf, 41
Daisan no shinjin (third generation of new writers), 208–16
Dazai Osamu, 100, 102, 111, 141, 179, 220
defeat: in Germany and Japan, 37–41, 66
Demetz, Peter, 91, 228, 229
democratization, 5–6; 45–46; of Germany, 41–43, 49–51; of Japan, 66, 67, 165–66, 167–68
Depression of 1930s, 5
Döblin, Alfred, 48, 92, 124, 132
documentary literature, 15, 194, 282, 283
Doppelgängertum, 12
Dorst, Tankred, 196
Dos Passos, John, 91, 92
Dostoyevsky, Feodor, 13, 175
Dutschke, Rudi, 88n
Dymshitz, Alexandr, 124

economic miracle. *See Wirschaftwunder*
economic recovery, 11–13, 81
Edschmidt, Kasimir, 126–27
Eichmann trial (1961), 15, 92, 194
Eliot, T. S., 233
emergency laws (*Notstandsgesetze*), 54, 94
Enchi Fumiko, 220–21
Endō Shusaku, 212, 222, 256
Engels, Friedrich, 253
Enzenberger, Hans Magnus, 84, 85, 282
Erhard, Ludwig, 88
Etō Jun, 138, 139, 142, 145, 163
Europe 1992, 20
European culture, 180–82
European Economic Community, 11
existentialism, 13, 217
extremist decrees (*Radikalenerlasse*), 94

Fanon, Franz, 257
Faulkner, William, 12, 91, 128, 190
"Five Great Reforms," 67

Fontane, Theodor, 128
Fort, Gertrude von le, 125
Forte, Dieter, 196
Foucault, Michel, 242, 257–58
Fradkin, Ilya, 124
Frank, Hans, 286, 287
Frank, Niklas, 286, 287–88
Freud, Sigmund, 15, 83
Friedländer, Saul, 95–96
Friedrich, Heinz, 91
Fujimori Seiichi, 146
Fukuda Tsuneari, 102

Gaiser, Gerd, 92
Gauch, Siegfried, 95
Genet, Jean, 257
German literature: anamnesis in, 228, 230; "first peak" novels in, 14, 191–94; and guilt, 82–83, 86, 129, 191; and postwar literary generations, 22, 46–47, 52–54; and postwar occupation of Germany, 123–33; "second peak" novels in, 194–98; and Third Reich, 88–96
Germany: capitalism in, 50; denazification of, 6, 43–44; and inability to mourn, 82–83, 282–83; inner migration in, 6–7, 125–27, 132; occupation of, 5, 6, 25–26, 45–46, 123–30
Glaser, Hermann, 36, 85
Glotz, Peter, 37
Goethe, Johann Wolfgang von, 129, 253, 264
Gomikawa Junpei, 111
Grass, Günter, 47, 48, 54, 88, 93, 191–92, 194, 196, 203, 282, 286
Greater East Asia Co-Prosperity Sphere, 5, 139
Green movement (West Germany), 16, 35, 55, 56–57, 280
Greenpeace, 280
Groll, Günter, 125
Grosser, Alfred, 124
Group 47 (Germany), 7, 47–49, 54, 84–86, 128, 132, 282
Group 61 (Germany), 195
Grundgesetz. *See* Basic Law

Habermas, Jürgen, 93, 243
Hagelstange, Rudolf, 125
Hamburger, Michael, 243
Haniya Yukata, 109, 173, 174, 180–81
Hara Tamiki, 112, 150, 256
Hashikawa Bunzō, 108
Hatta Yoshie, 256
Hauptmann, Gerhart, 129
Hayashi Fusao, 106
Heissenbüttel, Helmut, 229, 236, 241, 244
Heissenbüttel, Werner, 282
Hemingway, Ernest, 12, 91, 128, 132, 190
Heym, Georg, 130
Higashi Mineo, 219
Hildebrand, Klaus, 243
Hildescheimer, Wolfgang, 192
Hillgruber, Andreas, 243
Hindenburg, Paul von, 39
Hirano Ken, 102, 173, 174
Hirohito, 6, 10, 13, 67, 73, 209
"historians' debate" (*Historikerstreit*), 6, 23, 76, 94, 203–5, 237, 243, 285
Hitler, Adolf, 5, 7, 281
Hochhuth, Rolf, 93, 194
Hocke, Gustav René, 128–29
Hofer, Walter, 36
Hoffmann, E. T. A., 283
Hofmann, Gert, 201
Hohoff, Curt, 242
Hölderlin, Johann C., 128
Holocaust, 15, 23, 86, 282, 283
"Holocaust" television series, 17, 91, 95, 201–4, 285
Honda Shugō, 138, 172–74
Horst, Karl A., 242
Hotta Yoshie, 258
Huch, Ricarda, 129

"I" novel (*shi-shōsetsu*), 2–3, 12, 207, 212–14, 218–19
Ibuse Masuji, 116, 256
Ihara Saikaku, 220
imperialism, 4–5, 256
Inoue Hisashi, 222, 256
Ishikawa Jun, 144, 258

Japan: citizen movements in, 104–5, 106, 251; and civil censorship, 135–53; compartmentalization of culture in, 3, 45; and democratic literature movement, 163; economic growth in, 74–75, 104, 255; emperor system in, 45, 180–82, 264; "founding myth" of, 10, 22; intellectual climate in, 99–108, 249–50; occupation of, 5, 25-26, 45–46, 67–70, 101, 163–65
Japan Community Party. *See* Communist Party, Japan
Japanese literature: aestheticizing in, 115–116; and books, 252–253; and classical revival, 219–22; fatalism in, 113–15; and guilt, 101, 152, 216; and humanist dialectics, 174–80; and language, 107; and occupation of Japan, 101; and postwar literary generations, 18, 27, 70–73, 108–10; 208–16; 221; and novels of "secession," 222
Japanese national character. *See Nihonjinron*
Jaspers, Karl, 23, 85, 93, 94
Jens, Walter, 229, 236
Johnson, Uwe, 88, 191, 192, 196–97
Joyce, James, 91, 92, 191
junbungaku (pure literature), 111
Jünger, Ernst, 27, 28, 126: critics of, 241–44; utopian novels of, 238–41

Kämpfer, Wolfgang, 241
Kafka, Franz, 12, 13, 91, 129, 132
Kaga Otohiko, 110, 115
Kageyama Masaharu, 147–48
Kaifu Toshiki, 20
Kaikō Ken, 109
Kaikō Takeshi, 221
Kamei Katsuichirō, 183
Kamo no Chōmei, 116
Katō Shūichi, 71, 111, 112, 152
Kawabata Yasunari, 109, 111, 115, 141, 142
Kawakami Hajime, 101
Keene, Donald, 100, 102, 138, 142, 143, 216–17
Kempowski, Walter, 199, 200, 202, 203

Kielmannsegg, Peter Graf, 41, 42–43
Kiesinger, Kurt Georg, 88, 93–94
Kikuchi Kan, 141
Kinoshita Junji, 256
Kipphardt, Heinar, 282
Kishi Nobuske, 103
Klarsfield, Beate, 94
Klepper, Jochen, 126
Kluge, Alexander, 93, 192, 194, 202
Kobayashi Hideo, 102, 145, 146
Kobayashi Takiji, 141
Koeppen, Wolfgang, 12, 27, 47, 48, 86, 92–94, 191, 282; critics of, 228–38
Kogon, Eugen, 85
Kohl, Helmut, 23, 95, 285–86
Kojima Nobuo, 210–11, 213–15, 258
Kolbenhoff, Werner, 128
Kōno Takeo, 110
Konoshita Junji, 105
Korean War, 9, 10, 26, 74
Kraemer-Badoni, Rudolf, 234, 236
Kruger, Horst, 53
Kunzman, Richard, 137, 140, 151
Kurahara Korehito, 100, 169–72, 174
Kurahashi Yumiko, 222
Kurihara Sadao, 150
Kurosawa Akira, 252
Kursbuch, 94
Kuwabaro Takeo, 220

Lange, Horst, 85, 125
Langgässer, Elisabeth, 91, 92, 125, 126, 131–32, 191
Langhoff, Wolfgang, 83
Lectures Faction (*kōza-ha*), 168
Lenz, Hermann, 95, 199
Lenz, Siegfried, 131, 194, 195–96, 203, 237, 282
Leonhardt, Rudolf Walter, 54
Lepenies, Wolf, 243
Liberal Democratic Party (Japan), 16, 22, 73
Liberal Party (West Germany), 52
liberal reactionism (*ōtake*), 103
Lifton, Robert Jay, 283–84
Lu Hsün, 256
Ludendorff, Erich, 39

MacArthur, Douglas, 25, 67–68, 135, 137, 138, 167, 209

magazines (Japan), 65, 100–101, 251–52
Manchurian Incident (1931), 5, 76
Mann, Golo, 244
Mann, Thomas, 125–26, 129, 132, 138, 233
Manthey, Jürgen, 84
Marshall plan, 9, 44
Maruyama Masao, 69, 102, 103, 163, 252
Marx, Karl, 15, 253
Marxist writers (*Sengoha*), 102, 109, 208–9, 211, 214, 216, 217
Masamune Hakuchō, 109, 163
Matsubara Shin'ichi, 109
Matsuura Sōzō, 138, 142
Mayer, Hans, 83
Meckel, Christoph, 95
Meier, Christian, 95
Meiji Restoration (1868), 4, 264
Mengele, Josef, 286–87
Mengele, Rolf, 286–88
militarism, 4, 20, 50, 256
Miller, Roy A, 107
Mishima Yukio, 73, 109, 111, 115, 220
Mitchell, Richard, 138
Mitscherlich, Alexander, 23, 82, 83, 86, 93, 282–83, 285
Mitscherlich, Margarete, 23, 82, 83, 86, 87, 94, 282–83, 285
Miyamoto Yuriko, 141, 147
Mizoguchi Kenji, 252
modernism: in German literature, 190; in Japanese literature, 182–83
Moore, Joe, 169
Morgenthau plan, 123
Mori Ōgai, 253
Morimura Sei'ichi, 110, 112, 256
Moscow conference (1947), 51
Murakami Haruki, 252
Murakami Ryū, 110
Mushanokōji Saneatsu, 141

Nabeyama Sadachika, 173
Nagai Kafū, 100, 109, 144, 163
Nagai Takashi, 151
Nagayo Yoshirō, 142–43
Nakagami Kenji, 220
Nakajima Atsushi, 102

Nakamo Yoshio, 252
Nakamura Mitsui, 115
Nakamura Mitsuo, 101
Nakamura Shin'ichirō, 109
Nakano Shigeharu, 102, 147
Nakasone Yasuhiro, 76
national identity: 38; in Japan, 45, 106–8
National Socialism (Germany), 36, 42–43, 92, 95–96
nationalism, 20, 74, 182–83
NATO, 11
Natsume Sōseki, 141, 142, 253
Nazi Party (Germany), 192, 281
Neue Ostpolitik (New Eastern Policy), 52
new subjectivism, 18, 199–200, 221
newspapers (Japan), 252
Nick, Dagmar, 130
Nihonjinron, 106–8
Nipponism (Japanese cultural exclusivity), 19, 20
Nobusuke Kishi, 45
Nolte, Ernst, 243, 285
Noma Hiroshi, 109, 214, 215, 217, 218, 256, 258
North Atlantic Treaty Organization. *See* NATO
Nosaka Sanzō, 168–69, 171–72, 174
Notstandsgesetze. See emergency laws
Nuremburg trials, 6, 45, 53, 82, 255
Nuyama Hiroshi, 146

Oda Makoto, 72, 105, 256
Odagiri Hideo, 101, 112, 173, 174, 180
Ōe Kenzaburō, 12, 72, 109, 112, 218–19, 220, 221, 222, 256
oil crisis (1973), 16, 55
Ōoka Shōhei, 109, 146, 179, 215–16, 256
Organization of Petroleum-Exporting Countries (OPEC), 56
Ōshiro Tatsuhiro, 219
Ōta Yōko, 151
Ōtake Hideo, 103
Ozu Yasuhirō, 252

Pfeifer, Jochen, 93
Pirker, Theo, 41, 43
Plievier, Theodor, 91, 93, 129–30, 132

political activism, 13–16
political parties: postwar reestablishment of in Germany, 124–25
Postwar Group (*sengō-ha*), 101, 109
postwar reform (*sengō kaikaku*), 67–70
Potsdam conference (1945), 51
Potsdam Declaration, 65, 100, 165, 167
Prange, Klaus, 241
Press, Publications, and Broadcasting (PPB) Division, 136–38, 139, 140, 141, 143, 147
Pringsheim, Hans, 138
Pringsheim, Klaus, 138
Proletarian School of writers (Japan), 27, 100, 102, 207
protest movements, 14–16
public conscience, writer as, 20–21, 29, 280; in German literature, 279–88; in Japanese literature, 263–75
publishers (Japan), 253–54
purges, 6, 45, 137, 147

Raddatz, Fritz, 232
Radikalenerlasse. See extremist decrees
Rape of Nanking, 76, 255
Reagan, Ronald, 76
realism: in German literature, 128, 190; in Japanese literature, 171
rearmament, 10, 51, 74
Red Army, 16
Rehmann, Ruth, 95
Reich-Raniki, Marcel, 229–30, 236
Reitz, Edgar, 202, 203
Richter, Hans Werner, 47, 48, 82, 84, 85, 127–28
Rilke, Rainer Maria, 128
Romantic School (*Nihon Romān-ha*), 109
Roosevelt, Franklin D., 123, 128, 143
Roosevelt, Theodore, 140
Rubin, Jay, 103, 138, 142, 144, 163
Der Ruf (The Call), 7, 25, 47, 48, 82, 84, 85, 127–28, 132
Ruhmkorf, Peter, 91
Rutschky, Michael, 241, 243, 244

Sakaguchi Ango, 115, 144

Samuel, Yoshiko Yokochi, 139, 141, 142
San Francisco Peace Treaty (1951), 10, 74
Sanders-Brahm, Helma, 202
Sano Manabu, 173
Sartre, Jean-Paul, 190, 259
Sasaki Kiichi, 173
SCAP. *See* Supreme Commander for the Allied Powers
Scheel, Walter, 42
Schiller, Johann, 190, 253, 264, 283
Schlegel, August Wilhelm von, 283
Schlegel, Friedrich von, 283
Schmidt, Arno, 282
Schmidt, Helmut, 42
Schmittlein, Raymond, 124
Schneider, Peter, 95, 200, 205
Schneider, Rolf, 194
Schnurre, Wolfdietrich, 91
Schoenbaum, David, 41, 42
Schumacher, Kurt, 47
Schwab-Felisch, Hans, 230, 231, 236
Security Treaty (1952), 74
Security Treaty renewal (1960), 13, 72, 104, 251
sengō-ha. See Postwar Group
sengo kaikaku. See postwar reform
senso taiken (personal experience of the war), 65, 77, 109
Serizawa Kōjirō, 141
Shakespeare, William, 283
Shaku no Chōkū, 148
Shibata Shō, 105
Shiga Yoshio, 166–69
Shigeru Yoshida, 137
Shilloney, Ben-Ami, 138
Shimao Toshio, 109, 211
Shimizu Ikotarō, 115, 252
Shinsei (magazine), 65
Shiroyama Saburō, 105
shi-shōsetsu. See "I" novel
Shoda Shinōe, 150
Sichrovsky, Peter, 286
Social Democratic Party (West Germany), 47, 49, 52, 94
Soviet occupation of Germany, 123–24, 129
Spaulding, Robert M., 138, 147, 151–52

Speer, Albert, 45
Spiegel affair, 88, 92, 192–93, 198
Spielhagen, Friedrich, 128
Springer, Axel, 54
Stalin, Josef, 51
Stein, Gertrude, 233
Sternberger, Dolf, 50
Stifter, Adalbert, 128
Strauss, Franz Josef, 86, 88n, 192
student demonstrations: in Germany, 94, 194–95, 197; in Japan, 104
Stuermer, Michael, 243
Stunde Null. See zero hour
Supreme Commander for the Allied Powers (SCAP), 135–36, 138–39, 140, 141, 148, 149–50, 153, 171
surrender of Germany and Japan, 5, 66, 100
Suzuki Takao, 107

taishu bungaku (mass literature), 111
Takami Jun, 101, 144
Takamura Kōtarō, 101, 109
Takeda Taijun, 109, 258
Takei Teruo, 104
Takeuchi Yoshimi, 183, 256–58
Tamiya Torahiko, 113
Tamura Taijirō, 177–78
Tanaka Hidemitsu, 113, 115
Tanizaki Jun'ichirō, 100, 109, 143–45, 163, 220, 274
terrorism, 16
Thiess, Frank, 125–26
Tokuda Kyūichi, 166–67, 168
Tokyo war crime trials, 6, 24, 105, 255
Treat, John Whittier, 112
Truman Doctrine, 51
Truman, Harry S., 51, 209
Trümmerliteratur (literature of the rubble), 10, 14
Trümmerlyrik (poetry of the rubble), 130
Tsurumi Shunsuke, 104–5, 106, 107, 108, 177

U.S. Information Control Division (Germany), 125
Ulbricht, Walter, 48
Umezaki Haruo, 109

Valéry, Paul, 129
Versailles Peace Treaty, 4, 5
Vesper, Bernward, 95
Vietnam War, 14, 16, 24, 28, 104, 197, 219, 267–70

Walser, Martin, 38, 88, 192, 282
war crimes, 7–8; of Germany, 53, 283; of Japan, 45, 112
war crimes trials, 6, 15. *See also under names of specific trials*
war experience: in Germany, 280–88; in Japanese literature, 110–12
war responsibility: in Japan, 101–4, 180–82
Warsaw Pact, 11
Watanabe Kazutami, 182
Wegener, Paul, 129
Weiss, Peter, 85, 93, 192, 194, 196, 197, 282
Weyrauch, Wolfgang, 128
Wiechert, Ernst, 130–31
Wilder, Thornton, 91

Willoughby, Charles, 137, 151
Wirtschaftwunder (economic miracle), 52, 84–85; contributing factors to, 55–56
Wirtschaftwunder-Kinder ('68 generation), 52–55
Wolfe, Thomas, 128
Woolf, Virginia, 129

Yamabe Kentarō, 167
Yamaguchi Takao, 140
Yamamura Shizuka, 173
Yasuoka Shotaro, 212–13, 258
Yokomitsu Riichi, 141
Yoshida Kenichi, 151
Yoshida Mitsuru, 111, 145–46, 215
Yoshida Shigeru, 103, 151
Yoshimoto Takaaki, 102, 104
Yoshiyuki Junnosuke, 211, 220

zero hour, 10, 12, 22, 35–37, 47, 52–54, 65, 190
Zuckmayer, Carl, 132